Psychology of Personal
and Social Adjustment

HENRY CLAY LINDGREN
San Francisco State College

Psychology
of Personal and Social
Adjustment

AMERICAN BOOK COMPANY

NEW YORK   CINCINNATI   CHICAGO   BOSTON
ATLANTA   DALLAS   SAN FRANCISCO

LINDGREN: PSYCHOLOGY

MADE IN U.S.A.

E. P. 2

To ROBERT SILAS STEWART,

whose understanding, insight, and friendly criticism
have been of inestimable value in helping to develop this book.

Preface

One of the significant trends in mental hygiene today is the increasing amount of attention directed to what might be called "the psychology of normal people." This textbook is a product of that trend. Its purpose is to help ordinary, everyday people — people with the usual number of problems — to gain a better understanding of themselves and others so that they may live happier and more effective lives.

This book is also the product of the trend toward General Education. San Francisco State College has participated in this trend during the past few years by developing an integrated sequence of courses based on student needs and emphasizing the understanding of man and his physical and social environment. The basic offerings in the field of psychology have been drastically revised under this new plan. The old required course in psychology was one semester in length and consisted of a sampling of widely differentiated areas in psychology. The new course covers two semesters and has as its purpose aiding the student to understand himself and others and helping him with problems of occupational choice and adjustment, courtship and marriage, and attaining success in college. Today, after almost five years of experimentation and trial, both students and teaching staff are generally agreed that the new course does its work well. Its success has doubtless been due largely to the enthusiasm and flexibility of the teaching staff, who have met the challenge of the new course by developing curricular materials and methods appropriate to its philosophy and goals.

One of the difficulties from the start, however, has been the dearth of textbooks that help students to develop a more penetrating understanding of the behavior of themselves and of others. This textbook is an attempt to fill that need. It has been used successfully in three preliminary editions, and the present text has profited from cumulative revisions based on both student and staff reactions and comments. It should be noted that the success of

vii

this text in the teaching of psychology has led to its use in other courses — counseling and guidance, mental hygiene, and teacher education — at San Francisco State College and elsewhere.

Perhaps one of the attractions of this text for the student is the fact that its viewpoint is dynamic — that is, it attempts to explain behavior as well as to describe it. Its concepts are drawn from the works of a group of writers in psychology and cultural anthropology who have much in common, even though they are not always completely in agreement: Erich Fromm, Harry Stack Sullivan, Karen Horney, Donald Snygg, Arthur W. Combs, Fritz Redl, Theodore M. Newcomb, Clyde Kluckhohn, and many others.

A note should be included regarding the source of the case material used illustratively throughout the book. The situations and cases described are drawn largely from my experiences and from material I have collected through the years. However, fictitious names have been substituted for those of real persons, all identifying data have been altered, and details, events, and characters have been changed, when not essential to the point being developed.

Although this book bears the name of a single author, it is to some degree the result of the collaboration of many persons. Chief among these are the many students I have taught throughout the years, whose reactions have helped to deepen and enrich the meaning of what I have written. In addition, there are my colleagues at San Francisco State College, who have read and criticized the preliminary editions as well as portions of the later revisions: Robert S. Stewart, Louis S. Levine, David Freeman, Margaret Jessen, Leslie Navran, and Hilda Taba. I am also grateful for help received from J. M. Winans, of Sacramento State College; Malcolm MacLean, of the University of California at Los Angeles; Wolcott C. Treat, of San Diego State College; Charles C. Collins, of Contra Costa Junior College; and Herman Peters, of Chico State College. Finally, it is to my wife, Fredi, that I am most indebted, for it is she who has suffered and worked with me through the seemingly endless rewriting and revising necessary to the development of any textbook attempting so ambitious a task as this one.

HENRY CLAY LINDGREN
San Francisco State College

Contents

Contents

I ... *Introduction to the Study of Human Behavior*

This book is written for the "average" or "normal" student — the individual who has made a reasonably successful adjustment to life and its problems, but who would like to be even more successful. Most of us fall within the limits of this concept of normality. We get along with others most of the time, but we realize that our relationships with others could often be pleasanter or more rewarding; we are for the most part satisfied with ourselves, but there are times when we are disappointed or annoyed with our own behavior; we are aware that we are able to accomplish and learn many things, but often the results fall short of our expectations.

Today the most "normal" or emotionally mature persons cannot help being affected by the tensions that are present in society. The international situation, marked by open warfare and undeclared "wars of nerves," affects the individual both directly and indirectly — directly because of the possibility of his becoming personally involved in some aspect of warfare, and indirectly because international events influence conditions that in turn may affect his welfare. As this is being written, tuna fishermen in California are unable to market their catch profitably because canneries can buy frozen tuna from Japan and Latin America at lower prices. Yet we are reluctant to protect local fishermen with a tariff on imported tuna because Japan needs to export to us to build herself economically; because Latin America needs dollars in order to continue to buy our manufactured products; and because we are afraid to alienate either Japan or Latin America, since we need friends badly during times of international tension. Thus the international situation makes life more difficult for tuna fishermen and their families.

I

Another situation affecting the lives of individuals today is the lack of stability in modern society. We change jobs more often than we did fifty or a hundred years ago, our families move more frequently, and the problems that face us change and shift with dizzying speed. One year our chief problem is unemployment; the next year we are shorthanded at the defense plants. Or we move from an economy of scarcity to one of plenty in a relatively few months. We build up savings accounts as hedges against the future, only to have their value cut in half by inflation. In truth, times like these demand the utmost in emotional health and maturity.

Emotional Matuirty and Mental Health. The assumption underlying this book is that emotional maturity is the chief component of mental or emotional health. In other words, the author assumes that the greater the emotional maturity of the individual, the greater will be his ability to withstand the disintegrating effects of the social tensions of the world around him and to live a happy and useful life. The emotionally mature person is one who has learned to use his emotions constructively and effectively, without injury to himself or offense to others.

The concept of emotional maturity can be more readily grasped by comparing the emotional life of adolescents with that of adults. According to Franz Alexander, adolescents are young men and women biologically full-grown, but in many respects children. As he says,

One has the impression that they do not know what to do with themselves in their newly acquired status. Their insecurity manifests itself in self-consciousness, both about their body and their personality. They do not know what to do with their hands and feet, there is a lack of spontaneity in their movements and speech and a constant effort to overcome their own feeling of awkwardness. A full-grown body is entrusted to an inexperienced mind (1).*

Alexander goes on to say that adolescence is characterized by an excessive competitiveness and a necessity to prove oneself an adult. When the adolescent falls short of what he considers to be adult standards, he feels inadequate and insecure; and he attempts to compensate for or overcome this feeling by boastfulness, aggressive behavior, and competitiveness.

The essence of the mature state of mind, according to Alexander, is the conquest of insecurity and the ability to take oneself for

---

* Numbers in parentheses refer to references at the end of the chapter.

"You're worried, depressed, can't sleep, and feel insecure.
Forget it — you're normal!"

The Saturday Review

granted. Presumably, because the mature adult has tested his abilities against the realities of life in adolescent competition, he knows what his capacities are. He has proved himself to others and to his own satisfaction. Thus he is not as preoccupied with himself as is the adolescent and is able to turn his attention outward — to his social and physical environment.

Alexander further characterizes the mature person as creative, productive, and altruistic. Whereas the energies of the adolescent are absorbed in growth and in reducing the anxiety produced by his feeling of insecurity and inadequacy, the mature person finds that he has surplus energy, which may be devoted to creativity, productivity, and aiding others. However, Alexander recognizes that there are times when even the most mature person meets problems that tax his resources to the utmost. At such times there is a tendency to regress to less mature behavior — as we say, to become "childish." Thus even the most mature person can at times become irritable, depressed, ill-tempered, and unreasonable.

Finally, Alexander sees the mature person as one who is flexible and adaptable, who can face the facts of the outside world and can accept his own limitations realistically. Therefore the adult who cannot accept the fact of changed conditions and who insists on "living in the past" and adhering to by-gone behavior patterns lacks some elements of emotional maturity.

Thus psychological or emotional maturity is not the same as physiological or even chronological maturity. We expect people to become psychologically more mature as they grow older, but this does not always occur. Physiological maturity perhaps can be retarded by certain conditions, but it inevitably arrives. Not so with psychological maturity. Becoming twenty-one years old automatically grants us legal maturity, but it does not automatically give us emotional maturity, any more than an officer's commission makes him a "gentleman." Emotional maturity is something that must be achieved, worked for. Many adults never become emotionally mature, for their attitudes and behavior remain fixed at an adolescent or even a childish level. They are excessively shy, chronically irritable, always belligerent, or exclusively pleasure-seeking. Hadley Cantril characterizes the immature person as one whose scope of behavior is limited to that which is appropriate to persons younger than he, who is unable to obtain satisfactions associated with adult behavior (2). Kimball Young points out that many adults are quite mature in some areas of behavior, and immature in others (3). For example, he says, a man may behave in an objective, consistent, and responsible manner in accumulating wealth, but may exploit his friends and his family in a wholly unreasonable, selfish, and immature manner.

Attainment of Emotional Maturity through Growth. The process of becoming emotionally more mature may also be described as a process whereby an individual demonstrates the following kinds of growth: (a) growth in his ability to understand, tolerate, accept, and respect himself and others; and (b) growth in his capacity for self-reliance, self-direction, responsibility, and productivity. The term "growth" is particularly appropriate here because psychological changes in the direction of maturity tend to come slowly, sometimes gradually and evenly, sometimes unevenly, through a process of spurting ahead and dropping back, with progress and improvement apparent only after a considerable period has passed.

The fact that emotional maturity comes so slowly explains why many who try to "improve their personalities" through taking "charm courses" or through practicing social techniques can see no changes of the sort they desire even after several weeks or months of study. Actually, this is an advantage, because the slowness of growth enables all elements of the personality to adjust to and accommodate newer patterns of behavior. People who change too readily are in danger of becoming *too* adjustable, *too* likely to change with every new situation. Such people tend to lack firmness of purpose and stability; they are all things to all men.

Growth in Understanding. Understanding plays a key part in the definition of emotional maturity we have given above. Through understanding we come to have better insight into our own actions and feelings, as well as those of others. That is to say, we are more realistic about ourselves and others and have a better grasp of the causes and effects of human behavior, including our own. It takes understanding to solve the problems that arise in our lives as a result of misunderstandings, and understanding helps protect us against misinterpretations that threaten peace of mind and our relations with others.

The emotionally mature person is one who understands, who has a good grasp of the realities of life. The immature person, on the other hand, is likely to distort or misinterpret the events and relationships he perceives. For example, the relations between an immature individual and persons in positions of authority may be strained because the former tends to interpret all actions of the latter as though they were directed against *him*. He may have a tightening in his stomach or even fear arrest when he passes a policeman, even though he has committed no crime *and has no logical reason to be afraid of policemen*. The mature person is better able to deal with persons in authority, because he knows what his rights, privileges, and abilities are, and because he is aware of the kinds of individuals with whom he is dealing. Because the immature person does not understand himself and others, he becomes the victim of unreasonable fears; whereas the mature person, having insight into himself and others, can cope with the realities of life without becoming unduly upset. He knows what he may reasonably expect and what to do about it when it occurs.

Growth in Tolerance. The abilities we have mentioned in our definition of growth in emotional maturity are listed in order from the most intellectual to the most emotional. Understanding is largely an intellectual process, though it must be accompanied or preceded by certain emotional conditions — readiness to learn, relative freedom from hate and fear — before it can take place. Tolerance is somewhat more tinged with emotion, though it is still largely an intellectual process. Presumably the person who can understand is ready to take the next step — tolerance.

The ability of an individual to be tolerant is largely dependent upon his freedom from unreasonable fears. If he is beset by such fears, he finds tolerance difficult because he tends to see threat or danger where none exists. On the other hand, the emotionally mature person finds it easier to be tolerant, because his more realistic approach to life enables him to reject feelings of being threatened as unreasonable and unrealistic, unless of course, he has some actual basis for fear.

It is often difficult to draw the line between reasonable and unreasonable fears. Perhaps we can demonstrate the difference with a situation involving a husband, his wife, and his mother. The wife is able to understand and tolerate her mother-in-law. She can recognize her fine qualities as well as her personal problems. She is aware of the fact that her mother-in-law can be very helpful at times but that she is also a lonely woman, who probably would like to have her son for herself alone. Therefore, the wife resists any suggestion that her mother-in-law live with them, because she has a real basis for being afraid that such an arrangement would cause trouble. She finds that she can tolerate her mother-in-law's visiting them for approximately two weeks, but no more. Because the wife is a psychologically mature person, she can tolerate her mother-in-law as a person and as a temporary visitor, and she does not have to be unreasonably afraid of her occasional visits. If the wife were immature, if she lacked understanding and tolerance, she might insist that her mother-in-law never visit their home; she might attempt to force an unnecessary showdown upon her husband and demand that he choose between her and his mother. The wife's fear of a permanent visit by the mother-in-law is reasonable; her fear of occasional visits would be unreasonable.

A tolerant person is one who recognizes the need for give-and-take relationships in life. He has learned that the best defense is not offense, but, rather, the promotion of the idea of mutual non-belligerency — "I won't attack you, with the expectation that you won't attack me; maybe it will take some time to convince you that I will not attack you, but I'm willing to wait."

Growth in Acceptance. Tolerance is a neutral state; taken in isolation, it means neither acceptance nor rejection. But presumably the person who has been able to reach this state is now ready to learn that he needs people and that they need him. Acceptance is more emotionally tinged than tolerance. The accepting individual is one who is willing to go beyond the live-and-let-live philosophy of the tolerant person and to take a few steps in the direction of the other person or persons. If the wife in the preceding case is accepting as well as tolerant, she may attempt to establish a sort of mother-daughter relationship between herself and her mother-in-law. She may make a special effort to learn to know her mother-in-law as a person, to seek some common area of interest.

When we characterize the mature person as "accepting," we do not mean that he will accept *everyone*, or even that he will regard others uncritically. Rather, he is able to accept people unless he has good and realistic bases for not doing so. He is able to seek out their company and enjoy them, because he has learned that he does not have to fear them.

Growth in Respect. The mature person can also permit himself to appreciate and value himself and others, when such appreciation is appropriate. He is actively aware of the gifts and competencies of himself and others. He has an appreciation of the trials that both he and his acquaintances have suffered, trials that have, in part, made them the kind of persons they are today. He is sensitive to the kinds of difficulties people experience in their everyday living, and he admires them for maintaining their integrity and purpose in spite of pressures.

There is a logical next step in the sequence of understanding, tolerance, acceptance, and respect: it is love. The mature person should be genuinely fond of himself as a person. This does not mean that he should be self-centered or completely wrapped up in himself, as we usually picture persons who are imbued with self-love, but it does mean that he must like himself. It is the psychologically immature person who hates, despises, or continually depreciates himself. And because a mature person can like himself and enjoy his own company on occasion, he can also like others and enjoy their company. Because he can love himself, he can also love those whose welfare is important to him — his spouse and his children. He can feel a love for mankind, because he also feels a love for himself and those who are near and dear to him.

Self and Others. It is to be noted that we have linked the self and others as the objects of the attitudes or processes we have described above. The reason for this linkage is the intimate relationship between attitudes toward oneself and toward others, a relationship confirmed by research findings (4, 5, 6). A person who consistently despises himself (unconsciously or openly), despises others (unconsciously or openly); and a person who consistently despises others similarly despises himself. An individual who has keen insight into his own motivation also has keen insight into the motivation of others. An individual who consistently finds others unpredictable and stupid, subconsciously believes himself to be unpredictable and stupid.

Growth in Capacity for Self-direction. As the individual becomes more mature emotionally, he will find himself freer to develop his capacity for self-direction, self-reliance, responsibility, and productivity. Similarly, as he becomes more self-directive — that is, comes to rely on his own ability to gather facts and evaluate them, and is thus freed from having to depend on the opinions of others — he will find himself in a better position to understand, tolerate, accept, and respect himself and others. As he learns about the realities of life and finds that he can cope with its problems, he becomes increasingly self-directive and begins to take more responsibility for his own actions and for his relations with others.

This means, in part, that his emotional difficulties with other persons will not lead him to place the blame solely on himself or others, but rather will cause him to accept some of the responsibility for the unfortunate relationships, at least to the point of attempting to analyze and to understand the causes. The more he can accomplish in this direction and the more he can understand, tolerate, accept, and respect himself and others, the more he will be freed to use his individual talents productively. The mature person is one who is helpful, productive, creative, and able to perform these functions effectively and with reasonable efficiency.

Factors Impeding Growth toward Emotional Maturity. Just as the healthiest of us harbor disease germs and are afflicted by minor ailments like colds, athlete's foot, and tooth decay, each of us has his complement of neurotic or irrational fears, which he has inherited from his past experiences. Just as there probably has never been an ideally healthy person, there are no persons who are completely free from neurotic feelings. However, in the process of becoming more mature emotionally, people do master or at least immobilize some of the neurotic components of their personalities. It is the purpose of this book to help students to understand some of the common elements that form the basis of neurotic or irrational fears and feelings.

"Neurotic," as used in the above sense, refers to those aspects of the personality which are immature and which are not attuned to reality. Thus, in a mild way, forgetting to set the alarm clock at night is neurotic, because the reality of tomorrow demands that one get to school on time. Such forgetting is not necessarily done on purpose, but is very likely conditioned by the individual's conscious or unconscious desire to "sleep in" the next morning. We are not disturbed by this kind of neurotic behavior, unless it becomes habitual. An example of behavior somewhat more neurotic is that of the inability to accept suggestions or criticisms, even when they are appropriate. Many of us are so hypersensitive that criticism disturbs our relationships with others.

We shall have much to say about neurotic needs and feelings, partly because psychologists have found out more about maladjustment than they have about adjustment, and partly because it is through the study of the forces producing maladjustment that one learns about the forces retarding one's own growth toward emotional maturity. If we are to come to grips with these forces and reduce their effectiveness, we must know their nature. Otherwise we grapple with them blindfolded, or submit to them passively because we feel we cannot cope with the unknown.

The Personality in Its Environment. To a very large degree this text is concerned with understanding the personality of the individual, how it grows and develops, and how it copes with and is formed by the forces of its environment. The study of ourselves and others thus is essentially a study of personality. However, personality as seen by the psychologist is different from personality as seen by the man in the street. C. M. Harsh and H. G. Schrickel see personality as embodied in the concepts of stimulus value, character, and temperament (7).

Stimulus value is the superficial aspect of personality. This is the aspect we have in mind when we say, "He has a pleasant personality." Personality in this sense is the outside shell of the person, that part he presents to the world. This is what we try to change when we endeavor to "improve our personalities." This is the aspect of personality at which so much advertising is aimed — billboards, magazine advertisements, radio and television commercials urge us to believe that others will think better of us if our hands are smooth as a result of using a certain hand lotion, if we are taller because of wearing "platform" shoes, if we can speak to the waiter in French, if we use sterling silver instead of plate, and so on and on.

Character is the innermost or "true" self, as compared with the more superficial social selves or roles that the individual may use in various places and at particular times. Character is based on the values or moral, religious, and philosophical beliefs of the individual.

Temperament has reference to the underlying emotions and feelings of the individual, particularly his habitual emotional pattern. Some people are slow to react, others over-react. Some are easygoing, others are hard and spiteful.

The man in the street recognizes stimulus value, character, and temperament as separate and distinct aspects of the individual. When he thinks of "personality," the chances are he has in mind the stimulus-value or mask aspect. He thus sees personality as separate from character and temperament. However, the psychologist sees stimulus value, character, and temperament as related aspects of a unitary whole that is *his* concept of personality. Personality to the psychologist is the sum of these factors, but it is much more than the sum, because it is also the pattern that unifies the whole; it is the emotional cement that holds these factors or aspects together and provides consistency and continuity. And particularly does personality give each of us the *stamp of individuality*.

Environment Defined. There are two aspects of environment that enter into the discussion of personality in this text. The first is the environment as seen or perceived by the individual. This is what is usually meant in this text by the simple term "environment." The environment as perceived by others, and particularly by the objective observer, is termed in this text "the physical and social environment."

In its effect on personality, the environment as perceived by the individual is by far the more important.* Let us take, for example, the situation faced by several individuals who are temporarily out of employment and who drop in at a local state employment office on a certain morning to pick up their unemployment compensation checks. The physical and social environment is similar for all of them, although there are minor differences — the room is the same, the amount of compensation is the same, the clerk greets them in much the same manner, although his reaction to each individual is conditioned or affected by the individual's attitude. We, as the observers, must admit that *the physical and social environment* is much the same for each of these unemployed men. However, *the situation as perceived* by each of them is quite different. The first man feels humiliated by the necessity of drawing his check; he feels that it is a reflection on his integrity and self-reliance. The second man regards his receipt of the check as a minor victory; he has schemed and plotted to get that check. The third man receives his check with apathy tinged with hostility; essentially he cares neither whether he works nor whether he is drawing unemployment com-

* For a more extended discussion of this approach to the study of personality, see D. Snygg and A. W. Combs, *Individual Behavior.* New York: Harper, 1949.

pensation, but he resents the pressure of the employment office to force him to seek work. The reaction of each of these men is determined largely by his personality pattern, which in turn is shaped by the kinds of experiences he has had in his life. If we were able to understand the personality patterns of these men, we would be able to predict their behavior and attitudes. The important point to remember is that, whichever of the two approaches to environment we use, an individual's environment as he senses and perceives it is peculiar to *him:* two persons could no more have the same environment than they could have the same skin.

Topics Dealing with the Personality in Its Environment. The first portion of this book focuses on the individual and his relations with himself; the second portion deals with the individual and his relations with others. In some ways this is an artificial division, inasmuch as the individual cannot be considered apart from his relations with others, and relations with others are of course influenced by the individual's concept of himself. However, in this text these two aspects are considered different viewpoints of the same body of information and understanding.

The first two chapters following the Introduction deal with the self and its development and the ideas of motivation and perception. The next two chapters deal with the development of normal emotionality and anxiety. Chapters 6 and 7 deal with two forms of immature behavior, shyness and overdependency.

Chapters 8 and 9 are transition chapters, forming a bridge from the portion of the book stressing the individual to the portion stressing social relationships. They are concerned with the determinants of personality, and particularly with the forces of the social environment which play upon and shape the personality, which control and direct the behavior, attitudes, and beliefs of the individual. The second of these two chapters is largely concerned with the effects that social class and status have upon the personality.

Chapters 10 and 11 deal in general with the phenomena of group behavior — what functions groups play in the life of the individual, what happens within groups, and how communication takes place. Chapters 12, 13, and 14 are concerned with problems of occupational adjustment and vocational choice. Chapters 15 and 16 are concerned with problems that arise in getting an education. Chapter 17 deals with courtship and marriage, and Chapter 18 deals with those forces within and without the individual that cause him to deviate from the social norm. The final two chapters are concerned with synthesizing concepts from the previous chapters and applying them specifically to the problem of better mental health.

The Dynamic Approach. The discussions of personality growth and development in this book treat the subject from the dynamic point of view, in that the emphasis is on behavior as the product of the individual-as-a-whole, the *total* personality interacting with its environment. Furthermore, our concern is as much with the *causes* of behavior as with behavior itself. Our chief method of understanding behavior is that of becoming acquainted with its causes.

The dynamic approach to human behavior involves a number of assumptions: 1. All behavior is caused. 2. All behavior is purposive. 3. Causes and purposes are multiple. 4. Behavior is a continuing process. 5. Behavior involves the total human organism.

"Common Sense" and the Dynamic Approach. One of the characteristics of these assumptions is that they are contrary to the dictates of "common sense." "Common sense," as used here and elsewhere in this book (always with quotes), refers to popular beliefs — concepts that seem to be confirmed by the senses and/or concepts typical of the man in the street. Many popular beliefs are essentially correct, such as the idea that married couples who have children are less likely to have divorces than couples who do not have children. But many other popular beliefs have been disproved by scientific experiments. For example, many of us still believe that heavier objects fall faster than lighter ones, even though Galileo proved this idea false centuries ago. Other common beliefs, which are without basis in fact, are that red-haired people are quick-tempered, that animals can see in total darkness, that slow readers read with more understanding than fast readers, and that studying spelling twenty minutes a day will give better results than studying it ten minutes a day. Because so much of what we commonly believe is without scientific basis, it is not surprising that psychology and the other sciences are constantly discovering facts and developing concepts that are radically opposed to "common sense." *

All Behavior Is Caused. The assumption that all behavior is caused is basic to all scientific research, the object of such research being the

---

* "Common sense," as we have used it in this paragraph, is of course different from another legitimate meaning of the phrase — that of "good sense."

discovery of the *causes* of certain kinds of behavior with a view to learning what scientific laws govern them. "Common sense" is less concerned with cause than with dealing with the behavior itself. For example, if a two-and-one-half-year-old child is discovered emptying dresser drawers, the "common sense" approach is to punish him so that he will learn not to do it again. However, the psychologist is interested in the cause of the behavior as well as in its prevention. He finds that children tend to grow out of this stage as they become more mature and that the arrival of more mature behavior is not expedited by punishment. Because of his research, the psychologist is able to predict (a) that children in this age group are likely to be negative and disruptive in their behavior, and (b) that they normally grow out of it in a few months.

"Common sense" tends to be impatient with the scientist's intense preoccupation with locating and analyzing causes. "Common sense" dictates that symptoms be dealt with directly. As an example, let us consider those individuals who suffer from gastric ulcers. Their need, as they see it, is to be relieved of the pain and inconvenience of the ulcers. For many years ulcers were dealt with directly — that is, people with ulcers took medicine designed to relieve the pain, took enforced rests, etc.; and surgeons cut out the ulcerated portion of the stomach. But very few ulcers were permanently cured. Then it was discovered that ulcers were caused by hydrochloric acid in the digestive juices attacking the lining of the alimentary canal. Treatment then took the form of special diets consisting of food that was quickly digested and had a soothing effect on the stomach lining. Many ulcer patients considered this kind of treatment a nuisance: they wanted to live life as they always had lived it, eating what they pleased. They were annoyed at having to change, and they wished that treatment could be directed at the immediate cure of the symptom. Then it was discovered that there is a relationship between a repressed need for dependency or repressed hostility, or both, and the occurrence of an ulcer (8). Although this discovery shed new light on the causes of the ulcer, it actually made the problem of dealing directly with it, or even with the acid causing it, infinitely more complicated than before. Now it was a matter of dealing with an intricate personality problem that required psychotherapy. It is not surprising that many patients refuse to undertake psychotherapy for their ulcers, partly because it runs counter to "common sense" — that is, that a pain in the stomach can be due to a state of mind — and partly because they fear that psychotherapy may change them and their way of life. In essence such people would rather remain the kinds of persons they are and keep the ulcers than get rid of them at the price of having to change.

Thus as scientific research progresses, it moves further and further from the symptom as it searches out the causes of the causes of the causes. And as it moves from the simple and obvious symptom into its causal background, it moves from the realm of "common sense."

All Behavior Is Purposive. This idea strikes at the very roots of "common sense," which perceives much of human behavior as senseless and purposeless. If we follow the dictates of "common sense" in this matter, we are faced with the necessity of surrendering to what appears to be the inevitable stupidity of mankind, or becoming cynical, or taking steps to *force* people to act sensibly in spite of their perverse nature. The psychologist's approach, on the other hand, is quite different. Since he assumes that all behavior has a purpose, his task is to discover that purpose. No matter how senseless and unreasonable human behavior appears, he knows that it serves some purpose or purposes for the doers; he knows that if he can discover the purposes, he can understand and predict the occurrence of this behavior and perhaps even undertake to control and redirect it.

There is no denying that his task is a difficult one. It is complicated by the fact that people are commonly unaware of the most important purposes underlying their behavior and that the same act can serve different purposes for different people — this, too, without their being aware of it.

Multiple Causation. The assumption that *causation is multiple* is supported by research and investigation wherever and whenever it is conducted scientifically. This assumption is of course contrary to "common sense." If we ask why a certain man eats at noon on a certain day, the "common sense" answer is that he is hungry, he is in need of food. Yet he may be well-nourished; his breakfast may have been adequate to maintain him all day. There is no denying that he has pangs of hunger as a result of contractions of his stomach, but investigation shows that these are largely due to the fact that he always eats at noon, that his stomach expects food at that time. Furthermore, his desire to eat at that time may be dictated by a wish to relax from the activities of the morning, to renew social contacts with his acquaintances over the lunch table. And he is motivated by the penalties incurred in *not* eating: a disruption in the day's routine, which is very unsettling; the unrelieved tension of continuing his morning's work; the displeasure of friends who expect him to eat with them; as well as the hunger pangs. Each of the above-named forces is in itself complex and is itself caused, in turn, by other forces. There is no such thing, scientifically, as a "simple act," since in any act there are whole constellations of forces operating. Some of these forces are understandably stronger than others, but they all have an effect.

Behavior Is a Continuing Process. The premise that behavior is a continuing process frequently appears to be violated in scientific writing, for in order to provide a graphic description of the forces and processes that are operating, it is frequently necessary to "freeze the action." This technique is followed in the next chapter, where various aspects of the personality are described as though they were "things" rather than processes. Furthermore, in each individual or group of individuals a countless number of processes go on at a given time. Nor does any human process actually come to an end, but continues, blending sometimes imperceptibly into other processes in whose cause it may have been a factor.

Behavior Involves the Total Human Organism. The popular, "common sense" concept is that "mind" and "body" are separate entities, that they frequently operate independently of each other, and that any part of the organism can operate independently of other parts. However, we now know that there is a close relationship between what used to be considered body (somatic) processes and mind (intellectual) processes. Glandular secretions affect thinking; attitudes affect bodily functioning. It is difficult or impossible to determine for any given action where somatic components end and where psychic or "mind" components begin, since every act or behavior sequence has components that have origins in, concurrently involve, and affect both "mind" and "body" processes. Furthermore, an action performed by one area of the human organism has been produced by, involves, or will eventually affect all other areas of the organism.

For example, as I sit at the typewriter producing this textbook, the mechanical task of punching the typewriter keys directly involves my fingers and arms. The blood that feeds these limbs is pumped by the heart and is refreshed by oxygen absorbed in the air sacs of the lungs. The blood stream also nourishes the brain, and the eyes follow the words as they are typed. The neural system performs its function of sending and receiving impulses; the whole organism is mobilized to a state of tension focused on producing these ideas, sentences, and words. This paragraph is produced by me as an organism *operating as a whole*, not by separate parts of me working in co-operation with other separate parts.

What the Dynamic Approach to Human Behavior Means. To persons who are in the grip of "common sense," the psychological problems of life tend to seem baffling and unsolvable. To them, man's apparent inability to solve the problems besetting him means either that the problems cannot be solved or that man is too stupid to apply the obvious solutions. Therefore, the man in the street is likely to accept with a fatalistic shrug such phenomena as crime, war, corruption, prejudice, and insanity, not to mention the occasionally peculiar and sometimes irrational behavior of himself and his acquaintances. The continued existence of these phenomena he attributes to "human nature," and therefore accepts the irrational as unchangeable or inevitable. Thus he assumes that nothing can be done to improve or change humans or their behavior.

However, the mature person, armed with concepts of dynamic behavior, rejects the human-nature hypothesis, for to accept it would mean that there would be no point in looking for the causes of man's apparent irrationality. He is interested in understanding human behavior, and this means looking for its causes. By probing and searching into the causal background, he finds that much of what the man in the street accepts as baffling and inexplicable can, in fact, be explained. He finds that human behavior can, within certain limits, be predicted and controlled. Therefore he is more at ease, more confident, and more psychologically secure.

The psychological benefits to be gained from understanding ourselves may to some extent be compared with those that have resulted from a better understanding of our physical environment. Except during the most recent period of man's sojourn on earth, he has been baffled and terrorized by plagues, floods, earthquakes, and storms. Since he knew neither the causes nor the nature of the forces involved, he was inclined to attribute these catastrophes to the revenge of the gods, or the actions of angry demons, or fate. As long as this attitude persisted, it acted to prevent him from investigating and understanding these events, for he feared that any attempt to study them would anger the gods, who would then punish him with new horrors. Today this feeling of helplessness against the elements is gradually being dispelled. Since we have learned much about the causes of these catastrophic events, we are better able to cope with them and to defend ourselves against their effects. We have techniques whereby we can investigate, control, and prevent both diseases and floods; we are aware of the kinds of forces present in earthquakes and can construct buildings to withstand them; and we can forecast storms and build the kinds of houses that will protect us from their violence. Furthermore, once catastrophes have occurred, we can bring skilled help and resources quickly to rehabilitate the stricken area. Thus, because we have an improved understanding of the phenomena of our physical environment, we can deal with them more realistically and consequently have less to fear from them.

Similarly, if we can understand ourselves and others better, we are in a position to act more realistically and resolutely, with much less fear, anxiety, and insecurity, and can live happier and more productive lives because we have been freed from some of our fears.

SUMMARY

This book is written for the "average" or "normal" student, who has made a reasonably good adjustment to life and its problems, but who would like to improve his ability to deal with his personal problems as well as with those forced on him by a rapidly changing society. The assumption on which this book is based is that the greater the emotional maturity of the individual, the more able he is to deal with personal and social problems. Emotional maturity is not something we automatically attain with physical maturity; yet, the process of becoming emotionally more mature is, like becoming physically mature, one of growth. As we become emotionally mature, we find that we are more able to tolerate, accept, and understand ourselves and others, and that we increase our capacity for self-reliance, self-direction, responsibility, and productivity. Emotional growth may be stimulated by increased understanding, or it may be impeded by surrender to neurotic or unrealistic fears.

In many ways, this book is the study of the development and functions of personality and the environment with which it must cope. Personality is described as the totality of the factors and processes that make us functioning individuals; environment is regarded as the total of events and situations as seen by the observer. The approach stressed in this book is dynamic: it is concerned with the causes of behavior, its purposes, its multiple origins, its continuity, and its involvement of the total human organism. It is recognized that much of the material to be discussed will run contrary to popular belief, or "common sense." It is assumed that the mature person will be more likely to use the dynamic point of view in order to attain a more adequate understanding of himself and others, and that the feeling of psychological security he will derive from this understanding will aid him in developing more satisfactory patterns of living.

REFERENCES

1. F. Alexander, "Emotional Maturity," *Mental Health Bulletin of the Illinois Society for Mental Hygiene.* 26:1–4; 1948. Reprinted by permission of Dr. Franz Alexander and the Illinois Society for Mental Hygiene, Inc.
2. H. Cantril, *The "Why" of Man's Experience.* New York: Macmillan, 1950. P. 128.
3. K. Young, *Personality and Problems of Adjustment.* New York: Appleton-Century-Crofts, 1940. Pp. 424–425.
4. R. R. Sears, "Experimental Studies of Projection: I. Attribution of Traits," *Journal of Social Psychology.* 7:151–163; 1936.
5. E. Sheerer, "The Relationship between Acceptance of Self and Acceptance of Others," *Journal of Consulting Psychology.* 13:169–175; 1949.
6. D. Stock, "The Self Concept and Feelings toward Others," *Journal of Consulting Psychology.* 13:176–180; 1949.
7. C. M. Harsh and H. G. Schrickel, *Personality: Development and Assessment.* New York: Ronald, 1950. Pp. 4–8.
8. R. W. White, *The Abnormal Personality.* New York: Ronald, 1948. Pp. 433–439.

SUGGESTED READINGS

L. F. Shaffer, *The Psychology of Adjustment.* Boston: Houghton Mifflin, 1936. See Chapter 1, "Human Conduct and Scientific Method."

H. A. Carroll, *Mental Hygiene*, 2d edition. New York: Prentice-Hall, 1951. The first chapter deals with the extent of the problem of mental disease as a basis for mental hygiene, behavior disorders in college, and the mental hygiene point of view.

— H. C. Lindgren, *The Art of Human Relations*. New York: Hermitage, 1953. See Chapter 1, "The Importance of Self-Understanding."

P. M. Symonds, *Dynamic Psychology*. New York: Appleton-Century-Crofts, 1949. Chapter 1 deals with the application of the scientific method and the use of the dynamic approach.

F. L. Ruch, *Psychology and Life*, 3d edition. Chicago: Scott, 1948. See Chapter 1, "Psychology as a Science."

R. Stagner, *Psychology of Personality*, 2d edition. New York: McGraw-Hill, 1948. See the chapters in the introductory section dealing with methods used in the study of personality.

T. M. French, "Clinical Approach to the Dynamics of Behavior," in J. McV. Hunt, ed., *Personality and the Behavior Disorders*, Vol. I. New York: Ronald, 1944. Pp. 255–268. The use of the psychoanalytic method as a research tool in studying personality.

O. H. Mowrer, "What is Normal Behavior?" in L. A. Pennington and I. Berg, *An Introduction to Clinical Psychology*. New York: Ronald, 1948. Pp. 17–46.

F. C. Thorne, "The Clinical Method in Science," in R. I. Watson, *Readings in Clinical Method in Psychology*. New York: Harper, 1949. Pp. 49–63.

J. E. Anderson, *The Psychology of Development and Personal Adjustment*. New York: Holt, 1949. The first chapter deals with such problems as the causation of behavior and the use of scientific methods.

— H. Cantril, *The "Why" of Man's Experience*. New York: Macmillan, 1950. See particularly Chapter 1, "The Science of Man."

— L. J. Saul, *Emotional Maturity*. Philadelphia: Lippincott, 1947. See particularly Part One, "The Achievement of Maturity."

II ... *The Development of*
Personality: The Self

The First Step: Understanding the Self. In the introductory chapter
we stressed the importance of understanding oneself and others as
a means of stimulating growth in the direction of emotional maturity.
It is our intention in this chapter to describe how the self develops
and how it meets the needs of the human organism of which it is a
component. Part of the explanation of our behavior lies in our
experiences, and these experiences, in turn, are related to the ways
in which we meet our needs.

When psychology was merely a lesser branch of philosophy, it
was much concerned with the self. Then there came a period when
psychology was endeavoring to establish itself as a science, when it
adopted the methodology of the natural sciences and concentrated
on the precise measurement and description of small areas of
behavior. In recent years, however, psychologists have begun to
realize that greater progress in understanding humans and their
behavior would come through studying the complete individual,
the person-as-a-whole, as personified by "the self" or "the ego."
Part of the motivation for this approach has come from psychoanalysis, with its concern for strengthening the ego through psychotherapy; and part has come from the study of personality by people
like Gordon W. Allport, Muzafer Sherif and his collaborators,
Prescott Lecky, G. H. Mead, Donald Snygg and Arthur W. Combs,
and Carl R. Rogers (1, 2, 3, 4, 5, 6, 7).

Research into the Nature of the Self. The problem of understanding
the self is to a large extent unsolved because of the difficulty of
conducting research in an area which is not well defined and in
which the nature of the thing being studied is in a state of constant

change. Nevertheless some real progress has been made, although many of the conclusions are still on a speculative level.

Scientific research usually starts with the formulation of a problem, which, in the case of the self, might be: What is the nature of the self? How can the self be distinguished from that which is not self? How does the self operate? The second stage is the development of hypotheses or shrewd guesses as to the solutions to the problems posed. The third stage involves testing the hypotheses through series of experiments or observations under controlled conditions. This third stage of research is comparatively easy for the natural scientists, who deal with relatively stable materials and processes that permit controls to be established. However in psychology and the other social sciences, the research problems are infinitely more complex, and the precision of the natural sciences is seldom matched. In spite of these difficulties, psychologists are making discoveries of the nature and causes of human behavior and, within limits, are able to predict and control it.

So far, the research conducted by psychologists has been roughly of three types. Some psychologists restrict their research to those areas in which conditions can be rigorously controlled. Experiments of this type produce information regarding minute segments of behavior, but they have not contributed as much to the general understanding of human behavior as have other types of research. Another kind of research specializes in the development of new and ingenious techniques and designs for conducting experiments and observations. Included in this category are statistical techniques that can be used to extract reliable and valid conclusions from data hitherto defying analysis. A third type of research is "clinical research," which results in the development of "working hypotheses" based on the observation of skilled observers. Most of what we know about the self has come from the latter type of research, although an increasing amount of knowledge is coming from a combination of the second and third approaches. For example, Rogers and others have studied the self through observing emotionalized attitudes toward the self as evidenced by persons undergoing psychotherapy, and changes in the perception of the self during psychotherapy (8).

Essentially, clinical research consists of those careful, shrewd, and insightful observations that skilled workers make in their attempts to help individuals and groups with their psychological problems. Working hypotheses grow out of such observations, fortified and supported by the comparison of notes and discussion of cases with other clinicians, as well as by repeated trials of the resulting hunches under varying circumstances. This means of studying personality was developed largely out of necessity. Persons in urgent need of help with their psychological problems cannot wait for the results of the precise, painstaking, and detailed kind of research that may eventually yield the basic truths of personality dynamics. Furthermore, it is often difficult, impossible, or undesirable to carry on experiments with persons who are in the process of receiving psychological help. Finally, the fact that psychotherapists *are* meeting with a reasonable degree of success in aiding their clients is an indication that the working hypotheses clinicians have developed concerning the nature of personality have a fair degree of validity (9). And since there is no difference, as we shall discover, between the *kinds* of problems faced by the average individual and those faced by persons under psychological treatment, it would appear that working hypotheses regarding the nature of the self developed under these conditions would have general application to both "disturbed" and "normal" persons.

The Concept of the Self. Because the chief purpose of this book is to help the student to understand himself and because this is not a textbook of theories of personality, we shall not attempt here a review of the various theories or working hypotheses regarding the nature of the self. Rather, the reader is referred to the writings of those who give extensive explanations of these hypotheses (1, 2, 3, 4, 5, 6, 7, 8, 10). However, in order that we may have some frame of reference within which to carry on a discussion of the nature of the self, we shall describe some of the ideas regarding the self that Rogers has so ably brought together and synthesized in his recent book *Client-Centered Therapy* (11).

Rogers visualizes each individual as the center of a continually changing world of experience, some of which is experienced consciously, but most of which is not. Individuals think, feel, and act in response to their world in terms of how they experience or perceive it, and the way in which they experience or perceive their world is to them "reality." A portion of the world as perceived by the individual gradually becomes differentiated from the rest of his

world, and this becomes the self. The self is that portion perceived
to be within the control of the individual. Thus objects or events
outside the body may under some circumstances be felt to be a
portion of the self, especially if the individual sees them as being important to his welfare, or, as we say, if he is "ego-involved" in them.

As the individual has more and more experiences, he begins to
organize his reactions into a fluid (changeable) but nevertheless
organized and consistent pattern, which Rogers calls "the self-
structure" or "self-concept." This self-concept is the individual's
way of looking at himself; and his thinking, feeling, and behaving
are for the most part consistent and harmonious with his self-concept.
That this is so is not remarkable — his thoughts, feelings, and
actions are merely his ways of meeting his needs as he sees them.

The Concept of Needs. As we stated in the introductory chapter,
one of the assumptions of the dynamic approach to the study of
human behavior is that human behavior has purpose. Its purpose
is to meet the needs of the individual. A need is a tension or im-
balance that persists until it is reduced, relieved, or eliminated
through some kind of satisfying activity. Needs may be met directly
or indirectly. For example, hunger is a need that expresses itself
in a craving for food, but some people satisfy this craving temporarily
by smoking a cigarette. For them, this need can be met at least
temporarily by a wider range of satisfactions than is possible for
nonsmokers. Needs are usually complex. The tensions some people
feel at dinner time are not relieved by food alone; dinner for them
is a ritual that involves both eating and communicating with others.
People of this type feel frustrated if they have to eat alone, for the
need to communicate is left unsatisfied. For most of us, mere food
is usually unsatisfying; it must be prepared and served in a manner
acceptable to the standards of our group, or it is not considered
fit to eat. However, when we have been forced to go without food
for prolonged periods, the sheer need for food of *any* kind takes
precedence, and we are satisfied with any sort of nourishment,
whether it is prepared "properly" or not.

Snygg and Combs state that the basic human need is to preserve
and enhance "the phenomenal self (12)." In other words, all our
behavior — thoughts, feelings, and actions — is directed toward
keeping ourselves alive, intact, and functioning and toward improving our living situation, if possible. And by "ourselves" in this

context is meant the persons, things, and relationships which are important to us and which we identify as "ours."

For the purpose of our discussion, we are going to distinguish several levels or stages in the one basic human need as outlined by Snygg and Combs. The system we shall use in this book is based on one developed by A. H. Maslow, which has the advantage of being simple, but which permits discrimination of needs according to various levels of emotional maturity (13). Maslow sees needs as ranked in a hierarchy, ranging from the most physiological to the most psychologically mature and "civilized." A somewhat modified version of his system, which we shall term the "basic needs," is as follows:

First level. The most essential body-needs — to have access to food, water, air, sexual gratification, warmth, etc.

Second level. Needs that relate to physical safety — to avoid external dangers or anything that might harm the individual.

Third level. Needs that relate to love — to be given love, affection, care, attention, and emotional support by another person or persons.

Fourth level. Needs that relate to maintaining satisfying relationships with others — to be valued, accepted, and appreciated as a person; to be esteemed and respected; to have status; and to avoid rejection or disapproval.

Fifth level. Needs that relate to achievement and self-expression — to be creative and productive; to perform acts that are useful and valuable to others; to realize one's potentials and translate them into "actuality."

There are two things that should be noted about the order in which these needs are listed. In the first place, they are listed in the order of their importance to the individual. In other words, the needs for air and water are important for the continuance of life itself, whereas the need for status is not. In the second place, the individual's ability to meet "higher" needs depends on the extent to which he has been able to meet his "more essential" needs. For example, it is difficult for an individual to work efficiently if he feels that he is not appreciated by his group or if he feels that he is not loved. Or, our normal receptivity to love can be lessened or impaired by unmet needs for food, water, or sleep.

Development of the Self during Early Infancy. Perhaps the best method of explaining the foregoing theories or working hypotheses regarding the nature and operations of the self is to describe several stages in the development of the individual and interpret them in terms of the concepts of the self and the basic needs.

The newborn infant has no self as we have defined it, because he is not sufficiently able to tell the difference between himself and his environment. As far as he is concerned, his mother's breast is as much a part of him as his own fist. It is some time before he realizes that the breast "belongs" to his mother and the fist "belongs" to him. He meets first-level needs according to the pattern of his temperament — vigorously or placidly, quietly or noisily, etc. When he falls or hears a loud noise, he perceives this as a threat to his needs for physical safety (second level), and he reacts with screams of fear or rage. He reacts to frustrations of his needs on the first level in much the same way. Naturally, when first- and second-level needs go unmet consistently, the child's health is very likely to be affected. He easily falls victim to disease, and he fails to develop at a normal rate. However, we consistently overlook the fact that the need for love is almost as essential as are the needs at the first and second levels. According to H. Bakwin,

Infants under six months of age who have been in an institution for some time present a well-defined picture. The outstanding features are listlessness, emaciation and pallor, relative immobility, quietness, unresponsiveness to stimuli like a smile or a coo, indifferent appetite, failure to gain weight properly despite the ingestion of diets which in the home are entirely adequate, frequent stools, poor sleep, an appearance of unhappiness, proneness to febrile episodes, absence of sucking habits. (14)

On the other hand, if the needs at the first three levels *are* met, the normal child will grow and flourish.

Development of the Self during Later Infancy. It is difficult to say when the self makes its first appearance. Perhaps it is when the infant begins to smile at his parents, some six or eight weeks after birth. Perhaps it is when he sets out to explore his crib or his own body. In any event, sometime during the first year of life, the child has some glimmerings of being a separate entity. He comes to recognize his name. He begins to develop needs on the fourth level, as is indicated by his expecting things from other members of his family. He learns that his mother will feed him, that his father will toss him in the air, and that his brothers and sisters will try to make him laugh or will try to hurt him, as the case may be.

Other functions of the self begin to bud and blossom. The child learns to enjoy the society of others; he appears to realize that they are important to him and that he is important to them. He is acquisitive — he wants things for himself, he makes wild grabs at things he should not have, and he clings to them and resists attempts to wrest them from his grasp. He put things into his mouth, for he still operates very much on the first level of need-satisfaction. He becomes very much aware of his physical environment and wants very much to explore it. As he grows and matures, he discovers that he *can* explore it — first by looking and listening; later by feeling, reaching, and grasping; and then by crawling. And in conducting his explorations, he very gradually learns the difference between his self and that which is not his self. His sense of reality, as observed by adults, is highly inadequate, for he does not know what parts of his environment he can control, he does not know what is dangerous and what is safe, and he does not know what is his and what is not his.

Early Childhood. Although these early explorations may prove satisfying to the child, in that they help him to find out "who he is," it is inevitable that they will bring him into conflict with the standards of his social group, particularly if he lives in a middle-class home. For example, he is likely to offend our sense of the importance of property and possessions, because, as his explorations grow more vigorous, he will pull books off their shelves, knock ash trays on the floor, pull over lamps, and relieve himself at inopportune times and in inappropriate places. This is understandable, because his behavior is impulsive, spontaneous, and uninhibited by reason or moral standard. Sooner or later he is likely to be punished for these acts. If punishment comes too early, he will not understand why he is being punished; but if it comes when he is able to associate punishment with breaking or dirtying things, he will be close to the next step in his development, which is to refrain from doing certain things as a means of avoiding punishment.

Viewing the situation from a different point of view, the child sees punishment as a threat to his self-structure or self-concept. Up till now he has perceived himself as the object of inexhaustible love. But now his parents are apparently withholding love from him, and his needs for affection are being momentarily frustrated. For all he knows — his sense of time is poor — they may be withholding love forever. In the past his parents have expressed their love for him by cuddling, caressing, or soft words; but now their harsh words or slaps seem to him the opposite of love — rejection. His expectation of love and security forever and ever has been rudely terminated; his self-structure is temporarily disorganized as he attempts to cope with this disturbing situation.

Normally, the child adjusts to these necessary restrictions when he is mature enough to discover what his parents expect of him, incorporating the parental expectations into his own self-structure. Some children accept restrictions as a matter of course; but many, if not most, do not accept them without going through one or more periods of rebellion. During these periods, the child is, in effect, fighting against the necessity of having to change his self-concept, and the battle is not over until he yields to the reality that he must accept the change.

In the first stages of developing these new controls over his behavior, perhaps he accepts the limits placed upon him by his parents only when they are in the same room with him. Then he learns that he must inhibit his behavior even when they are absent. For instance, when he spilled the ink on the rug, those parents, by some unknown powers of black magic, discovered that it was *he* who had done this thing! And he was punished and scolded for it, even though they did not see him do it! Maybe he did not even spill the ink — that is, maybe he did not *remember* spilling it, or was *unaware* that he had spilled it — but there was this ink stain, and he was punished! What can you do against such all-powerful, all-knowing parents, who possess such magic powers, *who can make you so afraid of what you might let yourself do?*

Although not every child has experiences and feelings like those described, most children in our middle-class culture do have some emotional conflict in the course of learning to restrain their impulses. In the second or third year of life,* the child begins to learn that he cannot trust himself to follow his impulses, for doing so would lead

---

* Psychologists do not agree as to the exact period when guilt feelings first assert themselves. Some report their appearance in the first year of life, while others place them in the second or third year. The eminent psychiatrist-writer, Gerald H. J. Pearson, denies flatly that there is any evidence of a "superego" (which in Freudian terminology is the source of guilt feelings) before two years of age (15). In any event, if any guilt feelings appear before this time, they probably do not constitute much of a force to be reckoned with.

him into trouble with those very important people — his parents. In order to protect himself from what (to him) appears to be the threatened loss of love — that is, punishment or rejection — he is forced to change his self-structure by incorporating into it something that will stop him the next time he feels like breaking or dirtying his parents' possessions. He accomplishes this change by taking over his parents' standards and by modifying his expectations of himself. By taking over his parents' standards, he accepts the thesis that some things are "wrong" or "bad"; by accepting their interpretation of his behavior, he comes to expect that he will do things that are "wrong" or "bad" if he is not careful to restrain himself. When he does misbehave, he feels guilty and conscience-stricken, because he has not lived up to his expectations; he feels that he has let himself down. He may react to this by punishing himself directly: for example, by slapping his own hands. Or, more likely, he reacts to his feelings of guilt by his own characteristic way of expressing frustration — having temper tantrums, blaming others, being irritable and "negative," biting his nails, acting babyish, etc.

"Conscience" is the term we use in everyday language to describe this restraining and punishing aspect of our self-structure, whereas the Freudian term "superego" is used by some psychologists. Essentially, conscience is a pattern or way of reacting to ourselves, a pattern that children adopt from their elders (16). Even as adults we are not immune from its effects, for it continues to operate much as it does in childhood, by punishing us with feelings of guilt for our real or fancied misdeeds. However, adult consciences are usually more benign and mellower than the consciences of children. Because the physical punishment they receive from their parents is less painful than the guilt inflicted by conscience, many children magnify their misdeeds out of all proportion and often tell their parents about some mischief that otherwise would have gone undiscovered. Sometimes, merely to *think* of violating standards of conduct is sufficient to arouse feelings of guilt. Some children, particularly those who live in homes where there are too many restrictions, will restrict *all* activities, because they feel that it is safer to do so than to run the risk of disapproval by their own consciences or their parents.

The "Terrible Twos." Inasmuch as the process of adopting parental standards, reforming the self-concept, and developing a conscience creates such problems of adjustment during the third year of life, psychologists have come to look for a stormy and negativistic period in the lives of most children during this stage of development (17). Figuratively speaking, the normal child does not give up easily what he considers to be his right of self-determination in exchange for parental standards; hence, this period of life is marked by sporadic skirmishes with parental authority. However, in the end he must surrender, if his behavior is to develop in the accepted patterns of his cultural group. If surrender can come happily and peacefully, so much the better, because it will be easier for him to conform later on to the many demands and restrictions society will place upon him. For example, if the child learns at home that he should not strike or curse the members of his family, it will be easier for him to conduct himself in a nonaggressive fashion in the society outside of home.

Later Patterns of Conformity. As the child grows and matures, the functions of his conscience take on a more positive character. Although conscience continues to be a source of guilt and anxiety, even in the normal child, it is less likely to inspire the behavioral disturbances characteristic of the two-and-one-half-year-old. As the child learns to know his parents better, and thus perceives them differently, his attitude toward them changes. And since his attitude toward his conscience (internalized parental standards) is a carbon copy of his attitude toward his parents, he will change his feelings toward his conscience very much as he changes his feelings toward his parents. He normally comes to admire the parent of his own sex and tries to copy his behavior in different ways. Girls pattern themselves and their behavior after their mothers; and boys, after their fathers. During these early years, their parents appear as pillars of strength and righteousness, and children have the feeling that if they do the things their parents do, they will be as strong and as blameless.

As the child becomes involved with social groups outside his family (playmates, school, etc.), he comes in contact with new sets of standards, which he incorporates into his self-structure, much as he incorporated parental standards at an earlier age. Now he finds himself bothered by guilt feelings not only as a result of "being bad," but also as a result of "being different." These guilt feelings express themselves in terms of a sense of shame at departing from established

"According to the book, we got the right idea in child training, dear . . . could be we got the wrong child . . ."

George Lichty and the Chicago Sun-Times Syndicate

The "terrible twos" are a difficult period — particularly for parents.

practices within the group (18), or as a fear of being different, or as a fear of being rejected or ostracized by others if one is very different. Thus the college student who inadvertently appears at a formal dance in sport clothes feels almost as miserable as a five-year-old who is tortured by guilt feelings because he was successful in getting his younger sister punished for something he had done.

Areas of Conflict in the Development of the Personality during Preschool Years. The growth and maturation of the self and its functions do not always proceed peacefully and comfortably. Growth is often an uncomfortable process: it involves adjustments and readjustments. Changes are difficult enough for an adult; they are even more painful for the child, who does not have the wealth of experience and the hopeful expectations that help the adult accept the discomfort of change more or less philosophically. For the child, adjustments and change always mean giving up something. Perhaps it is something he has never really had, but the feeling is still there. For example, when he accepts the necessity of a conscience with its restrictions, he gives up the right to do as he pleases. When a younger brother or sister arrives in the family, the older child is forced to give up his monopoly on his parents' love and attention or the favored place of the family's youngest, as the case may be. Thus adjustments and change always mean giving up a familiar and comfortable pattern for a strange and unknown one. This is one of the reasons why children need more emotional support and understanding during periods of change. Yet change, disturbing as it is, is necessary if children are to grow emotionally and intellectually, as well as physically.

Toilet-training is one example of the kind of conflicts that develop out of the need to adjust to the standards of society. Children naturally prefer to relieve themselves wherever and whenever they please, but such behavior is frowned upon by most societies. Parents therefore enforce standards of behavior at variance with the children's desires, standards demanding that they give up the infantile pleasure of relieving themselves at will. In the eyes of the child, a "compromise" is reached: he is not required to give up urination and defecation altogether, but he must relieve himself at appropriate times and in specified places. Thus society does not insist that basic needs be forever throttled or frustrated, but inhibited and controlled.

The standard of society becomes incorporated in the child's self-structure, so that when it is violated, he feels guilty and unworthy. However, before he arrives at the point of accepting his standard of behavior, there are usually lapses, which are punished by scoldings, expressions of disapproval, spankings, etc., the type of punishment depending on the custom of the parents and their cultural group. Although it may not be easy for the child to give up infantile pleasures, he eventually does so in deference to the demands of the standard that has become a part of his self-structure.

Perhaps one way of summarizing the foregoing discussion of conformity, conscience, superego, and guilt feelings is to state that these processes of the personality represent the attempts of the self to meet those needs of the individual concerned with maintaining satisfactory relations with others. In essence, the problem of the self, in this respect, is that of finding the best ways of satisfying basic needs without trespassing on the rights of others. As the child establishes the necessary controls over his impulses, he prepares the way for his acceptance as a participating member of society.

All growth has an aspect of achievement and creativity about it, and children and adults alike take pride in being able to accomplish something today that they could not do yesterday. Even though growth is often uncomfortable (it involves change, and change, as we have said, usually involves some discomfort), to have met the challenge of one's environment, to have mastered a difficult situation, gives most of us a thrill of pleasure, because such feats help to satisfy our need for achievement and self-expression.

Later Development of the Self. As the individual's experiences become more complex and as he becomes more dexterous, skillful, and competent, he normally finds himself less concerned with the basic needs and more concerned with needs at higher levels. As he finds roles in life that are comfortable to him, he finds that he needs to worry less about control of his impulses, for as he plays these roles, the problem of emotional control tends to take care of itself.

These principles can be identified in the kinds of problems that arise in connection with employment. Even in the initial stages of vocational choice, the problem of meeting the needs for food, shelter, and clothing are of relatively minor importance, particularly during periods of full employment. The individual is not concerned with selecting *any* job that will keep the wolf from the door, but rather with selecting the job that will permit him to do the kinds of things he enjoys and to be with the kind of people he likes. It is true that the immature person may look upon a job solely as a source of income, but this attitude vanishes with emotional maturity.

In essence, when we express a preference for a job that permits us to do the kinds of things we enjoy, we are stating a preference for a job that gives us an opportunity to be creative, to express ourselves in terms of our individual talents. When we stress the desirability of congenial companionship in our work, we are aware of the need for acceptance by others. We might also insist that our work give us a feeling of importance, thus meeting the need for status.

The emotionally mature adult also organizes his life so that he can give aid and support to others. This is further indication that he is less concerned about his own basic needs, which he has learned will be met in ways that are incidental to his meeting needs on a higher level. In other words, he will see to it that the activity that meets his needs for creativity, self-expression, and acceptance by others will also help to meet his needs for food, shelter, and love. Therefore, he organizes his behavior efficiently, in order to meet the maximum number of needs with any given act or type of behavior. Thus when a salesman has a good week and brings home a bonus check, he is meeting needs at all five levels. The check will buy food and pay the water bill; it will help with the payments on the house; perhaps some of it will go for taxes, which help pay the firemen and policemen who provide protection of various kinds. His wife will be proud of him, because she knows that he put forth this effort partly for her sake. His fellow employees will recognize that he is "one of the top men on the sales force." And he himself will take pride in his accomplishment. Behavior of this kind is particularly satisfying because it helps to meet needs of various kinds at all levels.

The self normally operates to organize and direct the activities of the individual in ways that will enhance his ability to meet all his needs and to maintain a high level of mental health. And the healthy self is one which not only is able to withstand the internal pressures of the basic needs and the external pressures of the environment, but which is able to meet both needs and pressures with increasing efficiency. In so doing, it aids the individual in understanding, tolerating, accepting, and respecting himself and others, and in becoming self-reliant and productive.

SUMMARY

This chapter was concerned with the nature and development of the self or ego. Much of our current understanding of the self is based on working hypotheses which, though based on clinical research, have been found to be useful and workable. The self is seen as that portion of the individual's world of experience with which he is identified and which he perceives to be within his control. As the individual matures, his reactions become organized into a pattern, which we call the self-structure or self-concept.

The individual behaves in ways that he expects will meet his needs as he sees them. Needs may be classified in a hierarchy ranging from the most biological to the most social and most civilized. Infants are concerned with meeting only basic needs, including the need for love; but as they become older, they become more concerned with needs involving relations with others. In order to meet these latter needs, it is necessary for children to modify and restrict the expression of their basic needs. The realization that they must change comes with greatest impact during the third year of life for most children, and this period is often marked by much negative behavior. Children normally emerge from this stage of development with a rudimentary conscience, composed of parental standards they have incorporated into their self-concept. This conscience helps them to live in relative peace with others, because it makes them aware of guilt feelings when they violate their adopted standards.

As children grow older, they learn to conform to other standards of behavior, particularly those of groups of playmates. Their consciences also take on more positive characteristics; not only do they inhibit certain kinds of behavior, but they also encourage children to pattern themselves on those characteristics they admire in their elders and their friends. However, growth is not usually an easy matter, inasmuch as it involves giving up older and more comfortable patterns of behavior for new and strange patterns. Nevertheless, if children are to become adequate and mature adults, they must be able to maintain satisfactory relations with others, which means, in turn, that they must be sensitive to the needs of others.

As children grow to emotionally mature adulthood, they find themselves less and less concerned with the need to meet needs at lower, more biological levels, and more concerned with needs involving acceptance by others, creativity, and self-expression. In organizing their behavior to meet as many needs as possible through any given behavior sequence, they find that the lower level needs virtually take care of themselves.

REFERENCES

1. G. W. Allport, "The Ego in Contemporary Psychology," *Psychological Review.* 50:451–478; 1943.
2. M. Sherif and H. Cantril, *The Psychology of Ego-Involvements.* New York: Wiley, 1947.
3. M. Sherif, *An Outline of Social Psychology.* New York: Harper, 1948.
4. P. Lecky, *Self-Consistency: A Theory of Personality.* New York: Island Press, 1945.
5. G. H. Mead, *Mind, Self, and Society.* Chicago: University of Chicago Press, 1934.
6. D. Snygg and A. W. Combs, *Individual Behavior.* New York: Harper, 1949.
7. C. R. Rogers, *Client-Centered Therapy.* Boston: Houghton Mifflin, 1951.
8. C. R. Rogers, "Significance of the Self-regarding Attitudes and Perceptions," in M. L. Reymert, ed., *Feelings and Emotions.* New York: McGraw-Hill, 1950.
9. J. Wilder, "Facts and Figures on Psychotherapy," *Journal of Clinical Psychopathology and Psychotherapy.* 7:311–347; 1945.
10. S. Freud, *The Ego and the Id.* London: Hogarth, 1935.
11. C. R. Rogers, *Client-Centered Therapy.* Boston: Houghton Mifflin, 1951. Chap. 11, "A Theory of Personality and Behavior."
12. D. Snygg and A. W. Combs, *Individual Behavior.* New York: Harper, 1949.
13. A. H. Maslow, "A Theory of Human Motivation," *Psychological Review.* 50: 370–396; 1943.
14. H. Bakwin, "The Emotional Deprivation in Infants," *Journal of Pediatrics.* 35:512–521; 1949. Reprinted by permission of Harry Bakwin and the *Journal of Pediatrics.*
15. G. H. J. Pearson, *Emotional Disorders of Children.* New York: Norton, 1949.
16. N. Cameron, *The Psychology of Behavior Disorders.* Boston: Houghton Mifflin, 1947.
17. A. Gesell and F. L. Ilg, *Infant and Child in the Culture of Today.* New York: Harper, 1943.
18. A. Kardiner, *The Individual and His Society.* New York: Columbia University Press, 1939.

SUGGESTED READINGS

W. C. Langer, *Psychology and Human Living.* New York: Appleton-Century-Crofts, 1943. See particularly Chapters 8, 9, and 13, although the whole book (less than 300 pages) is well worth reading for a comprehensive treatment of this subject from the combined standpoint of psychoanalysis and the "needs concept."

G. Murphy, *Personality: A Biosocial Approach to Origins and Structure.* New York: Harper, 1947. A much longer and more sophisticated treatment than Langer's. Part IV is particularly concerned with the origins and evolution of the self.

R. Stagner, *Psychology of Personality,* 2d edition. New York: McGraw-Hill, 1948. Again, the entire book is well worth reading. Chapter 9 deals specifically with the self.

H. Cantril, *The "Why" of Man's Experience.* New York: Macmillan, 1950. An interpretative book, which grows out of the author's wide experience in the field of psychology. See particularly Chapter 6, "The Nature of the 'Me.'"

P. M. Symonds, *Dynamic Psychology.* New York: Appleton-Century-Crofts, 1949. A dynamic treatment of the development and maintenance of the "self-structure." An excellent source that will be appropriate to much of the discussion in this text. Specifically related to this chapter are Symonds's chapters "Introjection and the Superego" and "The Ego and the Self."

C. Thompson and P. Mullahy, *Psychoanalysis: Evolution and Development.* New York: Hermitage, 1950. A short and easily read description of the leading viewpoints in psychoanalytic thinking. See particularly Chapter 3, "The Ego and Character Structure."

L. E. Cole and W. F. Bruce, *Educational Psychology.* Yonkers, New York: World Book, 1950. See Chapter 9, "The Development of the Self into a Mature Person."

O. S. English and G. H. J. Pearson, *Emotional Problems of Living.* New York: Norton, 1945. A readable and dramatic description of the development of personality from the orthodox Freudian point of view.

D. Snygg and A. W. Combs, *Individual Behavior.* New York: Harper, 1949. A theoretical consideration of the dynamics of the self from the aspect of how the individual views himself, his behavior, and his environment. This viewpoint is incorporated in some of the discussion of personality dynamics later in this text.

M. Sherif and H. Cantril, *The Psychology of Ego-Involvements.* New York: Wiley, 1947. An important book, based on sound research, particularly helpful in the understanding of attitudes and the relationship of the individual to his social environment. See particularly the chapters entitled "The Genetic Formation of the Ego," "Re-Formation of the Ego in Adolescence," and "The Ego in Psychoanalysis." The last-named chapter is a highly critical discussion of the stand taken on this subject by such writers as English and Pearson.

C. M. Harsh and H. G. Schrickel, *Personality: Development and Assessment.* New York: Ronald, 1950. A well-integrated discussion of the various theories of personality.

R. W. White, *The Abnormal Personality.* New York: Ronald, 1948. Chapter 4, "The Integration of Personality," is a brief, readable discussion of the self-concept.

K. Young, *Personality and Problems of Adjustment.* New York: Appleton-Century-Crofts, 1940. See Chapters 9 and 10.

G. Murphy, *An Introduction to Psychology.* New York: Harper, 1951. See Chapters 21–23.

J. McV. Hunt, ed., *Personality and the Behavior Disorders.* New York: Ronald, 1944. In Part I, see D. V. MacKinnon, "The Structure of Personality," for a discussion of the various theories of personality, and O. H. Mowrer, "Dynamic Theory of Psychology," for a discussion of personality that synthesizes several points of view.

E. H. Erikson, *Childhood and Society.* New York: Norton, 1950. A treatment of the relationship that develops between the child and society in the process of his growing up. A restatement of Freudian principles in the light of anthropological research.

E. T. Prothro and P. T. Teska, *Psychology.* Boston: Ginn, 1950. See Chapter 3, "Psychology's Central Problem — The Individual."

N. Cameron, *The Psychology of Behavior Disorders.* Boston: Houghton Mifflin, 1947. See Chapter 4, "Language, Thought, and Role-Taking in the Behavior Disorders." An approach to personality development that sees the later growth of the ego and superego largely as a learning of adaptive roles.

H. C. Lindgren, *The Art of Human Relations.* New York: Hermitage, 1953. See Chapter 2, "Why We Behave as We Do."

III ... *The Functioning of the*
Unconscious Processes

Unconscious Motivation. William Alanson White, the eminent psychiatrist and teacher, once said that our failure to take into account the factor of unconscious motivation has probably been "the cause of more inadequacies in the understanding of human behavior than any other thing (1)."

White's statement has important implications for those of us who are attempting to understand ourselves and others. In other words, if we are to make any progress in such understanding, we shall have to abandon the "common sense" idea that people always know why they do things, and approach the study of ourselves and others with the assumption that people may *think* they know why they do things, *but usually they do not.* That is to say, people can often find some reasonable explanation for their behavior, but usually the explanation they find is not the important one and often is completely irrelevant.

To use a homely example, let us consider the situation of Mr. and Mrs. Benbow:

Mr. and Mrs. Benbow were thinking of getting a divorce. Their lawyer believes in helping married folk stay together, and so he asked them, "Tell me, why do you *really* want a divorce?" At first, they were somewhat taken aback by this inquiry, but finally Mr. Benbow spoke up and said that the thing that exasperated him most was that he had to get up and get his own breakfast, whereas his wife slept all morning. Mrs. Benbow countered by saying that the same thing happened in every household she knew of and other husbands didn't object, so why should he? Furthermore, if anyone wanted to know what *she* objected to, it was that Mr. Benbow was so untidy that she spent half her time picking up his clothes from the floor. At this point, the lawyer moved deftly into the argument, and before the Benbows knew it, they had agreed to stay together on a trial basis: Mrs. Benbow was to get Mr. Benbow's breakfast, and Mr. Benbow was to hang up his clothes.

Now, a month later, they are back in the lawyer's office. It didn't work. Each scrupulously carried out his side of the bargain, but still it didn't work. When their lawyer presses them to account for their incompatibility, the Benbows give additional reasons like the ones they gave the month before, but this time they resist any attempts to effect a compromise. They have learned their lesson and they want their divorce.

The Benbows probably never will be *consciously* aware of the real reasons why they do not get along. They *will* be able to find "logical" explanations which will sooth their pride and which will be more or less acceptable to their friends, but these superficial excuses will serve only to keep them from finding out the real reasons for their incompatibility. The fact that the Benbows insist on their divorce indicates they are at least dimly aware that there is a hidden basis for their inability to get along; hence, they resist any further attempt at a reconciliation.

The lawyer in this anecdote is like many of us who take the explanations given by ourselves and others at face value. He was unable to effect a reconciliation because he assumed that the things the Benbows complained about were the *real* bases of their difficulties; hence, his suggested remedy that they compromise their points of difference did not touch upon their basic unwillingness or inability to adjust to each other. However, it is to be admitted that had the Benbows really been willing and able to adjust to each other, the lawyer's suggestion might very likely have helped them to start rebuilding their marriage. But even so, their efforts probably would not have been based on any understanding of the hidden dynamic elements involved.

Like the Benbows, the people we know are always explaining their behavior. Usually these explanations are not in themselves important — they are supplied as a means of making the explained behavior acceptable to themselves and others. It is not important whether or not we accept the statement of a friend that he cannot go golfing with us because his wife wants him to paint the back porch. The important thing at the moment is that he is unable to go. However, if he is *always* too busy with something else and is *never*

Philip Bonn and Children's Bureau

Most people who get into trouble are unaware of the real bases of their antisocial behavior. This boy is being helped by a school counselor to gain a better understanding of and insight into his problems.

able to go golfing, then we begin to suspect that he does not like to go out with us, or that he does not like golfing, or that his wife does not permit him to go out with the fellows — or what *does* he mean when he gives these excuses? Perhaps we shall never find out what he really means, but the chances are that we shall do him an injustice if we assume that he *intentionally* invents these reasons, just as we do the Benbows an injustice if we assume they intentionally thought up reasons for their incompatibility that turned out to be unimportant when put to the test.

Since instances like the ones we have described above are exceedingly common in everyday life, it follows that we shall be unable to make even a start at understanding ourselves and others unless we are able to accept the proposition that much of the causation of our behavior lies beyond the limits of our awareness, that it is, in effect, unconscious.

Unconscious Processes and "Common Sense." As we have indicated previously, the concept of unconscious motivation does not meet with sympathy or acceptance on the part of the man in the street, inasmuch as it is diametrically opposed to "common sense." "Common sense" assumes that most of us "are in command of our faculties"; that we should be able to know why it is that we do things; that people who do not act "sensibly" — that is, in their own interests — are stupid, lazy, or crazy; and that anyone who gives an explanation for his behavior contrary to the observable facts — as the Benbows did — is obviously lying. "Common sense" holds further that every sane person can behave logically and reasonably if he so desires, that if we do not behave logically and rationally, it is because we have *chosen* not to do so. Another "common sense" belief is that any one, if he exercises enough will power, can change his "personality" and that anyone who is unable to do so lacks "will power" or is "weak-willed."

Unfortunately, people fit the patterns prescribed for them by "common sense" only to the extent that their unconscious processes permit them to do so. There is much evidence, some experimental and some to be found in everyday life, demonstrating the unconscious nature of the forces that motivate our behavior.

Everyday Evidence Supporting Unconscious Motivation. Careful, well-intentioned people *do* forget things they have every logical reason to remember. A student memorizes theorems for an examination and can write them out letter-perfect. When he tries to remember them during the examination period, they are gone, apparently beyond recall. Yet, later in the day, they come to mind without effort on his part.

A girl has the habit of gnawing her lower lip; she feels that it attracts notice, and she would like to stop. Yet no matter how hard she tries, she cannot break herself of this habit.

A student sits down to study an important lesson; he reads a certain paragraph. Each sentence is clear and sensible; but when he has finished the paragraph, he cannot remember what is in it. Even though he reads it over several times, he cannot make himself grasp the sense of the passage.

A girl takes a class in public speaking; she knows it is essential for her to speak on her feet in front of the group. She makes a good appearance before her bedroom mirror, but she is never able to speak before the class. Furthermore, she is unable to discover why she can make a speech in one place and not in another.

An employee would like to make a good impression on his boss and thus smooth the way for promotion. Yet, every time he meets him, he finds himself stuttering and mumbling, unable to say anything of importance.

Two drill-press operators work side by side in a certain manufacturing plant; one has a perfect safety record, and the other has an accident on the average of once every two months (the last one nearly cost him the index finger of his right hand). Yet each tries equally hard to be careful.

What is this mysterious force that prevents us from behaving sensibly and logically? What is this power that forces us to be shy, awkward, to say inappropriate things, to be generally ineffective, particularly at times when it is important to make a good impression? Why should we forget things we know so well? Why shouldn't we be able to concentrate whenever the need arises?

The answers to these questions may be found in the theories or working hypotheses that have grown out of clinical observations and out of research in social psychology. These theories are all useful; some explain certain situations better than others.

Some Explanations of Unconscious Processes. One theory, developed by Harry Stack Sullivan, states that we tend not to accept new situations as "new," but rather in terms of situations with which we are already familiar. We should like to believe that the new situation is the same as a more familiar one we have been able to cope with in the past, one with which we feel more or less comfortable. Because we are somewhat afraid of a new situation (afraid, perhaps, that we shall not be able to handle it), we approach it with some anxiety, which, in turn, serves to blot out those details of the new situation that make it different from the old situation (2).

This hypothesis helps to explain why the girl who is unable to speak before the class cannot understand her behavior. She tries to convince herself that the situation of speaking before a class and speaking before her mirror are essentially the same, whereas it is evident that for her they are not. Her inability to accept this difference serves to relieve her of the necessity of finding out why she is afraid of groups.

Sullivan's explanation of unconscious processes is similar to that put forth by Rogers. Rogers states that the individual can react to his experiences in three ways: 1. He can recognize an experience and accept it as having some relationship to his self-structure. 2. He can ignore an experience because he does not perceive it as having any relationship to or meaning in his self-structure. 3. He can deny the meaning of an experience or distort its meaning, because he perceives it as inconsistent with his self-structure (3).

Thus an individual who has difficulty in speaking before a group can react to this situation in three ways: 1. He can admit that he is shy and that speaking before groups frightens him. 2. He can ignore the situation and go on speaking badly, refusing to be concerned about it. 3. He can deny the fact that he speaks badly or can distort the situation by blaming the audience for being unsympathetic, by excusing himself for having had insufficient time to prepare his speech, by criticizing his teacher for not having given him enough training, etc.

Rogers believes that the third type of response covers the kind of reaction the psychoanalytic school of psychologists terms "repression," * which means the unconscious process whereby certain

* Psychoanalytically oriented workers distinguish between "repression" and "suppression." Repression refers to the *unconscious* process whereby a thought, memory, or feeling is eliminated or kept from awareness, whereas suppression refers to the *conscious* process of deliberately putting something out of mind, usually by turning the attention to something else. For example, an individual deliberately may suppress the memory of an unhappy love affair by playing a game of tennis. On the other hand, he cannot remem-

thoughts, feelings, and occurrences are cut off from the individual's awareness because he fears that if he were to become aware of them, he would become anxious and upset. Freud described the "unconscious" as an "area of the mind," a sort of repository of those aspects of our personality and experiences that we would consider infantile, disgusting, humiliating, or otherwise upsetting (4, 5). Later theorists in the field of psychoanalysis tend to think more in terms of *unconscious processes*, a concept that they find more useful than Freud's formulation (6).

In his synthesis of various theories of personality, Rogers describes the unconscious aspects of personality in terms of certain experiences being "denied symbolization (7)," and he refers to "organic experiences and needs which have not been symbolized (8)." In other words, there are certain aspects of our lives and ourselves that, for some reason or other, we cannot or do not put into words. As we say, they exist on a "subverbal level." Thus the adolescent who has inadequate knowledge of the sexual side of life might not be conscious of sexual needs, partly because he knows just enough to feel guilty about these new strong feelings, but does not know enough to be able to translate his feelings into words. He might tend to deny even to himself that he has such feelings.

Snygg and Combs speak of a "narrowing of the perceptual field under tension," which means that when people are tense and anxious, they tend to be less observant and less aware of their environment. As these authors say, "the girl too concerned over her appearance entering a room is only too likely to be unaware of the disastrous carpet edge in her path (9)." In some ways, this theory is similar to that of Sullivan's, in that the girl's anxiety operates to blot out certain aspects of the situation under observation. Although her optic nerves may actually register the details that should mean "torn carpet ahead — danger!" she is so concerned with her appearance that this impression is denied admission to consciousness.

Experimental Evidence to Support the Concept of Unconscious Processes. A number of the experiments that serve to demonstrate the existence of unconscious processes are studies in the field of perception. These

---

ber the name of the fifth grade teacher who humiliated him or even the humiliating circumstances, inasmuch as this memory has been repressed as too uncomfortable and painful.

experiments show how people will unconsciously distort or deny what they see, feel, and hear because they are influenced by certain forces or values without being aware of such influences.

In an experiment conducted by Sherif, persons who expressed certain opinions when alone, modified them to conform to the opinions of others when the experiments were repeated in a group setting. Yet almost to a man they stated that the group opinion had no effect, even though the evidence indicated that the group opinion was the most important factor in bringing about the change. Since they had nothing to gain by distorting the truth and since their denial of having been influenced was so close to being unanimous, we may assume that they were actually unaware of the fact that they *were* influenced (10).

Erica M. Weingarten noted that individuals who were evaluating others tended to be influenced in their judgment by their own problems of adjustment and that they were likely to see more problems in areas in which they themselves were psychologically insecure (11). Inasmuch as the individuals in this study were presumably attempting to render judgments as objectively as possible, it would appear that this bias operated unconsciously.

Elliott McGinnies and Warren Bowles found that students tended to remember more easily those pictures of faces that had been identified with occupations of the greatest value to them (12). Here the needs of the self-structure had an unconscious influence on both perception and learning. Similar findings were reported by Leo Postman, J. S. Bruner, and Elliott McGinnies in a study demonstrating that students recognize words of high value more quickly than words of low value (13).

It is beyond the scope of this chapter to review all the research demonstrating directly or indirectly that the internal and external pressures and forces experienced by us tend to influence our thoughts, feelings, and actions in ways beyond our awareness; but the interested reader may find material relating to this subject in the experiments and writing of Postman (14), A. I. Hallowell (15), Bruner (16), Bruner and Postman (17), Albert Pepitone (18), Mason Haire and W. F. Grunes (19), Eugene E. Levitt (20), and R. S. Lazarus and R. A. McCleary (21).

There is also experimental evidence to support the psychoanalytic theory of repression. I. M. Rosenstock found that when he presented to subjects printed sentences at various levels of readability, those sentences containing material theoretically most likely to be repressed were the very ones students found harder to read and whose meanings they were most likely to distort (22).

Donald V. McGranahan asked his subjects to reply with adjectives to a list of 100 nouns. Whenever they replied with an adjective pertaining to color, they received a mild electric shock. After a while, some of his subjects not only stopped naming colors, but apparently failed to think of them at all (23). In other words, they tended to repress replies pertaining to color from their consciousness when faced by this situation.

How Unconscious Processes Operate in Everyday Life. Even though it constitutes a denial of reality, repression nevertheless often serves a useful function in that it enables us to adjust more easily to the demands of life, relatively unhampered by unpleasant thoughts and feelings and unaware of contradictions in our behavior. It enables us to perform tasks and operations that would be difficult or impossible if we were bothered by recurring painful reminders of past failures or by other disturbing thoughts and memories. For instance, George Jones undertook a career in physical education, completely unaware that his vocational choice was dictated by his unconscious needs to dominate others, to run things, and to acquire power and status. In some ways, these are unpleasant, sinister, and socially unacceptable motives. Since he was unaware of these needs, he was free to continue his career with confidence and enthusiasm. One might with reason argue that George's relations with others may suffer because of these needs; but since his self-concept is that of a man who is humble, modest, and self-sacrificing, it is questionable whether he would be able to accept the picture of himself as he appears to others without becoming greatly upset. In the light of this fact, life is probably easier for George (if not for others) because the unpleasant aspects of his personality are denied admission to consciousness.

As we stated in the previous chapter, our conscience or supergo plagues us with guilt feelings whenever we indulge in thoughts and actions that run contrary to the accepted standards of our culture. These feelings often cause us to repress certain thoughts that might otherwise lead us to perform forbidden or disapproved acts. Some actions that are disapproved are violations of moral standards, while others involve certain patterns of behavior that are less "stylish" than others. For example, there is a tendency in our culture to repress feelings that would lead to an emotional display. We disapprove of weeping in public, and this attitude leads us to repress feelings of deep sorrow, particularly when we are with others. We condone kissing in public on certain occasions, provided it is more or less formal and perfunctory. But if a nine-year-old girl throws her arms around her mother and effusively kisses her — say, on a streetcar or in a department store — the mother is likely to be embarrassed and to scold the child. These are examples of a cultural pattern which stresses *emotional control*, and which regards the expression of strong emotions as babyish, immature, unmannerly, or even abnormal. Thus the typical American not only expresses *less* emotion than, say, the typical resident of the Mediterranean countries, but will often deny that he feels any emotion at all when faced by situations that would evoke considerable emotionality on the part of the Mediterranean person. In our "flight from emotion," we often try to present ourselves as calm, reasonable, competent, efficient, and cheerful persons, even though we may not feel this way. We stress the intellectual aspects of our behavior and attempt to deny to ourselves and others the presence of strong feelings.

Like many other patterns of behavior we display as adults, the repression of strong emotion begins in childhood. Parents in our culture do not generally permit children full expression of their fear and rage impulses. Children who cry are hushed and distracted, even though the crying may be justified. Partly because adults do not permit themselves to cry, they become very upset when children cry, and they often seem to take it as a personal affront when they cannot stop a child's crying instantly. Striking another child or, particularly, a parent, is forbidden; it leads to punishment or parental disapproval (threatened loss of love). Children come to learn, too, that symbolic attack in the form of curses or threats is disapproved. They also discover that it does not pay to have even hostile or fearful thoughts, because such thoughts sometimes lead to hostile or fearful behavior and, in turn, to ridicule or disapproval or punishment. They learn that it is less painful to repress such thoughts. The success of this repression can be demonstrated by the fact that although probably all children have at some time or other had conscious desires to kill one or both parents, only a minority of adults remember ever having had such a desire. Not only is the murder of parents frowned on by our culture, but it arouses our own moral indignation that we should have such ideas, for they contradict the real love we feel toward our parents. Inasmuch as we cannot tolerate an ambiguous situation within ourselves — that is, one in which we have feelings of both love and hatred toward our parents — repression resolves the dilemma for us by blotting our hostility from consciousness.

How Successful Are We in Repressing Our Feelings? We have mentioned some of the advantages to be gained by repressing our true feelings, but the gain is not all on the positive side. The primary purpose of repression is to hide feelings from our own selves, so that we may not be plagued by guilt feelings and anxiety. Its secondary purpose is to hide our feelings from others. In actuality, we do a much better job of hiding our feelings from ourselves than we do from others. One of the ways in which we reveal our true feelings is through slips of the tongue. The behavior of Mr. Falstaff illustrates this fact.

Mr. Falstaff disapproved of his secretary's untidy desk, but he still liked her as a person and valued her as a generally effective employee. Since he did not want to hurt her feelings, he refrained from criticism. Yet every time he passed her desk, piled high with documents, manuals, and correspondence waiting to be filed, he cringed inwardly. On one occasion, he revealed his real feelings. He approached her desk with a letter that needed correcting and said, eyeing her desk, "Miss Franklin, will you fix up this litter?" What he really meant to say was, "Will you fix up this letter?" but his true feelings struggled for expression and resulted in the slip of the tongue. Mr. Falstaff flushed and stammered and said that he hadn't meant that at all, but Miss Franklin knew what he meant.

Unconscious feelings do not always reveal themselves through such obvious means as a slip of the tongue. Usually they express themselves to others through subtle little mannerisms, quirks, facial expressions, tones of voice, etc.

Miss Primrose, the English teacher, finds it necessary to assure her classes at least once each day that she has their best interests at heart. The very fact that she finds it necessary to reassure them is a clue to her students that something is amiss; and, if this in itself were not revealing, her cold and hostile tone makes it doubly clear how she feels about students. She further reveals herself by her defensive attitude whenever she believes that her motives are being questioned by parents, her fellow teachers, or her principal.

Mrs. Larkspur is always saying, "My family comes first in everything." Yet she is "up to her ears" in club work to the extent of spending afternoons, evenings, and week ends in the service of her organizations. Her very behavior is a clue pointing to the strong probability that, unconsciously, she either dislikes her family or despises her role as a wife and mother or, at best, really prefers organizational activities to homemaking.

The two individuals described above are genuinely and sincerely unaware of their true feelings; and if their sincerity were questioned, they would stoutly defend their good intentions. Yet we have learned better than to accept statements like theirs at face value; instead, we base our judgments of people on their true feelings, which they reveal indirectly. We are usually able to see through the verbal barrage behind which people often try to hide their real feelings. This is the ability termed "empathy."

The Importance of Empathy. Empathy, as used in this sense, is the ability to be *aware* of the feelings and attitudes of others without necessarily *sharing* them. We gain this awareness by observing the speech, facial expression, posture, and body movements of others. As the four-year-old says, "I know my Mommy's mad, 'cause she *walks* mad." Empathy is the result of sensitive and acute perception. Like other forms of perception it may be sharpened or dulled, depending on the state of our emotions. Sometimes anxiety can serve to sharpen empathic awareness, but usually it operates to distort it.

The following illustrations show how a lack of empathy can result in failure in human relationships.

Judge Fine said to the prisoner at the bar, "Joe, you come from a good family; you know better than to earn a living by stripping cars. Your wife and daughter need you as a law-abiding breadwinner. You're no good to them in jail. I'm going to let you go back to them for one more chance." Joe answered, "Your Honor, you're so right. I've been a heel; I can see how wrong I've been. I'll turn over a new leaf." A month later he was back in jail. The fact is that Joe has a neurotic need to steal, to break the law, to be punished — a need of which he is completely unaware.

If Judge Fine had been empathic, if he had been sensitive to Joe's *feelings*, he would have treated Joe as a person with a psychological problem, not as one who can be helped merely by a kind gesture.

Jerry McGovern is a junior member of the Mountain Climbers' Club, and he attended a meeting called for the purpose of laying plans for the annual dinner. The club has always had their dinner at the Black Derby, an expensive custom, costing $10 a plate. Jerry got up and argued against this, pointing to the increasing costs of living, and stating that a good dinner might be had at the Blue Sombrero at $3 a plate. He said the food was not as fancy as that at the Black Derby, but he had eaten there with other groups, and he knew that the members would have a good time. The older members opposed the change, but Jerry beat down their arguments one by one. A vote was taken, and the Blue Sombrero won by a slight margin. Jerry felt good because he had fought the good fight and won; and his cup was full when some of those who opposed him congratulated him on his victory. However, a week later, a notice went out to the members to tell them that, because there was a flaw in the procedure followed at the last meeting, the board of directors met to reconsider the matter of the annual dinner meeting, at which time they decided it would be "safer" to have the dinner at the Black Derby, according to previous custom.

If Jerry had been more empathic, he would have sensed the reluctance of the older members to accept the suggestions of a junior member, delivered so aggressively and so logically that they felt inferior and inadequate and were placed on the defensive. Unconsciously, they felt a need to revenge themselves for the humiliation they had suffered. Jerry did not permit himself to be aware of this situation, because he was so intent on proving his point and defeating the older members.

The Elwood Locksleys are not speaking to each other. Elwood says that he loves his wife, but he cannot understand how she can be so unreasonable. When she suggested that they buy an automatic washing machine at the cost of three-hundred-odd dollars, he asked her to justify the expenditure of such a sum. She stated that washing with her current nonautomatic washer was a backbreaking job. Elwood suggested that the clothes be sent to a laundry. She replied that this was a ridiculous idea, and asked if he had considered the costs of laundry service as well as the fact that commercial laundries wear out clothes twice as fast as home washing. Thereupon Elwood, who is a cost accountant, whipped out a pencil and proved that even with higher costs and clothes wearing out twice as fast, it would be cheaper over a ten-year period to patronize the laundry than to invest in an automatic washing machine. Result of the discussion: the Elwood Locksleys aren't speaking.

If Elwood were more empathic, he would realize that the automatic washer is more than a mere household gadget to his wife — it is a symbol of status. The fact is that most of the wives in the neighborhood and all of the wives in Mrs. Locksley's bridge club have automatic washers, and she feels inferior to them because she does not have one. The possession of an automatic washer would reassure her that she is "as good as they are." The refusal of her husband to purchase the washer makes her feel even more inferior and inadequate, because she interprets it to mean that he does not understand or care about her feelings, and furthermore perhaps he does not love her as much as he should.

Communication of "Feeling-tone." The situations described above are typical of the difficulties we all have at certain times when some aspects of our self-structure prevent our being empathic. Most of us are capable of empathizing most of the time, and as we empathize with one another, we find our actions and attitudes conditioned or affected by one another's feelings. This amounts to a sort of communication or exchange of "feeling-tone" that takes place below the level of consciousness. In many, if not most, situations involving two or more persons, the interchange of feeling-tone at the unconscious level is of greater importance than the verbal exchange at the conscious level.

Otto Spiel was a competent bookkeeper with the Eldorado Packing Company. He was making $250 a month, but he wanted to make more. He saw no chance for promotion in his division, unless someone died or retired. On the other hand, he heard stories of the financial killings some of the salesmen were making. He decided that if he was to progress with the Eldorado Packing Company, it had to be in the field of selling. However, in order to break into the selling field, he felt that he had to have something more to offer management than experience in bookkeeping, and so he attended evening college and completed a two-year course in merchandising with a high scholastic average. Convinced that he knew the answers and formulas needed for success in the selling field, he applied to the personnel department of the company for transfer to the sales force. They were impressed by his academic record and granted his request.

Now, a year later, both the sales department and Otto are disappointed by the results of the change. Otto is not sure why he has failed, and the sales department puts it down to the lack of sales personality, whatever that is. The reasons for Otto's difficulties would be apparent if we could listen in on a conversation between him and a prospective customer.

Otto's approach to his customer is technically proper. He politely inquires after the health of his customer and talks about the weather and a few general subjects before getting down to business. He mentions a new line his company is pushing, and goes into a description of the advantages in stocking the line — low introductory cost, tie-in with premiums, support by newspaper and billboard advertising, etc. But his customer doesn't buy. He is overstocked with a similar merchandise; this kind of thing goes poorly at this time of year; he is suspicious of items that have to be pushed; he got stuck on the last deal like this; and so on. After a while, Otto retires from the scene as gracefully as possible.

Another salesman using the same approach and much the same words would have succeeded where Otto failed. Why?

Otto's difficulty is that he resents what he considers to be the role of a suppliant — *asking* people to do things for him. He despises himself when he has to "lick the boots," as he puts it, of people who are "not as good" as he is — that is, have less education or are foreign-born. He realizes, of course, that it would be highly improper to reveal his true feelings about his customers, and so he endeavors to conceal them. If we were to discuss this feeling of resentment with him, he would deny that it has anything to do with his failure to sell. The truth is, of course, that when he is trying to sell, he is successful only in keeping his feelings of contempt from himself. His manner of speaking and his gestures are only too revealing. His prospective customers probably could not say exactly why they do not buy from Otto. They might give the same reasons they gave Otto, because they, too, are repressing the real reasons. After all, no one really likes to be the object of scorn or contempt. At best, they are probably aware only that Otto rubs them the wrong way. Is it the air of superiority or condescension? Is it the lack of real warmth in Otto's smile, in Otto's greeting? Is Otto too stiff and mechanical in his sales talk? Does Otto seem unsure of himself? Whatever it is, his customers feel uneasy, uncomfortable, somewhat irritated, and even hostile when the sales interview is over.

Otto, too, feels that he is failing, that he is not impressing his customers as he should. Yet he is unable to admit to himself that he is a failure as a salesman, and so he tries harder to succeed. But the harder he tries, the more tense he becomes, and the sales resistance of his customers increases accordingly.

Another common situation demonstrating the communication of feeling-tone is that of the speaker who is competent and learned, but who raises the anxiety level of his audience by apologizing for his inadequacies, or by spending an overlong period to warm up to his subject. Good speakers, on the other hand, are characterized by their high level of empathy. They are very sensitive to the mood of their audience, and when they note symptoms of restlessness and boredom, they change their pace or tell a story, or at least move on to another topic less likely to arouse tension or hostility.

Teachers, too, are in a position to use or misuse the communication of feeling-tone. Some teachers are technically competent, but so unsure of their relations with others that they attempt to "cover up" by being grim or pedantic or hypercritical. Teachers of this sort usually succeed in communicating the very feelings they are trying to hide, with the result that the class becomes tense, hostile, or just bored. Other teachers are able to empathize with their students to the point that they can determine whether students understand or are confused, whether they are receptive, or whether they are in a mood calling for a change of pace and subject matter.

A demonstration of the exchange of feeling-tone between teachers and their classes is provided by the study of N. L. Gage and George Suci, who found that those teachers who estimated student opinion on school affairs more accurately — that is, who were more empathic — also tended to receive higher ratings from their own students (24).

The communication of feeling-tone is essential, too, in courtship. Two people may meet accidentally and discuss the weather or the latest television program in a casual fashion. Yet while this desultory conversation proceeds, there is an exchange of feeling-tone, and each may begin to feel the effects of mutual attraction and warm feelings. This love-at-first-sight phenomenon leads to other meetings, until the participants are sufficiently aware of their feelings to make them a subject for communication on the conscious level.

In the situations we have described above, the words spoken at the conscious level do not necessarily give clues to the communication taking place at the feeling level. And, as we have indicated, the latter type of communication really plays the more important part in attitude formation, motivation, and the course of action people actually will take.

The Place of Empathy in Everyday Living. There are no easy solutions to the problem of the salesman who dislikes people or the teacher who infects his students with his own insecurities. The use of empathy as a basis for getting along with others is in reality a part of the larger problem of attaining higher levels of emotional maturity, of coming to understand and accept oneself and others. Empathy is improved through the normal processes of emotional growth and not through learning techniques or by practicing the tone of voice that conveys the most "warmth." The latter approaches to personality change are essentially attempts to change the outward appearance without changing one's basic nature. Putting a honey-jar label on a vinegar bottle may make the bottle more attractive, but it does not change the acidity of its contents.

The individual who is really interested in change, who is prepared to give up some of his cherished concepts, must, as we have indicated, begin by understanding himself and others. Empathy is an essential tool in furthering such understanding, and the problem is more likely one of *permitting* one's empathy to function rather than of *learning* empathy, for we are normally empathic. As Sullivan and others have discovered, even infants communicate empathically with their world (25, 26, 27). L. B. Murphy found that three-year-olds showed definite signs of being able to empathize with their age-mates (28). Theodore M. Newcomb points out that the behavior of others seems less arbitrary and more understandable when one can empathize. He gives the example of the child who first says to himself, in effect,

"Mother is now hearing me say 'I won't' and she is getting ready to send me to my room, because that is what she always does." But later, when he is more mature and better able to empathize — that is, put himself in mother's place — he is able to say to himself, "Mother is now hearing me say 'I won't' and she's feeling pretty angry this time because she's busy getting supper (29)."

Thus the ability to empathize, like other psychological processes that contribute to general effectiveness, grows with maturity. And, like other processes, it can be impaired or rendered less effective by the pressure of neurotic needs. For example, Rosalind Dymond found that persons with high empathy tended to have better emotional adjustment than persons with low empathy (30).

The story of Jerry McGovern, cited above, who wanted the Mountain Climbers' Club to change the place of its annual dinner, might serve as an illustration of what happens when empathy is impaired by anxiety. If he had been sensitive to what the members were feeling, instead of merely listening to what they were *saying*, he might have gone about his campaign in a more conciliatory and less threatening manner. Perhaps he would not have undertaken it at all, realizing that having an annual dinner at the Black Derby had deep and inexpressible meaning for many of the members. Furthermore, being more sensitive to the feelings of others might have helped him become more sensitive to his own real and underlying motives in proposing the change. Was he trying to compete for the leadership of the club? Or was he merely attempting sabotage by trying to start a small rebellion against the established order? Was his plan based on careful analysis of the club's objectives and traditions? Was his aggressive attack a compensation for feelings of inadequacy and inferiority?

The best arrangements for human understanding are found in situations in which the individuals concerned are prepared to recognize, tolerate, accept, and respect others' feelings as well as their own. In situations of this kind, each individual empathizes with other individuals and is able to develop insight and understanding of his own feelings and motives.

SUMMARY

An awareness of the fact that the motivation of all human behavior is deeply rooted in the unconscious processes is essential if we are to understand ourselves and others. Indeed, much human misunderstanding is based on our lack of awareness of this principle, opposed, as it is, to the dictates of "common sense." Yet everyday life is full of incidents that demonstrate, through their inconsistencies and contradictions, the existence of unconscious processes.

One explanation of unconscious processes is that we attempt to deny the presence of elements that would make new situations appear different from more familiar ones. Another theory states that we tend to deny admission to consciousness or to distort experiences that are inconsistent with our self-structure. Still another concept states that we tend to repress or unconsciously "force out of our minds" thoughts and feelings that might cause us to experience anxiety. Experiences that we cannot or will not put into words also tend to remain on the unconscious level. Some psychologists speak of our tendency in times of stress to "narrow our perceptual field" or to ignore certain details of the situation in which we find ourselves.

The unconscious process termed "repression" is sometimes helpful in our everyday activities in that thoughts and feelings that might upset us and thus interfere are removed from consciousness. Our culture encourages us to go to extremes in this regard by placing us under some compulsion to repress feelings that in other cultures are permitted free expression. However, repression is not always successful, and feelings find indirect ways of expression in spite of our efforts. Sometimes they express themselves in slips of the tongue, but more usually they are revealed through such clues as the tone of voice, body posture and bearing, gestures, and mannerisms.

The ability to put oneself in another's place and sense his attitudes and feelings is an unconscious process termed "empathy." It is highly necessary if one is to understand others and communicate with them effectively. If we are not empathic, we are in danger of being chronically disappointed in others. Thus we must be aware of how others feel, which is frequently at odds with what they say. At the same time, we must be aware of our own feelings, which have their effect on others through the medium of mutual exchange of feeling-tone.

REFERENCES

1. W. A. White, "Medical Philosophy; from the Viewpoint of a Psychiatrist," *Psychiatry.* 10:191–194; 1947.
2. P. Mullahy, ed., *A Study of Interpersonal Relations.* New York: Hermitage, 1949. Pp. xxvi–xxvii.

3. C. R. Rogers, *Client-Centered Therapy*. Boston: Houghton Mifflin, 1951. Pp. 503–507.

4. S. Freud, *A General Introduction to Psychoanalysis*. New York: Boni and Liveright, 1920. Pp. 248–261.

5. S. Freud, *New Introductory Lectures on Psychoanalysis*. New York: Norton, 1933. Pp. 101–102, 111.

6. K. Horney, *New Ways in Psychoanalysis*. New York: Norton, 1939. Pp. 18–21.

7. C. R. Rogers, *Client-Centered Therapy*. Boston: Houghton Mifflin, 1951. P. 503.

8. C. R. Rogers, *Client-Centered Therapy*. Boston: Houghton Mifflin, 1951. P. 509.

9. D. Snygg and A. W. Combs, *Individual Behavior*. New York: Harper, 1949. Pp. 110–111.

10. M. Sherif, "Group Influences upon the Formation of Norms and Attitudes," in T. M. Newcomb and E. L. Hartley, eds., *Readings in Social Psychology*. New York: Holt, 1947. Pp. 77–90.

11. E. M. Weingarten, "A Study of Selective Perception in Clinical Judgment," *Journal of Personality*. 17:369–406; 1949.

12. E. McGinnies and W. Bowles, "Personal Values as Determinants of Perceptual Fixation," *Journal of Personality*. 18:224–235; 1949.

13. L. Postman, J. S. Bruner, and E. McGinnies, "Personal Values as Selective Factors in Perception," *Journal of Abnormal and Social Psychology*. 43:142–154; 1948.

14. L. Postman, "Toward a General Theory of Cognition," in J. H. Rohrer and M. Sherif, eds., *Social Psychology at the Crossroads*. New York: Harper, 1951. Pp. 242–272.

15. A. I. Hallowell, "Cultural Factors in the Structuralization of Perception," in J. H. Rohrer and M. Sherif, eds., *Social Psychology at the Crossroads*. New York: Harper, 1951. Pp. 164–195.

16. J. S. Bruner, in R. R. Blake and G. V. Ramsey, eds., *Perception: An Approach to Personality*. New York: Ronald, 1951. Pp. 121–147.

17. J. S. Bruner and L. Postman, "Symbolic Value as an Organizing Factor in Perception," *Journal of Social Psychology*. 27:203–208; 1948.

18. A. Pepitone, "Motivational Effects in Social Perception," *Human Relations*. 3:57–76; 1950.

19. M. Haire and W. F. Grunes, "Perceptual Defenses: Processes Protecting an Organized Perception of Another Personality," *Human Relations*. 3:403–412; 1950.

20. E. E. Levitt, "Cognitive Distortion and Ego Involvement," *Journal of Personality*. 19:212–220; 1950.

21. R. S. Lazarus and R. A. McCleary, "Autonomic Discrimination without Awareness: a Study of Subception," *Psychological Review*. 58:113–122; 1951.

22. I. M. Rosenstock, "Perceptual Aspects of Repression," *Journal of Abnormal and Social Psychology*. 46:304–315; 1951.

23. D. V. McGranahan, "A Critical and Experimental Study of Repression," *Journal of Abnormal and Social Psychology*. 35:212–225; 1940.

24. N. L. Gage and G. Suci, "Social Perception and Teacher-Pupil Ratings," *Journal of Educational Psychology*. 42:144–152; 1951.

25. H. S. Sullivan, *Conceptions of Modern Psychiatry*. Washington, D. C.: William Alanson White Psychiatric Foundation, 1947. P. 9.
26. J. Bowlby, *Maternal Care and Mental Health*. Geneva: World Health Organization, 1951.
27. P. Greenacre, "The Predisposition to Anxiety," in S. S. Tomkins, ed., *Contemporary Psychopathology*. Cambridge: Harvard University Press, 1943. Pp. 16–35.
28. L. B. Murphy, *Social Behavior and Child Personality: An Exploratory Study of Some Roots of Sympathy*. New York: Columbia University Press, 1937.
29. T. M. Newcomb, *Social Psychology*. New York: Dryden, 1950. P. 309. Reprinted by permission of T. M. Newcomb and The Dryden Press, Inc.
30. R. Dymond, "Personality and Empathy," *Journal of Consulting Psychology*. 14:343–350; 1950.

SUGGESTED READINGS

I. Hendrick, *Facts and Theories of Psychoanalysis*. New York: Knopf, 1934.
–C. Thompson and P. Mullahy, *Psychoanalysis: Evolution and Development*. New York: Hermitage, 1950. Particularly Chapter 4.
–J. Dollard and N. E. Miller, *Personality and Psychotherapy*. New York: McGraw-Hill, 1950. See chapters entitled "Social Conditions for the Learning of Unconscious Conflicts" and "The Unconscious: How Repression is Learned."
S. Freud, *An Outline of Psychoanalysis*. New York: Norton, 1949.
–P. M. Symonds, *Dynamic Psychology*. New York: Appleton-Century-Crofts, 1949. Chapter 10.
–W. C. Langer, *Psychology and Human Living*. New York: Appleton-Century-Crofts, 1943. Chapter 12.
–A. H. Maslow and B. Mittelmann, *Principles of Abnormal Psychology*, Rev. edition. New York: Harper, 1951. Chapter 4.
H. C. Lindgren, *The Art of Human Relations*. New York: Hermitage, 1953. Chapter 3, "Beyond the Limits of Awareness."

IV... *Emotion: Threat, Anxiety, and Hostility*

Threat. If there was anyone ten-year-old Jud Knudsen hated, it was Miss Morales, his fourth-grade teacher. Whenever there was any trouble, she blamed him. Even when there wasn't any trouble, she was always picking on him. But Friday was really the pay-off. Friday morning, Jud sort of accidentally spilled ink on Sandra's hair ribbon. Sandra sat in front of him and she was always trying to get him mad by calling him names under her breath during arithmetic drill, so she had it coming to her. But when she found ink on her hair ribbon, she went and told Miss Morales, and Miss Morales made Jud wear the ink-stained hair ribbon all day — even on the playground. Of course all the kids teased him, tripped him, and, worst of all, called him "sissy."

Resentment smouldered inside Jud all week-end long, and he thought of all kinds of things that he would like to see happen to Miss Morales for having done this to him. He thought of several ways to murder her; he thought of burning down her house; he thought of letting all the air out of her automobile tires. Then, as he was walking home from Sunday School across the fields, he almost stumbled over a large snake. It gave him quite a fright at first, till he realized it was only an old king snake. Then he got his big idea.

At ten o'clock the next day, Miss Morales was announcing that it was time for the art lesson and if the monitors would come forward, she would give them the drawing paper to hand out. So saying, she opened the bottom drawer of her desk and looked into the eyes of the biggest snake she had ever seen. Miss Morales screamed a little scream, then a bigger scream, then a long wailing scream . . . and fainted in a heap on the floor. The class sat in their seats, shocked, unable to move. Jud shrank back in his seat, horrified at what he had done. He felt so ashamed. He wished he were dead.

Threat. Patrick Ross sat on a stool in his own bar, clenching and unclenching his fists. He had just been talking to his lawyer. The

60

judgment of the court was that the former Mrs. Ross was to get one-half of the community property and alimony of $500 per month. Mr. Ross slipped off the bar stool, stood staring at it for a few seconds, and then heaved it into the bar mirror. He then went behind the bar and smashed each bottle, one after the other, against the edge of the sink, as customers and bartenders scurried out of the door. He was trying to smash the furniture when the police came to take him away.

Need-satisfaction. As Edward O'Donnell, junior at State, stood in the registration line to pick up his program book, he found himself talking to an attractive girl who had transferred to State and who was also a junior. During the long wait in line, he was able to tell her about the college, to give her advice as to the kinds of courses she should take, what instructors to avoid. He also told her some things about himself — what clubs he belonged to, what courses he was taking, what his vocational plans were.

During the first day of instruction, he was pleased to find her in not only one, but three of his classes. As they had lunch together, he said, "You know, I was sort of hoping we'd get together in some of my classes, and here you are in *three* of them! Isn't that a coincidence?" "Yes, isn't it?" she agreed.

Varieties of Emotion. The purpose of these three anecdotes is to portray the expression of emotion as it appears in two basic kinds of life situations. Jud Knudsen, Miss Morales, and Mr. Ross were all involved in situations which they perceived to be threatening and which called forth emotionally toned behavior associated with threat. Edward O'Donnell and his friend were drawn together by the mutual expression of a desire for need-satisfaction.

Essentially, emotion is a state of generalized excitement that expresses itself in changes in feeling-tone and bodily condition. When we are enraged we *feel* enraged, and others are made aware of our feelings by our actions. The feeling of rage is accompanied by such bodily changes as increased blood pressure, faster heart beat, increased secretions of the adrenal glands, inhibition of the digestive processes, increased skin moisture, and a dropping or rising of the skin temperature. Similar conditions accompany or consti- tute the expression of other strong emotions in response to threat (for example, panic), or in response to a desire for need-satisfaction (for example, sexual passion). Some examples of emotions of a milder sort that appear in situations involving threat are feelings of irritation, boredom, annoyance, resentment, and displeasure. Still others are timidity, apprehension, shyness, and hesitancy. Emotions of a milder sort associated with need-satisfaction occur in the form of enjoyment, curiosity, interest, friendship, and acceptance.

Various Theories regarding Emotion.   Some psychologists think of the bodily changes themselves as constituting the emotion, and they consider feelings to be the awareness of bodily change.   Other psychologists think of the emotions as accompanying or resulting from the bodily changes.   In all probability, emotions, feelings, and bodily changes are all aspects of the same condition.*

Emotions may also be considered one aspect of our attempts to meet our basic needs, particularly those needs more closely related to our biological processes.   Thus emotions are more closely related to those functions of the self which are subverbal, which lie below the threshold of awareness.   Many of our unexpressed emotions are primitive, impulsive, and antisocial, and therefore we tend to repress them from consciousness.   No one remembers when he first learned to fear, when he first learned to express anger and love. Since these feelings have their roots in the unconscious processes of our personalities, we are unaware of how much they affect our daily lives.   As we stated in the previous chapter, every one of our acts, thoughts, and beliefs has its unconscious, emotional bases, as well as the conscious and logical reasons we ascribe to it.

An example of this is the problem faced by Harold Ratto:

Eighteen-year-old Harold has volunteered for the Air Force.   When he is asked why he did this, he says that he would be drafted anyhow, and that he may as well go while he can make his choice.   He believes this and his friends accept it as the real and logical reason.   But this does not explain why Harold does not go into defense work, where he would likely be draft-exempt, and it does not explain why he does not enjoy civilian life as long as he can.   Consider these other factors in Harold's life: 1. All the fellows who graduated from high school with him are in the service or are about to go in. 2. Quarrels between Harold and his parents have increased in frequency during the past year, and he is beginning to feel that they do not appreciate the fact that he has grown

---

* For a review and discussion of various theories pertaining to emotion, see M. L. Reymert, ed., *Feelings and Emotions.* New York: McGraw-Hill, 1950. See particularly Sections I and II.

up and can make his own way in life. 3. His girl friend is carrying on a "pen pal" correspondence with two soldiers overseas. 4. Harold is really afraid of going into the service, but he has always handled his fears by putting on a bold front and acting as though he were not afraid. Each of these conditions has an important bearing on Harold's decision, but he is unaware of their influence. Because of these conditions, he has strong needs to appear as brave as the other fellows seem to be, to attempt to live up to what he thinks his girl friend expects of him, to break loose from parental domination. These are the *emotional* reasons why he has volunteered for the Air Force, and these are the *important*, though unconscious, reasons.

This does not mean that emotions remain entirely in the realm of the unconscious. The stronger they are, the more we are aware of them; and the more socially acceptable they are, the more we are conscious of them. Thus a mother may not be conscious of a mild hostile feeling toward her child, although she is aware of losing her temper. On the other hand, she is conscious of a feeling of pleasure the first time the child says the word "mama."

Emotion may be classified in terms of the action seen by the individual as appropriate. Thus, those emotions we commonly associate with *fear* occur in situations that the individual interprets as calling for flight, panic, or immobilization ("freezing" with horror); emotions commonly associated with *anger* occur in situations that the individual interprets as calling for attack, for hostile, aggressive action; and emotions commonly associated with *pleasure* occur in situations that the individual perceives as calling for movement toward the source of the stimulus.

Therefore, *the "real cause" of the emotion is the perception of the individual.** If an individual feels that he is being or has been or will be attacked, thwarted, deprived, or frustrated, he will react to the situation with the emotional behavior he feels to be appropriate; and the appropriateness of this behavior will depend on whether he sees the situation as calling for flight or for attack. If he feels that his needs are being, have been, or will be satisfied, or that he is being aided in his attempt to satisfy them, he will react with emotional behavior appropriate to need-satisfaction.

---

* Physiological states may often predispose us to perceive certain situations or events as threatening or as pleasure-producing. A person who is hungry is likely to be irritable about any occurrence that does not propel him in the direction of food, and a person whose system is deficient in calcium may be inclined to be gloomy or pessimistic.

"Don't be scared. He's dead."

The emotion generated by an individual depends on how he perceives his situation, rather than on its objective reality.   In the above cartoon, the bridge players perceive the mouse as a threatening object, even though it is powerless to harm them.   Their fear is just as genuine as it would be if the mouse were a poisonous snake.

Snygg and Combs write as follows on this subject:

A very large part of what a person is describing when he speaks of his "feelings" is made up of his awareness of the bodily conditions which he differentiates at that moment out of his field [of perception]. These "feelings" are his description of his field [of perception] at any given moment and usually contain some reference to body states. For example, when I say that "I feel fine," what I am describing is the nature of my field [of perception] at the moment, including the state of my body (1).

Emotion is a state of tension or readiness to act. This tension represents the reaction of the organism to the perception of the possibility of need-satisfaction (self-enhancement) or the perception of threat (maintenance of self). . . .

What the individual describes as his emotion is actually his account of his personal relation to the situation. The greater the personal reference in any situation, the greater is the degree of emotional experience for him (2).

In other words, it is the way in which the individual perceives and evaluates the situation, consciously or unconsciously, rather than the situation itself — that is, how it appears to an outsider — that determines his emotional reaction. For example, tennis may be for one individual a fear-provoking situation, because he is timid, is not a good tennis player, and is humiliated when he feels he is "making a spectacle" of himself. For a second person, tennis may be a rage-provoking situation, because he usually plays with his brother, whom he dislikes, and who, he is convinced, does not play fair. Every time he plays he loses his temper and finally stalks off the court in a rage. For a third person, tennis may be a pleasure-provoking situation. He may enjoy the exuberance and grace that may be expressed or displayed in this game. To the outsider, one tennis match is much like another, but these three players see tennis so differently and have such different reactions, that we concede that, as far as they are concerned, the situations *are* different.

The Dynamic Quality of Emotions. Feelings and emotions have a quality of "strength" that often gives the individual who is trying to control them the sensation of struggling with a force stronger than he. When we *feel* angry, we wish to *act* in an angry manner. If the feeling is very strong, we may fight to keep it under control; but if it is too strong, it may take over, in which case we behave in enraged fashion, although most of us do not go as far as Patrick Ross did, in the anecdote at the beginning of this chapter. In everyday adult life, temper tantrums like these are rare. A customer who feels offended by a salesperson may *feel* like striking him, but he compromises with this feeling by permitting himself a sarcastic remark. On the other hand, a man cutting firewood in the forest who cuts his finger may fly into a paroxysm of rage, swear at the top of his voice, and throw the axe across the clearing. If he were with others, rather than alone, he might express his anger differently, according to the mode of the group. The expression of anger is conditioned by the "permissiveness" of the situation (for example, when we are alone or with our families and close friends we may permit ourselves more latitude in emotional expression) or by the demands of our self-concept (for example, we may see ourselves as the kind of persons who never get angry, in which case we would repress or suppress the more obvious forms of angry behavior).

Reactions to Threat. Emotions resulting from perceptions of threat are the expressions of our feelings toward the negative forces of our environment — the forces that threaten to interfere with our attempts to behave as humans, or that threaten life itself. Both fear and rage are stimulated by situations we perceive to be actually or potentially dangerous, frustrating, or depriving. Whether an individual reacts to a given situation in terms of fear or rage depends on how he interprets the situation and his role. If he sees himself powerless to deal with the situation, he may react with behavior characteristic of fear — that is, he may run away or may *feel* like running away. If he feels competent to deal with the threatening situation, he may act in an aggressive manner.

How we deal with "threat" — that is, situations involving danger, frustration, or attack — depends on the kind of persons we are (our self-structure), and upon the kinds of solutions we have learned to apply to our life problems. Some persons habitually react to threat by running away, figuratively and literally. Some persons react to threat by seeking protection of those who are more powerful than they; this is the solution by dependence on others. Some become immobilized, as did Miss Morales when she discovered the snake — solution by inhibition. Others attack the source of the threat, as Jud Knudsen did when he placed the snake in Miss Morales's desk drawer; or, if the direct approach is inconvenient or unavailable, they "displace" their anger by attacking innocent bystanders or by destroying things, as Patrick Ross did. Still others react to threat by using defensive tactics, such as arguing and lying, while others surrender to the threatening situation, because they feel that to fight or to flee would be useless.

The mature approach to threatening situations is to view them as occasions calling for skill and intelligence — that is, as problems to be solved. The individual who reacts to threat in this manner may decide that he should flee, fight, or conform. Or he may be able to avoid the situation or reduce its threatening potential. The chief difference between the emotional and the problem-solving approaches is that the former is impulsive and the latter is more deliberate. One of the difficulties in adopting a rational approach to threatening situations is that the unconscious nature of emotions often makes them difficult to identify and to cope with; an individual may take many pains to work out what he feels is a rational plan of procedure, only to discover that he was duped by his emotions into taking a distorted view of the realities of the situation.

Threat Motivates Much of Our Behavior. Persons who "take life seriously," who are sensitive to its potential dangers, and who are, as we say, "security-conscious" — most college students fall into this category — are more concerned with protecting themselves against possibilities of threat than they are with planning for pleasure. This may be because they see the world as a largely hostile environment against whose forces one must erect defensive barriers and from whose unwilling grasp one must wrest what security he can. On the other hand, it may be that the culture itself has saturated the psychological atmosphere with an ever present dread of the perils that may befall one in the future. There is also a cultural pattern stressing avoidance of situations that may evoke fear or anger. The result is that the typical middle-class person is so preoccupied with building defenses and laying plans against potential threat that when he does pursue pleasure he often seeks it not so much as an end in itself but as a means of forgetting the unpleasant side of life.

The puzzling yet fascinating thing about our attempts to defend ourselves against threat is that often the situation that produces the threat lies within ourselves rather than in the outside world. Thus we find ourselves in the paradoxical situation of erecting defenses against ourselves. What we find so alarming in ourselves is the subject of the remainder of this chapter.

The Nature of Anxiety. What psychologists call anxiety is an emotion resulting from the perception of threat. As far as bodily
processes are concerned, the symptoms of severe anxiety are a rapid
heart beat, a feeling of tension, an increase in perspiration, accelerated breathing, trembling, a feeling of dread or apprehension, and
an overwhelming desire to fight or flee. Which of these symptoms
will appear depends on the individual's perception of the situation,
his temperament, the kinds of experiences he had during his formative years, and his self-structure. Richard Hogan defines anxiety
as "the affective response to threat, which occurs when the individual
perceives his experiences as contrary to or incongruent with his
expectations, particularly when he is aware that his own thoughts,
actions, or feelings are not in keeping with his self-concept (3)."*

Most of the time we are not consciously aware of our feelings of
anxiety, either because we repress them or because the situations
evoking them appear only mildly threatening. A good example of
repression of anxiety may be seen in the film "Unconscious Motivation," in which the experimenter has planted a neurotic conflict in
the minds of two students under hypnosis and has suggested that
when they awaken they will be unable to remember the conflict
situation, although it will cause them to have feelings of guilt and
anxiety. As they awaken from their hypnotic sleep, the experimenter
asks his subjects how they feel. The young man says that he feels
all right. But even as he says it, he shows signs of tension and
anxiety: he squirms, rubs his hands together, and bites his finger-
nails. It is not until the other student states that she is upset and
the experimenter has pointed out to the boy that he is rubbing his
hands together that he can admit he is really quite uncomfortable (4).
The fact is that anxiety is so painful that we will go to great lengths
to avoid it; and, if we cannot avoid it, we will try to deny to ourselves that we are anxious, perhaps in the hope that if we ignore
the feeling it will go away.

Differences between Anxiety and Fear. Among most Western cultures,
fear, even *reasonable* fear, carries the stigma of cowardice and disgrace. This makes it difficult or impossible for many of us to admit
to ourselves (for fear that we might reveal it to others) the existence

---

* For a thorough discussion of philosophical and psychological theories regarding
anxiety, see the first portion of R. May, *The Meaning of Anxiety*. New York: Ronald,
1950.

of any feelings remotely resembling fear. Inasmuch as anxiety resembles fear, we reject fearful or anxious expressions or impulses as unworthy, and hence baseless. We are much more comfortable if we can believe that we do not have these feelings.

The word "anxiety," used psychologically, is more closely related to the German word *Angst* (fear) than it is to the meaning more commonly given it. It has the quality of "dread" or of apprehensiveness. Fear involves the awareness of an immediate and present situation which is dangerous, which may actually harm the individual. You are crossing the street and are narrowly missed by a speeding automobile. Immediately you are aware of a feeling of weakness, there is a "sinking feeling" at the pit of your stomach, and your heart begins to pound. These are symptoms of fear.

Anxiety, too, is associated with awareness of danger, but of a danger which is less immediate, which impends — a *possible* danger, a danger which *might* occur. Fear results from some *specific* object or occurrence — a narrow escape, seeing a black widow spider on one's clothing, being shot at, or, as it happened with Miss Morales, finding a snake in a desk drawer. With anxiety, the threatening situation cannot be so readily defined or identified; hence, there is a tendency to exaggerate its dangers. A student who always gets A's is always plagued by anxiety when he takes an examination — he is afraid of failing; a hard-working employee is made anxious by the mild reprimand of a supervisor — he wonders if it means that he will be fired; a conscientious student's anxiety is aroused at receiving a summons from the dean's office — he knows he has done nothing wrong, but still he wonders if he has committed some misdemeanor, unknown even to himself.

Fear is a strong, sometimes violent emotion that tends to impel some sort of action — usually an attempt to escape from the threatening situation; whereas anxiety is a vague, persistent, and pervasive emotion, characterized by a feeling of disorganization, inadequacy, or helplessness as to the individual's capacity to cope with himself, with others, with life in general, or with some specific situation. Through anxiety, the individual is made aware of a threatening situation — that "something is wrong." Yet this "something" is intangible, and the immediate cause of his feeling of anxiety is obscure. Since the individual is unaware of why he has this feeling, he tends to blame it on situations, other persons, or objects that

actually bear only indirect relationships, if any, to the true cause
of his feelings.

Sources of Anxiety. One explanation of the cause of anxiety is that
it results from the feeling that someone (particularly a "someone"
important to us) disapproves of us or rejects us. It does not matter
whether the rejection or disapproval is real or imagined — if we
interpret an event or a situation as "rejection" or "disapproval,"
we are almost certain to display some of the symptoms of anxiety.

Anxiety first appears in infancy. As Phyllis Greenacre describes it,

> The child reacts with a puckered, worried, or tense expression when
> people around it are cross or gloomy. This may come through an associ-
> ation of mild discomfort (the restricting, frustrating sensations of being
> held or handled by a tense and jerky nurse or mother) with the gloomy
> expression which it sees; nevertheless the infant soon seems to make the
> connection directly, an anxious nurse being reflected in an anxious
> baby. . . . (5)

As Greenacre describes the situation, the infant becomes anxious
because he is able to sense the feelings of others around him (empathy); since his welfare is so dependent on how his parents feel,
particularly on how they feel toward him, it is easy to see how their
unfavorable moods would arouse his anxiety. An infant has no
sense of proportion; he has no way of distinguishing between a mild
frustration and a major one. Therefore, he reacts to *any* perceived
threat as though it were cataclysmic. His reaction is one of anxiety
— a feeling of discomfort, painful and intense, which constitutes
one of the most upsetting, depressing, and terrifying experiences
an individual ever undergoes. On a "feeling level" it is something
like a blow on the head (6).

If this description seems overdrawn, observe the actions of an
infant who does not get his bottle when he feels he should, or who
suddenly realizes that he is not being held by his mother but by a
stranger, or who has been put to bed to sleep when he wants to stay
up with his parents. The intense emotion he displays is a clue to the
pain, discomfort, and terror he feels.

Inasmuch as an infant cannot distinguish between the external
situation that evokes his anxiety and the feeling of anxiety itself, it
follows that he will learn to fear the feeling of anxiety as much as
the frustrations causing it.

Anxiety as Caused by Inner Conflicts. Another way of looking at anxiety is to see it as the result of conflicts between various needs. Lawrence I. O'Kelly considers conflict and frustration a prime cause of anxiety (7). Norman Cameron states that conflict tensions perpetuate neurotic difficulties (8).

Anxiety may be produced by the necessity to deny or to frustrate some biological and some neurotic needs in order to live at peace with ourselves and others. Sometimes we must deny some kinds of needs in order to be the kinds of persons we would like to be or think we should be. The college student who has an opportunity to go to the movies with a girl friend, but knows that he ought to stay home to prepare an assignment, is faced with an anxiety-producing conflict. No matter what he decides to do, some anxiety will result. He may not be aware of anxiety — that is, he may not perceive his behavior as conditioned by anxiety, but may see it as an inability to concentrate, if he remains at home, or as twinges of guilt, if he goes to the movies. His problem really is one of avoiding the solution that would result in the most anxiety and of selecting the one that would result in the least anxiety; and one of the decisions he must make is whether or not to tolerate much anxiety now in exchange for less anxiety later.

The basic conflict that produces anxiety was regarded by Freud as the result of the opposing forces of instinctual drives, on the one hand, and the ego and superego, on the other (9). According to Freud, the instinctual drives attempt to force the individual to do things that are not condoned by society. In the earliest years of childhood, this brings the child into conflict with his parents' wishes; and his persistence in behavior that is personally — that is, biologically — satisfying but socially disapproved brings parental punishment and disapproval, which are interpreted by the child as rejection or "loss of love." The anxiety called forth by this prospect helps to subdue and control the instinctual drives and to channel them into more socially acceptable outlets.

Anxiety Arising from Nonconformity. Still another interpretation of anxiety and its cause is that of Sullivan and Fromm, to the effect that anxiety is generated by conformity (and particularly *blind* conformity) to the dictates of others (10, 11). Conformity is learned in childhood, in the form of obedience to parental demands. This is certainly a necessary condition of child rearing, if children are to behave in ways that do not violate the rights of others.   However, some children learn the lesson of conformity *too* well, usually because of excessive demands on the part of their parents, and grow up to be adults who are incapable of thinking or acting for themselves.

Miss Harris is one of these people.   Although she is very susceptible to colds, she has been assigned working space in the draftiest corner of the office.   She stays where she was put, suffering and sniffling in silence, rather than speaking to the boss and asserting herself. Even the thought of this mildly nonconformist behavior is enough to cause her sleepless nights.   On the other hand, she knows that the sensible thing to do is to speak to the supervisor, and she feels helpless and inadequate and angry at herself for not doing so.   Since the accepted pattern is not to assert oneself to persons in authority, not to question an order, Miss Harris may even change jobs rather than ask that she be permitted to work in another part of the office.   There are many "Miss Harrises" in adult life.

Anxiety Caused by Perceptual Rigidity.   Miss Harris's behavior can also be seen as a tendency to repeat previously learned patterns of behavior in situations that mark them as inappropriate.   Through our experiences in childhood we learn methods (acquire "habits") of meeting and dealing with situations in rather consistent ways, and these patterns persist in later life.   We also form certain "pictures" or expectations of ourselves and others and these, too, persist in later life.   Frequently we are aware that these patterns of behavior and our expectations are inappropriate, but we are unable to give them up.   We are aware that the circumstances of reality call for different behavior and different expectations, but we seem to be unable to act differently.   This awareness that our actions and expectations are inappropriate gives rise to anxiety for the reason that we feel helpless to deal with a situation.   If we were to give up our unrealistic (neurotic) attitudes and modes of behavior, we would be able to deal more competently with a situation, but we are usually unable to do so.   Of course, these neurotic expectations and behavior patterns were originally developed in childhood as defenses against anxiety-producing situations;   they served us well then, and we cling to them now because the thought of the anxiety, with its implications of disapproval and rejection, is too painful.   This is one of the reasons why neurotic patterns of adjustment are so difficult to change, why "personalities" cannot be altered overnight by will power, "success classes," and "charm schools."

The case of Clare Lucas is illustrative of perceptual rigidity.

Clare Lucas was dominated by her mother. Her mother criticized and belittled her until she came to believe that she really was an inadequate, helpless, and stupid person. The feeling was decidedly contrary to reality, because she was on the honor roll in high school and college, and her intelligence test scores placed her in the top 10 per cent of the general population. Her mother died prior to her graduation from college, but after her graduation Clare married a professional man whose mother was also a dominant woman. Before long she was repeating the pattern of her childhood. It so happened that Clare's husband had been able to declare his independence from his mother, and he was much annoyed to see her continuing to exercise control over the household by demanding and getting obedience from his wife. This situation caused a number of quarrels, during the course of which he would get Clare to admit that there was no logical reason why she should consult with his mother about every move, and she could see how it was damaging to his ego for her to consult with his mother instead of with him. Yet the next occasion calling for a decision would find her telephoning her mother-in-law to ask her opinion.

Clare adopted her submissive and dependent behavior as a way of coping with a dominating mother; in effect, it was the price she felt she had to pay in order to retain her mother's love and approval. She grew to expect helplessness and inadequacy from herself and strength and direction from her mother. Her behavior served to protect herself as a child from the feeling of anxiety that would result from her mother's rejection or disapproval. These patterns of behavior and attitudes were inappropriate in her new life as a married woman, but they were so habitual and so basic a characteristic of her self-structure, that she was unable to change them. The very thought of behaving any differently toward her mother-in-law caused her to have severe feelings of anxiety; on the other hand, her husband's admonition that she was behaving in a manner which was not only unrealistic but which damaged their marital relationship also produced anxiety. The early behavior that was contrived to protect her from anxiety became in turn a producer of anxiety in a different setting, but because of the rigidity of her personality pattern, she was unable to change her behavior or her expectations.

As is usual in such cases, she was also aware of a strong feeling of guilt at not meeting her husband's expectations.   Yet if she had altered her behavior to suit him, she would have felt guilty at not deferring to her mother-in-law.   Like so many, she was caught in a situation bound to produce anxiety and guilt no matter which way she turned.

Anxiety Arising from Disappointment or Loss.   Another source of anxiety, which is similar in many ways to the one just described, is the situation in which an individual has been encouraged by his parents to set a high level of aspiration for himself and is unable to live up to expectations.   In effect, he feels guilty at disappointing his parents, and this guilt produces anxiety, because he feels helpless to cope with the situation.   This type of problem is described in greater detail in Chapter 6, "The Struggle against Shyness and Feelings of Inferiority."

An anxiety pattern related to fears of rejection, withdrawal of love, and disapproval in childhood is that appearing in the person who has lost status, thinks he has lost status, or fears he is about to lose status — status being defined here as the place one holds in the regard of others.   To be aware of a real or imagined threat to one's status awakens the feelings of childhood that were called forth by the disapproval or rejection by the parent.   We are not always consciously aware of conditions that are threatening to a feeling of status, just as we are not always conscious of the resulting anxiety and our anxious attempts to cope with these threats.   The situation of Robert Duncan illustrates this anxiety pattern.

Suppose we listen in on a meeting of the freshman class.   They are discussing the Spring Dance, and the issue being hotly debated is whether they should gamble on hiring a "name band," with the expectation that the expense would be paid for by an increased number of admissions, or whether they should "play it safe" by hiring some "home-grown" talent.   Defending the home-talent group is Robert Duncan, a handsome lad with a condescending, lofty manner, who is much resented by his fellow classmates.   Robert produces a number of cogent, realistic arguments as to why the class cannot afford a name band — shaky finances, another big dance the same week end, lack of spirit in the freshman class — but his classmates meet each of his arguments with vigorous opposition.   At times they make sarcastic and resentful remarks.

Plainly, the freshman group is "rejecting" Robert.   Yet, if we were to ask Robert later what happened at the meeting, he would probably complain about his inability to convince the group of the most sensible course to follow. If we should probe deeper and ask him if he felt rejected by the group, he would probably say that he felt irritated by their stupidity and unreasonableness, but that he was unaware of any attempt to *reject* him. Nevertheless, if we had a sound recording of the meeting, we would be able to identify statements definitely indicating the group's rejection, as well as statements by Robert of a defensive nature, statements showing at least an unconscious feeling of being rejected and an attempt to defend himself against rejection. His irritability grew out of his anxious awareness that he was unable to cope with the situation, that he lacked status with the group, and that they rejected and disapproved of him. Not *consciously* aware that he had lost status, he nonetheless took steps to protect this status, thus indicating genuine but unconscious awareness of threat.

Anxiety Arising from Feelings of Inferiority. Still another cause of anxiety, which, like the others described here, is not essentially "different" but approaches the subject from a different angle, is the feeling of helplessness that arises in us when we perceive that we are not as important or as powerful as we thought we were as children. Since this concept is covered in much greater detail in Chapter 7, "The Struggle to Become Independent and Self-reliant," in a discussion of overdependence, it will be mentioned only briefly here. This type of anxiety appears in persons who are unable to admit to themselves that in some ways they are inadequate or inferior or have failed. Some people maintain this attitude of make-believe omnipotence with relation to all or most of their life situations; probably most of us are overconfident to a greater or lesser degree in a few types of situations. When the balloons of our false pride are punctured, we may react to the situation with any of the various symptoms of anxiety.

One of the characteristics of anxiety as it affects most of us is that it is accompanied by a general feeling of inadequacy and helplessness. However, we may repress our feelings of inferiority and instead be aware of a strong feeling of resentment. Thus in some instances anxiety may masquerade as fear, whereas at other times it may appear in the form of rage. In either case, we often blame others for our feelings, and that, in turn, enables us to ignore the possibility that the source of our anxiety is really ourselves.

For example, the person who suffers from severe stage fright may feel that he is really afraid of his audience. However, it is quite apparent that the audience can do him no bodily harm, that what he very likely fears is *failure*, which may lead to loss of status and self-respect; he is afraid that he might not live up to his expectations of himself. His fears actually derive from his own feelings of inadequacy and his real or imagined inferiority. Persons who have a record of successful performances before audiences have no logical reason to feel inadequate; yet, many of them continue to suffer from stage fright.

Another case in point is that of Mr. Jensen, part owner of an electrical appliance store, who takes elaborate precautions to protect himself from being swindled by his partner. He says that he does this because it does not pay to trust anybody in this world. Superficially it appears that Mr. Jensen is motivated by a natural fear and is taking necessary steps to protect himself against the source of his fear — his partner. However, since he has never been cheated by a business associate, one wonders whether he has real cause to suspect his partner's honesty. In all probability, Mr. Jensen's real problem is that he cannot trust himself. He is not consciously aware of this, but the anxiety and guilt generated by this mistrust are sufficient to cause him to take more than necessary precautions. Unconsciously attributing one's own motives to others, termed "projection," is a very common form of defense mechanism, which will be discussed more fully in the following chapter.

Interpersonal Relations the Chief Source of Anxiety. Our discussion up to this point has been concerned with anxiety as it grows out of our relationships with others. The various theories we have discussed all involve, in some way, the idea that anxiety is related to our fear of being rejected, disapproved, or thought inadequate by others. Even when our anxiety arises from disappointment in not being able to live up to our own expectations, we should not overlook the fact that these expectations are molded by our concepts of persons we would like to emulate. In these cases we are made anxious by the disapproval of others as expressed through our own consciences or superegos.

By the time most of us are ready for grade school, we have learned that the most severe expressions of disapproval are called forth by one of two kinds of behavior: sexual activity or aggressive behavior of a hostile nature. Because of this, most middle-class children learn to be afraid of impulses that may lead to forbidden acts of a sexual or aggressive nature (12). Furthermore, this fear of sexual or hostile-aggressive impulses is carried into adulthood and becomes a prime source of much of the anxiety experienced by persons in our culture.

The depth and intensity of the anxiety produced by the frustrations and inhibitions of these impulses vary widely with the age of the individual, his temperament, and the other characteristics of his personality, as well as with the situations he must experience. When Freud conducted his clinical explorations, it appeared to him that the frustration of sexual impulses was the prime source of emotional maladjustments, and this may well have been true for the Victorian era and the people whom Freud studied. Although even today sexual frustrations are an important source of anxiety for most people in our middle-class culture at various times in their lives, at least one group of students of personality feel that conflicts involving hostile aggression (the expression of hostile feelings) are usually more important than sexual frustrations as producers of anxiety (13).

The Repression of Hostile Impulses. Anxiety resulting from hostility-aggression conflicts is the result of a combination of factors in our culture, partly related to a misapplication of Christian ethics, partly related to a way of life inherited from the burgher culture of the Reformation, but mostly related to our relationship with figures of authority and power in our middle-class culture today (14, 15).

Parental figures loom large to the child, from the standpoint of physical size and power, as well as of status and prestige. Early in life the child finds that he cannot stand up for "his rights" by striking a parent or even by "talking back." Regardless of how well he learns this lesson at home, he relearns it at school, where he comes in contact with other figures of authority who are as powerful, inexorable, unpredictable, inconsiderate, and disapproving as his own parents seem to be. The child learns that he has few, if any, rights of self-determination and that his rights are those that others have determined for him — the rights to be sheltered, protected, guided, loved, and nourished. Self-expression is permitted only if it is channeled into predetermined and specified paths, in conformity with the expectations of adults. Children who violate this pattern are regarded as disrespectful, unworthy, or "spoiled"; adults disapprove of them; other children are encouraged to reject them. Adults are likely to reward, praise, or refrain from disapproving of a child who is submissive, retiring, modest, and nonassertive, who lives up to their expectations, and who expresses himself in conventional fashion, in conformity to the expectations that adults have for children. The child who engages in the more open forms of hostile-aggressive behavior — fighting, stealing, swearing, "talking back" to parents or teachers, and being destructive — discovers that this behavior will earn the rejection and disapproval of adults.

Although we are eventually successful in teaching most children to deny themselves the expression of feelings in ways that violate the mores of our culture, we are unable to teach them to eliminate the hostile feelings that would normally produce this antisocial behavior. These feelings still seek expression, and there are only two socially approved modes of expressing it: self-punishment and competition.

Expression of Hostility through Self-punishment. If hostility is expressed through self-punishment, it operates through the medium of our conscience or superego. What happens is something like this: the perception of a threatening situation arouses feelings of hostility in the individual, but he has learned that hostility, if freely expressed, leads to aggressive behavior, which results in punishment, disapproval, and rejection, and that these, in turn, produce feelings of inadequacy and insecurity. The individual's conscience or superego, furthermore, has incorporated within itself a cultural-moral standard that disapproves of hostile-aggressive behavior; the conscience or superego therefore acts to "punish" the individual for having entertained such dangerous and immoral impulses. This punishment takes the form of guilt feelings or feelings of inferiority and inadequacy. The individual may therefore express hostile feelings by speaking of himself in a depreciating manner, by withdrawing from social contact, by sabotaging other behavior that might possibly lead to the approval of others, or by engaging in other forms of behavior that have a tinge of self-abasement or self-punishment. This sounds like a painful way to live, but this kind of individual has found that he incurs less anxiety if he punishes himself than if he seeks or even contemplates seeking more open and aggressive expression of his hostility.

Expression of Hostility through Competition.   The other socially acceptable way of expressing hostility is through competition. Lessons in competition start at home.   The child who is more successful in learning what it is his parents expect of him, and who can discipline himself to behave in accordance with their expectations, is the one most likely to avoid disapproval and to gain approval. He is the one who tends to be most favored, who gets more than his share of privileges, advantages, and other tokens of love and affection.   Even an only child learns to compete.   His task is to draw the attention of his parents away from their other interests; he works hard to get as much of his parents' time and attention as possible.

When the child goes to school, he learns to compete with a vengeance.   In order to produce results that society recognizes as "learning" or "progress," our teachers pit children against one another, urge them to emulate and to surpass fellow pupils.   In the competitive school situation, as far as students are concerned, the end product of "education" is not the skill or knowledge that adults see as the desirable outcome, but rather the marks (symbols of adult approval) that they will receive for their efforts.   Thus, most schools do a rather good job of teaching children to compete and to learn what kind of behavior is expected of them in a competitive situation.

There is no question but that competitive skills have their psychological advantages.   They enable the individual to express his normal feelings of hostility and frustration in a manner that is usually less dangerous to others than the more violent forms of antisocial behavior.   Furthermore, the competitive situation frequently enables an individual to gain status, and it occasionally affords him with opportunities to express himself creatively.   Finally, competitive skills will stand an individual in good stead in fending for himself in a competitive and sometimes hostile society.

However, there are some severe limitations to this way of life. Unfortunately, once having learned to compete, many individuals go on competing in life situations where competition is inappropriate or undesirable.   Thus a person with an overdeveloped competitive approach to life competes with his fellow workers, his fellow lodge and fraternity brothers, and even with his spouse for attention, recognition, economic rewards, position, prestige, status symbols, and/or power. It is difficult or impossible to build really sound and permanently satisfying human relations on a competitive base. Although competition is admittedly useful as a means of coping with the economic and power factors in life, it does not in itself provide a satisfactory way of life.

Competition differs from self-punishment in that it is directed toward one's fellows rather than toward oneself. In our culture it is valued more highly than self-punishment, because it is more likely to bring rewards of approval, power, and economic, political, and social success. The successfully competitive person is rewarded by our culture, provided he does not violate moral or legal codes, whereas the self-punishing person meets with mild approval or disapproval or is ignored altogether.

Reduction of Hostility through Creativity. There is a third solution to the problem of anxiety, hostility, and aggression, that of creative expression, which may be exhibited in a wide range of activities, from child rearing to bridge building, from document filing to javelin throwing. Creativity is a positive, nonhostile form of enterprising behavior; it is the result of a drive to master the physical or social environment or to achieve self-expression rather than an attempt to injure or destroy. However, there are many forces in our culture that tend to discourage this solution. Creative people have to develop their individuality, for there are times when they must think and act differently from others, rather than conform blindly. And there are times when they must refrain from competition in order to use or to express their talents more adequately. Inasmuch as our culture places great value on conformity and competition, it often tends to discourage creativity on the part of the individual. Original creativity is both condoned and applauded when displayed by persons of power, prestige, and authority, but the unknown person, the person of little power, often finds many forces operating to inhibit or impede creative expression. Furthermore, individuals like the self-effacing Clare Lucas, who have learned too well *not* to assert themselves, have great difficulty in becoming creative; the self-punishment solution seems less dangerous and provokes less anxiety. On the other hand, individuals who have learned to solve their problems through competition or a "drive for power" may not find creativity satisfying. It is difficult to find satisfaction in creative effort when what one really wants to do is to dominate or surpass others.

Persons who are not committed to life patterns of self-punishment, competition, or unquestioning conformity find that they can reduce some of their anxieties in a satisfying way through creative activity. Sometimes creativity is learned in childhood, but all too often, because of restrictive home and school environments, creativity must be postponed till the individual can enjoy the relative freedom of mature adulthood. Some adults find creative expression in hobbies, some find it in vocations, some find it in community-service activities, some find it in social-welfare work, some find it in homemaking, and some find it in participating co-operatively in group activities.

It is much to the credit of schools that goals involving creativity and co-operation are written into the curricula at all stages of education. However, these goals are seldom attained, either because teachers themselves do not know how to help students learn the techniques and attitudes that go with co-operation and creativity, or because the school situation, through its traditional emphasis on patterns of submission, conformity, and competition, does not permit or encourage such instruction.

Hostility in Everyday Living. Mr. and Mrs. Nelson illustrate the operation of hostility in a "real-life" situation.

Mr. Nelson has a tender, ever-loving, if somewhat oversolicitous wife. He feels anxious and irritable when she brings him his pipe and slippers, when she cooks his favorite dishes for supper, when she sympathizes with his ailments. Not only is Mr. Nelson anxious and irritable, but he is upset because there seems to be no observable reason for these feelings. He expresses his resentment openly when his wife appears vulnerable, such as when she exceeds her budget, or when she neglects her housework; and if queried as to the reason for his feeling of hostility, he would probably say that it was due to his wife's careless habits. And yet there is this feeling of discomfort that comes over him at inappropriate times, when his wife is doing her best to make him feel comfortable. He cannot account for this feeling, and it makes him feel guilty, since he knows his wife's intentions are of the best.

Mr. Nelson's trouble is that he had an overprotective, over-solicitous mother, who used to go away on long trips. When his wife is solicitous, he has an unconscious fear that she, too, will leave him, that she, too, is as undependable as his mother was. It may be that, after a number of years, Mr. Nelson will learn that he does not need to expect such inconsistent behavior from his wife; in the meantime, his hostility may cause much discomfort. It would probably ease the situation somewhat if he could discuss this problem with his wife, but he finds it difficult to do so — it is such an unreasonable feeling, and he does not wish to offend her.

Mr. Warner is a foreman in a lithography plant. He is a competent, conscientious craftsman and is well-liked by his men in spite of his gruff manner. The plant manager has learned, after long association with Mr. Warner, that he must never give him orders or instructions. This means that he turns each job over to Mr. Warner with a written statement of what the customer expects. Co-ordination between various departments of the plant is worked out by the plant manager and supervisors in committee, thus eliminating the necessity for direct orders to Mr. Warner on these matters. Occasionally it is necessary to make emergency changes in jobs or in plant operation. At these times the manager discusses the situation with Mr. Warner and then *asks* him what should be done.

Until this method of dealing with Mr. Warner was evolved, relations with Mr. Warner's department were exceedingly difficult. Whenever a suggestion was made with regard to a job, Mr. Warner threatened to quit. Occasionally he walked off the job for a couple of hours, only to return and pick up where he left off. When given orders involving his department, he would glower and sulk and on occasion would subtly sabotage operations in a way that left him technically in the clear. A number of times management considered whether they should let him go, but were deterred by the fact that Warner was a very competent man, who got out jobs on schedule and who usually did flawless work. The present plan of dealing with him was worked out by the plant manager, a person with unusual insight and a willingness to minimize his own importance in order to get the work out.

The source of Mr. Warner's difficulty is also found in his childhood experiences. He grew up in a rigid, punitive, authoritarian home. Instead of becoming submissive like his brothers and sisters, he rebelled frequently and openly against parental domination. He ran away from home at the age of fourteen and went to sea. After a checkered vocational career, he learned the lithographer's trade and went to work for his present employer. Much of his hostility is absorbed in his work, which is essentially creative. Management in the plant is helping Mr. Warner to solve his problem by refraining from parentlike, authoritarian patterns of behavior and by giving him opportunities to be self-assertive and to participate in the management of the plant.

A phenomenon that occurs commonly, but that is not ordinarily recognized as an expression of hostility, is boredom or apathy. The boredom of a class in college or high school is a by-product of the authoritarian situation. Often the student is given little choice regarding the course he takes or the content thereof. Furthermore, the authoritarian atmosphere of the school encourages him to leave full responsibility for his education to the instructor. This in turn enables the student to disassociate himself from the course objective. He comes to feel that the goals of the course are the instructor's, not his. Naturally, this is an unhealthy orientation. The student is not able to grow intellectually unless he can take some responsibility for his growth. He realizes that he is not taking responsibility, that he is not permitted responsibility, and he feels resentful. Sometimes he is forced to take responsibility before he is ready to do so, and he resents this also. At other times, the student has been so benumbed into a pattern of not accepting responsibility for his own learning that whenever he is required to do so, he resents it. Altogether, the authoritarian situation within the school leads to resentment — a form of hostility — that expresses itself in boredom and apathy.

SUMMARY

Emotion is a state of generalized excitement that expresses itself as changes in feeling and bodily condition. Basically, emotions can be classified as (a) reactions to the perception of threat and (b) reactions concerned with need satisfaction. Emotions are further characterized by whether the individual feels impelled to attack, flee from, or move toward the source of stimulation. Fear and rage are emotions commonly associated with the perception of threat; pleasure and affection are commonly associated with perceptions involving need-satisfaction.

Anxiety is an emotion aroused by the perception of threat. It is similar to fear in many ways. It differs from fear in that it is stimulated by dangers removed in point of time or distance, whereas fear is prompted by dangers in the immediate and present situation. Fear is a strong and sometimes violent emotion, whereas anxiety has a vague or persistent quality. Nevertheless, anxiety is a very painful emotion, which we normally try to avoid at all costs. It may be aroused by an awareness of disapproving and reflecting attitudes on the part of others, by conflicts between opposing needs, by nonconformity to prescribed standards, by perceptual rigidity, disappointment or loss, feelings of inferiority, and the repression of hostile impulses.

The avoidance of hostile and aggressive behavior is a major problem in growing up in our culture, inasmuch as we disapprove of most of the direct forms of aggressive behavior. We try to resolve this difficulty by teaching children to be submissive, in which case they turn their hostility upon themselves; or to be competitive, in which case they turn their hostility on others in some socially approved way. A third solution to the problem of hostility is that of creative expression. This is an outlet which we have not used to any great extent, but which has great potentiality.

REFERENCES

1. D. Snygg and A. W. Combs, *Individual Behavior*. New York: Harper, 1949. P. 105. Reprinted by permission of Harper & Brothers.
2. D. Syngg and A. W. Combs. *Individual Behavior*. New York: Harper, 1949. Pp. 107–108. Reprinted by permission of Harper & Brothers.
3. R. Hogan, *The Development of a Measure of Client Defensiveness in the Counseling Relationship*. Ph. D. Thesis Abstract, University of Chicago, 1948.
4. L. F. Beck, "Unconscious Motivation." Association Films.
5. P. Greenacre, "The Predisposition to Anxiety," in S. S. Tomkins, ed., *Contemporary Psychopathology*. Cambridge: Harvard University Press, 1943. Pp. 16–35. Reprinted by permission of Harvard University Press and *The Psychoanalytic Quarterly*.
6. P. Mullahy, ed., *A Study of Interpersonal Relations*. New York: Hermitage, 1949. Pp. xxii–xxiii.
7. L. I. O'Kelly, *An Introduction to Psychopathology*. New York: Prentice-Hall, 1949.
8. N. Cameron, *The Psychology of Behavior Disorders*. Boston: Houghton Mifflin, 1947.
9. S. Freud, *The Problem of Anxiety*. New York: Norton, 1936.
10. H. S. Sullivan, *Conceptions of Modern Psychiatry*. Washington, D. C.: William Alanson White Psychiatric Foundation, 1947. P. 10.
11. E. Fromm, *Escape from Freedom*. New York: Rinehart, 1941. P. 206.

12. A. Davis, *Social-class Influences upon Learning.* Cambridge: Harvard University Press, 1948. Pp. 31–37.
13. K. Horney, *The Neurotic Personality of Our Time.* New York: Norton, 1937.
14. E. Fromm, *Escape from Freedom.* New York: Rinehart, 1941. P. 206.
15. E. Fromm, *Man for Himself.* New York: Rinehart, 1947.

SUGGESTED READINGS

R. May, *The Meaning of Anxiety.* New York: Ronald, 1950. The first half of this book is a philosophical-psychological study of various theories regarding the nature and origin of anxiety.

N. R. F. Maier, *Frustration: The Study of Behavior without a Goal.* New York: McGraw-Hill, 1949. Maier develops an interesting approach to the study of frustrated and motivated behavior through his experiments with rats.

L. J. Saul, *Emotional Maturity.* Philadelphia: Lippincott, 1947. Chapters 6 and 11 deal with hostility, violence, and guilt.

P. M. Symonds, *Dynamic Psychology.* New York: Appleton-Century-Crofts, 1949. Chapters 2, 3, 4, and 6 deal with drive, frustration, aggression, and anxiety.

N. Cameron, *The Psychology of Behavior Disorders.* Boston: Houghton Mifflin, 1947. Chapter 5 deals with need, frustration, and conflict.

R. W. White, *The Abnormal Personality.* New York: Ronald, 1948. Anxiety and defense are discussed in Chapter 6.

A. H. Maslow and B. Mittelmann, *Principles of Abnormal Psychology*, Rev. edition. New York: Harper, 1951. An outstanding book in its field; of particular interest is Part II, which deals with psychodynamic processes.

L. I. O'Kelly, *An Introduction to Psychopathology.* New York: Prentice-Hall, 1949. Chapter 3 consists of a brief but thorough discussion of the dynamics of anxiety.

J. C. Coleman, *Abnormal Psychology and Modern Life.* Chicago: Scott, 1950. Chapter 3 deals with personality development and adjustment.

L. C. Steckle, *Problems of Human Adjustment.* New York: Harper, 1949. See particularly Chapter 3, "Emotional Living."

J. E. Anderson, *The Psychology of Development and Personal Adjustment.* New York: Holt, 1949. Chapters 10 and 11 deal with motivation and the development and control of emotions.

H. C. Lindgren, *The Art of Human Relations.* New York: Hermitage, 1953. See Chapter 5, "Anxiety: Friend or Foe?"

G. Murphy, *An Introduction to Psychology.* New York: Harper, 1951. A readable discussion of the physiological aspects of emotion may be found in Chapter 8.

E. T. Prothro and P. T. Teska, *Psychology: A Biosocial Study of Behavior.* Boston: Ginn, 1950. Recommended for an extended study of emotional behavior from the standpoint of physiology and social development. See Chapters 3, 4, 5, and 6.

F. L. Ruch, *Psychology and Life*, 3d edition. Chicago: Scott, 1948. See Chapter 4, "Motivation: Biological and Social"; Chapter 5, "Emotions: Inner Springs of Action"; Chapter 11, "Emotional Development: Experimental Findings"; Chapter 12, "Emotional Development: Clinical Findings"; Chapter 13,

"Reactions to Frustration." An adequate treatment from the standpoint of reports of experiments and the physiological aspect of emotion.

W. Dennis, *Readings in General Psychology.* New York: Prentice-Hall, 1949. Sections 4 and 5 deal with experiments and basic points of view in the study of emotion and motivation.

E. L. Hartley, *et al.*, eds., *Outside Readings in Psychology.* New York: Crowell, 1950. Sections 10 and 11 present reports of experiments and important papers in the study of motivation and emotion.

W. L. Valentine, *Experimental Foundations of General Psychology*, Rev. edition. New York: Farrar, 1941. See chapters on drives and motives, motives and incentives, frustration, the development of emotional behavior, and emotion in adults.

V... *Emotion: Patterns of Defense and Escape*

The Effects of Anxiety. Whereas the previous chapter was concerned with the nature, causes, and development of anxiety, this chapter will be concerned with the expression of anxiety, the behavior of anxious people.

In the previous chapter we described anxiety as a largely negative force, in that it limits, hinders, and inhibits the individual who is trying to actualize his potentialities — that is, who is "trying to be himself." Actually, this is largely true of the individual who has too much anxiety, is troubled by "neurotic anxiety." Neurotic anxiety, according to May, is a reaction to threat which is out of all proportion to the real danger, which involves repression and internal conflict, and which leads to the development of various forms of neurotic defense mechanisms (1).

May distinguishes neurotic anxiety from "normal anxiety," the sort of anxiety which is a reaction to threats to values that the individual holds essential for his existence as a personality, and which does not lead to kinds of reactions typical of neurotic anxiety (2). Normal anxiety is necessary to our functioning as emotionally mature individuals. Those who are lacking in normal anxiety are not considerate of the rights of others and have little incentive to learn or to plan for the future. The brash, impulsive individual who is insensitive to the feelings of others, who lives only for the moment, behaves in this immature fashion because he lacks normal anxiety.

On the other hand, neurotic anxiety, or an overabundance of anxiety, will also lead us to behave in ways that are immature.

87

Often this behavior takes a defensive turn, in that we try to rid ourselves of our anxious feelings by defending ourselves against the events, persons, and situations that we feel are threatening us and causing our anxiety. Inasmuch as the last place that we are likely to look for the cause of anxiety is within ourselves, it is only natural that we should look for it elsewhere. If our anxiety is caused principally by feelings of inferiority and inadequacy, our attempts to seek relief by dealing directly with our environment may appear to the objective observer to be inappropriate, ineffectual, or even grotesque and ludicrous. Yet, irrational as this behavior appears, it may still serve some useful function for us, in that it does serve to reduce the intensity of our anxiety, even though not eliminating it.

An example of this phenomenon may be found in the behavior of Clare's stepfather, in the mental hygiene film "The Feeling of Hostility." The stepfather suffers from repressed and unexpressed hostility toward his wife, brought about, in part, by the fact that she is disappointed in him as a husband. One morning, after a brief conversation carried on against the background of a hurried breakfast, a situation marked by polite coolness, surface indifference, and submerged hostility, he dashes off to catch his bus, only to have it drive off just as he gets to the street corner. At this point, he gives vent to all his pent-up hostility, jumps up and down, shakes his fist at the back of the retreating bus, and shouts imprecations (3).

On a superficially objective basis, his behavior is ridiculous, inasmuch as it will not bring the bus back; as a matter of fact, the bus driver is out of earshot. When the stepfather eventually arrives at the office, a few minutes late, he scolds a subordinate who is unfortunate enough to arrive a little later than he. Note that his wife, whose disapproval aroused his hostility, guilt, and anxiety, is not the target of these verbal attacks. Presumably, all day long he will engage in angry fulmination at persons, events, and things that irritate him. Although his relations with others and his efficiency as a worker suffer, his behavior *does* relieve him of the need to express his hostility toward his wife. Thus his behavior, irrational as it appears, is actually effective, in a perverse sort of way, in that it helps relieve some of the pain of his anxiety.

Another illustration is that of the eight-year-old girl who sucks her thumb whenever she feels worried or depressed. Although this immature form of behavior does not solve any problems for her in the world of reality, she finds it satisfying because she has learned to find comfort in sucking. And since it comforts and satisfies her, it allays her anxiety.

Defenses against Anxiety. The patterns of behavior we use to protect ourselves from feeling anxious are identified by a number of different classifications by psychologists: "behavior mechanisms," because they reveal themselves in certain patterns of behavior; "defense mechanisms" and "escape mechanisms," because they aid the individual to defend himself against the feeling of anxiety or to escape from anxiety; and "mental mechanisms," because these patterns of behavior are in actuality based on attitudes and points of view, and so are "mental." Some psychologists classify these patterns under the heading of "nonadjustive behavior," because they do not help the individual to meet life problems realistically. Actually, these mechanisms act as a sort of anesthetic, in that they dull the pain of living but actually do nothing about removing the basic cause of the anxiety.

The major part of this chapter will be devoted to a discussion of various kinds of mechanisms, classified under titles commonly used by psychologists. The difficulty about any system of classification is that any act undertaken to defend the individual against anxiety can be included under a number of different headings. The broad classifications used in this chapter are substitution, self-deception, and retreat. Although there are mechanisms that can be classified simultaneously under all three of these headings, the author feels that this system of classification, even though fairly arbitrary, will aid in understanding some of the dynamics involved.

Adjustment through Substitution

The essential characteristic of the mechanisms discussed in this section is that they grow out of the frustration experienced by the individual in his attempt to meet his basic needs. In order to ward off the anxiety that would result from failure to satisfy his needs, he permits himself to be content with a second-choice goal, one that he accepts as a substitute for the original, more desirable goal.

Compensation. Many types of mechanisms are compensatory in nature in that they involve the overdevelopment of one kind of activity as a substitute for failure or deprivation in another kind of activity. Students who are thwarted in their attempts to make

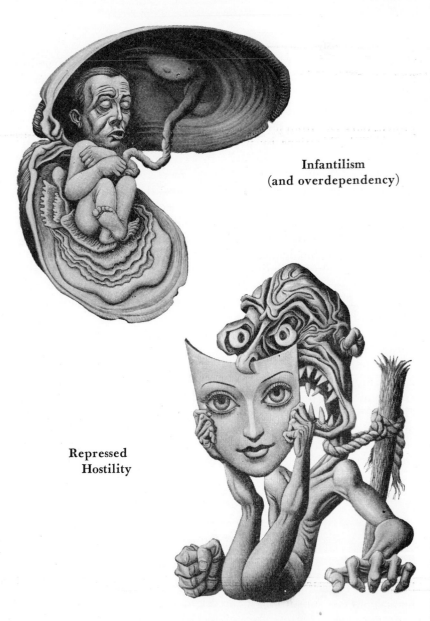

**Infantilism
(and overdependency)**

**Repressed
Hostility**

These five drawings by Boris Artzybasheff portray in dramatic form some of the neurotic conflicts and personality patterns that we develop in our attempts to deal with our anxiety.

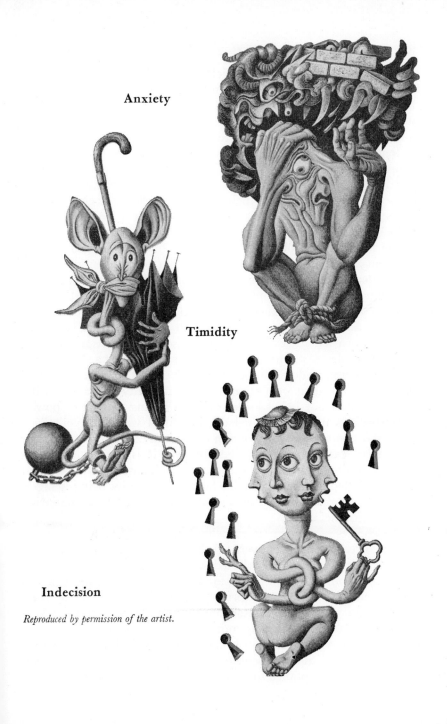

Anxiety

Timidity

Indecision

Reproduced by permission of the artist.

a good showing on the playing field frequently compensate for this failure by working for top grades in class. Secretly, there is nothing they would like better than to be football or tennis stars; since this success is denied them, they attempt to make up for it by surpassing in fields in which they have more ability. Another large group of students find themselves unable to succeed in the classroom and compensate for this by excellent performance in athletics. This does not mean that all good students and all outstanding athletes are compensating through their excellent performances for weaknesses in other fields, but this description *does* fit a large proportion of the students who excel in sports and in the academic field. Some people feel that the outstanding showing made by Negro athletes in recent years is due partly to an attempt to compensate for the success denied people of their race in other activities of life.

Another common example of compensation is that of the short individual who is pugnacious and "cocky." We say that he is compensating for his size by adopting a belligerent attitude toward others. However, the explanation is not so simple, inasmuch as not all short people are pugnacious. The chances are that a short person who compensates does so because of feelings of inferiority and inadequacy, brought on perhaps by the inability to find security, by a feeling of not being loved, or by a feeling of lack of power. These feelings may be focused on, identified with, or symbolized by his short stature. The adoption by an individual of *any* behavior mechanism cannot be explained simply; it is always due to a complex constellation of events and forces. Thus when we say that someone is "compensating for his lack of stature by being belligerent," we are referring to the *symbol* of his feelings of inferiority, not to their chief cause.

The choices of compensatory behavior frequently appear strange and involved to the observer. A boy may steal an automobile primarily because he feels rejected and humiliated by his parents. The automobile may symbolize for him the affection he wants so badly; and his stealing may serve symbolically as a hostile act that enables him to revenge himself on his parents, who have denied him the love to which he feels entitled. A girl may become sexually involved with a gang of boys because she feels unloved and unaccepted at home. She compensates for this lack by gaining attention and a form of acceptance from others. Since this form of behavior is considered undesirable in our culture, her activities may also be classified as an attempt to punish her parents for rejecting her (4).

Sublimation. Sublimation is a specialized form of compensation. Of all the types of mechanisms, it meets with the greatest social approval. A person who employs this mechanism reaps a double dividend, psychologically speaking, for he not only reduces anxiety but is able to act in a way that will aid him in gaining approval and acceptance from others. Some psychologists consider creative activity a means of sublimating anxieties that arise from the suppression of the sex drives; others consider it a means of meeting a normal and basic human need. Probably it plays a dual role for many of us.

Sublimation involves the substitution of a socially approved goal for one that is less likely to be approved. The person who has conformed to social pressures by repressing his hostility may release it in a positive way through playing in competitive sports, the more aggressive and the more vicious the better; through business activity of a competitive nature; through playing games like poker, chess, and billiards; or through some such type of vigorous physical activity as chopping wood, mowing the lawn, or digging postholes. All these activities are of an aggressive nature, and some of them even have a tinge of hostility.

Other Forms of Substitute Activity. There are other forms of substitute activity that are not classified as sublimation, because they meet with less social approval. Some people compensate for frustration and threat by overeating; others take refuge in oversleeping. For some people, hoarding wealth or material possessions is a way of compensating for the feeling of being deprived. Still further down the scale of social disapproval are masturbation, excessive drinking, sexual perversion, and the use of narcotics — all forms of substitute behavior employed by individuals in their attempts to cope with anxiety.

Conformity. One of the commonest means of avoiding anxiety is the type of mechanism variously identified as identification, introjection, and conformity. This is a type of approach we all use. When we meet a new group of people for the first time, we usually observe closely to see how the others act and behave, to learn what the proper "norm of behavior" is for the group. Frequently we center our attention on one person, usually one whom the group accepts as its natural leader, in our search for cues as to proper behavior. We then participate with the group by copying the behavior that appears to be acceptable. The adoption of this mode of approach protects us from being rejected by the group and thus experiencing unnecessary anxiety.

It may be said that the child builds up the strength of his conscience or superego processes by identifying himself with his parents and with other significant adults. By copying their behavior and adopting their attitudes, he protects himself from any behavior that might result in their disapproval.

Identification, introjection, and conformity are, of course, necessary processes in learning to cope with life, and they aid us in avoiding much unnecessary anxiety. However, an individual can become so concerned in doing what others do that he is unable to develop in directions which would be personally satisfying or rewarding to him, which would lead him in original and individually creative directions that would not necessarily be in conflict with the moral code of the group. He is in the position of the twelve-year-old girl who was being interviewed about her attitude toward comics. "She said: 'I like Superman better than the others because they can't do everything Superman can do. Batman can't fly and that is very important.' When asked whether she herself would like to fly, she replied: 'I would like to be able to fly if everybody else did, but otherwise it would be kind of conspicuous (5).'" For her, even the joy and freedom of flight would be dangerous because of its nonconformist element.

Phantasy or Daydreaming. Phantasy or daydreaming serves as a substitute for the attainment of goals which would be satisfying, but which are either socially disapproved or are, in the estimation of the individual, beyond his reach. Virtually everyone indulges in some daydreaming. Some daydreams consist in making plans for the future that may or may not serve as the bases for action at later dates, while other daydreams are more obvious substitutes for the desired activity. Adults tend to conceal their daydreams, but children display them openly in make-believe play. Little boys in cowboy outfits gallop through the streets in pursuit of imaginary cattle and horse thieves. Little girls pretend that they are mothers and enact the routines and rituals of homemaking. Some children between the ages of three and ten conjure up for themselves imaginary companions who have rather stable characteristics and predictable behavior (6). Sometimes daydreams approach the vividness of hallucinations, as is exemplified by one little girl's sending her mother out into the rain to bring in an imaginary playmate who was presumably getting soaked.

One study of a group of college students indicated that all tended to indulge in daydreaming to some extent. Phantasies of vocational success, money or possessions, and sexual activity were reported by more than 90 per cent of both sexes. Other popular daydreams involved physical feats, mental feats, physical attractiveness, and worry. "Saving," "physical strength," and "grandeur" dreams appeared to be more popular with men, while women preferred dreams of "physical attractiveness" and "martyrdom (7)."

Daydreams do not necessarily have to be pleasant in nature. Some individuals, particularly those who are masochistically inclined — that is, who use self-punishment as a way of handling hostile feelings — prefer dreams of the "suffering hero" or "martyr" type. The person who feels he is mistreated or unloved may imagine himself the victim of a tragic accident, meeting death in a heroic manner. His cruel and unthinking family are, of course, heartbroken because they had never appreciated him properly when he was alive; they are flayed by their guilt feelings.

At the opposite end of the scale is the "conquering hero" type of daydream, in which the dreamer is able to realize some fond hope for status and prestige. By way of illustration, a third-string quarterback might imagine that, because of injuries to other players, he is put into the game at the crucial moment, and, by a dramatic and daring play, wins the game singlehanded. Naturally he is acclaimed, and his teammates and classmates wonder how the coach could have overlooked such a phenomenal player.

Modern civilization has provided us with "canned phantasies," in the form of movies, radio programs, and television shows, which are mass-produced for the millions. No longer do we have to develop our own daydreams; we can have them brought to us by a flick of the electric switch, or we can view them in technicolor at the neighborhood movie. Through the process of identification, we are enabled to incorporate these manufactured dreams into our own repertory, where they serve as models for more dreams of the same type.

Regression. This maneuver permits us figuratively to "turn back the clock" in thought or action. Presumably the individual meets with a frustration or other anxiety-producing situation, to which he reacts by reverting to behavior that was satisfying at a former period in his life. Thus when marriage turns out not to be the idyllic, never-ending honeymoon that the movies tell us it should be, or when sex relations arouse anxiety, some husbands or wives give it up as a failure and return to their parents' homes, there once again to take up the role of the happy, carefree, and dependent child, who could expect nothing but complete love and indulgence.

An eight-year-old child, who gave up bed-wetting at the age of three, moves to a new home. During the strains and trials of adjusting to the new dwelling, he may regress and wet his bed for several nights until he comes to accept his new home and the loss of the old one.

To a certain extent, most neurotic behavior is regressive, in that the individual affected tends to act in a less mature manner than otherwise. Thus a person under the stress of anxiety may flare up and lose his temper easily, or his language may revert to that of a person several years younger, or he may burst into tears. When children are frustrated, their play patterns become less mature (8). Even animals who have learned to solve certain simple problems will regress to earlier stages if placed under stress (9).

Compulsiveness. Compulsive behavior is characterized by an irresistible urge to do, say, or think something in a ritualistic manner or according to a set pattern. This kind of behavior may be preceded by a feeling of tension (anxiety), which is relieved by carrying through the compulsive act, or the compulsive act may serve to prevent or forestall anxiety. The act itself usually has no directly discernible connection with the anxiety; it is almost as though it serves as a kind of magic spell that protects the individual from anxiety. Compulsions are very common in everyday life. Smoking is a common compulsive act, and one of the reasons why veteran smokers have difficulty in breaking the habit is that they cannot tolerate the anxiety that arises when they leave off smoking.

As Henry Galvin walks down a corridor, he absent-mindedly touches the frame of each door he passes. As we watch him, he never misses; sometimes he has to go a few steps out of his way to perform this ritual.

When we speak to him about it, he looks a little sheepish; he says he has tried several times to stop, but it is too hard to give up.

As we interview Miss Stevens, we notice that while she talks, she straightens the books and papers on her desk, carefully seeing that each book does not protrude beyond the others. Then we remember that she is always straightening books and papers. Furthermore, she cannot pass another desk without stopping to push in any drawers that are sticking out, even if they are not out more than a fraction of an inch.

If we were to look over Dr. Simpson's shoulder at staff meetings, we would discover that he is an "O-filler." He always brings a magazine with him, and, as the meeting goes on, he carefully and methodically fills in one "O" after the other until the meeting is over. He participates in some heated arguments, too, but he never misses an "O."

As nine-year-old Johnny Petri walks down the block, he is careful not to step on any of the cracks in the sidewalk. As he walks, a rhyme runs incessantly through his head: "Step on a crack, and you'll break your mother's back."

Compulsions like the ones described above are normal, although sometimes mildly annoying — they may cause us embarrassment when others point them out to us. With those who are more deeply disturbed than most of us, compulsive behavior may become more and more peculiar and may eventually interfere with normal, everyday life. The compulsive drinker is one example; the person who must check and recheck everything beyond all reason is another.

Obsessions and Phobias. An obsession is an idea that usually accompanies a compulsive act. For example, a college student may be obsessed with the idea that girls do not like him, and he may compulsively blurt out some impolite or ridiculous statement whenever he has to talk to one.

A phobia is a strong, unreasoning fear, directed at some external object. A common phobia is that directed at snakes, small animals, and spiders. Phobias like these do not usually interfere with normal adjustment. However, other phobias can be more disturbing to a happy and useful life — fear of high places, closed places, darkness, moving vehicles, open spaces, or any other aspect of the physical or social environment. Phobic fears are not especially strong in persons with merely the normal amount of neurotic anxiety; but when they become so strong that they interfere with the conduct of a happy and useful life, some sort of psychotherapy is indicated.

Phobias are quite common in small children. Many a perplexed parent wonders how and where his child picked up an intense, unreasonable fear. An illustration of a child's phobia is cited by O. S. English and G. H. J. Pearson:

A four-year-old girl had a pronounced phobia of dogs. If one appeared three blocks away she became panic-stricken and rushed into the house or clung to her mother screaming. It made no difference whether the dog was large or small, friendly or hostile, good-natured or vicious; its appearance produced an anxiety attack. This fear of dogs did not follow any attack or injury by one, but began suddenly. When she was convalescing from an attack of pneumonia, she suffered a night terror. In the early hours of the morning she began to scream and did not recognize any person in the room. When her father came toward her, she shouted for him to go away. When her mother asked what the matter was, she said there was a dog under her mother's bed. When the father approached her, she screamed, "Go away. You're a dog." After some little time her terror subsided and she fell asleep quietly. On waking the next morning she was perfectly calm, but from that day on her fear of dogs was present (10).

The therapist who handled this case was able to discover that the real source of the little girl's phobia was a threatened break between her mother and her father. Her selection of a dog as the phobic object was tied up in a complicated psychological manner with the normal tendency of the child to confuse phantasy and reality and to assign animals' roles to humans, and vice versa. The important point English and Pearson make is that parents and physicians are misled into thinking that the phobic object (the dog, in this instance) is of great importance, whereas the real cause of the phobia lies in the child's feeling about himself and his relations with his parents.

Psychosomatic Symptoms. The popular press has had much to say in the last few years about psychosomatic disorders, and the evidence is steadily mounting that certain types of physical complaints are partially due to or are closely associated with the amount and kind of anxiety experienced by the individual. A study of asthma by French and others reports that the "asthmatic personality" is characterized by anxiety, overdependence on parents or parental substitutes, and a low degree of self-confidence (11). A study of persons suffering from high blood pressure (essential hypertension) and migraine headaches reveals that they tend to react to frustration and conflict with intense rage and hostility, which is always severely repressed (12). These are but a few of the patterns of personality characteristics found by investigators to be associated with disorders formerly classified as entirely physical and treated as such. Other physiological symptoms that are thought to have a definite emotional involvement are peptic ulcer, colitis, many forms of constipation, many cases of rheumatoid arthritis, and many kinds of skin rash (13).

Like the other emotions of the rage-threat variety, anxiety is physically disturbing. It is thus reasonable to assume that repeated shocks to the body occasioned by the emotional changes and tensions of anxiety may eventually result in the malfunctioning of certain organs, which in turn may produce the kind of symptom termed psychosomatic. The field of psychosomatic disease is an area in which psychologists and physicians can do much, working co-operatively, in uncovering causes and developing therapeutic methods. Any research done in this area will make slow progress for a number of reasons. First, society is more concerned with therapy and the welfare of the patient than with research, and this attitude, praiseworthy as it is, means that research must play a secondary role. Second, the controlled experiment of the psychologist's laboratory cannot be duplicated easily with patients, because conditions are so variable, because symptoms have been developing over periods of varying lengths, and because it is difficult to assemble a sufficiently large number of cases on which to base valid conclusions. Third, many patients are convinced that their symptoms are physiological; hence, they resist the idea that there is any psychological or emotional involvement. Unfortunately, because of the prevalent attitude regarding mental disease — that is, that it is a disgrace — the implication that an ulcer or a "low-back pain" may have an emotional basis is interpreted by many patients as a veiled insult. Their first reaction, when such a possibility is mentioned, is, "You mean this is all in my mind? I tell you I can *feel* these pains!"

Because of these difficulties, our knowledge of psychosomatic disease is based on a rather small amount of research pieced out with a considerable framework of hypothesis and clinical insight. As a result, we have one group of medical practitioners claiming that many physical disorders not only are caused largely by emotional upset, but should be treated primarily through psychotherapy;

whereas another group insists that these disorders are physical, and diagnoses and treats them through surgery, drug therapy, and other nonpsychological forms of therapy.

If we accept the evidence that many diseases are caused or at least conditioned by the shocks and tensions of anxiety, it would appear that psychosomatic symptoms are similar to the other mechanisms of defense and escape in that they, too, serve the purpose of helping the individual to avoid greater anxieties through suffering physical pain and smaller amounts of anxiety. Thus the girl who has "fallen out of love" with her fiancé, but who neither wants to face the fact nor break the news to him, may develop a severe headache as she starts out on a date with him. Of course he is disappointed, and she is annoyed with herself, but there is no course open but for her to be taken home. Like so many mechanisms, her headache serves several purposes. It helps her get out of an unwanted date, and it accomplishes this without too much guilt and embarrassment. In fact, she gets considerable sympathy. The pain of the headache is her punishment for not having played fair with herself and her fiancé, and of course worrying about the headache keeps her from worrying about her lack of constancy in love. Probably the most important factor, however, is self-punishment, since this is the recurring theme in many psychosomatic illnesses. The physical symptom and its accompanying pain are the means whereby the individual punishes himself for not having lived up to his own expectations or for having done something he considers unworthy, despicable, or immoral.

Accident-proneness. The self-punisher may also express this need in an equally dramatic form — through accidents. Physicians, psychologists, and safety engineers in industry are beginning to discover that the establishment of safe working conditions is only one step in the elimination of accidents, for they must still reckon with the accident-prone employee. For many such employees, the accident also serves as an expression of hostility that they cannot allow themselves to express more directly through assault, verbal insult, theft, or even through demanding rights. In one study of persons who were victims of recurrent accidents, it was found that most of them were unable to give free expression to their hostility. Some of these patients had tried to "sublimate" their hostility through sports or through their vocation; when these attempts failed, they turned to the "accident solution," directing the aggression against themselves. There seemed to be a desire for shock, for personal hurt, a symbolic "attempt at suicide." The investigators found that some of the accidents served a useful emotional purpose, such as the need to prevent loved ones from leaving the victims (14). A man whose wife was about to leave him might unconsciously permit himself to cross the street in a careless manner so that he would be seriously injured by an automobile. Since his motivation is unconscious, he sees himself as an innocent and unfortunate victim of circumstances, whose wife will be obliged to stay with him and nurse him back to health.

This explanation of accidents is of course contrary to the dictates of "common sense," as is the entire concept of accident-proneness. "Common sense" would have us believe that all accidents are something which "happen" to people, that they are occurrences over which the victims have no control. That such is not the case is indicated by research revealing that 12 to 15 per cent of employees are responsible for almost 100 per cent of industrial accidents and that certain combinations of personality traits apparently identify the accident-prone person psychologically (15).

Another kind of person who tends to be accident-prone is quite the opposite of the self-punisher. He expresses his hostile impulses too openly, for he does not have sufficient normal anxiety. One study of taxicab drivers who had a high rate of accidents showed that they came most frequently from homes marked by evidences of instability. As children they were frequently in trouble with the school and with juvenile authorities. As adults they never stayed very long on any job; very often they were fired. Their personal lives were marked by evidences of disregard for others, an emphasis on material values, and a desire for immediate satisfaction of impulses without concern for the consequences. These attitudes tended to be reflected in their driving, which showed similar tendencies of hostile aggressiveness, impulsiveness, lack of consideration for others, and disrespect for authority (16).

Suicide. The supreme gesture of the person who is self-punishing and who cannot tolerate anxiety is suicide. Countries like Sweden, Germany, and America, which produce many individuals of the self-punishing type of personality, have high suicide rates and relatively low homicide rates; whereas countries like Spain, Italy, and Ireland, where local cultures permit freer expression of emotions, have high homicide rates and low suicide rates. This difference appears to support the theory that suicide, like homicide, is really a form of hostile aggression, and that the tendency to commit suicide is related to the culture in which one lives. Probably most middle-class people in our culture contemplate suicide at some time in their lives (17). Thoughts of this sort evidently tend to be phantasies of the "suffering hero" type, discussed above. Relatively few individuals are sufficiently anxious and depressed actually to lay plans for suicide, and even fewer carry them out. Most would-be suicides make no secret of their plans; thus the safest rule to follow if someone threatens suicide or mentions plans for suicide is to persuade him to seek immediate psychiatric or psychological help.

It is difficult to draw a sharp line between suicide and accident-proneness. Many accidents are probably unconscious suicides or at least concealed suicides, as witness the case of the eighteen-year-old boy who crashes into a fence while speeding at eighty miles per hour down a winding road in a roadster with lights out. There is certainly a strong desire for death here — the surest escape from the pangs of anxiety and guilt.

Adjustment through Self-deception

There is no sharp division between those mechanisms which reduce anxiety by substitution and those of the self-deception variety, which protect the individual from his anxiety by disguising the existence of threat or denying its existence. A person who employs a substitution type of mechanism when he "sublimates" his hostility or his sexuality, employs simultaneously a self-deception type of mechanism (rationalization) when he tells himself in effect that the substituted activity is what he preferred all along, or that it is better and more satisfying than the activity whose pursuit he abandoned. In this way self-deception helps to make substitute behavior appear reasonable and palatable.

Repression. Repression, which was mentioned in Chapter 3, "The Functioning of the Unconscious Processes," is the basis of all forms of neurotic behavior, including the mechanisms discussed in this chapter, and is itself a mechanism. Its purpose is to hide from consciousness those deeds, feelings, and impulses that are immoral, undesirable, embarrassing, upsetting, and anxiety-laden.

Repression operates to keep the conscious self insulated from the anxiety radiated by the repressed material; or, viewed from another point of view, it keeps the individual from perceiving or being aware of conditions that would upset him, that would produce anxiety and guilt.

Rationalization. Rationalization is a mechanism that can often be identified in everyday life. It consists of the attempt to explain or justify an act, an attitude, a thought, or a feeling on what are meant to be reasonable or logical grounds, irrespective of the "true nature" of the underlying motivation. In common parlance rationalization is called "giving alibis," "making excuses," or "fooling oneself." The poor workman traditionally blames his tools for his failures. Mr. Gimlet forgot to mail a letter inviting his mother-in-law to visit for a couple of weeks; he explains this by saying that he was very much concerned with an important business deal. It is true that the business deal was very much on his mind, but the real reason for his forgetfulness is his desire to have his mother-in-law stay away. When she is in the house, Mr. Gimlet, a dependent person, does not get the attention from his wife that he feels is his due.

Rationalization is a convenient mechanism because it so successfully beclouds the issue that we can go about the business at hand unhampered by worries concerning the cause of our behavior. When Mrs. Gimlet asks her husband, "Oh, *why* did you forget to mail my letter to Mother?" he is actually unaware of the *true* reason, buried as it is in his unconscious processes. However, he has *this other reason,* which is very handy and which directs the attention of both persons away from his sin of omission and toward the fact that he has business worries. By attempting to turn himself from an object of criticism into an object of pity or sympathy, he successfully blocks himself from ever finding out why his mother-in-law makes him uncomfortable, and he avoids the upsetting truth that he is greatly dependent on his wife for affection and attention. Thus rationalization keeps Mr. Gimlet from finding out what ails him and Mrs. Gimlet from finding out how her husband really feels about her mother. Not only does Mr. Gimlet retain his "self-respect" — that is, his idea of himself as a strong, dominant male, who does not need to be dependent on anyone — but he maintains workable relations with his wife.

In other words, if we did not rationalize, if there were no mechanism to conceal the secret, unconscious motives of ourselves and others, the results would be disturbing, to say the least. The impossibility of anyone telling "the whole truth and nothing but the truth" at all times is burlesqued in the high school play "Nothing but the Truth," in which the hero must tell the truth for twenty-four hours; the result is chaos, and the moral is that in most social situations it is not wise to tell all that one knows or feels. Many things are better left unsaid.

Rationalization plays an important part in our culture, largely because of the emphasis we place on "reason" — we constantly are urging one another to "be reasonable." Yet in our very search for reason we are unreasonable. A parent catches his child stealing and he thunders, "Why did you take that money?" This is an unreasonable request: Can the child *really* account for his reason for taking the money? If the child *were* consciously aware of the needs he is meeting, would they be accepted by the parent as a "reasonable" explanation? The fact is that the adult who asks such questions does not really expect to get reasonable answers. He behaves in this irrational way because he has a need to express his horror and anxiety; he is trying to cope with such thoughts as "My child is a *thief!*" "Have I been a poor parent and is the guilt really mine?" "What will the neighbors think?" "What if they find out?" "How can my child *do* this thing to me?" Caught in the web of these anxious feelings, he can only lash out with the question "Why did you do it?" in the vain hope that the child can produce some explanation indicating that what appears to be a crime is not actually a crime, that the parent is not really at fault, that the whole thing is a mistake.

Rationalization occurs in connection with many other mechanisms; it serves to help the individual feel that his behavior, which appears peculiar to others, is really quite sensible and reasonable. Thus the housewife who spends several hours each day cleaning her house thoroughly does so "because someone might come"; the person who has to wash his hands every half hour or so does so "because of germs"; and the compulsive drinker drinks "to be sociable."

Logic-tight Compartments. Sometimes rationalization is facilitated by a system of logic-tight compartments that enables an individual to do things opposed to his principles or to explain his behavior by statements that are logically incompatible. By way of illustration, a church deacon who is also a real estate broker may take advantage of a client through a technicality in a contract. He may be altruistic and humanitarian with his friends, his family, and his fellow church members; but when it comes to money, "business is business," or, as the Yankee farmers were reputed to say, "Friendship's one thing, an' hoss tradin's another." Another example is that of the parent who thrashes his boy soundly, and then says, "*This* will teach you not to hit people!"

Perceptual Rigidity. A very common kind of mechanism, one that seldom penetrates awareness, is rigidity of perception. Rigidity as used in this connection refers to our tendency to react to a new situation as though it were a familiar one or to a new acquaintance as though he were someone previously known.

John McGuire was dominated by his father and his teachers as a child. He always felt helpless and inadequate with them. When John became an adult, he was unable to stand up for his rights with persons in authority. He reacted to his boss as though his boss were his father — that is, his expectations of his boss were much the same as the expectations he had formed regarding his father. This neurotic misevaluation was supported whenever his boss did anything that reminded him of his father; he ignored anything his boss did differently from the way his father would have done it, because such action did not fit the picture he had of his boss. John was completely unaware that he was a victim of perceptual rigidity; only the objective observer acquainted with John's childhood and employment situation would be in a position to see the parallel relationship between John's reaction to his father and his reaction to his employer.

In actuality, most of our judgments regarding people are based on previous experiences with others who for some reason appear to us to be similar. Thus we find ourselves being affable to a saleswoman who reminds us of our Aunt Martha, who was a very friendly, easygoing person. On the other hand, we are on our guard and are unnecessarily sharp with a bus driver who reminds us of the dentist who used to say, "It isn't going to hurt a bit," though it always did. Like other mechanisms, perceptual rigidity protects us from anxiety, for it helps us to feel that each new person does not represent a new problem. In the first few seconds of meeting a stranger, we have him classified according to the people he reminds us of. Even though we are actually misjudging him, we are at ease and confident, or alert and suspicious, depending on our experience with the person he resembles. We are relieved of the necessity of studying him and drawing up a set of evaluations; since we have made our judgment of him we are free to deal with him in accordance with our expectations — we think we can stop worrying about the kind of person he is.

The disadvantages of this sort of evaluation are obvious. In the first place, the saleswoman is *not* Aunt Martha, no matter how much she resembles her. She is really a different person. Probably our misjudgment will not matter here, because our contact with her is brief; we may never see her again. Thus prejudgments based on perceptual rigidity usually cause us little difficulty, for most of our contacts with others tend to be on a formal, superficial basis. Occasionally, however, they can lead us into serious problems, such as those faced by the woman who could never trust men enough to marry one of them because her own father was prone to make elaborate and attractive promises that he never carried out. Inasmuch as she reacted to all men in the light of what she had "learned" from her experience with her father, it was impossible for her to permit herself to become emotionally attached to any man, no matter how trustworthy he might seem to others.

In the second place, prejudgments — that is, prejudices — based on perceptual rigidity may actually prevent our learning to know other people. Cy Barnum is spared the necessity of becoming acquainted with persons of Mexican origin; he "knows" that they are shiftless and lazy. Mr. Barnum carries this concept of Mexicans over to each person of Mexican parentage he meets or hears about. Furthermore, perceptual rigidity enables him to maintain his logic-tight compartmentation, because the prejudgment it produces enables him to ignore any evidence that does not fit this picture.

One further point should be made about evaluations colored by perceptual rigidity: they reflect the values and needs of the person making the evaluation. Thus the dependent person tends to see others as sources of help and support, even though there is no objective evidence on which such a perception may be based. The suspicious person tends to see others as untrustworthy, as possible competitors, or as threats to his security. This tendency to attribute one's point of view, one's failings, one's personality traits to others is called "projection."

Projection. Projection is a mechanism that protects us from guilt and anxiety by freeing us from the knowledge of our more or less undesirable traits, while at the same time giving us an opportunity to condemn them in others. Thus persons who would really like to give rein to their dependency needs, but who have learned to feel so guilty about them that they have repressed them from consciousness, tend to be the ones who will harshly condemn others who display behavior that may be characterized as "lazy" (dependent). Others, who have repressed their sexual longings because of the "sinful" nature of such feelings, will condemn others for engaging in any kind of behavior that has possible "immoral" implications, regardless of whether such condemnation is justified. Such people can always be depended upon to attack sex education in the schools, or the "bare-midriff" sports costume, or adolescent dating. They rationalize their disapproval by saying that such behavior leads to licentiousness and immoral conduct, even though the evidence to support this contention is lacking.

In its broader sense, projection is a mechanism by which we "project" our personality on our physical and social environment. We are all acquainted with the phrase "looking at the world through rose-colored glasses." To a person who is in a pleasant mood, his physical and social environment seems pleasant. He is optimistic about events whose outcome may be highly dubious; he trusts people about whom he might otherwise be suspicious. On the other hand, consider the individual who is susceptible to Blue Mondays. No matter how promising and hopeful an event may be, he tends to interpret it in its worst possible light; he finds the general outlook depressing; he is convinced that his best and most loyal friends have let him down.

Projection is not only affected by moods — it also reflects the characteristic personality patterns of the individual. Psychologists have capitalized on this latter tendency by constructing and standardizing tests known as "projective techniques." These tests present the individual with ambiguous or neutral stimuli that he must interpret. For example, the Rorschach test consists of a series of ink blots that in themselves have no meaning. The individual is asked to tell the administrator of the test what he thinks he sees.   Since the ink blots themselves are completely meaningless, anything the individual sees will be the result of what he has a need to see or feels inwardly compelled to see.   The skill in interpretation of the results of this and other projective tests lies in the psychologist's ability to determine what emotional stresses and pressures are expressing themselves in the responses given and what personality characteristics would be associated with the emotional stresses revealed.

Displaced Hostility.   Another form of self-deception is displaced rage or displaced hostility — that is, being angry at or attacking an innocent person or object as an expression of aroused hostility. The pinball-machine player misses an easy one and gives the machine a kick that causes it to show "tilt."   The carpenter hits his thumb while driving a nail and angrily knocks a panel out of the fence he is building.   The high school social science teacher is reprimanded by the principal for having an unruly class.   When he comes home in the evening, he speaks sharply to his son and quarrels with his wife.   In each situation the individual is prevented from expressing his rage at the source of his frustration or threat.   Unable to tolerate the anxiety that would result from the repression of his rage, he expresses it by mistreating a piece of equipment or an innocent bystander.   The pinball-machine player and the carpenter are themselves at fault; since they are unable to express hostility toward themselves, they attack what they would like to feel is the source of their frustration.   The teacher would like to tell his principal that the criticism is unjust.   Since for realistic or neurotic reasons he cannot bring himself to do so, his family must suffer.

Scapegoating.   A special form of displacement or projection is the scapegoat mechanism.   This usually occurs in groups of people who are frustrated or threatened and who feel unable to deal with problems on a realistic level.   Thus a group working in an office under an autocratic and critical supervisor will tend to select as a scapegoat a more or less defenseless member of the group, preferably one who differs from the rest to some marked degree, whose behavior is unconventional, or even one whose work is better than that of the rest.   The group will blame this person for most of the things that go wrong in the office;   they may hold him responsible in some way for every frustrating and annoying situation that exists. There is no logic behind such behavior, unless it is the logic that strong and hostile feelings must find some kind of expression.

One of the most dramatic examples of scapegoating in recent years was the persecution of the Jews by the Nazis in Germany. Through the skillful use of propaganda devices, the Nazis were able to magnify the relatively small amount of existing prejudice against the Jews into a nationwide crusade of hate, which culminated in the destruction of millions of innocent persons. Jew-baiting thus served as one of the means whereby the attention of the German people was distracted from the realities of the national and international scene. This situation, in turn, fitted in nicely with the plans of the Nazis to seize political power and to exploit the German people and their neighbors to the utmost.

Reaction Formation. Still another form of adjustment through self-deception is the mechanism called "reaction formation." The individual who uses this defense against anxiety is one who is so disturbed (unconsciously) by what he feels are unworthy tendencies in himself that he acts in an opposite manner. Paul Martin, as a boy, had a violent temper. As an adult he has a well-developed drive to achieve social and financial success. Inasmuch as the expression of rage is incompatible with these goals, he represses all feelings of rage, resentment, irritation, or anything that even remotely resembles hostility. Because he so fears his own hostility, he over-reacts, he develops a role in which he is too pleasant, too nice, too friendly. Sometimes he is upset when people characterize him as insincere, which, in reality, he is. Yet this mask performs a necessary function in that it dispels anxiety by over-compensating for his temper. Another sort of reaction formation occurs in those who become so concerned about what they consider are immoral tendencies in themselves that they become prudish and develop overly narrow, overly conventional patterns of life.

Adjustment through Retreat

A person who attempts to avoid anxiety through retreat does so by figuratively burying himself in some kind of activity demanding so much emotional involvement that he becomes less sensitive to the actual problems troubling him. Or he may insulate himself from reality by taking refuge in the anesthetic forgetfulness resulting from excessive consumption of alcohol or narcotics.

Depression. Depression is an example of the retreat variety of mechanism. In the film "Feeling of Depression," the "hero" wards off anxiety by succumbing to a long period of depression, the cause of which he attributes to business difficulties. When his wife and his business partner suggest that he see a doctor, he says there is nothing a doctor can do for a business that is "on the rocks." In reality, the business difficulty is not as serious as he perceives it; it merely serves as a rationalization for his neurotic depression, which is actually due to feelings of guilt and unworthiness caused by his unconscious hostility toward his younger brother and his unconscious feeling that he is unworthy of his dead father. However, by feeling depressed and blaming it on the business, he does not look himself in the eye, psychologically speaking, and see his hostility and guilt for what they really are. This would be too anxiety-provoking and would disturb his conscious mental picture of himself as a kind, worthy, and responsible individual (18).

In some instances, the depressed person feels that he has been deprived of something which is rightfully his but which cannot be recovered because of circumstances, or because he feels that he is unworthy. Actually, he resents the deprivation, but instead of expressing his feeling of hostility openly, he relapses into inertia and immobility. He draws within himself and refuses to participate in certain activities, particularly those that normally provide him with the most pleasure. Essentially, depression is a self-punishing method of adjustment.

Shyness. Shyness, which is discussed at length in the following chapter, is another form of adjustment through retreat that results in inertia and immobility. By withdrawing from active participation, the shy person feels that he protects himself from exposing his inadequacies to public gaze. When he does something that causes him to become the object of public attention, his anxiety rises to a high level. By remaining silent, by seeking the anonymity of the crowd, by shrinking from the limelight, he is able to minimize his anxiety.

Hyperactivity. The inactivity of depression and shyness form one kind of defense; hyperactivity forms another. Some persons escape from anxiety by a veritable "flight into activity." By becoming involved and overinvolved in an endless sequence of activities, the hyperactive person is kept so busy that he does not have time to be anxious. His attention is so taken up with carrying out the activities he has scheduled for himself that he is unable to become aware of the emotional problems causing his anxiety. He must fight constantly against his tasks becoming too routine, for, when this occurs, his attention may wander to the anxiety he is endeavoring to escape. Thus he may adopt a dilettante approach to life, going from one activity to another, seldom or never completing a task, frequently promising more than he can deliver. The man who has "too many irons in the fire" is a common figure in the business and professional world.

Drugs and Alcohol. The person who takes refuge from anxiety in drugs or alcohol differs from other persons who employ mechanisms only in that his method is chemical rather than emotional. In our culture the habitual escape from anxiety through alcohol and drugs is not condoned because of the likelihood that habitual users may become burdens on, if not menaces to, society.

Because addiction to alcohol and drugs constitutes a graver social problem than other forms of psychological escape from anxiety and guilt, there has been more research in this field than with other types of mechanisms. Giorgi Lolli sees addiction to alcohol as "an expression of lopsided growth; infantile traits in one part of the personality coexist with mature traits in another. . . . [The addict] is an impulsive person who faces great difficulty in resisting his instinctual drives (19)." The research literature dealing with the existence of an "alcoholic personality" was reviewed by Edwin H. Sutherland, H. G. Schroeder, and C. L. Tordella, who found researchers largely in disagreement, and concluded that "no satisfactory evidence has been discovered that justifies a conclusion that persons of one type are more likely to become alcoholics than persons of another type (20)." However, Victor H. Vogel, Harris Isbell, and K. W. Chapman assert that "a vast majority of narcotic drug addicts are fundamentally emotionally immature, childlike persons, who have never made a proper adaption to the problems of living (21)."

Psychosis. Mental patients occupy more than half of the hospital beds in the United States. Relatively few persons troubled solely by neurotic difficulties are committed to mental hospitals; the bulk of these patients suffer from some form of psychosis. Psychotic persons differ from neurotics in that they have solved their life problems by a "flight from reality" and hence are more or less incompetent to manage their own affairs. According to O'Kelly, psychotic behavior develops from an attempt to reduce anxiety.

He states further that the psychotic person is one who either has not used the usual neurotic techniques for dealing with anxiety or has been forced to abandon them in the face of his inability to solve his problems (22). As we have indicated previously, neurotic behavior is characterized by its lack of logic and good sense, as well as by its tendency to ignore the realities of life. Psychotic behavior also lacks good sense and is not attuned to reality, but the gap between the psychotic individual and reality is much greater than that between the neurotic and reality. The unrealities of psychotic behavior are on such a large scale, they are so elaborate, they are dispelled with so much difficulty, and they so threaten the welfare of the individual concerned that he must be placed in an institution where he may receive therapy, or at least the care he is unable to provide for himself.

Psychotherapy

Who Needs Psychotherapy? No discussion of emotional adjustment and maladjustment would be complete without some consideration of the measures that have been developed to aid individuals whose adjustment problems have overwhelmed them, or threaten to do so, or whose general emotional adjustment might be improved.

There are five broad classes of individuals who may be aided by psychotherapy. The first and most obvious are those persons whose emotional and social adjustment is so impaired that they require intensive therapy and, usually, hospitalization: the psychotic group.

The second group consists of those persons who have severe problems of emotional adjustment that interfere with their health, happiness, creativity, efficiency, and relations with others, but not so much so that they have lost contact with reality or are "menaces to themselves and to society." These individuals, called psycho-neurotics, do not usually require hospitalization but are much in need of psychotherapy to aid them in relieving symptoms of anxiety and fearfulness, extreme sensitivity, egocentricity and heightened self-awareness, emotional immaturity, psychosomatic complaints, and generalized dissatisfaction and unhappiness.

A third group consists of social deviants — persons who attempt to solve their problems through recourse to alcohol, drugs, crime, and other illegal behavior. (See Chapter 18, "Patterns of Devia-tion: Antisocial and Abnormal.") These individuals are mentioned here because their problems are primarily problems of adjustment that are frequently amenable to psychotherapy.

A fourth group consists of individuals whose problems of adjustment and whose symptoms are not as severe as those of the group characterized as psychoneurotic. These are individuals who are coping with life and its problems but whose search for happiness and better interpersonal relations would be aided by recourse to psychotherapy. Included in this group are those who are fairly productive workers but whose marital relations suffer from their emotional immaturity; those who are not alcoholics but who drink somewhat more than they should; and those who are fairly effective professional workers but who could be more effective if they were emotionally more mature.

A fifth class of individuals are those who are reasonably happy and secure but who through some catastrophe or some unusual situation have been subjected to psychological pressures that are extraordinarily severe. An example of this class is the individual who has a reasonably good emotional adjustment but who in wartime is exposed to enemy fire on the front lines for a period of several weeks. Under conditions of constant danger and privation, otherwise well-adjusted individuals become emotionally disorganized, but can be helped by psychiatric first aid. The Army discovered that these individuals could usually be returned to combat duty in a short time.

Who Provides Psychotherapy? Psychotherapy is provided by professional workers who are variously classified as psychiatrists, psychoanalysts, clinical psychologists, and psychiatric social workers.

Psychiatrists are medical doctors who have completed three years' advanced training of a psychological nature, have passed the examinations of the American Board of Psychiatry and Neurology, and have been issued diplomas by the Board. Actually, any licensed medical doctor may practice psychiatry, but there is an increasing tendency to restrict the use of the title "psychiatrist" to those persons who have had this specialized training. A psychiatrist may or may not have had psychoanalytic training.

Psychoanalysts are persons who have themselves been psychoanalyzed and who have been trained to give psychoanalytic therapy. Most of the persons in the United States who are trained to do this work are doctors of medicine and are also psychiatrists. However, a few psychoanalysts, called "lay analysts," do not have medical training.

Clinical psychologists do not have the M.D. degree but are trained to perform a variety of professional functions in addition to psychotherapy, particularly in the fields of psychological research and diagnosis. Indeed, there is a tendency for many, if not most, departments of psychology to emphasize research skills in training clinical psychologists. However, for the purposes of the present discussion, we are concerned primarily with their therapeutic functions. The clinical psychologist usually receives his training in psychotherapy through specialized graduate course work and through supervised experiences in clinical settings. The American Psychological Association has in recent years sought to improve the standards of clinical training by the inspection and certification of colleges and universities offering training programs in clinical psychology.*

A psychiatric social worker is a person who has had training beyond the bachelor's degree in principles and techniques of social case work, as well as special instruction in the problems of dealing with persons with psychoneurotic or psychotic difficulties. The advanced training also involves experience in a clinic or mental hospital under psychiatric supervision.

Because of the severe shortage of professionally trained psychotherapists, many persons in need of this service have turned for help to the large number of counselors who work for governmental or private agencies or are in private practice. The psychological training of these workers varies from zero to the equivalent of that of the clinical psychologist or the psychiatric social worker. Some of these persons do an excellent job of psychotherapy, while others confuse their clients, or exploit them, or both. In general, school and college counselors, ministers, and guidance workers employed by social welfare agencies provide a better service than those counselors engaged in private practice who do not have clinical training. However, in any event, the individual in need of psychotherapy takes a greater risk when he entrusts his case to the indi-

---

* For a discussion of the role of the clinical psychologist, see C. R. Rogers, "Where Are We Going in Clinical Psychology?" *Journal of Consulting Psychology.* 15:171–177; 1951. For an extensive coverage of training programs and problems, see V. C. Raimy, ed., *Training in Clinical Psychology*, New York: Prentice-Hall, 1950.

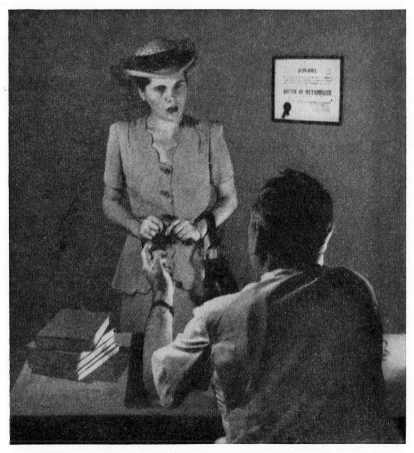

Persons who seek professional help from psychotherapists should be careful to locate reputable and ethical practitioners. The degree of Doctor of Metaphysics, appearing on the diploma hanging on the wall, is neither recognized nor accepted by any of the professional organizations that have prescribed standards of training and competence for practitioners of counseling or psychotherapy.

vidual who lacks clinical training. On the other hand, facilities for psychotherapy fall so short of adequate in most communities that individuals desiring psychotherapy have no choice but to obtain this service from persons who lack clinical training. Probably the best recommendation that can be made under the circumstances is that they ask local social welfare agencies or members of the psychology department of local colleges and universities for information about psychotherapists who have been certified as ethical. Unfortunately the individual who looks up "psychologists" in the advertising section of his telephone book is given little or no protection. Psychiatrists, being doctors of medicine, must have a license to practice; there is no difficulty here. But in most states, anyone can call himself a "psychologist" or a "psychoanalyst," regardless of whether or not he has had any training or education. Professional groups of psychologists are endeavoring to have laws passed by state legislatures providing for the licensing or certifying of psychologists; so far they have been successful in a few states.

The Nature of Psychotherapy. The more drastic forms of psychotherapy — electric shock, lobotomy, metrazol, and insulin (termed "somatic therapy"), as well as confinement — are reserved for the more deeply disturbed psychotic patients who do not respond to the verbal forms of psychotherapy. It sometimes comes as a surprise to students to learn that the most effective form of psychotherapy and the method used almost exclusively with all persons suffering from emotional maladjustments, except psychotics, consists of *talking to a psychotherapist.* The first reaction is, "How can *talking* help?" "What good can *talking* do if I am troubled by headaches?" or "I have *talked* to everybody and anybody, and it hasn't done any good."

The answer to these objections is that psychotherapy is more than merely talking; it encourages self-exploration, self-knowledge, and insight through a personal-interview type of relationship. Psychotherapy goes under a variety of labels — for example, directive and nondirective therapy, personal counseling, psychoanalysis, marriage counseling, and group therapy. These are actually descriptive terms rather than distinct varieties of therapy. For instance, it is possible for *group therapy* to be conducted in ways that are *nondirective* or *directive.*

The chief characteristics of any of these forms of therapy are as follows: 1. The client or patient is enabled to relieve pent-up feelings through frank discussion (catharsis). 2. He comes to identify symptoms of behavior of which he has hitherto been unaware. 3. He is enabled to gain understanding and acceptance of his difficulties. 4. He is helped to develop behavior which is more desirable and more "reality-oriented," which enables him to eliminate, diminish, or avoid the objectionable symptom, on the one hand, or enables him to "live with it," on the other.

The process of therapy may also be viewed as a "learning situation" in that the patient is "re-educated" by the therapist to the end that his anxiety is reduced and his behavior and life goals become more realistic, more reasonable (23).

Norine Corbett is a fussy, precise person, who must do her work over several times before she is satisfied. She also suffers from severe headaches and stomach upsets. She went to see a doctor about her headaches and her gastric troubles, and he, finding nothing organically amiss, referred her to a psychotherapist. During the course of the first few interviews, the psychotherapist discerned (but did not disclose) a relationship between her bodily symptoms and her obsessive-compulsive habits; and this, in turn, he connected with her relationship to her mother, both as an adult and as a child. Miss Corbett's first problem was to recognize that she has a neurosis. (This was difficult for her to do, because the chief function of her headaches and stomach-aches is to prevent her from becoming very objective about herself.) Having gained this much insight, her next problem is to discover why she developed the neurotic symptoms. As she comes to face her problems successfully, she will learn that many of her fears concerning herself are baseless, and this insight will reduce the threat she feels, which in turn will reduce her feeling of anxiety. The reduction in anxiety will help to eliminate or to lessen the annoying symptoms, because they will not be needed for their original purpose — that is, to defend her against the feeling of anxiety. The role of the psychotherapist in this process is to *help* Miss Corbett, not to tell her what is wrong with her. Eventually, with the psychotherapist's help she will come to discover some of the meanings in her behavior that he was able to discern rather early in the psychotherapeutic relationship.

Various psychotherapists perform their helping function in different ways. Some aid the client with interpretations of behavior (directive therapy; psychoanalysis), while others accept and reflect the client's statements and refrain altogether from making interpretations (nondirective, client-centered therapy). It is difficult or impossible to say which kind of therapy is the more successful; perhaps the safest generalization is that the more experience a therapist has and the better his reputation, the more he is able to help his clients (24, 25).

The chief factors that help to make psychotherapy successful are as follows: (a) a genuine desire on the part of the patient to overcome his difficulty; (b) the belief that he can be helped by psychotherapy; and (c) the opportunity to discuss his problem with a trained, experienced person in a relaxed, permissive, and accepting atmosphere. As the patient learns that he is accepted for who he is rather than for what he does, he will find that he can talk about matters he has hitherto feared to mention to others because of the possibility of criticism or ridicule. Thus he can eventually permit himself to lower his defenses and look at his problems objectively, with a minimum of anxiety.

Essentially, psychotherapy is a learning situation wherein one learns new means of dealing with life and unlearns the older, unrealistic, and neurotic methods. As with other learning situations — for example, in school — the therapist cannot learn *for* the client; his function is to create an atmosphere in which the client can find out for himself. Occasionally the therapist will help his client over some of the more difficult portions of the lessons in self-knowledge.

Group Therapy. The technique of group therapy deserves special mention, for it differs somewhat from the face-to-face relationship of the client and therapist. Group therapy is coming into greater use not only because it can reach more people but because it frequently enables the individual to obtain and to test insights more quickly and effectively than would be possible in individual psychotherapy. Inasmuch as neurotic traits invariably arise from an interference with interpersonal relations, it is often possible for the individual to learn through the medium of group psychotherapy just how it is that he affects others and they affect him. Furthermore, it is frequently easier for an individual to accept interpretations of his behavior from a group than from a psychotherapist.

By way of illustration, let us consider Larry Bellini, who attempts to bully others. This behavior pattern is so characteristic that he is certain to attempt to dominate any group consisting of persons equal to him in status. At first the group undergoing therapy will tolerate his bullying, but soon it will become impatient and will express its resentment openly. Perhaps Mr. Bellini will not accept the accusation on the part of the first or even the second group member that he is attempting to bully, but when the entire group agrees on this point, he will reluctantly admit that perhaps he does try to push people around. On the other hand, if Mr. Bellini's treatment were confined to individual psychotherapy, it might take months for him to see himself as a bullying individual. Furthermore, as Mr. Bellini continues to participate in the group, he will be enabled to search for and to discover other and more effective ways of working with other people.

SUMMARY

This chapter has been concerned with the kinds of defensive behavior we employ to protect ourselves from that painful awareness we term "anxiety." These defenses were classified under three broad headings, admittedly overlapping: substitution, self-deception, and retreat.

The anxiety provoked in the individual by frustration in his attempt to meet his needs is sometimes warded off by his accepting lesser goals as substitutes for the more desirable ones. Examples of substitution mechanisms are compensation, sublimation, identification, phantasy, compulsions, obsessions, phobias, psychosomatic disorders, accidents, and suicide.

Some kinds of behavior operate to disguise anxiety or deny its existence; these were discussed under the heading of self-deception. These mechanisms include rationalization, perceptual rigidity, projection, displaced hostility, scapegoating, and reaction formation.

Some persons attempt to avoid guilt and anxiety by retreat into forms of behavior that prevent their becoming consciously aware of either the anxiety or its source. These forms of behavior are depression, shyness, hyperactivity, addiction to drugs and alcohol, and psychosis.

All persons use mechanisms of defense to a greater or lesser degree, and the extent to which these mechanisms are employed is a measure of general adjustment. Deeply disturbed persons (psychotics) differ from normal people in that their symptoms are more numerous or more involved, with the result that these persons are to a large degree out of contact with reality. Although relatively few persons reach the point of psychosis, a large proportion of the population is plagued intermittently or constantly by problems of adjustment serious enough to impair markedly their capacities to enjoy life and to be creative, productive, efficient, companionable, and co-operative. Thus there are many of us to whom psychotherapy, though not essential, would be beneficial.

Trained psychotherapists — psychiatrists, psychoanalysts, clinical psychologists, and psychiatric social workers — are not available in sufficient numbers to meet all the therapeutic needs of the community. Many of those for whom psychotherapy is desirable, even though not essential, therefore have to obtain treatment from persons who may be very effective but whose formal training does not meet the standards set by the medical and psychological professions. Caution therefore must be advised. Some of these workers are conscientious and able; others are more likely to hinder than help and may even exploit their clients financially.

The most effective forms of therapy for persons with nonpsychotic problems are the therapeutic interview and group therapy. By discussing personal problems with therapists who are accepting, permissive, and noncritical, most persons are enabled to gain insight into the nature of their problems, with the result that they are helped to lead lives of improved usefulness and increased happiness.

REFERENCES

1. R. May, *The Meaning of Anxiety.* New York: Ronald, 1950.
2. R. May, *The Meaning of Anxiety,* New York, Ronald, 1950. P. 194.
3. "The Feeling of Hostility." National Film Board of Canada, 1948.
4. B. Safier, *et al.*, *A Psychiatric Approach to the Treatment of Promiscuity.* New York: American Social Hygiene Assn., 1949. Publication No. A-741.
5. K. Wolfe and M. Fiske, "The Children Talk about Comics," in P. F. Lazarsfeld and F. N. Stanton, eds., *Communications Research.* New York: Harper, 1949. Pp. 26–27. Reprinted by permission of Harper & Brothers.
6. A. T. Jersild, F. V. Markey, and C. L. Jersild, "Children's Fears, Dreams, Wishes, Daydreams, Likes, Dislikes, Pleasant and Unpleasant Memories," *Child Development Monographs, No. 12.* New York: Teachers College, Columbia University, 1933.
7. L. F. Shaffer, *The Psychology of Adjustment.* Boston: Houghton Mifflin, 1936.
8. R. G. Barker, *et al.*, "Experimental Studies of Frustration in Young Children," in T. M. Newcomb and E. L. Hartley, eds., *Readings in Social Psychology.* New York: Holt, 1947. Pp. 283–290.

9. L. I. O'Kelly, "An Experimental Study of Regression. I. Behavioral Characteristics of the Regressive Response," *Journal of Comparative Psychology*. 30:41–53; 1940.

10. O. S. English and G. H. J. Pearson, *Emotional Problems of Living*. New York: Norton, 1945. Reprinted by permission of W. W. Norton & Company, Inc.

11. T. M. French, *et al.*, *Psychogenic Factors in Bronchial Asthma*, Parts I and II. Psychosom. Med. Monographs IV. Washington, D. C.: National Research Council, 1941.

12. E. Weiss, *et al.*, "Emotional Problems of High Blood Pressure," *American Journal of Psychiatry*. 107:264–270; 1950.

13. F. Alexander, *Psychosomatic Medicine*. New York: Norton, 1950.

14. I. Csillag and E. Hedri, Jr., "Personal Factors of Accident Proneness," *Industrial Medicine*. 18:29–30; 1949.

15. P. J. Moorad, "Human Factors in Accident Liability," *Industrial Medicine*. 16:494–498; 1947.

16. W. A. Tillman and G. E. Hobbs, "The Accident-Prone Automobile Driver: A Study of the Psychiatric and Social Background," *American Journal of Psychiatry*. 106:321–331; 1949.

17. G. N. Raines and S. V. Thompson, "Suicide: Some Basic Considerations," *Digest of Neurology and Psychiatry*. 18:97–107; 1950.

18. "Feeling of Depression." National Film Board of Canada, 1950.

19. G. Lolli, "The Addictive Drinker," *Quarterly Journal of Studies on Alcohol*. 10:404–414; 1949.

20. E. H. Sutherland, *et al.*, "Personality Traits and the Alcoholic," *Quarterly Journal of Studies on Alcohol*. 11:547–561; 1950.

21. V. H. Vogel, *et al.*, "Present Status of Narcotic Addiction," *Journal of the American Medical Association*. 138:1019–1026; 1948.

22. L. I. O'Kelly, *An Introduction to Psychopathology*. New York: Prentice-Hall, 1949.

23. E. J. Shoben, Jr., "Psychotherapy as a Problem in Learning Theory," *Psychological Bulletin*. 46:366–392; 1949.

24. F. E. Fiedler, "A Comparison of Therapeutic Relationships in Psychoanalytic, Nondirective, and Adlerian Therapy," *Journal of Consulting Psychology*. 14:436–445; 1950.

25. F. E. Fiedler, "Factor Analyses of Psychoanalytic, Nondirective, and Adlerian Therapeutic Relationships," *Journal of Consulting Psychology*. 15:32–38; 1951.

SUGGESTED READINGS

General Psychology

H. W. Hepner, *Psychology Applied to Life and Work*, 2d edition. New York: Prentice-Hall, 1950. See Part Two, "Understanding the Individual's Behavior through the Adjustment Concept." A discussion of various mechanisms and methods of psychotherapy.

F. L. Ruch, *Psychology and Life*, 3d edition. Chicago: Scott, 1948. Chapter 13 deals with mechanisms under the heading, "Reactions to Frustration." See also Chapter 14, entitled "Psychotherapy and Readjustment."

J. E. Anderson, *The Psychology of Development and Personal Adjustment.* New York: Holt, 1950. See Chapter 18, "Inadequate Adjustment."

G. Murphy, *An Introduction to Psychology.* New York: Harper, 1951. See particularly Chapter 23, "Defense of the Self."

E. T. Prothro and P. T. Teska, *Psychology: A Biosocial Study of Behavior.* Boston: Ginn, 1950. See Chapter 7, "Reactions to Conflict."

E. L. Hartley, *et al.*, eds., *Outside Readings in Psychology.* New York: Crowell, 1950. Section XV is entitled "Personality and its Disorders."

Abnormal Psychology

L. I. O'Kelly, *An Introduction to Psychopathology.* New York: Prentice-Hall, 1949. The entire book is an extended treatment of what is briefly discussed in this chapter.

A. H. Maslow and B. Mittelmann, *Principles of Abnormal Psychology*, Rev. edition. New York: Harper, 1951. Like O'Kelly's book, this one is an extended treatment of the subject matter in this chapter.

N. Cameron, *The Psychology of Behavior Disorders.* Boston: Houghton Mifflin, 1947. Again, an extended treatment of the subject matter in this chapter.

J. C. Coleman, *Abnormal Psychology and Modern Life.* Chicago: Scott, 1950. See comment above.

R. W. White, *The Abnormal Personality.* New York: Ronald, 1948. See comment above.

Mental Hygiene

K. A. Menninger, *The Human Mind*, 3d edition. New York: Knopf, 1948. A popular but sound treatment of the problem of mental hygiene.

O. S. English and G. H. J. Pearson, *Emotional Problems of Living.* New York: Norton, 1945. An orthodox Freudian approach to the problem of emotional maladjustment, with particular reference to developmental periods in childhood. Interesting reading.

H. A. Carroll, *Mental Hygiene: The Dynamics of Adjustment*, 2d edition. New York: Prentice-Hall, 1951. Chapters 7, 8, 9, and 10 deal with adjustment to frustration, psychoneuroses, and psychoses; Chapter 14 deals with psychotherapy.

L. F. Shaffer, *The Psychology of Adjustment.* Boston: Houghton Mifflin, 1936. An older book, but a classic in its field. Part II deals with varieties of adjustive behavior.

F. McKinney, *Psychology of Personal Adjustment*, 2d edition. New York: Wiley, 1949. Mechanisms are discussed in a portion of Chapter 5.

P. M. Symonds, *Dynamic Psychology.* New York: Appleton-Century-Crofts, 1949. Most of the chapters in this book deal specifically and extensively with mental mechanisms.

L. J. Saul, *Emotional Maturity.* Philadelphia: Lippincott, 1947. See Chapter 14, entitled "Fight and Flight."

Psychotherapy

L. A. Pennington and I. A. Berg, *An Introduction to Clinical Psychology.* New York: Ronald, 1948. Chapter 13 deals with the psychoses and psychoneuroses;

Chapter 14, projective tests; Part IV, various means of psychotherapy; Part V, the relationship between psychiatry and clinical psychology.

G. H. J. Pearson, *Emotional Disorders of Children*. New York: Norton, 1949. A thoroughly Freudian coverage of this subject, including some discussion of psychotherapy with children along psychoanalytic lines. Contains case material.

F. Fromm-Reichmann, *Principles of Intensive Psychotherapy*. Chicago: University of Chicago Press, 1950. Approaches the subject from the standpoint of the newer psychoanalytic school as represented by Fromm, Horney, and Thompson.

J. Dollard and N. E. Miller, *Personality and Psychotherapy*. New York: McGraw-Hill, 1950. An attempt to synthesize the findings of psychological research of the laboratory type with the findings of clinical research. Part II, dealing with the basic principles of learning, may prove difficult reading for the beginning student in psychology; but the balance of the book presents stimulating points of view and hypotheses that do not appear in most texts — for example, communication and therapy, therapy as a learning problem.

C. R. Rogers, *Counseling and Psychotherapy*. Boston: Houghton Mifflin, 1942. A pioneer book on the nondirective or client-centered approach to psychotherapy. Interesting and controversial. Much case material.

C. R. Rogers, *Client-Centered Therapy*. Boston: Houghton Mifflin, 1951. A more recent treatment of nondirective therapy.

S. R. Slavson, *Analytic Group Psychotherapy*. New York: Columbia University Press, 1950. A treatment of one form of group therapy by a leader in the field.

H. F. Dunbar, *Mind and Body: Psychosomatic Medicine*. New York: Random House, 1947. A semipopular, highly readable discussion of the psychological origin of many diseases. Cases cited.

F. Alexander, *et al.*, *Psychoanalytic Therapy: Principles and Application*. New York: Ronald, 1946. An authoritative discussion, stressing brief therapy. Contains case material.

R. R. Grinker and J. P. Spiegel, *Men under Stress*. Philadelphia: Blakiston, 1945. A discussion, well documented by case histories, of occurrence and treatment of neuroses that developed in the Air Force under stress of war conditions on the ground and in combat.

T. Reik, *Listening with the Third Ear*. New York: Farrar, 1949. A chatty, intimate account of psychoanalytic treatment as seen through the eyes of the analyst.

K. Horney, *New Ways in Psychoanalysis*. New York: Norton, 1939. See particularly Chapter 16, which deals with psychoanalytic therapy.

S. G. Law, *Therapy through Interview*. New York: McGraw-Hill, 1948. A book written by a psychiatrist for general medical practitioners, composed largely of a discussion of simulated but realistic cases as they might be handled by the general practitioner. Very interesting reading, although the first chapter may be difficult for beginning students in psychology; a clear presentation of a modern approach to psychotherapy and psychosomatic medicine.

VI... *The Struggle against Shyness*
and Feelings of Inferiority

The Prevalence of Shyness. In one form or another, shyness, feelings of inferiority, and the inability to relate to others constitute the commonest group of problems faced by college students (1). This appears to be true generally of "normal" individuals. For example, investigators in one study found that 52 per cent of "nonproblem" children showed symptoms of shyness, as compared with 42 per cent of "problem" children (2).

A glance around the college classroom will reveal the prevalence of shyness. During the typical hour's discussion in a group of twenty to forty students, not more than a quarter to a third will participate voluntarily, and even the most heated discussion rarely involves more than two-thirds of the class. Furthermore, in classes where discussion is voluntary, not more than half of the average class will participate to any large extent during the course of an entire semester; and even those students who become actively involved in discussions will complain privately of feelings of shyness. The complaints of participating and nonparticipating students are remarkably similar: they are unable to speak as often as they would like; they cannot think of the right things to say; they worry about the impression they are making on the rest of the class; when they speak they cannot think of the right words; or they can talk in a small group but have trouble in a large group. The symptoms of shyness thus appear to be well-nigh universal among college students.

Why Students Do Not Participate in Discussions. It is the writer's experience that when students express themselves in private about their reasons for nonparticipation they give essentially the following explanations: 1. "I haven't anything to say." 2. "I can't think of anything to say." 3. "Someone is always saying what I have to say better than I can." 4. "I get more out of sitting and listening to others than I do out of participating actively." 5. "I am too self-conscious." *

As we have learned from the first five chapters of this book, explanations of this kind cannot be accepted at face value. The first four explanations tend to be rationalizations that serve to cover up the real reasons for nonparticipation. The fifth is the exception. It is a frank admission of a basic cause, and the statement made by the student shows good insight into, if not acceptance of, the kinds of feelings that result in the behavior we call shyness.

When we examine shyness from the dynamic point of view, when we look for the emotional background that causes it, we can identify at least four causal aspects, largely buried in the unconscious processes of the nonparticipator.

Vulnerability. Vulnerability is basic to most shyness. The shy person fears that if he speaks up he may expose himself to failure and ridicule. Since in our culture failure is loaded so heavily with feelings of guilt and inadequacy, he feels that the risks that may be incurred in speaking outweigh any possible gain. Actually, this is unrealistic, because it is usually difficult to "fail" merely through making a statement in a class discussion. And as far as exposing himself to the ridicule of others is concerned, most of the group are so engrossed in trying to think out what *they* will say, or in analyzing the *content* of what has been said, that the possibility of criticism is rather unlikely.

However, the panic experienced by the shy person who is forced to speak before the class is so genuine that it does constitute a real problem, one that we cannot dispose of merely by calling it illogical and unrealistic. His feeling of panic has all the characteristics of anxiety. Essentially, as we will find, he is afraid of failure according to his own standards, rather than according to standards that may have been set by the class.

Feelings of Inferiority. One of the reasons the shy person is so sure he will fail is that he is victimized by his own feelings of inferiority.

---

* One student wrote, "On the few occasions when I speak up in class I wonder to myself, 'I suppose they think that I wear these shoes every day and wonder if I don't have another pair I can use, or perhaps they think my hair needs washing and how awful I look!'"

"Mom, what can I do to overcome being such an introvert?"

Feelings of inferiority are particularly acute and troublesome during adolescence and young adulthood.

Fred McKinney characterizes an inferiority feeling as an emotional reaction to an assumed failure, and contrasts it with *knowledge* of inferiority, which is something quite different (3). People react to feelings of inferiority in various ways. Some overcompensate by becoming arrogant or domineering, but the shy person submissively accepts his own evaluation of himself, at least as far as expressing himself in public is concerned. His defense is not aggressive attack, as it is with the person who overcompensates, but withdrawal. The first two of the "typical" reasons for nonparticipation cited above — "I haven't anything to say" and "I can't think of anything to say" — reveal inferiority feelings in that they imply either a repression of ideas worth saying or the existence of a feeling that may be described as "What *I* have to say isn't worth saying."

The hypothesis of repression is supported in part by the fact that shy people often find that they have many good ideas when they attempt to express themselves in writing. Furthermore, many who feel that they have nothing to say actually *do* think of a number of contributions they could have made to a discussion, once the opportunity to speak has passed.

The implication that one has nothing worth saying points to what Karen Horney calls the "self-effacing" personality, one who does not dare permit himself to feel consciously superior to others and must therefore act the part of inferiority (4). However, it is only fair to note that when the nonparticipating person states that he has nothing to say, he does so in all honesty and sincerity, since he is not consciously aware either of the depth of his feelings of inferiority or the possibility of his enacting a self-effacing role.

Guilt Feelings. The third aspect of nonparticipating behavior is the probable presence of guilt feelings. Perhaps not all nonparticipants are afflicted with neurotic feelings of guilt, but the situations in our culture predisposing one to guilt feelings are so common that most of us are exposed to them at some time or other during the early, formative years of our lives. These feelings have their origin in the authoritarian conditions of home and school, which discourage "showing off," "talking out of turn," "talking back," and free self-expression in general. It is not so much that we were actually punished for such behavior (although sometimes we were), but rather that we learned to feel ashamed of not conforming to the expectations of adults in authority. The effect in later years of these early situations is that we tend to hang back and wait for persons in authority to speak before we express ourselves, if we do so at all.

Passive Participation. A fourth factor in this problem is that our culture encourages us to participate *passively* in many activities, to be onlookers rather than doers. (This, in turn, is related to the problem of overdependency, which is discussed in the next chapter.) The passive participator hopes that learning can be a passive process, that better results will come from listening to a discussion than from participating actively in it. The passive participant feels that as long as he sits on the sidelines, so to speak, he is in a strategic position: he does not have to commit himself, and he can wait until one side appears to be winning before he does commit himself.

Although it is true that some learning may take place through identification with the more active participants, it is also true that for the most part the passive participant is the loser, in that he robs himself of the opportunity to learn more effectively through becoming involved in the learning process. There is a growing feeling among psychologists that really significant learning takes place *only* when individuals have invested something of themselves in the process (5). Learning is a process of intellectual and emotional growth, and neither the nonparticipator nor any other person can have someone else do his growing for him!

Passive participation as a way of learning provides all too neat a solution to the prohibition on aggression so implicit in the middle-class pattern of life. Passive participation is nonaggressive, and the shy person is thus enabled to avoid becoming involved in the sometimes rough-and-ready give-and-take of open discussion. Since he does not participate actively, he is required neither to defend nor to attack; he does not have to risk any emotional involvement if he does not wish to; he is able to stand aloof and secluded; and he thus feels safer and less vulnerable.

The four aspects of nonparticipating behavior overlap. By being passive, the nonparticipant feels less vulnerable; he can protect himself from the exposure of what he feels are his inferior talents; and by not participating he can avoid feeling guilty for "showing off" or asserting himself.

Nonparticipating behavior *appears* to satisfy the nonparticipant, but appearances are sometimes misleading. Many shy people are keenly unhappy about their nonparticipation, and only the fear of attendant anxiety keeps them from participating. When, later, they think of the things they could have said, they feel guilty for having let themselves down. Thus they often incur some of the very anxiety they are trying to avoid by nonparticipation.

Why We Feel Shy and Inferior. Psychologists have proposed a number of reasons to account for nonparticipating behavior, withdrawal from social contact, feelings of inferiority, and other symptoms of the shyness category. Jane Warters suggests that they are due to constitutional defects, mental deficiency, social disapproval, and to imaginary causes, with the last-named factor being stressed (6). Fritz Redl and William W. Wattenberg attribute some cases of timidity and shyness to parental overprotection during childhood (7). L. F. Shaffer considers withdrawing types of behavior are due to parental severity, overprotection, or lack of contacts with other children during the formative years of childhood (8); while McKinney states that feelings of inferiority are related to the gap between what one hopes for and aspires to (level of aspiration), and what one actually accomplishes (9).

Another possible source of such feelings is what Horney calls "the pride system (10)," a concept that resembles McKinney's hypothesis. She proposes that anxiety, feelings of inferiority, and self-contempt result from the gulf that lies between the goals of a neurotically exaggerated "idealized self" and the potential accomplishments of the "real self." The idealized self is that aspect of self-concept concerned with the ideals, standards, and expectations which the individual has set for himself and which he feels he has not yet attained. It is derived largely from such sources as: (a) the qualities and achievements the individual admires in his parents and other significant persons in his life — it does not matter whether these qualities are genuine or supposed, as long as the individual *thinks* that they are present and incorporates them into his system of values; and (b) the expectations and hopes which the individual's parents (and other significant persons) have for him, or which the individual *thinks* they have for him.

How the conflict between the overidealized self and the real self can result in feelings of inferiority and inadequacy are illustrated by the case of Lucy Christopher, who was never able to become more than a typist, although she had a high level of ability and a college degree.

Lucy despised herself for not being like her father, who was out-spoken, forceful, and "always right." He criticized his daughter because she was not positive and always seemed so uncertain, although on the few occasions when she asserted herself, he became irritable and abusive. However, Lucy came to feel that her father wanted her to be like him and she patterned her idealized self accordingly. When she incorporated these qualities into her idealized self, she was of course unaware that her father's behavior was a façade that helped him to compensate for *his* feelings of self-doubt, insecurity, and inferiority. Actually, her father was so wrapped up in maintaining his own defenses that he was hardly aware that his daughter felt he expected her to play the kind of life role he played.

Lucy's case is an example of feelings of inferiority caused by failure to meet self-imposed standards. Even if Lucy had been able to attain greater vocational success, the chances are that she would never have achieved satisfaction. As Walter Langer says about this kind of person, even though she might attain success in the eyes of everyone else, she would still be dissatisfied and would goad herself on to even greater efforts, believing always that she had failed (11). In the school situation, this outlook is typical of persons who are never satisfied with anything less than a "perfect" mark.

The neurotically exaggerated version of the idealized self has an important quality: as far as its owner and victim is concerned, it is infallible. He may have grave questions about himself, his social and physical environment, and the state of the world, but he is unable to question the standards set for him by his idealized self. Since he is never quite able to meet these standards, he is constantly forced to say to himself, in effect, "I have failed. And I have failed *not* because my standards were too high, too ideal, or inappropriate, but because I am inferior, inadequate, and unworthy."

Disparities between the Real Self and the Unrealistic Idealized Self. There are three ways in which the unrealistic idealized self may constitute itself an inappropriate and impossible standard of behavior: 1. There may be a wide, unbridgeable gulf between the idealized standards and the actual potential of the individual. 2. The idealized standards may themselves be internally incon-

sistent.   3. The kind of self-structure that would be in keeping
with the standards and goals of the idealized self may be incongruent
or at variance with the real self, or the self-structure of the individual.

An example of a wide gulf existing between the real and the
idealized self of a boy of nineteen follows:

> The boy's father and mother are clever, facile, socially mature indi-
> viduals, active in lodge work and in civic affairs.   The boy often finds
> himself in situations that necessitate his meeting and talking with his
> parents' acquaintances, and he finds that he is unable to be an accom-
> plished conversationalist like either of his parents.   He is depressed
> because he cannot attain the standards that he *feels* they have set for him,
> even though he may be capable of very effective relations with persons
> of his own age.   Inasmuch as he has set a standard impossible of accom-
> plishment — that is, that of acting like adults more than twice his age —
> he is doomed to disappointment and failure.   Yet he persists in trying
> to achieve this standard because he expects it of himself and feels that
> others, too, expect it of him.

Probably most idealized selves have some internal inconsistencies
and contradictions.   An example of this type of orientation is found
in the person who believes that he *always* should be frank and honest
and *never* hurt anybody's feelings.   These are ideals that at times are
mutually incompatible: if one *always* is frank in expressing his opinion, he is bound, at times, to hurt the feelings of others.

Examples of incongruities are found in people whose idealized
selves are quite different in nature from their real selves.   A son
may use as the model for his idealized self a father who is striving,
driving, practical, and matter-of-fact.   The son may be by nature
artistic, warm, friendly, and dramatically inclined.   He can never
attain the standards of his idealized self except possibly in a highly
artificial manner.   Failure to achieve these unnatural standards,
however, can cause him pain, frustration, anxiety, unhappiness,
and even guilt.

The Unrealistic Idealized Self in the Adolescent and Young Adult.   The
greater the gap or disparity between the idealized self and the real
self, the greater is the possibility of developing anxiety and guilt.
The gap is likely to be wider during adolescence and early adulthood
than at any other time, although some individuals pass through early
and middle adulthood and into old age without having bridged

the gap that separates them from their idealized self. The contribution that adolescence makes to the maturing personality is a clarification of the individual's picture of himself as the person he would like to be (12, 13). However, since most young people are more or less subject to pressures and influences that result in some measure of anxiety and guilt, the idealized self of the typical adolescent and young adult is to a greater or lesser degree subject to some distortion of the kind we have described. Many of us learn through the maturing experiences of everyday life that some of our goals are unattainable or inappropriate, but others of us seem less able to learn this. In any event, unless most of the neurotic distortions are worked out of the self-picture, the individual will be plagued by some feelings of inferiority and inadequacy. Thus it is not surprising that shyness and social inadequacy head the list of problems that concern college students. Furthermore, the typical adolescent has not had an opportunity to try out life roles and to settle on the one he will play as a more mature adult. When he has tested himself against life and tried out his idealized self in a variety of situations, he will be in a better position to determine which of his expectations are realistic.

For the adolescent or the young adult, the expectations of his parents and the significant adults in his life are more real and more commanding than his own more or less tentative self-concepts. A boy of nineteen may have fondness for or a talent in mechanical work, but his father may expect him to try for a career in law. He may insist that the boy enter college and prepare for law school. Inasmuch as the boy has not had an opportunity to try himself out in a pre-engineering curriculum or in some kind of mechanical trade, he does not know but that his father is right. In other words, he is not in a position to have developed realistic expectations for himself. Therefore, it is not surprising that he is unsure and hesitant.

The Effect of Maturity on the Idealized Self. Growing older normally results in greater emotional and intellectual maturity, and this, in turn, brings with it increased self-understanding and insight. As we come to understand ourselves better, we become more aware of our capabilities and limitations and thus can modify and refocus our idealized self until it provides us with the kinds of goals which can actually be achieved and which will help rather than hinder us in charting the activities of life. However, understanding, insight, and maturity are not usually acquired automatically with the passing of years. Going from one level of emotional maturity to another usually involves some anxiety, some willingness to sacrifice neurotic and childish satisfactions for more mature kinds of behavior. This is certainly true of the shy person, for in order to behave in a more mature fashion, he must abandon his place on the sidelines and participate more actively in the group. It is not easy to change the pattern of shyness, and such changes as occur must take place over a long period of time, for shy persons do not conquer their shyness in a day, a week, or even in one or two months. The story of John Malloy can perhaps illustrate better than a theoretical discussion the long and tedious road that leads from a life limited by shyness to one of greater active participation and social usefulness.

John Malloy grew up in a middle-class home in a small town. He was the oldest of four boys. His father, an accountant for the railroad, had started as a telegrapher. He was ambitious for his sons, the whole family worked and saved in order to send all four boys to college, and great things were expected of all of them, particularly of John.

John was a painfully shy, timid, and retiring boy. He was frequently beaten by other boys, he disliked vigorous sports, and he was constantly humiliated by his younger brothers, who excelled at aggressive play. His methods of escape were to read, go on long walks in the woods and country, and work in his home chemistry laboratory. He was not active socially in high school, but made almost straight A's. As a result of this record he was selected as valedictorian for the graduating class.

He now looks back on the graduating exercises as the most painful event in his whole unhappy pre-college career. He does not know to this day how he was able to struggle through his speech. He has never been able to discuss it with his family, and they, with rare consideration, have never mentioned it to him. Even today, he avoids returning to his home town for fear of reactivating that horrible memory. Occasionally he finds himself reliving the sleepless nights that led up to the momentous event, his becoming sick at his stomach the morning of graduation, the grim look on his father's face when he suggested that he was too sick to go on, his feeling faint and weak at the sight of the audience. Then the fatal words that introduced him. As he stood before the audience, his knees almost gave way and he gripped the microphone to support himself. The only thing he really wanted to do was to run far away. Why he stayed, he does not know. How he was able to remember the speech, he does not know. It was just as though he were standing far-off and someone else was giving it.   Why the audience applauded, he does not know — the speech must have sounded ghastly.

John went to a college in another state.   He found that his academic talents and his interest in chemistry brought him honors and attention. He even was persuaded to join a fraternity.   However, in all things he studiously avoided situations that might lead to speaking before groups and invested most of his time and energy in chemistry.   He graduated with honors and Phi Beta Kappa.

However, he took no real pleasure in his success.   As far as he was concerned, he had failed.   His father had hoped that he would work his way through college, but jobs were hard to get and he had earned only half his expenses.   His father had wanted him to go into something practical, like business administration, but he had wasted his time on chemistry, just because he couldn't keep away from it.   In 1937, when he graduated, a man with a bachelor's degree in chemistry was not very employable, and so he could not even support himself.   It is probable that he could not have successfully competed for a job.   He was so depressed by what he felt was complete failure that he seriously considered suicide.   To make matters worse, he was in love with the daughter of a dean, in defiance of his father's specific orders that he was not even to look at a girl until he was ready to support a wife.

But in the end it was his fiancée who helped pull him through.   She urged him to visit the college placement bureau.   The counselor at the placement bureau suggested that he put in his name for a fellowship in ceramic technology.   Much to his surprise he was granted the fellowship. This was the turning point in his psychological development.   Encouraged by this success, he married the dean's daughter, and she took a job while he worked through to his Ph. D.

During this period he began to "find himself" with respect to his real potentialities.   He was having real successes.   He was valued both for himself and for his useful talents.   He was able to achieve an independence of thought and action that he had never before known.   But he was still painfully shy.   Although he was capable of highly original thinking, most of it never saw the light of day.   He was unable to talk to his superiors with ease and confidence about anything, let alone his own ideas.

In the meantime, his idealized self was undergoing a marked reorganization.   The old ideas that he was a failure because he was unemployable and had not taken a business course were still there in essence, but he felt that he was now in a better position to attain a goal in keeping with his father's expectations.   He knew that he could have a teaching job in college with a Ph. D., but he felt that this was the easy way out. He felt that he would have to make his mark in business in order to be successful in his own eyes. When he had come to that decision, he made his first step — he took a course in public speaking. Although it was frightening at first to face a group and make an unrehearsed speech, he became quite successful, as long as he was facing the class. He still could not talk to his superiors, and when, as part of the course, he had to give a talk on ceramic technology to the local Rotary Club, there was a recurrence of some of the same symptoms he had had when he delivered his valedictorian address.

John took a trainee job with a ceramics firm after he got his Ph. D., but before his training period was over, he was drafted. He spent two years as a private before he was sent to Officer Candidate School. As soon as he was commissioned, he was given a job inspecting war plants manufacturing materials for use in chemical warfare. It was inevitable that he would think of improvements in the manufacturing and shipment of chemicals, but putting these ideas into circulation was another story. Fortunately, his commanding officer was a man of perception and understanding, who encouraged his junior officers to discuss matters with him. He recognized Malloy's ability and recommended him to the Pentagon. Malloy was transferred to Washington and in three years was the head of an office, with the rank of lieutenant colonel.

These three years were very difficult for John, both physically and psychologically. He involved himself intensely with the war effort, and it brought out abilities he had not suspected. In order to play his role as chemical expert, he had to make frequent appearances before groups of civilian officials and high-ranking officers. At these times he had to think on his feet and deliver opinions clearly and forcefully, as was expected of an Army officer. He found that he was more effective when he was answering questions than when he was delivering a prepared talk, and he learned to maneuver his audience into questioning him. He found that he could warm up his audiences with a funny story. He discovered that if he wrote out the first paragraph of a talk in detail, the rest came easily. He never became a polished, confident speaker, but he gave a competent talk, as long as he stayed with his own subject. After a few fiascoes which occurred when the discussion left his own subject, he avoided the discussion of matters outside his own field.

On leaving the service, Malloy sought out a small industrial ceramics firm undergoing expansion and talked the owners into making him a partner, with the position of plant manager. His wife helped him plan the strategy that resulted in this job, just as she had encouraged him and coached him in his previous roles. Today he is a one-fourth partner in a firm that grosses a half-million a year, as compared with seventy-five thousand four years ago. Much of the firm's growth has been due to

John's ability to work out production problems and to explain problems to his employees.

Even today he is a shy person. He still takes a back seat in meetings that do not involve his firm or his professional field. He avoids social contacts, and would not have become involved in civic affairs except at the urging of his wife and his partners. On the rare occasions when he has to address a group he has not met before, he has symptoms of acute stage fright. New acquaintances find him cold and remote. He is embarrassed by compliments and is embarrassed at having to give them. On the whole, however, he is a fairly well-adjusted individual, not often upset by psychological conflicts or frustrations. He has readjusted and remade his idealized self into something that closely approximates his real self. His accomplishments are very close to his expectations, and his expectations are reasonable and modest.

John Malloy was able to conquer the most troublesome aspects of his shyness by the following means:

1. He recognized that shyness is a major problem and he took steps to correct it.

2. He worked out a vocational role compatible with his abilities and within the realm of possibility.

3. He took advantage of opportunities that presented him with roles he could develop to his own advantage as well as to the advantage of his employers.

4. He was able to learn from his successes and was encouraged by them; he also learned from his failures.

5. He learned techniques that increased the chances for success.

6. He was able to accept his failures (to accept the fact that he *could* fail) without becoming unduly upset, and he was able to learn from these failures, instead of being defeated by them.

7. He practiced his role, constantly improving his competence as a speaker in his own field and thus eliminating much of his shyness.

8. He was able to achieve a large measure of emotional security by achieving successes largely by his own efforts and by modifying his life goals and his idealized self on the basis of his experiences in the world of reality.

Overcoming Shyness. We cannot all achieve the kind of financial success that came to John Malloy, but his case is in many ways a usual one. We note that he did not completely overcome shyness but that he did master it for all practical purposes. He did not achieve this victory at great cost to his personality — that is, he did not strive to become the glad-handing, so-called happy extrovert who has worked out a superficial technique enabling him to manipulate and exploit others. Rather, he achieved victory through finding out what his strengths and weaknesses were and through modifying his goals and standards to fit the realities he found in himself and in his environment.

SUMMARY

Shyness is one of the commonest problems faced by college students. The shy person is one who withdraws from social contact and participation because he feels particularly vulnerable to criticism and rejection by others. It is very likely that he is troubled by feelings of inferiority and guilt. Shyness and nonparticipation tend to be produced by our culture because it encourages passivity as a way of life.

Feelings of inferiority, which result in shyness and nonparticipation, are often due to the existence of a wide gulf between the individual's real self and his idealized self, between his actual accomplishments and his unrealistic expectations and aspirations. If we are unable to evaluate the facts of reality and our own abilities realistically, we tend to become overcritical of ourselves and our efforts.

The idealized self is formed in part from the expectations that others, particularly our parents, have for us, and in part from the idealized qualities we admire in our parents and other significant adults. It comes into particular prominence in adolescence and early adulthood, because this is the period of life when the individual attempts to find out "who he is" and tries to discover the roles he will play in life. Normally, he learns to modify the unrealistic expectations he has for himself, but sometimes this learning is blocked by neurotic anxiety, and he goes through life saddled by an unrealistic, idealized self. The greater the gulf between the real self and the idealized self, the more likely the individual is to be plagued by feelings of inferiority, inadequacy, and self-contempt, and the more likely he is to display behavior characterized by shyness, withdrawal, and nonparticipation.

Shyness and the feelings that accompany it are most effectively overcome by permitting oneself to become involved emotionally and actively in social situations, through learning what one can realistically expect of oneself and one's environment, and through modifying the goals of the idealized self until they are more realistic.

REFERENCES

1. C. W. Heath and L. W. Gregory, "Problems of Normal College Students and Their Families," *School and Society.* 63:355–358; 1946.
2. E. Martens and H. Russ, *Adjustment and Behavior Problems of School Children: A Description and Evaluation of the Clinical Program in Berkeley, California.* United States Office of Education, Bulletin 18, 1932.
3. F. McKinney, *Psychology of Personal Adjustment,* 2d edition. New York: Wiley, 1949. P. 617.
4. K. Horney, *Neurosis and Human Growth.* New York: Norton, 1950. Chap. 9.
5. C. R. Rogers, *Client-Centered Therapy.* Boston: Houghton Mifflin, 1951. Pp. 389–390.
6. J. Warters, *Achieving Maturity.* New York: McGraw-Hill, 1949. Pp. 152ff.
7. F. Redl and W. W. Wattenberg, *Mental Hygiene in Teaching.* New York: Harcourt, Brace, 1951. P. 152.
8. L. F. Shaffer, *The Psychology of Adjustment.* Boston: Houghton Mifflin, 1936. Pp. 176–177.
9. F. McKinney, *Psychology of Personal Adjustment,* 2d edition. New York: Wiley, 1949. P. 633.
10. K. Horney, *Neurosis and Human Growth.* New York: Norton, 1950. Pp. 111ff.
11. W. C. Langer, *Psychology and Human Living.* New York: Appleton-Century-Crofts, 1943. P. 169.
12. F. Redl and W. W. Wattenberg, *Mental Hygiene in Teaching.* New York: Harcourt, Brace, 1951. P. 92.
13. R. J. Havighurst, *Developmental Tasks and Education.* Chicago: University of Chicago Press, 1949. Chap. 5.

SUGGESTED READINGS

F. McKinney, *Psychology of Personal Adjustment,* 2d edition. New York: Wiley, 1949. See Chapter 15, "Self-Confidence."
J. Warters, *Achieving Maturity.* New York: McGraw-Hill, 1949. Chapter 8, "You and Your Feelings of Inferiority."
P. M. Symonds, *Dynamic Psychology.* New York: Appleton-Century-Crofts, 1949. Chapter 15, "Guilt and Self-Punishment."
L. J. Saul, *Emotional Maturity.* Philadelphia: Lippincott, 1947. Chapter 4, "Egoism, Competitiveness, and the Sense of Inferiority."
W. Johnson, "The Semantics of Maladjustment," in L. A. Pennington and I. A. Berg, eds., *An Introduction to Clinical Psychology.* New York: Ronald, 1948. A presentation of the development of neurotic patterns of life from the standpoint of IFD — idealization, frustration, and demoralization. This point of view

is also discussed extensively in Johnson's book, *People in Quandaries*. New York: Harper, 1946.

K. Horney, *Neurosis and Human Growth*. New York: Norton, 1950. A book that to a great degree inspired the writing of this chapter. A description of what happens when the individual becomes alienated from himself and becomes neurotically involved in striving for an impossible perfection.

H. G. Seashore, *All of Us Have Troubles*. New York: Association Press, 1947.

S. H. Krains and E. S. Thetford, *Managing Your Mind*. New York: Macmillan, 1943.

L. E. Travis and D. B. Baruch, *Personal Problems of Everyday Life*. New York: Appleton-Century-Crofts, 1941.

L. E. Bisch, *Why Be Shy?* New York: Simon and Schuster, 1946.

C. G. Wrenn, *Building Self-Confidence*. Stanford: Stanford University Press, 1948.

VII...*The Struggle to Become*
Independent and Self-Reliant

Interdependence and Overdependence. There is within any normal individual a strong drive or need to accomplish things by himself, without help from others. We note the expression of this desire in the gleeful satisfaction of the baby who has finally succeeded in getting a spoonful of mush into his mouth unaided. As adults, we take particular pride in accomplishments that are achieved without help. These thrills of pleasure and independence are all very normal and very satisfying. However, there are two kinds of situations or conditions that confront the individual as he endeavors to capture the feeling of personal accomplishment in his daily life. One of these is the necessity of interdependence and the other is the hazard of overdependence.

Interdependence is an essential condition of life in a complex civilization like ours. We cannot even prepare food for ourselves without using utensils made by others and sold to us by others. Even if our food consists of vegetables we have raised in our own gardens, they were cultivated with tools made and sold by others; and the laws and customs of the land, upheld by our fellow citizens and the police, protected our produce from theft.

Most of the time we accept the need for interdependence easily, even unthinkingly. We are so used to it that it is like the very air we breathe. We enjoy its obvious benefits, and, through co-operation with and service to others, make it possible for others to be dependent on us. Nevertheless, the ability to co-operate and serve others is a skill not easily attained. It has to be learned through the give and take of social interaction. Sometimes the learning is tedious or painful. Some never learn how to co-operate. The

140

childish, immature, and neurotic elements within us react against the necessity for co-operation and interdependence. Neurotic needs tend to be characterized by selfishness and impatience, qualities that make co-operative action difficult and sometimes impossible. Such needs often express themselves in the feeling that we will lose our freedom of thought and action if we admit that we have certain responsibilities to society or if we work co-operatively with others rather than independently. However, co-operation, responsibility, and interdependence do not threaten our need for self-reliance and independence; actually, we are in many respects freer because of them. Instead of having to spend most of our time in a hazardous struggle with the elements in order to acquire the minimum essentials of our livelihood, we have the essentials provided for us with minimum risk and effort through the interdependent relationships of our society. This gives us more time to develop our individual potentialities. Thus our very interdependence helps us to become more independent, even though it exacts a price in terms of responsibility and conformity to certain standards of conduct. It is true that the demands for conformity often result in a further loss of freedom, but this is a sickness of our society (which we shall discuss later), rather than a direct outcome of mutual responsibility and of interdependence.

The hazard of overdependence is of a different order. When we are feeling overdependent, we want to be cared for, helped, given gifts and tokens of affection, or attended in some way. Essentially, overdependency consists of the desire to be loved or given the tokens of love, without any obligation to reciprocate. Our normal dependency need consists of our need to be loved and to receive tokens of love; but one of the conditions of emotional maturity is that we be prepared to love as well as be loved, to give tokens of love and affection as well as to receive them. It is immature, neurotic, and unrealistic to expect to be always in the position of receiving.

Overdependency constitutes a real threat to self-reliance and independence, because it robs us of the desire to act on our own behalf and causes us to prefer having our problems solved and our needs met by others. Yet we are all more or less troubled by this neurotic need. The following list of everyday behavior patterns indicates the presence of a childish and unrealistic — hence, neurotic — longing for the "joys" of being completely dependent:

1. We like to see movies and read stories in which the chief characters *have their problems solved for them* by some stroke of fortune. These stories appeal to us because we can identify ourselves with the main characters and symbolically have *our* problems solved, too, without effort on our part.

2. Most of us enjoy being waited on. The chief attraction of "eating out" is not that the food is necessarily better but that we do not have to prepare it and serve it, and we do not have to wash the dishes.

3. We are envious of the kind of parasitical lives presumably led by the "idle rich," "café society," or the "international set." The fact that we would like to live this kind of life ourselves is reflected in the disproportionate number of plays and novels dealing with the lives of people who do not have to work for a living, who are dependent on staffs of servants.

4. Most of us feel relieved when luck or chance removes from our path some problem or obstacle that we could easily have surmounted. We like to have things "made easier" for us.

Roots of Our Dependency Needs. Our enjoyment of dependency appears to have its roots in infancy, when we received the complete love and attention of our fond parents. When we were infants, this love was given freely and without obligation; and, essentially, the overdependent person is one who tries to re-establish this vanished love relationship.

However, the young child does not regard himself as a "dependent person." As the psychoanalyst Sandor Ferenczi views it, the infant and the young child do not see themselves as weak and powerless creatures, whose needs are met by kind and generous adults, but as all-powerful, omnipotent creatures, whose needs are met by adults having no choice in the matter (1). As far as the infant is concerned, all he has to do is to "wish" for food, and he is fed. He may hear his own cries, but he is unaware that they are his. As his awareness of reality matures, he discovers that wishing is not enough; sometimes it does not bring food immediately, but both reaching and crying help. Later he learns words to express his commands, and he finds that both words and thoughts seem to have magic powers. Sometimes, when he says, "I would like some ice cream," ice cream is given to him. Or he wishes, "I hope we have some ice cream for dinner tonight!" And there *is* ice cream for dinner! In each instance he attributes the fulfillment of his wish to his command or wish, rather than to coincidence or to the indulgence of adults. And he "forgets" about the times when he asked for or wished for ice cream and received none, because these occurrences do not fit his picture of himself as important and "powerful."

The child is enabled to maintain this wholly unrealistic self-concept for a time because he does not have the means to find out how weak, helpless, and dependent he really is; he is unable to pierce the illusion of his omnipotence. Some of his first disillusionment comes when he encounters stubborn and unyielding situations. He tries to fit a square block into a round hole; in spite of many efforts, it will not fit, and he dissolves into tearful rage. Or his parents express disapproval and punish him. How *dare* they do this! Yet they have done it. When this realization sinks in, the false sense of security he felt in his omnipotence is violated, and rage and depression result. Actually, this stage is a necessary preliminary to the formation of the superego or conscience, for the child must learn that his parents are the powerful ones, not he. (See the section on the formation of the conscience or superego in Chapter 2.)

Surrender of the Omnipotence Myth. If emotional maturation proceeds normally, the child surrenders his idea of omnipotence in exchange for a more realistic approach to life. He is aided in doing this by his parents, who help him to become "immunized" against reality, such immunization consisting of small doses of uncomfortable, frustrating, and sometimes painful reality situations. With each such dose, the child becomes better prepared to deal with reality at increasing levels of difficulty, until, as an adult, he is able to cope with life's problems realistically and without parental guidance. Thanks to the "immunization," he has found that reality is not as bad as it looks: sometimes it is necessary to deal with it by solving problems; sometimes it is possible to live with it by making small changes or by accepting the frustration of some needs but not others. In growing up, the individual learns that his feelings of omnipotence were in reality a result of being dependent on his parents and that our society expects him as an adult to be independent and self-reliant in some situations and dependent and submissive in others. He learns that the power that comes through self-reliance and the power that comes through a sense of omnipotence are different: in the former, power comes through ability to understand and cope with oneself and one's environment; in the latter, power comes through the ability to take advantage of others.

Overdependence as an Immature Pattern.   Many children are not permitted or cannot permit themselves the loss of their dream; they cannot relinquish the thought that they may again be as omnipotent as they were as infants (2).   This may occur to children who are overprotected (who never get sufficient opportunity to experience the normal frustrations of reality), or whose basic needs for affection and security are chronically thwarted (in which event they maintain their dream as a support for their weak or inadequate self-structures).   As they grow up they never let go of the hope that they really can be omnipotent (if others will just co-operate), or that someday they will be omnipotent again (if things "break" right, or if they meet the "right" people).   All evidence to the effect that they are not, never will be, and never have been really omnipotent is repressed, rationalized, evaded, or rejected.

Here are a few examples of persons who are very much in the grip of the omnipotence dream:

1. The adolescent who cannot deny himself an automobile (a symbol of power in a power-oriented culture) and who "borrows" one in the optimistic expectation that no one will deny him this pleasure-object. Even though he is apprehended and punished, he cannot evaluate what has occurred, with the result that he will offend again and again.

2. In an attempt to avoid accepting evidence that would disprove his omnipotence, the individual who seeks refuge in alcohol, which helps to anesthetize him to the point where he does not have to admit the existence of a threatening and disillusioning environment.   Insulated against reality by alcohol, he is enabled to reinstitute the feeling of omnipotence he had as a child.

3. The woman who marries because she cannot cope with life alone. Her husband must be more than a breadwinner, for he must protect her against the unpleasant realities of life and he must provide her with constant reassurances of the love he has for her and the power she holds over him.   Such relationships tend to be selfish and one-sided; she is probably incapable of expressing genuine love and affection for him.

To the objective observer, these individuals are highly dependent, but they would deny any suggestions to this effect.   They want to have people love them — that is, they want to establish dependent relationships with others — but they are incapable of consistently offering love in return.

Dependency Conflicts in Adolescence.   Adolescence is the age at which the conflict between desires to be dependent and to be self-reliant reaches its height for most people in our culture.* It is at this stage that youth become the physical equals of adults and develop increasing interest in persons outside the family circle, particularly members of the opposite sex.

One source of conflict for the adolescent or young adult is his changing role. Society expects him to be more self-reliant and more able to cope with life independently. At the same time, society is inconsistent in its demands and expectations. Sometimes it expects him to be childlike (submissive, obedient, and dependent), and sometimes it expects him to act like an adult (self-assertive, self-sufficient, and independent). Sometimes it expects him to demonstrate mature behavior far beyond his years, and in the next moment it expects and encourages behavior on a wholly immature level. O. H. Mowrer describes society's inconsistency with respect to the adolescent as follows:

Our culture . . . places a very great and . . . a very unusual premium on rationality. Parents are forever demanding that the youngster behave rationally. But actually any culture is a considerable bar to the free exercise of rationality. Parents make conflicting demands — that the child be rational but also that he not question the wisdom of the culture. The adolescent who is painfully orienting himself to some form of compromise between his own needs and cultural demands discovers that his parents are by no means as rational as the ideals which they have preached to him would presuppose. This is a potent source of antagonism between parents and children and leads to mutual displays of aggression. Adults have compromised rationality with their culture and they very much resent any re-examination of these questions by their children (4).†

Adolescence in its literal sense means "becoming an adult," and

---

* The period of adolescence varies both physiologically and socially. Whereas 90 per cent of boys reach physiological maturity between the ages of 13½ and 17½, and 90 per cent of girls between the ages of 11½ and 15½ (3), the age of social maturity varies with the culture and the individual. For the purposes of this discussion, we shall consider the end of adolescence and the beginning of adulthood to be marked by considerable freedom from parental ties, the stage at which the individual becomes largely self-directing and self-reliant. For most middle-class individuals this would occur somewhere between the ages of sixteen and twenty-four, the period selected by Howard M. Bell as the definition for "youth" in *Youth Tell Their Story.* Washington: American Council on Education, 1938.

† J. McV. Hunt, *Personality and the Behavior Disorders.* Copyright 1944, The Ronald Press Company.

adult status is associated with independence and emancipation from family ties. However, the real goal of the adolescent is not to get rid of his parents but to work out family relationships on a give-and-take basis among equals (5). Unfortunately, his attempts at emancipation are not usually accepted in this light. Many parents regard the adolescent's attempts to participate in decision-making as direct attacks on their authority. Such an attitude leads to further parental restrictions, which in turn lead to further demands on the part of adolescents for independence.

Independence and complete emancipation from parental control have a certain false charm for the adolescent. He would like to be free from parental domination, but he is not really ready to take responsibility for his economic support or the consequences of his actions. This is partly because our culture prolongs the training of youth to a period of some twelve years from the time physical maturity is reached (6), and partly because adults are unable to give youth sufficient experience in situations that require responsibility and independent thinking.

Parental Attitudes and Overdependency. We have noted that the difficulties adolescents face in their struggle to be independent are aggravated by the fact that adults are frequently inconsistent in their dealings with younger people. An additional set of aggravating factors may be found in the relationships that develop between parents and their children under some conditions.

1. Parents have a *need* to have their children depend on them, and they often prolong and intensify the dependency relationship for this reason. It is hard for them to accept the fact that when children grow up, parents are no longer as necessary as they were (7).

2. It is important for some parents to have someone who needs their care, attention, love, protection, and support, because it gives them the feeling of being powerful and important. It helps to give them status in a world where many forces appear to conspire to make the individual feel helpless and impotent.

3. Having dependent children helps to insulate some people from the feeling of growing old. To have children break loose from the bonds of dependency and marry or move away brings parents to the sharp awareness that they are growing older, and they would like to postpone or avoid this feeling as long as possible.

4. Some parents are themselves insecure psychologically (perhaps they

"You've no idea of the prices! Guess what it's setting me back
just having you youngsters to dinner."

George Clark and the Chicago Tribune-New York News Syndicate

*Some parents unconsciously strive to keep their grown children in a state
of dependency, emotionally and financially.*

were and still are unable to solve *their* dependency problems) and cannot bear to have their beliefs and opinions challenged by maturing adolescents; hence, they contrive to maintain control and are successful for a time in continuing the dependency status of their children through denying them a voice in decision-making.

5. Some parents are unable to give their love freely and unconditionally. They *demand* the love and respect of their children, by reminding them of how they worked and slaved for them, only to find them inappreciative of these sacrifices (8). A similar feeling finds its expression, often in immigrant cultures, when youth are exploited by being assigned low-paying jobs in the family business. Such parents attempt to bind their children to these jobs with chains of gratitude, to the end that they feel guilty even about wanting to leave.

6. Other parents dominate and control their children by unconsciously "using" them to attain goals that they themselves failed to attain. In order to gain these ends, they force their children to subordinate their own wishes to parental aspirations, thus endeavoring to stifle attempts to become independent and self-reliant.

An excellent portrayal of an individual who was made overdependent through his childhood experiences is provided by the mental hygiene film "Overdependency (9)":

Jimmy had difficulties from the very beginning. His mother had not wanted any more children; yet, when she almost lost Jimmy at birth, she felt guilty about not having wanted him. During his childhood, she tried to make up for her initial rejecting attitude by babying him and protecting him from the normal difficulties of life. His father, too, always discouraged Jimmy's attempts to grow up and to engage in more mature activities. As a result, Jimmy's level of aspiration as an adult was well below what we expect in a normal, mature individual. He could not make decisions for himself, even on trivial matters; he always needed extra care and attention; and he lacked confidence and self-assurance. By mature, adult standards, he was a weak and ineffective person, unable to "bear his share of the load." However, through the help of a psychotherapist and an exceptionally mature and understanding wife, he was enabled to progress to a more satisfactory level of maturity and self-reliance.

The Normality of Dependency Needs among Adolescents.   The foregoing descriptions of the contributions parents make to the dependency problems of adolescents may make it appear that parents are solely to blame for the difficulties appearing at this stage of development.

Although there is no question that parents do make a large contribution, they do so largely as the unconscious agents of the culture. Thus, if our cultural standards are confused as to the role of the adolescent, parents too will be confused.

Yet there are some basic reasons why the adolescent himself must feel a normal need to depend on his parents, while at the same time he may wish to be emancipated. From the emotional point of view, the world appears to the adolescent as threatening and complicated, and so he desires the continued emotional support and security his parents can provide (10). On the social and economic side, he has not as yet learned the skills he needs to cope with life as an adult.

But there is still this conflict between the need to be dependent and the need to become a self-reliant adult. While the adolescent may enjoy some features of dependency — the stability of the parental home; not having to worry about food, clothing, and shelter; having the assurance of a reliable source of acceptance, attention, and love — he feels a resentment against his very needs for dependence. In some ways he enjoys being dependent, but he wishes that he did not have to be. Talcott Parsons feels that the "compulsive independence" displayed by many adolescents is a "reaction formation" against these unwanted dependency needs (11). In other words, the adolescent so despises himself for feeling or wanting to be dependent that he tends toward extremes in his search for independence. This shows up in rebelliousness, feats of daring, and defiance of authority.

Dependency Needs in Adults. In view of the confused situation that adolescents must face in their attempts to attain the relative independence of adult status, it is not surprising that most of us enter adulthood and even go on to old age with some of our dependency conflicts unresolved. Our problems are not made easier by the demands of the culture, which, with its emphasis on independence, self-reliance, and self-sufficiency (rugged individualism), makes us feel guilty, uncomfortable, or hostile when we try to meet even legitimate dependency needs.

Let us consider the case of Mr. Bond, who has been hospitalized with a disease requiring complete bed rest. He bitterly resents the doctor's order that he must stay in bed for a matter of weeks. He feels he should be at his business; there is so much to be done.

He complains to every visitor of his enforced inactivity, of what a crime it is to keep an active man cooped up in a hospital bed. Unconsciously, Mr. Bond would like to enjoy his enforced stay in the hospital. He *could* find the state of relaxation without responsibility and being waited on at every turn a completely delightful way to spend the next few weeks, but he cannot permit himself this enjoyment. He feels guilty at being so inactive, so useless, so helpless, so dependent. Mr. Bond has reacted violently to his dependency needs by denying them conscious awareness, by repressing them.

On the other hand, Mrs. Southwark, in a bed down the hall, has spent some time in the hospital at least once every year for the last decade. Whereas Mr. Bond has to be virtually dragged to see a doctor, Mrs. Southwark calls her physician at every indication of anything that could possibly be interpreted as a symptom of illness. Her colds *always* turn out to be something more serious. Her digestion is very poor, and she has had a number of operations. Perhaps we can find one of the clues to her behavior in the fact that doctors and nurses give her the kind of attention and care that she feels she does not get at home from her husband and children. Mrs. Southwark would resent any suggestion that her illnesses have anything to do with her unmet needs for love and attention (dependency needs), but we strongly suspect that with her dependency needs (which cannot be legitimately and openly expressed by adults in our culture) have been disguised and repressed and appear as needs for medical attention (which are considered a legitimate reason for dependent behavior in our culture).

Evidences of our conflicting feelings about independence are readily found in everyday life. Take for example the perennial problem of deciding whether to tip or not to tip or how much to tip. If we consider that after all the waiter (or the porter or the taxicab driver) is paid a decent wage and may even earn more than we do and hence decide not to tip him, we feel guilty and uncomfortable, for we have not lived up to the expectations of society. If we do tip, we feel exploited, inasmuch as we do not feel that we received full value for the extra compensation. If our funds are low, we feel doubly resentful. Management is aware of this conflict, and tries to solve the problem for us by posting "No Tipping" signs. Yet we go on tipping and despising ourselves for doing so.

Psychologically, part of this conflict results from the fact that giving a person a tip places him in a dependent status. The tip giver may project himself into the situation and may say to himself, in effect, "I would feel disgraced if I ever had to accept a tip from anyone." This is as far as most people go in their introspective activities. The next step in this line of reasoning, which few take, is the admission, "I wish *I* could receive gifts from someone. I wish *I* could be dependent, but this I cannot permit myself." Inasmuch as the tip receiver is "getting away with something" that the tip giver will not permit himself to do, the latter feels hostile and anxious.

Another illustration of our conflicting feelings about independence is our attitude toward "laziness" and "lazy" people. Essentially, a lazy person is one who is successfully dependent. He does not shift for himself, but somehow his needs are met. Part of our resentment has its basis in our fear that we are permitting ourselves to be exploited by him, but the chief source of our hostility lies in the fact that he is "getting away with something" that *we* would like to do but that we cannot permit ourselves to do. Seeing him successfully lazy reminds us of our own unmet dependency needs, and we are hostile and resentful of this reminder.

The dependency aspects of life have many perils for the insecure person. Having a natural need for love, affection, and friendship, he must eventually receive evidences of this regard in the shape of favors, gifts, and attentions. If he is oversensitive about feelings of dependency, he may not know how to receive these evidences of love and how to reciprocate. In short, he may be unable to accept the fact that all of us are dependent on each other for love and affection, and that the need for love and affection does not of itself make the receiver inferior or overdependent.

Dependency Feelings in the World of Work. Our feelings about even legitimate dependency are related to our feelings about inferiority and weakness. The dependent person and our own normal dependency needs are stigmatized because of the implication that they are weak and inferior. In a power-oriented culture like ours, weakness and inferiority are despised, and a dependent person is expected to despise himself for his weakness, his helplessness, and his inferiority.

According to Douglas McGregor, even persons who are in subordinate positions at work are sometimes led to resent their leaders, their own status, and their own failure to climb the occupational ladder, although this "failure" may not be due to any fault of their own.   Inasmuch as business and industry are organized along authoritarian lines, the subordinate is dependent upon his superiors for wages or salary, promotions, increases in salary, job security, satisfactory working conditions, and even for the job itself.   This dependence is not adequately recognized and accepted by our culture, for we tend to overemphasize the importance of the subordinate's own efforts in meeting his needs for status, security, etc., whereas much more depends on economic conditions and the desire of management to help him meet these needs.   McGregor believes that the relationship between the subordinate worker and his superiors is much like the relationship between a child and his parents, a relationship that the worker hoped he had outgrown in adolescence.   Furthermore, McGregor adds, although the adult is not consciously aware of this resemblance, the parallel is strong enough to reactivate some of the feelings he had toward his parents when he was a child (12).

Not only do the subordinate's relations with his superiors reactivate some of the emotional patterns of childhood, but they also aggravate any dependency conflict he may have carried over unresolved from adolescence.   Our culture teaches us, in effect, not to accept subordinate status, which it has characterized as being weak and dependent, and urges us instead to strive to become completely independent, to become "rugged individualists."   Therefore we feel impelled to work toward an independence that cannot really be attained.   The story of Abe Martinelli is an illustration of this phenomenon.

When Mr. Martinelli graduated from high school, he took a job as a service station attendant.   In this position he felt economically weak, inferior, and dependent.   He saw himself at the mercy of his employer, who was in a position to hire and fire at will, to change working conditions and hours of employment without notice, and to raise or lower his pay.   Mr. Martinelli could have sought protection through his union, but here again he was dependent on someone in higher authority.   Furthermore, he felt that working through his union robbed him of freedom of action, because he could no longer negotiate directly with his employer. When hard times came and Mr. Martinelli was laid off, he found himself dependent on the government for unemployment compensation and relief. When business became better and he again had a job, he decided that he would strive to place himself in a position where he would never have to depend on others again.

A few months later, he opened his own service station. Then, through good luck, hard work, and shrewd management, he expanded this modest holding into a chain of service stations, a distribution plant, and interests in a number of oil fields. Today, fifteen years after starting as a service station operator, he has 500 people on his payroll. The question is: Has he arrived at the point where he no longer has to depend on others?

Financially, Mr. Martinelli is somewhat more independent than he was before. He has more economic power, somewhat more freedom in planning his daily work schedule, and more status. But in many ways he is more dependent than before.

In the first place, he is dependent on his 500 employees. If they are not productive, his power can be destroyed almost overnight. Thus from the point of view of interpersonal relations he is more dependent than when he started.

In the second place, he is dependent on his customers. If for any reason they stop buying from him, his business is ruined.

Then there are countless chains of dependence that interlock with each other and help to integrate Mr. Martinelli's business with the rest of the economy. He is dependent on his bankers, on the oil refineries that supply him, on equipment houses, on the police and fire protection provided by the cities where his service stations are located, etc. Thus, in attempting to make himself independent, he has actually made himself more dependent. Or, rather, he has traded one kind of dependency for another kind of dependency.

Unconsciously, Mr. Martinelli feels this and resents it; he feels cheated of the independence he worked for. Here are two ways in which he might express his resentment:

1. He might fight this growing awareness of having to depend on so many employees by not trusting them, by trying to do all the work himself, even if it required 80, 90, or even 100 hours a week.

2. He might grudgingly accept his dependent status but express his hostility by badgering and criticizing his employees, by being a slave driver, by showing up at unexpected hours and in unexpected places to see whether people were really doing their jobs.

If Mr. Martinelli followed either of these solutions, his health, or his business, or both would suffer. His relationship with his employees would deteriorate and he might even fail financially. Since he is too intelligent to make either of these mistakes, he selects a third solution, one often elected by "smart" businessmen.

3. He swallows his resentment at having to depend on others. He may not be able to trust his employees, and he may want to show them how to do their jobs, but he hides his feelings behind a smiling, pleasant, and affable exterior. He may express some of his hostility in a culturally approved fashion by *competing* with his employees — that is, by working longer hours than his office force, producing better plans or sales campaigns than his sales force — but all in the superficially pleasant spirit of give and take.

The chief dangers of this solution lie in the possibility that it may not enable him to express sufficient hostility. His family relations may suffer as a result. Or the pent-up, internalized hostility and resentment may be too much for the lining of his stomach, and he may develop ulcers.

If Mr. Martinelli attains the goal that many of us daydream about — that is, if he eventually becomes a multimillionaire, surrounded by servants and sycophants — he will be even more dependent than before, for he will not only depend on others to carry on his business, but he will depend on others (servants) to care for his personal needs. Thus, complete independence, even the independence of the rugged individualist, is, in the final analysis, as mythical as the infant's state of omnipotence — it is, after all, another kind of dependence.

Dependence and Emotional Maturity. The question arises: Would it have been possible for Mr. Martinelli to have achieved financial success without having run afoul of his dependency conflict? The answer lies partly in the fact that the neurotic element in Mr. Martinelli's situation is not in his financial success as such, but in his reasons for undertaking his climb up the financial ladder in the first place. He began his quest for financial success so that he would not have to depend on others. Depending on others made him feel inferior and inadequate. Since his quest for power and independence was impelled by an unrealistic, and therefore neurotic, orientation to life — that is, he was attempting to reach a goal that never really existed — he was doomed to failure.

There are others who achieve financial success and who do so without violating principles of emotional maturity. Wealth and success come to them as rewards or even as by-products of their productivity and creativity. Their striving is the result not of their fear of being inferior or subservient to others, but rather of their strong desire to express themselves, to exercise their individual talents. These people are described by Fromm under the heading of "the productive character (13)." Their productivity and creativity are the result of inner drives to express their personality, and their effectiveness is in direct relationship to their freedom from neurotic needs, anxiety, and guilt.

The need to be dependent is not in itself a neurotic need. We all have dependency needs, and whether they are neurotic or normal depends to a large extent on how we regard them. If our dependency needs are exaggerated, as they are by Mrs. Southwark, whose case was mentioned above, or if we are ashamed or afraid of even normal and unavoidable dependency relationships, as Mr. Bond and Mr. Martinelli are, then our dependency needs are unhealthy or neurotic. On the other hand, when we can accept the fact that we are mutually dependent in our relationships with others, when we can accept our normal needs for "passive love relationships" (to be loved, cared for, attended, served, etc.), and when we can accept without rancor those unavoidable situations requiring us to submit to the authority of others — in other words, when we can accept the facts of our social environment and our own natural needs without feeling inferior, inadequate, or guilty — we have become emotionally mature and are freed from the neurotic restraints that impede productivity, creativity, and the natural drive to express our personalities.

SUMMARY

The need to be self-reliant and independent is normal and natural, but in order to meet it, we must cope with two kinds of forces or conditions in our culture. The first is the interdependence that is an essential part of life in a complex civilization, and the second is the attraction of the overdependent way of life. Interdependence is not a real threat to self-reliance and independence of thought and action, although it may appear so when it thwarts or frustrates our more self-centered needs, for it actually frees us from the necessity of devoting our lives to a struggle for existence. Overdependence consists of the desire to be given tokens of love and affection without the responsibility of reciprocating. It constitutes a real threat to independence and self-reliance. The fact that we all have some immature needs to be overdependent is revealed by our daydreams and our preferences for fiction in which problems are solved through chance and good fortune and in which the chief characters do not have to work for a living but are served and waited on by others.

Our enjoyment of dependency relationships has its roots in infancy, when we were completely dependent and enjoyed the complete love and attention of our parents without obligation on our part. As children, we were unaware of the nature of this dependence, but felt that the attention was accorded us as a right, perhaps because we were omnipotent. Some persons never grow out of this feeling of omnipotence and go through life demanding attention and unremitting love from others without obligation on their part to reciprocate.

Conflicts regarding feelings of dependency come to a head during adolescence and early adulthood. Youth want to become adult-like and assert their independence, but they find that the world of reality is full of complications and hidden dangers that cause them to desire continued parental support and protection. In some ways, parents would like their children to grow up and be responsible; in other ways, they would like them to remain childlike and dependent. They want youth to use their rational powers, but they do not want them to question the arbitrary and often irrational aspects of the culture. In the confusion and ambiguity of this situation, adolescents often rebel against authority, and then become helpless and dependent just when adults want them to be responsible and rational.

Since many of us enter adulthood with our dependency conflicts unresolved, it is not surprising that "our normal complement of neurotic needs" stems partly from this cause. The situation is aggravated by our culture, which is ambivalent with regard to dependent relations: on the one hand we learn to despise laziness, but on the other hand we aspire to the parasitical existence of the international set or café society; on the one hand we are taught to feel guilty about any form of dependency, but on the other hand our normal dependency needs would actually permit us to enjoy some passivity, some unobligated care and attention. Further, the structure of our society, particularly in the world of work, is authoritarian in nature, which means that the subordinate is bound to be dependent on his superiors. Thus our culture teaches us to play our dependent occupational roles with submissive obedience and at the same time to despise ourselves for being dependent. Some of us try to work our way out of this dilemma by striving for financial and occupational success, in the hope that if we can get enough power, we will be freed from the necessity to depend on others. However, this merely involves exchanging one kind of dependency for another, for the wealthy person finds that he too is dependent on others to carry out his wishes and support him in his accustomed style.

If we are to solve the dilemma of becoming independent in spite of our dependency needs, we must accept such needs as normal and we must, furthermore, accept those aspects of our environment which involve our mutual interdependence and which necessitate our submission to the requirements of the reasonable and rational authority of others. If the realities of the situation can be tolerated, the individual is then freed to expend his energies in creative production and in expressing his personality through the exercise of his talents and real potentialities.

REFERENCES

1. S. Ferenczi, "Stages in the Development of the Sense of Reality," in E. Jones, tr., *Sex in Psychoanalysis*. Boston: Badger, 1916. Chap. 8.
2. W. V. Silverberg, "The Factor of Omnipotence in Neurosis," *Psychiatry*. 12:387–398; 1949.
3. Alice V. Keliher, *Life and Growth*. New York: Appleton-Century-Crofts, 1938. P. 159.
4. O. H. Mowrer, "Dynamic Theory of Personality," in J. McV. Hunt, ed., *Personality and the Behavior Disorders*. New York: Ronald, 1944. P. 129.
5. F. Redl and W. W. Wattenberg, *Mental Hygiene in Teaching*. New York: Harcourt, Brace, 1951. P. 91.
6. O. H. Mowrer, "Dynamic Theory of Personality," in J. McV. Hunt, ed., *Personality and the Behavior Disorders*. New York: Ronald, 1944. P. 128.
7. L. F. Shaffer, *The Psychology of Adjustment*. Boston: Houghton Mifflin, 1936. P. 373.
8. K. Young, *Personality and Problems of Adjustment*. New York: Appleton-Century-Crofts, 1940. P. 416.

9. "Overdependency." Montreal: National Film Board of Canada, 1949.
10. R. J. Havighurst, *Developmental Tasks and Education*. Chicago: University of Chicago Press, 1949. P. 37.
11. T. Parsons, "Psychoanalysis and the Social Structure," *Psychoanalytic Quarterly*. 19:371–384; 1950.
12. D. McGregor, "Conditions of Effective Leadership in the Industrial Organization," in T. M. Newcomb and E. L. Hartley, eds., *Readings in Social Psychology*. New York: Holt, 1947. P. 428.
13. Erich Fromm, *Man for Himself*. New York: Rinehart, 1947. Pp. 82–106.

SUGGESTED READINGS

J. Levy and R. Monroe, *The Happy Family*. New York: Knopf, 1938. Chapter 1 deals with the relations of the adolescent to his parents.

E. Fromm, *Man for Himself*. New York: Rinehart, 1947. A significant contribution to the problem of overdependency and relations to persons in authority.

R. J. Havighurst, *Developmental Tasks and Education*. Chicago: University of Chicago Press, 1949. Brief, easily read, largely in outline form. See chapter entitled "Developmental Tasks of Adolescence."

K. Horney, *The Neurotic Personality of Our Time*. New York: Norton, 1937. See particularly the chapters entitled "The Neurotic Need for Affection" and "The Quest for Power, Prestige, and Possession."

R. J. Havighurst and H. Taba, *Adolescent Character and Personality*. New York: Wiley, 1949.

P. Blos, *The Adolescent Personality*. New York: Appleton-Century-Crofts, 1941. Contains illustrative case material depicting some of the conflicts of adolescence.

C. Zachry, *Emotion and Conduct in Adolescence*. New York: Appleton-Century-Crofts, 1940.

C. Zachry, "Adolescence," in the *Forty-third Yearbook*, National Society for the Study of Education. Bloomington, Illinois: Public School, 1944.

E. M. Smithies, *Case Studies of Normal Adolescent Girls*. New York: Appleton-Century-Crofts, 1933.

H. M. Bell, *Youth Tell Their Story*. Washington D. C.: American Council on Education, 1938. A survey of Maryland youth in the 1930's.

P. Blanchard, "Adolescent Experience in Relation to Personality and Behavior," in J. McV. Hunt, ed., *Personality and the Behavior Disorders*. New York: Ronald, 1944. Vol. II, pp. 691–713.

A. B. Hollingshead, *Elmtown's Youth*. New York: Wiley, 1949. The social class structure as it affects youth of a small midwestern town.

L. J. Saul, *Emotional Maturity*. Philadelphia: Lippincott, 1947. See Chapter 2, "Independence and Dependence."

O. S. English and G. H. J. Pearson, *Emotional Problems of Living*. New York: Norton, 1945. See Chapters 10 and 11 on development of personality and emotional problems that appear during puberty and adolescence.

K. W. Taylor, *Do Adolescents Need Parents?* New York: Appleton-Century-Crofts, 1938.

VIII... The Forces That Mold Us: Determinants of Personality

Why We Should Be Concerned with Personality Determinants. In our previous discussions of the ways in which we become the kinds of persons we are, we have focused our attention on the stresses and developments that are found "inside" the self, and have been only indirectly concerned with forces and conditions on the "outside." With this chapter, our emphasis moves to a consideration of these more or less external conditions and forces — forces which modify and channel the expression of our basic needs and which, in fact, predetermine certain needs and motives. These are the forces and conditions that make each of us resemble *all* other persons, *some* other persons, and *no* other persons (1).

The patterns we can discover in our inheritance and in those events and forces in our life that have affected us may be called *the determinants of personality.* Psychologists, sociologists, and anthropologists use several systems of classifying these determinants. For our purpose we shall use the following: *physical-situational* (forces that come from or are related to the physical environment), *biological-constitutional* (forces and tendencies that are physiological in nature), and *cultural* (forces that derive from interaction with others).

Physical-situational Determinants

Effects of the Physical Environment. Physical-situational determinants are the forces that affect all or most individuals who live in the same physical environment. The effects of forces in the physical environment may be detected in the grosser personality traits or cultural patterns that develop within groups of people living in various regions. The way of life of a whole tribe is affected because it lives in a desert country; another group develops national characteristics because it lives among mountains in the temperate zone; still another group wrests its living with great toil from barren soil and rocks; while another group lives amid plenty. All these factors have an effect on the personality of the total group and upon the personalities of the individuals who constitute these groups, for they share common experiences. Even when we know the physical features of the environment, we cannot safely predict what these personality characteristics will be; but as we study the individuals and the groups concerned, we can see how the interplay between the individual and his environment has resulted in some of the characteristics we observe.

The effect of the physical environment on personality has been ably demonstrated by Abram Kardiner and Ralph Linton in their report and analysis of the dry- and wet-rice cultures of Tanala-Betsileo, in Madagascar (2). Though these two cultures had basic similarities, indicating a common heritage, they were different in a number of respects. The *differences* were due primarily to the changes in the pattern of tribal life brought about by the adoption of wet-rice cultivation. And the cultural differences resulted, in turn, in personality differences.

Situational Determinants. Under the heading of situational determinants may be included those things that happen to people by chance or accident. A child may narrowly escape drowning, he may be the oldest or the youngest in his family, his family may be separated by divorce, he may grow up next door to a family of aggressive girls — again, we are not able to predict the exact effect these factors will have on the individual's personality, but we do know that they will have an effect to a greater or lesser degree. A chance meeting with an influential or a prominent person may affect the rest of an individual's life and, consequently, his personality. The school experiences of an individual will certainly have an effect: Does he live away from home while attending school? Is his school authoritarian or is it permissive? Does it have an "enriched" or an "impoverished" curriculum?

Biological-constitutional Determinants

Biological-constitutional determinants are those that are inherited, as well as those that have to do with a bodily defect, such as an amputation or a hearing loss resulting from disease. It is well to point out here that these classifications of personality determinants overlap and intermingle. For example, an amputation may also be a *situational* determinant, because it was due to an accident. It has *cultural* implications, because the culture influences the individual's attitudes toward his disability: Should he be ashamed of it? Should it be considered a badge of honor? Does it permit him to play a semidependent role as a pensioner? Although most bodily aspects have cultural implications, their origin enables us to classify them as *biological-constitutional*. Among these bodily characteristics are those described below.

Pigmentation of the Skin. Skin pigmentation has implications for personality, particularly if it differs markedly from the pigmentation of the dominant group. What effect it has depends partly on the culture — Negroes in Birmingham are treated differently from those in Chicago, and those in Chicago are treated differently from those in Johannesburg, South Africa.

Height. Height frequently has a noticeable effect on personality. We are all familiar with the tendency of many short people to be pugnacious and "cocky" and, as we indicated in Chapter 5, we can attribute this tendency partly to an effort to compensate the feeling that one is less adequate physically than a taller person. Research indicates that leaders tend to be taller and heavier than the average (3), but whether the height of a leader is due entirely to inherited tendencies or to other factors — for example, nutrition — is yet to be discovered.

Glandular Development and Activity. Glandular development and activity affect personality in a number of ways. Insufficient secretions from the thyroid gland, for example, can make a person lethargic and sluggish. Personality changes, as shown in altered attitudes and behavior, can be induced by the administration of glandular extracts and similar substances.

Temperament. Babies at birth show a number of personality traits that seem to have no relation to environmental forces. Some babies seem to have an inordinate need to be fondled and held. Others

Doris Day, from Frederic Lewis

The attitudes and feelings of our parents have great influence in the molding of our personalities.

do not seem to care whether they are held or not. Some babies take the breast enthusiastically, making loud smacking noises, while others appear to take feeding as a matter of course. Temperament has important implications for personality. The personality of the newborn child is constituted almost entirely by its temperament, and this is what forms the basis of the reaction of others to the child. Parents always have certain (largely unconscious) expectations for their unborn children. These expectations lead them to react in various ways to the temperamental pattern of the newborn infant. Parents who are prepared to love their babies, but who do not expect them to be nuisances, are upset by infants who demand much attention and are pleased by those who do not. Parents who have a need to lavish attention on babies have the opposite reactions. It is difficult to separate temperament from the other determinants of personality, for the emotional climate of childhood, which has so many important implications for personality, is compounded of parental expectations *that have been modified* by the parents' reactions to the actual behavior of their child. The temperament of the infant is not only an important ingredient in his budding personality, but it directly affects and conditions the emotional climate of his family, which, in turn, has *its* effect on his personality. This emotional climate not only tends to persist into childhood but also forms the basis of the child's expectations of himself, his self-structure. In this way, the temperament of the infant sets up waves and counter-waves of feelings, which constitute the forces molding his personality during its earliest stages.

Sexual Function. Whether one is male or female has a pronounced effect on personality, although many of the personality traits that we once considered to be determined biologically now appear to have their origin in the culture — that is, they are related to what the culture *expects* of its male and female participants rather than to any inherent, biological predisposition. For example, "common sense" tells us that women are born to be passive, dependent, and submissive, whereas men are born to be active, dominant, and aggressive. Yet the anthropologists find cultures where the men have personality traits we call "womanly" and where women not only possess "manly" traits but play occupational and social roles that are monopolized by males in our culture (4). Nevertheless, the fact that women are smaller and slighter and are peculiarly

equipped for childbearing has a pronounced effect on their personalities, irrespective of culture (5).

Body Type.   To one group of workers in this field, body type
appears to be related to certain personality characteristics.   W. H.
Sheldon and his associates base their theories on the fact that there
are three layers of tissue forming the structure of the body: the
endoderm, which forms the vital organs; the mesoderm, which
forms bone, muscle, and sinew; and the ectoderm, which constitutes
the outer layer.   Individuals whose physical structure represented
various emphases of these basic structural components were given
clinical interviews.   From the resulting data, Sheldon has related
certain personality types to certain body types (6, 7).   However,
criticism of the methodology that Sheldon used raises a serious
question as to the validity of his findings.*   Even if Sheldon's
findings are accepted, it cannot be said that he has demonstrated
that personality traits are *caused* by the type of body structure.   It
may be that to have a certain kind of temperament and to grow
up in a certain kind of emotional climate mean that one will develop
a certain kind of body.   Or, what is more likely, all these factors
may be interrelated without one necessarily *causing* another.

Psychologists differ in the emphasis they place on the importance
of biological-constitutional factors in personality development.
Some tend to stress the contribution of the interpersonal or cultural
factors and to ignore the biological-constitutional and the physical-
situational.   Clyde Kluckhohn and H. A. Murray adopt a middle-
of-the-road attitude.   They feel that *biological inheritance determines
personality trends and sets limits* within which these trends may be
developed.   They feel further that inheritance does much to determine the varying potentialities for learning, for speed of reaction,
for level of energy, and for frustration-tolerance; and does much to
determine the biological rhythms peculiar to the individual —
rhythms of growth, of the menstrual cycle, of activity, and of depression and exaltation (8).

Cultural Determinants

For the purpose of this discussion, cultural determinants of
personality will be arbitrarily divided into two areas: *role* and *group.*

* See R. R. Holt's review in the *Journal of Abnormal and Social Psychology* (45:790–795;
1950) of W. H. Sheldon, *et al., Varieties of Delinquent Youth.*   New York: Harper, 1949.

S. Stansfield Sargent defines an individual's role as "a pattern or type of social behavior which seems situationally appropriate to him in terms of the demands and expectations of those in his group (9)." Sargent points out that the roles of two individuals are not identical. Roles are also influenced markedly by the individual's expectations of himself, his self-concept or self-structure. And these expectations, of course, were originally adopted from the expectations that others had for him. As Sullivan says, "the self may be said to be made up of reflected appraisals (10)."

Position in the Family. In Western cultures, his position in the family has much to do with the role — hence, the personality — of the individual (11). Oldest sons in patriarchal families frequently develop "crown-prince" characteristics of behavior; they look upon themselves as "assistant fathers," are dominant, have a strong sense of responsibility, and tend to take themselves very seriously. Frequently the oldest child is the object of more anxiety on the part of the parents than are younger children; he is also likely to be more jealous (12). The middle child finds himself faced by the choice of competing with his older siblings, criticizing and depreciating them, or falling back to the level of the younger siblings. The youngest child tends to have his "babyhood" prolonged by his parents and siblings. Discipline tends to be less strict with him, and his siblings are likely to fight his battles for him.

Occupational Role. Of prime interest to the college student and psychologist is the part played in personality development by the occupational role. That certain personality traits are traditionally related to certain occupations is widely known. Consider the stereotype that Hollywood presents for the doctor: benevolent, patient, all-knowing, and authoritative. The college professor, too, has his stereotype: absent-minded, confused, impractical, and somewhat helpless. Ministers are benign, eloquent, charming, and somewhat pedantic. Hollywood has overlooked the bookkeeper and accountant, but they, too, seem to have their stereotype: careful, precise, neat, patient, modest, and submissive. The fact that individuals from one occupation differ in personality traits from individuals in other occupations has been the basis of a successful interest test, The Vocational Interest Blank for Men, by E. K. Strong, Jr. (13). (See Chapter 14 of this text for further discussion of this test.)

An incidental comment on the successful playing of occupational roles is in order. The general population frequently confuses good "role-playing" with "good adjustment." The doctor who conforms exactly to his stereotype and is precisely what his patients and his fellow workers expect of him may be markedly less successful in his other life roles. Is a man well-adjusted who has the *same* mannerisms, outlook, and approach to people, regardless of whether he is in his office, at his club, in the "bosom of his family," out hunting with his friends, playing golf, or playing bridge? Many persons learn to play their occupational roles so skillfully that we are often misled into overestimating their general level of adjustment.

The "Marginal" Businessman. An interesting variety of the occupational role is that played by the marginal businessman. He is an excellent illustration of how cultural forces, expectations of the dominant social groups, and self-expectations combine to form a rather pronounced personality pattern, which tends to be characteristic of marginal businessmen, irrespective of race or color.

Marginal businessmen have existed since the dawn of history. They are the individuals who do not "belong" to a community, who come in from the outside and endeavor to obtain and maintain a foothold in order, at first, to gain livelihood, and later, to flourish and become economically, socially, and politically powerful. Well-established members of the community usually view the outsiders with suspicion and hostility, and history is full of bloody persecutions of such newcomers. The marginal businessman has at various times been Phoenician, Syrian, Levantine, and Jew. The Chinese traders whose tin shacks sprinkle the South Seas are marginal businessmen, as were the Yankee traders who ranged over the Eastern Seaboard in the late eighteenth and early nineteenth centuries. In fact, Connecticut bears its present nickname, "the Nutmeg State," because of the reputation its peddlers had for selling wooden nutmegs, instead of real ones, to unsuspecting housewives.

Because the marginal businessman must subsist on leavings, because he is not established, and because life is grimmer and more hazardous for him than it is for the more secure members of the community, he tends to develop rather well-defined personality traits. He may find it necessary to become striving, aggressive, and ruthless. He learns how to stretch the mores of the community just as far as they will go and still remain inside the law. He works long hours; he cuts corners; he tries to produce more per hour and per day than do other workers in his occupation. These traits are both the result and the basis of his exclusion from normal social intercourse with the dominant culture, many of whose members may display the same personality traits. The members of the dominant culture tend to resent, despise, and fear him, even though they are responsible for his deprived status by refusing him participation in the normal economic life of the community (14).

Sex Roles. Well-defined in each culture is the sex role — the behavior, attitudes, and personal qualities society expects of each person according to his sex. As has been indicated above, much of the behavior that we think is related biologically to sexual differences is actually due to cultural expectations. Girls tend to be less active than boys, they prefer to play with dolls, and they are more verbal. Some of these differences may be related to inherited temperament, but for the most part they are the result of the expectations of the adults who dominate society. Girls are as strong as boys through childhood and early adolescence; but our insistence that girls play subordinate roles makes it necessary for them to gain their ends by less direct means than those available to boys. Thus girls learn to express themselves verbally rather than physically. In other words, girls behave the way they do largely because we *expect* them to do so; we encourage and reward them when they act like "little ladies"; we express disapproval when they do not conform to this stereotype. If boys behave like the little-lady stereotype, we shame them by referring to them as "sissies"; and we arrange situations, select companions, and promote experiences that will cause them to act in accordance with the little-boy stereotype. As a result, children who do not conform to the expectations of their sex roles learn to be ashamed of their deviant behavior.

Probably the best study of cultural influences on masculine and feminine qualities is that made by Margaret Mead of three New Guinea tribes who were racially similar and living in the same general area (15). She found the Arapesh to be peaceful, co-operative people, who minimize sex differences and accept human nature as intrinsically good. According to the Arapesh ideal, *both* men and women are nonaggressive, permissive, kindly, and maternal. The Mundungumor are a Spartan people, in many ways the opposite of the Arapesh. *Both* men and women of this tribe are expected to be sexually aggressive, jealous, violent, competitive, and vengeful. The Tchambuli have created a culture that empha- sizes artistic skills and ritual. Whereas the Arapesh and the Mun- dungumor have not developed differentiated sex roles for their members, the Tchambuli have clear and separate concepts of the kinds of persons women and men should be. Women should be persons who fish, manufacture, and control the power and economic life of the community. They should take the initiative in courting and be tolerant and appreciative of male activities. Men should be persons who are dependent, coquettish, who place much stress on show, and who spend much time in games and theatricals. Thus with the Arapesh, the ideals for both sexes correspond to our ideals of feminine personality and behavior; with the Mundungumor, the pattern is similar to our masculine stereotype; and the Tchambuli have assigned sexes roles that are in sharp contrast to the expecta- tions of men and women we have developed in Western culture.

It therefore appears that the personality characteristics that we associate with womanhood (submission, co-operation, aesthetic expression, etc.) are not so much biologically determined as they are the result of what the culture has led us to expect of women and what women have come to expect of themselves. As Clara Thompson says, no one knows what the essential womanly person- ality characteristics really are (16). Similarly, many of the person- ality characteristics we have come to associate with manhood (dominance, independence, aggression, etc.) are the result of the fact that our culture expects men to play competitive occupational roles in our patriarchal society (17).

The above discussion should not be interpreted to mean that psychologists and anthropologists have eliminated physiological differences as an influence in the personality traits that characterize the sexes. Undoubtedly the childbearing function of women places them in situations where they are required to be tender and moth- erly, and the larger size and strength of men leads them to engage in activities calling for vigor and aggression. However, these differences are not as crucial as they were in former days, nor are they as important as we commonly believe. The middle-class way of life, with the father becoming more closely involved in the care of children, has demonstrated that he can be as tender and as considerate as the mother. The larger size of the male is no longer the advantage it was formerly, because in modern life there is less and less premium placed on muscular strength in the performance of the tasks of daily life. Indeed, there are few occupations today in which women could not compete successfully with men. It is interesting to note, too, that when women enter occupations that are highly competitive, they can become as aggressive as any man.

Conflicting Roles. At any stage of life in our culture we commonly play a variety of roles (18). The doctor plays the roles of physician, club member, husband, father, member of a hunting party, golf enthusiast, and bridge player. Some of these roles are compatible; others may conflict. A common example of conflicting roles is that of the traveling salesman who also tries to be a good husband and father. His situation is difficult, because being a successful traveling salesman often involves being "on the road" twenty-five days out of the month, whereas being a good family man involves being at home most of the nights of the week. Similar situations are faced by persons in the entertainment industry: musicians, actors, and their agents. For these people, building a stable home life is exceedingly difficult, and divorce is much more frequent in their families than it is among the general population.

Conflict in role is also much in evidence when an individual changes his way of life; at these times he must go through an adjustment period that is often very painful for both him and his associates. Such a time of conflict and readjustment is the period when a child first goes to school, when he must surrender, at least for a part of the day, the security and satisfactions incident to his role of being protected, loved, nourished, supported, and of being the center of family attention. He must exchange all this for a role cloaked with anonymity, as he becomes a mere blur in a sea of forty faces. Many children find this abrupt change painful and frightening. Perhaps it conditions many to an eternal fear of school and education in general.

There are other times in life when a change of role is accompanied by conflict and anxiety: the change from being the only child to being the older child; the change from the role of high school student to that of the college student; the change from the role of student to that of employee; the change from a civilian to a soldier and back again; the change from the role of bachelor or maiden to that of spouse; the change from the role of a childless spouse to that of parent. The fact that some of these changes have joyful connotations in our culture sometimes blinds us to the realities — for example, that the bride and groom will inevitably go through a more or less painful process in adapting their expectations of themselves, of each other, and of married life to the facts of the situation. While marriage bestows its own particular kinds of rewards, it is not the state of unadulterated bliss that Hollywood and the slick magazines imply. Parenthood has its own special joys, but there are bound to be times when children are something less than satisfying and when each parent longs — momentarily, of course — for the days when he had fewer and less pressing responsibilities. There is no change of role that does not bring with it some problem of adjustment; and the more unrealistic the individual's expectations are, the more difficult the shift is likely to be.

Relationship of Roles to Adjustment. Roles are learned by the individual through a process of identification with another person or persons. Thus a pledge to a fraternity learns to play his role as a fraternity brother by identifying himself with the "typical fraternity man" and copying his behavior. The pledge is at first aware of a difference between himself and the other members of the group. Even though he has been accepted officially into the group, he still feels like an outsider; and until he learns the acceptable modes of behavior, belief, and conversation, he will continue to feel like an outsider. To be a nonconforming member of the group is to court rejection, because active, functioning groups will not for long tolerate deviation from their accepted standards of behavior. The pledge therefore conforms by learning his assigned role as a member of the fraternity. He learns this role through conformity to the accepted standards of the group and by identifying himself with the group's leaders or with typical group members. Thus, by learning and by actually playing the role of the fraternity man, he is able to eliminate the anxiety he felt as a newcomer.

The description of role-taking by the fraternity pledge is an everyday example of the use of this psychological device as a means of avoiding, controlling, and reducing anxiety. It is a mechanism we have all used many times. Sometimes we use it as the fraternity pledge did, as a way of becoming like the other members of the group; and sometimes we use role-playing as a means of compensat-

Family life is sometimes improved for both children and parents if the father and mother have opportunities to develop their personalities instead of jogging along in a rut.

ing for feelings of inferiority. A child who is weak or physically handicapped may compensate for this disability by learning to play the role of the bright student; or he may overcompensate and, like Theodore Roosevelt, learn to play the role of the rugged, aggressive individual. John Malloy, whose case was described in Chapter 6, "The Struggle against Shyness and Feelings of Inferiority," was enabled through developing his life roles to overcome much of his shyness.

The child who fails in the classroom may compensate for his feelings of frustration and failure by taking on the role of the bully, which enables him to attain satisfactions from physical domination of weaker individuals, sometimes the same ones who humiliate him in the classroom by their academic success. Still other frustrated children meet their psychological needs by adopting the role of the juvenile delinquent. In some instances the adoption of this role may be in answer to a chronic need for punishment or to a chronic need to fight back against overwhelming forces. In these cases, there is a definite pattern of expectations: the delinquent is expected by others to behave in a delinquent manner, and he himself expects this kind of behavior from himself, even though he may suffer feelings of remorse for his delinquency.

Group Determinants of Personality

Whereas role determinants operate to mold the personalities of *individuals* in specific situations, group determinants * of personality relate to the expectations that the social group has for *everyone* in the group. For example, our society expects that a person who plays the *role* of a military officer will behave in a brusque, efficient, forceful, and direct manner when he is operating in that capacity. These are the personality characteristics ascribed to the stereotype of the role of a military officer. But our society expects *everyone* to protect the young and weak, to appreciate the virtues of hard work and thrift, to defend the sanctity of the home. Similarly, *all* members of the group called the Boy Scouts of America are expected to lead lives marked by loyalty, courage, and courtesy.

Value Patterns. The broader aspects of personality are shaped by the value patterns of the culture. The culture determines what the

* Designated as "group membership determinants" by Kluckhohn and Murray (19).

standards of right and wrong behavior shall be — that is, what the norms are — what is important in the environment, what kinds of behavior shall be rewarded or penalized, and what the rewards and penalties shall be.

A study made by McGranahan of the attitudes of American and German youth illustrates how differences in cultural values affect personality patterns as revealed in attitudes. McGranahan compared several groups of postwar German youth, Nazis as well as anti-Nazis, with groups of contemporary American youth. In general he found marked differences between the American and the German groups, as well as between the Nazi and the anti-Nazi groups. Most of the differences were in the expected direction — that is, the Germans were more inclined to be subservient to authority, although the anti-Nazis were closer to the "American" norm. German girls were closer to the "German" end of the scale than were the German boys, indicating a greater tendency to conform to the national cultural stereotype (20).

Cultural values are pervasive, permeating virtually all aspects of group and individual life. Ruth Benedict compares two kinds of culture existing among the various Indian tribes of the Southwest. One variety, which she calls Dionysian, is violent, aggressive, and exuberant; it permits its members to indulge in extremes of various sorts. The other kind of culture, which she terms Apollonian, emphasizes peace, self-control, and moderate behavior. These basic life patterns are revealed in the dances, the ceremonies, the tribal customs, and every other aspect of interpersonal relations (21).

Some of the patterns and values that permeate the American culture are, according to Kluckhohn, an emphasis on material generosity and benevolence; a greater freedom for women than in other patriarchal societies; a feeling that rational processes are better than other means; a belief in a romantic individualism and the cult of the common man; a high valuation of change (ordinarily taken to represent "progress"); the conscious quest for pleasure; the glorification of science; a pattern of revolt against authority; the worship of material success; competition for power and prestige; a belief in mass production and mass education; and the belief in "the American dream" — "a vision of a society in which the lot of the common man will be made easier and his life enriched and ennobled (22)."

The cult of power in the United States sometimes takes the form of a tremendous respect, perhaps even worship, for those things that *symbolize* power. There is, for example, a tendency on the part of some to endow machines with almost human qualities. Thus we give automobiles and airplanes pet names; strong men shudder when wives clash gears in shifting; and many make real sacrifices to surround themselves with such household deities as electric cocktail shakers, freezers, and gadgets that start the radio and the coffee-maker simultaneously when it is time to get up.

The personalities of most individuals in our culture are also molded by the pattern of values that is the core of our middle-class ideology. This is so important a force that the following chapter will be devoted to it.

Cultural Determinants as a "Hidden Cause." Many kinds of behavior that we usually consider basic, biological, and universal — and therefore untouched by cultural influences — are actually the result of, or are strongly affected by, cultural forces.

The activity of babies is illustrative. One would assume that the activity of babies would be entirely a function of their temperament. For example, some babies seem naturally to be active, while others seem naturally to be quiet and passive. However, in one study of Zuñi Indian babies and white babies born at the same hospital, the observer found that approximately 10 per cent of the babies of both races could be classified as "hyperactive" at birth; and that by the time the same children were a year old, the number of white babies who could be classified as hyperactive was the same, whereas no Indian babies could be so classified (23). Presumably the reasons for the difference in development may be found in the differences between the Zuñi and American cultures. The Zuñi culture teaches its members to live peaceful, calm, satisfied lives; whereas the American culture stresses activity, progress, drive, and accomplishment. The American culture rewards the "progressive" individual; the Zuñi culture rewards the person who is calm and easily satisfied.

One would certainly think that the onset of the first menstrual period would be a function of a girl's biological inheritance; yet, a study of Danish girls growing up in Denmark reports that they had their first menstrual period at the age of fourteen, whereas Danish girls growing up in the United States first menstruated at the age of thirteen and one-half. Not only was this difference a significant one, but it could not be accounted for on the basis of either climate or diet (24).

The "natural" family ties that we accept as a norm in our culture are not found in all groups of people. For example, Balinese children learn not to depend on members of the family for warmth and affection. When Balinese children are about three years old, their mothers deliberately frustrate them by fondling other children in their presence and by offering them the breast and then withdrawing it. Because of this kind of treatment during childhood and because of the general atmosphere of the Balinese culture, its members learn to withdraw into themselves and not to depend on siblings or parents for emotional support (25).

Personality Determinants to Be Found in the Cultures of Subgroups. The discussion so far has dealt with the kinds of patterns of culture that exist on a national or tribal scale. In a nation the size of the United States there are, in addition to the national cultural patterns, thousands of subcultural patterns. These are superimposed on the national pattern, or, rather, are actually merged with it to form variants of the main pattern. Sometimes the subcultures develop value patterns that are at odds with the national pattern; for example, the mountaineer subculture in the South believes in taking the law into its own hands when conducting a feud. Sometimes the subcultural patterns operate only in special times and places, and therefore do not conflict with the national patterns; for example, the subculture of a Trappist monastery has a value system quite different from that of the rest of the country but its isolation gives little opportunity for conflict.

There is a rural-urban differentiation that forms a variation on the national pattern. In general, rural people tend to be friendlier, more neighborly (and more interested in their neighbor's affairs), and less interested in art, music, and the theater than city people. Suicides and mental disorders in general are more common in the cities (26).

Migrant workers develop standards that differentiate them from others in the areas where they work. They develop behavior which enables them to cope with a rootless and economically insecure kind of life, and which encourages a philosophy of "spend it while you have it."

Large manufacturing plants and other establishments employing many people tend to develop their own subcultures. Some plants present almost a military appearance. Supervisors and foremen bristle with authority; their conversations with their subordinates are brusque, curt, and to the point. Subordinates treat their superiors with polite deference and always make it a point to say "Sir." In other plants, the atmosphere is one of easy friendliness. Supervisors and foremen discuss matters with their subordinates in a casual, relaxed manner, and everyone is on a first-name basis. There may be no difference in the productive efficiency of the two plants, but the difference in emotional climate, and its effect on the personalities of employees, is considerable.

Foreign colonies represent subcultural variants in the total cultural pattern. Settling in a strange land creates its own fears and insecurities, and the process of adopting a new culture, like other psychological changes, is frequently a painful one. It is natural, therefore, for immigrants to attempt to protect themselves from the necessity of changing, or at least to attempt to slow down the rate of change, and the formation of a "Little Italy" or a "Chinatown" fills this need. The subculture thus created stands between the old and the new: its members do not think or talk the way they did in the "old country" (although they may believe that they do), nor are they completely under the influence of the new culture. Sometimes in their attempt to shield themselves from changing and taking on new value patterns, they tend to magnify the virtues of the culture they have left. Their anxiety also expresses itself in child-rearing practices: they expect their children to conform to the standards of the old country and thus create many problems for the young second-generation American, who must cope with rejection by his peers, on the one hand, and criticism and punishment by his parents, on the other.

Determinants Operate Unconsciously. It is important to remember that no one is consciously aware of having been influenced by the personality determinants that inhere in his biological heritage or his social and physical environment. Most of us accept the facts of our existence as natural phenomena, unaware that they are to a large extent the creation, in part, of the emotional and social climate that we ourselves, through our cultural group, have created. Zuñi parents probably think that all one-year-old babies are quiet and placid, just as we think it is normal for one-year-old babies to be active. We think it is the most natural thing in the world for parents to want obedient children, just as some American Indian tribes like to see their boys disobedient and refractory (27).

A graphic example of how attitudes become fixed in the personality is provided by a study in two Tennessee communities by E. L. Horowitz and R. Horowitz. The white parents of the communities were asked whether they influenced the attitudes of their children toward playing with Negroes. The parents stated that they felt that the discrimination displayed by the children was spontaneous and natural in origin. Yet further investigation indicated that the smallest white children played freely with members of both races and learned not to play with the Negro children only through increasingly severe disciplining by the parents. In fact, playing with Negro children was one of the most frequent causes of "getting a whupping." Not only were the parents unaware of having influenced the children, but the children themselves, when specifically queried about parental influence in this matter, frequently could not remember having received it and accounted for their not playing with Negroes by rationalizations — for example, "they're too dirty" or "they have diseases and germs (28)." There is nothing unusual about the fact that the parents were unaware of their role as vehicles for cultural values, nor is it unusual that the children should not remember the real bases of their discrimination. The people in these Tennessee communities were no different from the rest of the citizens of the world in that all of us have learned the values of our culture largely through unconscious processes. We do not remember how, when, and why we have come to be as we are.

SUMMARY

In order to understand more fully how we have come to be the way we are, we should have some knowledge of the forces that help to mold our personalities: the determinants of personality. These may be classified as physical-situational, biological-constitutional, and cultural.

Physical determinants are those that grow out of the physical environment. Situational determinants are those events or accidents or chance factors that have an effect on the personality.

Biological-constitutional determinants have to do with the physiological characteristics that affect our lives. They include our inherited traits, tendencies, and limitations, and physiological events, such as illness, amputation, and loss of sight or hearing. Temperament is an important contribution of the biological-constitutional determinants, because the individual's first personality is temperamental in nature, and it is on this initial behavior pattern that the framework of his personality is erected.

Cultural determinants are considered under two aspects: role and group determinants. Role determinants are those expectations that the group has of the individual in certain circumstances and situations. Most of us play a variety of roles. Sometimes we have to change a major role; this is often a difficult process because painful adjustments have to be made. Sometimes roles aid in adjustment: individuals are able to reduce anxieties by learning to play the roles that are appropriate to the kinds of persons they wish to be.

Those forces that affect the personality as a result of membership in a group, which includes a tribe or a nation, are called group determinants. Determinants of this sort operate through value patterns which are developed and adopted by members of the group and which become the bases of norms, or behavior standards. We are not consciously aware of the ways in which we assimilate these values or of how they affect our behavior. For the most part, value patterns and norms, like the other determinants of personality, operate outside our field of perception.

REFERENCES

1. C. Kluckhohn and H. A. Murray, "Personality Formation: The Determinants," in Kluckhohn and Murray, *Personality in Nature, Society, and Culture.* New York: Knopf, 1948. Pp. 35–48.

2. A. Kardiner, *The Individual and His Society.* New York: Columbia University Press, 1939. Pp. 251–351. (A brief version of the same material entitled "The Change from Dry to Wet Rice Cultivation in Tanala-Betsileo," may be found in T. M. Newcomb and E. L. Hartley, eds., *Readings in Social Psychology.* New York: Holt, 1947. Pp. 46–55.)

3. E. B. Gowin, *The Executive and His Control of Men.* New York: Macmillan, 1915.

4. M. Mead, *Sex and Temperament in Three Primitive Societies.* New York: Morrow, 1939.

5. C. Kluckhohn, *Mirror for Man*. New York: McGraw-Hill, 1949. P. 204.

6. W. H. Sheldon, *et al.*, *The Varieties of Human Physique*. New York: Harper, 1940.

7. W. H. Sheldon and S. S. Stevens, *The Varieties of Temperament*. New York: Harper, 1942.

8. C. Kluckhohn and H. A. Murray, "Personality Formation: The Determinants," in Kluckhohn and Murray, *Personality in Nature, Society, and Culture*. New York: Knopf, 1948. Pp. 35–48.

9. S. S. Sargent, "Conceptions of Role and Ego in Contemporary Psychology," in J. H. Rohrer and M. Sherif, eds., *Social Psychology at the Crossroads*. New York: Harper, 1951. Pp. 355–370.

10. H. S. Sullivan, *Conceptions of Modern Psychiatry*. Washington, D.C.: William Alanson White Psychiatric Foundation, 1947. P. 10.

11. J. H. S. Bossard, *The Sociology of Child Development*. New York: Harper, 1948. Pp. 108–117.

12. A. Davis and R. J. Havighurst, *Father of the Man*, Boston: Houghton Mifflin, 1947.

13. E. K. Strong, *Vocational Interests of Men and Women*. Stanford: Stanford University Press, 1943.

14. S. I. Hayakawa, *Language in Thought and Action*. New York: Harcourt, Brace, 1949. Pp. 191–201.

15. M. Mead, *Sex and Temperament in Three Primitive Tribes*. New York: Morrow, 1935.

16. C. Thompson, "Role of Women in This Culture," in P. Mullahy, ed., *A Study of Interpersonal Relations*. New York: Hermitage, 1949. P. 146.

17. T. Parsons, "Certain Primary Sources and Patterns of Aggression in the Social Pattern of the Western World," in P. Mullahy, ed., *A Study of Interpersonal Relations*. New York: Hermitage, 1949. Pp. 269–296.

18. R. Linton, "Concepts of Role and Status," in T. M. Newcomb and E. L. Hartley, eds., *Readings in Social Psychology*. New York: Holt, 1947. Pp. 367–370.

19. C. Kluckhohn and H. A. Murray, "Personality Formation: The Determinants," in Kluckhohn and Murray, *Personality in Nature, Society, and Culture*. New York: Knopf, 1948. Pp. 35–48.

20. D. V. McGranahan, "A Comparison of Social Attitudes among American and German Youth," *The Journal of Abnormal and Social Psychology*. 41:245–257; 1946.

21. R. Benedict, "Psychological Types in the Cultures of the Southwest," in T. M. Newcomb and E. L. Hartley, eds., *Readings in Social Psychology*. New York: Holt, 1947. Pp. 16–23.

22. C. Kluckhohn, *Mirror for Man*. New York: McGraw-Hill, 1949.

23. C. Kluckhohn, *Mirror for Man*. New York: McGraw-Hill, 1949. Pp. 21–22.

24. R. N. Franzblau, "Race Differences in Mental and Physical Traits: Studied in Different Environments," *Archives of Psychology* (*N.Y.*), 1935. No. 177.

25. G. Bateson, "Cultural Determinants of Personality," in J. McV. Hunt, ed., *Personality and the Behavior Disorders*. New York: Ronald, 1944. P. 731.

26. R. E. L. Faris, "Ecological Factors in Human Behavior," in J. McV. Hunt, ed., *Personality and the Behavior Disorders*. New York: Ronald, 1944. P. 740.
27. R. Benedict, "Continuities and Discontinuities in Cultural Conditioning," in P. Mullahy, ed., *A Study of Interpersonal Relations*. New York: Hermitage, 1949. P. 303.
28. E. L. Horowitz and R. Horowitz, unpublished study reported by G. Murphy, L. B. Murphy, and T. M. Newcomb, "Attitudes of White Children toward Negroes," in S. H. Britt, ed., *Selected Readings in Social Psychology*. New York: Rinehart, 1950. Pp. 447–451.

SUGGESTED READINGS

D. Haring, *Personal Character and Cultural Milieu*. Syracuse: University Bookstore, 1948. A compilation of important papers in the field of anthropology that contribute to the understanding of personality formation.

R. Stagner, *Psychology of Personality*, 2d edition. New York: McGraw-Hill, 1948. See Chapter 22 (written by A. H. Maslow), entitled "Personality and Social Values."

S. S. Sargent, *Social Psychology*. New York: Ronald, 1950. The entire book is useful, but see particularly the chapters entitled "Culture and Personality," "Social Roles," and "Social Change and Social Movements."

T. M. Newcomb, *Social Psychology*. New York: Dryden, 1950. A very useful book. See particularly the chapters entitled "Social Norms and Common Attitudes," "Role Behavior and the Self," "Culture and Personality," "Individual Adaptations to Role Prescriptions," and "Effects upon Individuals of Membership in Groups."

C. Kluckhohn and H. A. Murray, *Personality in Nature, Society, and Culture*. New York: Knopf, 1948. Most of the papers contained in this book bear on the subject of this chapter and the one that follows.

T. M. Newcomb and E. L. Hartley, eds., *Readings in Social Psychology*. New York: Holt, 1947. See sections entitled "Uniformities and Variations under Differing Social Influences," "Socialization of the Child," "Effects of Group Situations," and "Role and Status."

K. Young, *Personality and Problems of Adjustment*. New York: Appleton-Century-Crofts, 1940. See chapters entitled "Constitutional Foundations," "Groups and Culture," and "Personality, Society, and Culture."

E. H. Erikson, *Childhood and Society*. New York: Norton, 1950. Personality development in the child against a background of anthropological research.

IX... *The Forces That Mold Us:*
Social Class and Status

Social Class an Unpalatable Concept.   Most of us find social class and status difficult subjects to discuss.   We have a feeling that such ideas have no place in our way of life, that they are concepts foreign to our ideals of democracy and equality.   Some of us feel that social class exists only in the imagination of a few social climbers, while others believe that to accept the existence of a social class system implies that one is a snob.   Since the resistance to the idea that social status has any place in our way of life is so widespread, it may be well to examine the possible sources of this attitude.

For the middle-class person, the "average" man, to admit the existence of social classes, he must accept the fact that there are people "above" him and "beneath" him.   The implication that there may be people who "think they are better" than he is a potential source of resentment and hostility.   Furthermore, it is an apparent contradiction of one of the principles on which this country was founded, the concept that "all men are created equal."   The fact that "equality *before the law*" is the principle embodied in our basic documents does not alter the situation in the mind of the middle-class individual;   he simply does not perceive it that way.   He sees only that certain people "have more money" than others, and he believes with simple faith that when he has as much money as they, he will be accepted by them as a social equal.

The implication that *he* might think he is "better" than persons in a lower class also is a potential source of anxiety.   The fact is that the middle-class person *does* consider himself superior in many ways to members of the lower classes, but he is unable to permit himself to be aware of this feeling, since it violates his self-concept ("all men are created equal"). He sees the difference between himself and lower-class individuals largely as an economic difference — they are poorer than he. In a way, he would like to assume no responsibility for their status, inasmuch as he subscribes to the credo of "equality of opportunity"; hence, if they have not attained *his* economic status, it is because they have not used the opportunity available to everyone. Yet, in a way the existence of the lower classes makes him anxious, partly because he senses that although social and economic opportunity is more nearly equal in the United States than in other countries, it is not "as equal" as it might be. For example, most middle-class people owe their status to the fact that being born into the middle-class has given them a head start in education, personal associations, financial stability, and the other essential qualities and conditions of middle-class life.

Because the middle-class person is not permitted by his value system to become consciously aware of his real attitudes toward members of other classes, he tends to deny free expression to such feelings, and these repressed feelings become, in turn, a source of anxiety when aroused by a discussion of class differences.

Ignoring the Realities of the Class System. Inasmuch as it is impossible for the middle-class person to live in the midst of the class system and ignore it, he rationalizes its realities by translating the evidences of status into symbols he can discuss and accept with less anxiety. Since he has no difficulty in discussing money, he tends to oversimplify the class and status system by reducing it to financial terms — that is, he describes the situation by stating that some people have more money than others. He also recognizes that some people have higher political and managerial position than others; this he attributes to natural talents, money, education, good fortune, and to "political pull." While these analyses may be valid as far as they go, they tend to ignore the facts that money, position, and power have accrued to the benefit of some families more than others and that these more fortunate families are also the social leaders of the community.

Importance of Social Class System for the College Student. The "typical" college student, being a member of the middle-class group (or a member of the lower-class group who aspires to middle-class status and hence subscribes to middle-class values), usually does not perceive his attendance at college as having any relation to a social class system. For example, the author once asked a freshman class to break up into small groups and discuss the question: What does the social class system have to do with my being in college? When the class reconvened after a fifteen-minute discussion period, it was discovered that only one of the six groups had discussed the question assigned; instead, they had discussed the reasons why *they* thought they were in college. They had not consciously ignored the assigned topic; they had merely acted as though it did not exist. If the college student is to obtain a realistic picture of why he is in college as well as "how he got to be the way he is," he must struggle with his own tendencies to distort his perception of the realities of the class structure as they apply to him.

It is desirable that college students understand the dynamics of the class system, because much of their time and effort is expended in an unconscious attempt to (a) maintain their present middle-class status, (b) achieve a relatively higher position in the middle class than that which they now possess, or (c) change their present status from lower class to middle class. Furthermore, attending college is coming to be a ritual that most middle-class adolescents and young adults must undertake in order to be granted full status as members of their class.

In a study conducted by Benjamin Fine, the educational editor of *The New York Times*, three main reasons emerged as to the bases for the desire to go to college:

1. Students expected that having a college education would enable them to obtain jobs paying more money, with more security of employment.

2. They believed that a college education would assist them in climbing the social ladder — to meet the "right sort" of people, to be accepted in homes and social gatherings where they presently feel unwelcome.

3. They felt that a college education would give them cultural and intellectual enrichment and would give them insights into areas of life that would otherwise be unknown to them (1).

It will be observed that the first two of these three reasons definitely involve aspirations of social status and that the third has implications pointing in this direction, for one cannot participate with upper-middle-class persons unless one can "speak their language" and participate with them on the basis of a common intellectual experience — a college education.

A survey conducted by Elmo Roper for *Fortune* confirms the find-ings of Fine. Members of Roper's staff asked a representative sample of the "American public" a number of questions regarding college attendance. Results of the poll indicated that Americans feel that the chief value to be obtained from a college education is "preparation for a better job, a trade or profession, greater earning power (2)." Thus both Roper's and Fine's studies indicate the value we place on college training as a means of attaining and maintaining status in life. The fact that professional status, rather than social status, was mentioned as the desired outcome in Roper's survey is understandable in the light of our reluctance to accept the idea of social status in our conceptual frame of reference. Later in this chapter we shall discuss the close relationship between profes-sional status and social status.

Roper and his associates also found that "a better chance to get ahead in the world" ranks high, in the eyes of the American public, as an expected result of receiving a college education, although it is interesting that persons who had never attended college, or who had attended college but had never graduated, tended to rate this out-come higher than persons who had graduated from college.

Evidence Supporting the Existence of a Social-class System in America

Recognition of Class Differences. Evidence of the fact that most of us are actually aware of the existence of a class structure is presented in a survey conducted by Richard Centers, in which individuals con-stituting a representative cross section of the adult white male population (1,100 persons) were questioned as follows: "If you were asked to use one of these four names for your social class, which would you say you belonged in: middle class, lower class, working class, or upper class?" Of this group 3 per cent said they were in the upper class, 43 per cent identified themselves with the middle class, 51 per cent classified themselves in the working class, and 1 per cent felt they were in the lower class. One per cent said they did not know, and *only 1 per cent said they did not believe in classes* (3).

Another study, conducted by Allison Davis, Burleigh Gardner, and Mary Gardner, ably demonstrates the differences in attitudes displayed by residents of a Southern town toward other members of the community, as influenced by social rank. The terms used by the townsfolk are highly descriptive: "leading families," "fine old families," "the four hundred," "the society crowd," "plain people," "nice, respectable people," "good people, but nobody," "po' whites," "red necks," "he isn't our social equal," "she isn't our kind," "they're nothing but white trash," and "oh, they're plain people like us." On the basis of the townspeople's descriptions of their fellow citizens, the researchers were able to develop a three-class system of classification (upper, middle, and lower), which they further divided into subclasses: upper-upper, lower-upper, upper-middle, lower-middle, upper-lower, and lower-lower (4). This system has also been used by other researchers (5).

Nor are children exempt from the influences of the class system. W. Lloyd Warner and others, studying children's rating of other children in the fifth and sixth grades of a Middle Western community, found that *children of the upper and upper-middle classes were rated high by all other children* for such traits as good looks, liking for school, leadership, friendship, and other favorable personal traits, whereas *lower-class children were given low ratings* and were said to be bad-looking, dirty, and "people you would not want for friends (6)."

Differences in Behavior among Classes. Although the attitudes described in the studies mentioned above may be accepted as valid evidence of the existence of a class-and-status hierarchy, we also have reports by trained observers showing that people in each of the several classes not only *regard* themselves differently but *behave* differently. This evidence points to social classes as varieties of subcultures, with value systems of their own, which permeate the attitudes and behavior of their members.

One study, conducted by Martha C. Ericson, which compared child-rearing practices among middle-class and lower-class whites and Negroes in Chicago, reported that lower-class mothers were more likely than middle-class mothers to breast-feed their children. Lower-class mothers tended to wean their children later than did middle-class mothers. Proportionately eleven times more lower-class children than middle-class children were fed "at will" (rather than on a schedule). More middle-class children sucked their thumbs. Bowel-and-bladder training was started significantly earlier in middle-class homes than in lower-class homes, though children from both classes achieved "control" at approximately the same age. Middle-class children were expected to help at home

"First they give 'em to you, then they start nagging at you —
pick 'em up, pick 'em up, put 'em away, put 'em away."

*Helping to keep living quarters neat and orderly is a difficult but unavoidable
responsibility in the life of the middle-class child.*

between the ages of two and five almost twice as often as lower-class children. Middle-class children were expected to be in the house earlier at night; lower-class children began going to movies unaccompanied at earlier ages (7).

Classes differ widely, too, in sexual behavior. The material from the Kinsey Report, according to the interpretations of Eli Ginzberg, indicates that the incidence of premarital sexual intercourse among members of the lower classes is seven times higher than among the upper and middle classes. Ginzberg attributes this difference to the fact that the middle-class male must postpone sexual gratification until he is economically self-supporting, whereas the lower-class youth feels he has nothing to gain by postponement (8).

Universality of Status Systems. Actually, we should be surprised if there were *not* a status system in America, in view of the fact that status systems or hierarchies of some kind appear wherever and whenever humans gather together. Even animals develop hierarchies and status systems. Flocks of chickens, for example, have a "peck order" — there is one chicken or small group of chickens who can peck any other chicken in the flock, but who cannot be pecked back. At the other extreme there are chickens who can be pecked by all others but who cannot peck back (9, 10). The evolvement of some kind of status system seems inherent in group living.

Functionally, a status system appears to be a necessary thing. If a group is going to function, some sort of leadership is necessary in order to aid the group in achieving its own aims. Leaders must be followed; otherwise they are not leaders. And leaders must have prestige, or no one will follow them.

Every culture has its own ways of designating its leaders. We reward them with economic power (money) and the power to control our behavior. We give them titles that symbolize their rank and status — president, superintendent, chief of police, foreman, assistant sales manager, dean, captain, boss, teacher, consulting engineer, senator, corporal, and so on.

There is considerable evidence that we tend to lean heavily on the upper classes (including the upper-middle) for our leadership. F. W. Taussig and C. S. Joslyn found that 10 per cent of the American population produces 70 per cent of the leaders in business, and that 50 per cent of the leaders in business had fathers who were also businessmen (11). Even labor is not immune. P. A. Sorokin studied the backgrounds of labor leaders, as compared with those of the rank and file, and discovered that a far greater percentage of the leaders had *not* come from laboring families but from families in professional, managerial, and business occupations (12). A study of college women, made by J. Carpenter and P. Eisenberg, compared those who displayed dominant traits with those who were submissive. They found that the dominant group tended to come from levels of higher socio-economic status and prestige (13).

Rewards of Leadership and Status. Theoretically, economic rewards in our culture are presumed to be assigned roughly on the basis of utility — that is, the person whose services are deemed to be of greater use to society receives the greater reward. Thus the leader receives a greater reward than any one of his followers because his services are felt to be more valuable. This theoretical relationship also applies to status — the more valuable the services, the higher the status. In the popular mind, the three factors are tied together: status, economic reward, and utility of services. Actually, however, matters often do not work out according to this formula. From the standpoint of indispensability, the services of a garbage collector rate higher than those of a sales clerk; yet the latter ranks higher on the status system, though he often receives a lower economic reward. A streetcar motorman provides services more indispensable than those of a highly skilled designer of jewelry, but the latter receives a higher economic reward and is accorded a higher status.

Another way of computing the value of services is to assume that the wage earned (the price paid by society for services) is a direct expression of what society considers to be the value of the services. In the popular mind, this is further translated to mean that the price paid the individual for his services is an indicator of his worth as a person. The next logical step is the linking of these factors — social status, value of services, value of the individual as a person — and all are held to be theoretically and roughly equal.

This distortion of reality leads to considerable resentment at times. The teacher is aware that, though he has a higher social status than that of the plumber, the latter may receive higher wages. If the teacher believes that wages should reflect individual worth and status, he is made anxious and hostile by this apparent contradiction. Since he, like most other Americans, cannot speak directly of social status, he vents his chagrin and hostility by complaining about the nonappreciative attitude of society toward teachers and about his investment in four, five, or six years of professional training, which brings him a lower wage than the plumber, who did not attend college. This attitude, of course, ignores the facts that plumbing is a closed trade into which relatively few persons are able to obtain entry; that plumbers must complete an apprentice- ship that may take from four to six years; that on a country-wide basis and over a lifetime period, the total earnings of the average teacher exceed those of the average plumber; and that persons who are suited, by reason of personality, to the work done by teachers are seldom suited to the work done by plumbers.

In general, the high hourly wages obtained by members of the working class (roughly, most of the upper-lower and much of the lower-middle classes) are regarded with resentment by members of the white-collar group, partly because the latter feel that these high wages are a threat to their status and partly because, reluctant to press their wage demands collectively and aggressively as have members of the working class, they have been unable to make corresponding economic progress. Since they believe that the worth of the individual is reflected in the amount of his income, they interpret their lower hourly incomes to mean that society considers them inferior. This interpretation constitutes a threat to their self-concepts, which rank white-collar status higher than "blue- collar" or working-class status.

Distinguishing Characteristics of Social Class

Essentially, an individual's social class status is determined by the persons with whom he associates and who accept him as an equal at work, in their homes, and at social gatherings. One tends to participate most freely and most frequently with the members of one's own class. Or, to use a definition by Davis and the Gardners, a social class is "the largest group of people whose members have intimate access to each other (14)."

Bases for Classification. It is apparent that class cannot be deter- mined on the basis of finances alone, although there is no question that wealth plays a part in such determination. Gunnar Landtman, after reviewing much anthropological data, came to the conclusion that wealth operated to support and to perpetuate class differences rather than being the cause of them (15). Actually, the kind of occupation an individual follows has a much greater influence on his social status than the extent of his wealth or income. As Max Levin says, "the status-conferring aspect of occupations is not exclusively dependent upon the income level inasmuch as our hierarchical class structure is only partially related to economic factors (16)."

Warner and his associates have conducted extensive researches into the bases upon which we assign persons their status in the class system (17). They have learned that the *source and kind* of income are as important as, if not more important than, the *amount* of money received. The upper classes hold their status by virtue of having *inherited* their money. In some localities, in order to qualify a family for upper-class status, this income should come from securities; in other areas it should come from the land — farms, ranches, plantations. These sources of inherited income are generally considered to be more "respectable" than income from an inherited family business, unless the business is particularly large, respectable, and well-known. Persons in the upper-middle and lower-upper classes tend to receive their income from fees, if they are doctors, lawyers, and consultants of various kinds, or from salaries, if they are executives, or from the profits of their businesses and investments. However, most of the people in the middle class derive their economic power from salaries. As one goes up the status scale, salaries are generally figured on an annual basis; going down the scale, the pay period shortens, and at the bottom, pay is usually figured on a weekly basis. Working-class income, which is called *wages* rather than *salary*, is usually figured on an hourly basis.

Warner and his group emphasize the importance of *how* one spends his income as a basis for assigning class status. Yachting, polo, and golf figure largely as amusements attractive to people at the upper end of the status spectrum. Clubs and lodges play important parts in determining status. In every community there are groups to which only the members of the upper class belong. For example, Charles Gray, the upper-middle-class hero of J. P. Marquand's *Point of No Return* is a member of the Oak Knoll Club, which he knows is "not as good" as the older country club at Hawthorn Hill. Members of the Oak Knoll Club are inclined to view Hawthorn Hill as "stuffy," but at the same time, any of them would have given much to become members of Hawthorn Hill. Similar situations exist in most real-life communities.

The kind of house and the district one lives in are important indicators of status. Older houses in run-down districts are inhabited for the most part by members of the lower class, while newer districts tend to be populated by the middle classes or lower-class members with middle-class aspirations. Newer houses tend to be preferred by middle-class individuals, while upper-class members often prefer older houses in "respectable" parts of town or in exclusive suburbs. These are a few of the criteria that Warner and his group have used in appraising social status in the communities they have studied. The proportions of the population of Yankee City, a New England community, that they assigned to the various classes are listed in the table below.

Distribution of Population by Class (17)

Class	Number	Per Cent of Total Population
Upper-Upper	242	1.44
Lower-Upper	262	1.56
Upper-Middle	1,715	10.22
Lower-Middle	4,720	28.12
Upper-Lower	5,471	32.60
Lower-Lower	4,234	25.22
Unknown	141	0.84
	16,785	100.00

James H. S. Bossard recognizes four distinguishing features of the American class system. 1. Social stratification is reinforced by ethnic * differences, in that persons from ethnic groups, particularly those whose immigration was more recent, are assigned lower status in the social system. 2. Both class and ethnic distinctions are further reinforced by religious differences. 3. The relative mobility found in the American class system makes it easier to move up or down the social ladder in the United States than elsewhere. However, as certain areas become more stable and more settled, class lines tend to become more rigid. 4. The class system also includes a caste (a class that has become hereditary), which occupies a fixed place in the social structure. Although there may be mobility over class barriers, there is relatively little if any movement over caste bar-

* *Ethnic.* Racial and/or national.

riers.   Nonwhite groups in this country find their opportunities for social participation with white groups more or less severely restricted by caste lines.

Bossard also distinguishes between the three main classes by their attitudes toward children.   He states that upper-class members tend to want children in order to guarantee and to fortify the family's position.   The child is under considerable pressure, as he grows to maturity, to maintain the family prestige and good name and to carry on family traditions.   Lower-class families, while they do not lack love and affection for their children, "tend to regard them as a sort of inevitable price which fate exacts in payment for sex relations."   Children become an acute burden as their number increases and the family income and facilities become proportionately less able to accommodate them.   Lower-class families are less permanent;   there is more divorce, desertion, and temporary, illegal unions.   To a large extent, the lower-class child is reared by the mother and punished by the father.   The chief emphasis is that children must not be an annoyance or a nuisance.   Children must keep quiet and not disturb the neighbors, which is understandable in view of the cramped living quarters with thin walls.   Children are expected to be obedient — to stop what they are doing at once or to suffer the consequences of physical punishment.   Whenever possible, children are put to work to augment the meager family income.   Middle-class children grow up in an atmosphere of rigidly controlled behavior, with a strong emphasis on conformity to established patterns.   In order to achieve conformity, children are reasoned with and, when they deviate, are likely to be punished by nonphysical means (18).

Patterns of Personality as Influenced by Social Class.   In the foregoing section, we have described how the individuals who comprise the different classes behave.   This behavior comes into even clearer perspective when we consider the emotional background and value patterns for the different classes.

In his studies of lower-class and middle-class groups, Davis found the lower-class group to be composed of individuals who are impulsive, aggressive, and more openly emotional than middle-class individuals.   Lower-class members permit themselves far more gratification of sexual impulses and rage impulses than do middle-class persons.   Whereas middle-class children are trained to fear, repress, and suppress impulses that may lead to sexual or openly aggressive behavior (fighting, stealing, swearing), slum children learn to engage early and frequently in such behavior. Middle-class children learn to express their hostile feelings through competitive efforts, initiative, or ambition, whereas lower-class children express their hostility openly, through direct aggression (19).

The Middle-class Pattern. Other personality characteristics of the middle-class person may be observed in the following excerpt from a definition of "middle class":

. . . a social class resting between the aristocracy and the proletariat on the social scale, characterized by its cult of respectability, . . . indefatigable business and professional enterprise, and usually by its moral inhibitions. In the middle class, cleanliness is next to godliness, and idle time is lost forever. The greatest goal in life is to be independent, the next is to work, but usually not with the hands in direct production. . . .

Middle class . . . is a term designating a heterogeneous section of the population, made up chiefly of small businessmen and industrialists, professional and other intellectual workers with moderate incomes, skilled artisans, prosperous farmers, white-collar workers and salaried employees. . . . Whatever unity they possess lies in their educational standards, their standard of living and ideals of family life, their mores and recreational interests. They constitute the overwhelming bulk of the Protestant Church membership and a considerable element of the Catholic Church and Reformed branch of the Jewish community (20).

Harsh and Schrickel characterize the middle class as follows:

The distinguishing quality of middle-class motivation is that it stems largely from social insecurity. Upper-middle-class individuals, not born to security like those above them in status, develop an anxiety toward losing the status which they hold only on sufferance. Members of the lower-middle-class are fearful of the loss of steady income or respectability, which would send them down into lower-class life. The middle-class way is a distinct pattern, with the high valuation it sets on property and other concrete symbols of achievement; its emphasis on belonging to the "right" fraternal and other formal organizations; its injunctions to "self-improvement" through "discussion" groups, book clubs, art, and music gatherings. These are persons who have been culturally trained to resist the immediate calls of the flesh; to invest in future status rather than to enjoy the moment; and to maintain stoically one's status, not in any final sense, but as a potential springboard to higher status. This anxious striving is usually well ingrained in the middle-class adolescent and young adult. From it comes the sustaining power, the drive to keep them on the self-sacrificing climb to socio-economic security — and possibly the reward of higher status. The adaptive anxiety of the middle-class adolescent who is "upward mobile" is by no means essentially irrational or primitively fearborn. In our society it is intelligently oriented and evaluative of status facts. Middle-class anxiety is doubly effective in that it entails awareness of the punishment of loss of present status and it fires the ambition to achieve the rewards of social prestige, power, and security for one's own; rewards that one can readily see being enjoyed by "successful" persons around him. The average middle-class adolescent, for example, has developed adaptive anxiety which will keep him, most of the time, from the pleasures of sexual intercourse until he has established himself economically and can afford to support a girl in the style and status to which she is accustomed (or aspires). This is particularly true of the boy who goes to college. The Kinsey Report shows this individual as reverting more to masturbation as a sexual outlet than does his lower-class grade school educated contemporary (21).*

Social Status and the Sexes. Other social-class characteristics affect the personalities of people. As one goes down the social scale, the status of women lessens, and, conversely, as one goes up the scale, their status increases. Wife-beating, for example, occurs almost exclusively among the lower classes. Lower-class men enjoy more leisure than do their wives, and their leisure-time activities are entirely "masculine." In the middle class, women are accorded a position more nearly approaching equality; marriage becomes more a partnership; men are expected to participate in housework and child care. Such participation is found less often in the lower classes. In the upper classes, one finds women playing a dominant role. This dominance is achieved partly through the abdication by men of the position of social leadership and partly through the fact that women live longer than men, which enables upper-class women to inherit the wealth accumulated by their husbands or brothers. Upper-class women dominate the clubs and other social organizations that operate upper-class group activities.

The role of the sexes in the classes has other implications for the personalities of their members. The dominant way of life in the lower classes puts a premium on physical strength and more or

---

* Charles M. Harsh, and H. G. Schrickel, *Personality*. Copyright 1950. The Ronald Press Company.

less open aggression; in the middle classes, it is intellect and "progress," based on ambitious, competitive striving; in the upper classes, prestige, tradition, and diplomacy are the way of life.

Determinants of Personality. The implications of these social-class patterns as determinants of personality are rather clear. Much of the behavior that middle-class people accept as "natural" and "normal" is natural and normal only for middle-class members and grows out of the norms and standards of behavior of the middle-class culture. This means further that large groups of people in the population follow patterns of behavior that impress middle-class members as being "crude," uncouth, and delinquent, on the one hand, or as snobbish and standoffish, on the other. The tendency is for the middle-class person to be intolerant of such behavior and to hold the individuals who display such behavior patterns personally responsible for their conduct. The fact is, however, that most of the individuals in question *had no choice in the selection of their personality characteristics, for they were superimposed or dictated by the cultural pattern of the social class in which these individuals were reared.*

Thus we can *expect* persons who were reared in a lower-class environment to be impulsive, more openly friendly or aggressive, and less able to plan and save for the future. We can *expect* middle-class persons to repress their emotions, to be more reserved, to be striving and competitive, to value "progress," to postpone the gratification of their needs in favor of some future reward, and to be more concerned about planning for economic security. And we can *expect* upper-class members to be concerned about prestige, to emphasize diplomacy, social graces, tradition, and "family." In following these patterns, individuals are merely carrying on the cultural patterns they have lived with from birth.

Adjustment Problems Growing Out of the Class System

Misunderstandings Arising from Cultural Differences. As the social classes attempt to live together and participate in the larger culture of which they are a part, it is understandable that differing attitudes, emotional patterns, and value systems can cause difficulties. Some of these conflicts would be much reduced and perhaps even avoided if the participants were aware that these differences are due not to personal peculiarities but to differences in cultural norms or values.

However, inasmuch as we have so rigidly schooled ourselves to ignore the existence of the social-class system and the effects that our membership in a social class have upon us, we are unable to see these differences in true perspective.

Marital Difficulties. A relatively common problem is that faced by individuals who marry outside their class. These individuals are generally unaware of the strikingly different behavior patterns that characterize the classes. If they *are* aware of class differences, the effect of this awareness often only strengthens their resolve to prove that "love is above social class." A woman who marries a man from a class higher than her own has to meet the veiled or open criticism and snubs of her husband's relatives. Frequently she is denied full participation in social affairs or is maneuvered into situations that will prove embarrassing. Her "uncouth" mannerisms are called to her husband's attention by well-meaning relatives. If she attempts to retain her friends, her husband may not approve. In the meantime, *her* friends and relatives are quick to point out instances that indicate to them that she is snubbing them or is flaunting her new status. Whatever she does is either resented by her oversensitive friends and relatives or is cause for criticism or ridicule on the part of her husband's family. Similar trials, perhaps not quite so severe, await the man who marries "out of his class." This does not mean that marriages between members of different classes uniformly end in failure; many of these individuals are able to weather the stresses and trials and work out marital arrangements that endure. However, it is certain that interclass marriage partners face far more hazards than those who marry members of their own class, and a much higher proportion of interclass marriages end in divorce.

Difficulties in School. Allison Davis paints a grim picture of the fate of the lower-class children in the public schools, which almost universally subscribe to middle-class standards. The kind of behavior accepted in lower-class homes (see above) meets with punishment or criticism at school. Essentially these children are rejected for what they are — members of the lower class, who know no other behavior pattern. Partly for this reason, there is a tradition of hostility between members of the lower class and the school. Money is usually in short supply among slum-dwellers, tenant farmers, and migrant workers, and they frequently view the school as a device of "the bosses" to rob the poor of the income that might be received from a working child. Furthermore, they regard education and learning with suspicion and distrust. A child of the lower classes does not boast about good marks; instead, he boasts of how he made a fool of the teacher or how many aggressive acts he was able to commit without being caught. Or he may boast of how much punishment he was able to absorb. Inasmuch as the school is organized by the middle class to teach middle-class behavior standards, it is diametrically opposed to the behavior standards of the lower classes and makes no provision to meet the needs of lower-class children (22, 23). The result, as A. B. Hollingshead reports, is that lower-class children find in school an atmosphere that is both hostile and frustrating. They attend only because the law forces them to, and only as long as the law requires. Where attendance laws are loosely enforced, they will not attend at all. If a member of the lower class completes high school, it is because he has aspirations of becoming a member of the middle class (24).

Status Aspirations and Upward Mobility. Another very common adjustment problem is that of the individual who aspires to a higher social status. If social status is imagined as consisting only of money and possessions, unforeseen frustrations may result, as they did for the junk dealer who moved, during the war, from a home in the working-class district to one in the most socially acceptable district in the city. He had been on very friendly terms with his neighbors in his former place of residence, but he was completely unsuccessful in making social contact with his new neighbors. At first he was puzzled, then hostile, and later embittered and resentful. Whether an understanding of the social class system would have helped him to adjust to his new neighborhood is questionable, but it might have caused him to decide against such a move, and thus saved him much unhappiness.

The problem of tensions arising from "upward mobility" is also faced often by the worker who has completed high school and is employed as a skilled worker in an industrial plant. He wishes to be promoted but feels frustrated because the company has a policy of requiring college education as a prerequisite for all positions of higher status than his. This is a common situation, for there is an increasing tendency among employers to insist on and expect a college degree of persons who are hired as trainees for positions of responsibility or who are promoted to positions of responsibility. While this policy is not universal, there has been a marked trend toward it for many years.

Where the drive is strong, the frustrated individual will take night-school training and correspondence courses, or will leave his job to obtain higher education. Some individuals cannot bring themselves to make this sacrifice because of family obligations — small children, paying for a home and a car, etc. Others make the sacrifice in spite of these encumbrances. In both groups of individuals, tensions and anxieties increase — in the first group, because the way upward seems blocked by insurmountable obstacles, and in the second, because surmounting such obstacles involves physical and psychological strains, financial insecurity, and sacrifices by all members of the family.

Still another solution involves leaving the job and entering business on one's own. Millions of Americans do this, and the vast majority of them either fail or find that being one's own boss is not what they expected. Regardless of whether one succeeds or fails as an independent businessman, much frustration, tension, and anxiety result from attempting to cope with the insecurities, the long hours, and the disappointments of operating one's own business. It appears that if one strongly desires to rise in social status, frustrations, anxieties, and tensions will result, regardless of whether or not the attempt is made or how it is made.

Many are successful in attaining higher social status, for the middle class shows a marked increase in size each decade; but many fail and are embittered. Perhaps those who succeed do so because they realize that high status means more than merely making more money. They realize, for example, that the widest, most open, most available, and most traveled road up the social scale is education and that this is the surest way for the lower-class person to become middle-class and for the lower-middle-class person to become upper-middle-class. Whatever rewards accrue from a college education in the way of personal satisfaction, one of its chief advantages is that the college degree serves as a sort of stamp of approval — it certifies that the individual is entitled to provisional acceptance by middle-class members as a coparticipant in the middle-class culture.

Middle-class Values and Mental Health. We live in a society that, although divided into class levels, is actually dominated by a set of values largely middle-class in nature. Our laws, schools, government services, and international policies are colored largely by the values drawn from our middle-class ideology. Essentially we are a middle-class nation, and it has been our adherence to middle-class values — perseverance, hard work, practicality, utilitarianism, and good sense — that has made us the nation we are today. We take great pride in being what we are and in our ability to attain the goals we have set for ourselves, both as a nation and as individuals.

The problem as far as the individual is concerned is how to live within the framework of middle-class values and to reap the benefits that accrue from the middle-class way of life, but at the same time to minimize as much as possible the psychological wear and tear that results from competitive effort and striving for higher status. The emotionally abrasive effects of this never-ceasing struggle may be observed in the high incidence of psychoneurosis, psychosomatic disorders, anxiety, and general unhappiness. Our problem is not so much "how to eat our cake and have it," as it is how to live a comfortable, middle-class life and keep our anxiety level at a minimum. One of the surest ways to avoid raising our anxiety levels is to set goals for ourselves which are within reach and which may be reached with reasonable effort. Another way to avoid undue strain is to enjoy the goals we have successfully achieved for ourselves without continually setting new and more difficult ones to struggle toward.

The contribution of this chapter to this problem is largely one of attempting to acquaint the college student with some of the facts of the class structure, to help him understand how his very presence in college and how the time and energy that he is expending, are a part of his attempt to achieve and maintain the middle-class pattern of life. In many respects, the typical college student's goal is not a personal one, freely and privately chosen, but is rather the goal that his subcultural group has chosen for him. If he can accept the fact that he is unconsciously influenced by the values of his subculture, in this and other respects, this acceptance may be a starting point for other kinds of self-understanding.

SUMMARY

Social class and status are not easily discussed in our culture. We tend to reject the idea of class because it does not fit our concept of ourselves and of our society. On the other hand, certain phenomena, certain kinds of behavior, and certain personality traits are understandable only if we are aware of the dynamics of the social class structure. An understanding of the social class system is particularly important for the college student, inasmuch as his very presence in college is the result of a middle-class pattern of behavior which dominates his life and which compels him to seek to improve or maintain his status.

There is considerable evidence, experimental and otherwise, that demonstrates the existence of a class system in America. Much of this evidence comes from surveys in which people are asked to classify themselves and members of their community. There are data, too, that show how people from various social levels differ in their behavior and attitudes. Indeed, we would be surprised not to find a status system of some kind in America, since such systems are universal, existing even among some of the infrahuman animals. Status systems are necessary in a group situation of any complexity, because group members need someone to act as the leader and take responsibility for the welfare of the group. Leaders are drawn chiefly from the upper levels of the social status system.

The rewards in our social system are power, prestige, and wealth. However, they are not divided evenly according to social rank. For example, many lower-class individuals earn more money, at least on an hourly basis, than many middle-class persons. This discrepancy confuses middle-class people who are in this situation, since to them it represents a reversal of the natural order of things.

Financial rewards are actually incidental to the social structure. Wealth permits the upper classes to maintain their status, but it tends to be the result rather than the cause of their ascendancy. Research workers have found that there are characteristics more important than wealth in determining social status. Social stratification in the United States is reinforced by ethnic and religious differences, it permits mobility both up and down the social scale, and it is marked by caste barriers, which are used to restrict the activities of certain groups. The various classes distinguish themselves by certain well-defined personality traits. The lower-class group tends to be more impulsive and nonconforming; the middle-class group tends to be more restrained, status-conscious, and practical; the upper-class group tends to value family, ritual, and social functions.

The existence of class barriers tends to lead to misunderstanding, partly because the members of each class see the behavior of members of other classes as violations of their own class standards, and partly because there is a tendency to ignore the existence of the social distances separating the classes. Certain value patterns, like the emphasis on striving for success that marks the middle-class way of life, produce anxieties and other adjustment problems. There is a need for the student of mental hygiene to understand the dynamics of the social class system in order that he may become more aware of the forces that mold himself and his fellow men.

REFERENCES

1. B. Fine, *Democratic Education.* New York: Crowell, 1945. P. 176.
2. E. Roper, "Higher Education," a *Fortune* Survey, September, 1949.
3. R. Centers, "The American Class Structure," in T. M. Newcomb and E. L. Hartley, eds., *Readings in Social Psychology.* New York: Holt, 1947. Pp. 481–493.
4. A. Davis, B. B. Gardner, and M. R. Gardner, "The Class System of the White Caste," in T. M. Newcomb and E. L. Hartley, eds., *Readings in Social Psychology.* New York: Holt, 1947. Pp. 467–475.
5. W. L. Warner, M. Meeker, and K. Eells, *Social Class in America.* Chicago: Science Research, 1949.
6. W. L. Warner, M. Meeker, and K. Eells, "Social Status in Education," *The Phi Delta Kappan.* 30:113–119; 1948.
7. M. C. Ericson, "Social Status and Child-Rearing Practices," in T. M. Newcomb and E. L. Hartley, eds., *Readings in Social Psychology.* New York: Holt, 1947. Pp. 494–501.
8. E. Ginzberg, "Sex and Class Behavior," in D. P. Geddes and E. Curie, eds., *About the Kinsey Report.* New York: New American Library of World Literature, 1948. Pp. 131–145.
9. T. Schjeldruppe-Ebbe, "Social Behavior of Birds," in Carl Murchison, ed., *A Handbook of Social Psychology.* Worcester: Clark University Press, 1935. Chap. 20.
10. A. M. Guhl, "Heterosexual Dominance and Mating Behavior in Chickens," *Behavior.* 2:106–120; 1949.
11. F. W. Taussig and C. S. Joslyn, *American Business Leaders.* New York: Macmillan, 1932. P. 241.

12. P. A. Sorokin, "Leaders of Labor and Radical Movements in the United States and Foreign Countries," *American Journal of Sociology.* 33:382–411; 1927.
13. J. Carpenter and P. Eisenberg, "Some Relations between Family Background and Personality," *Journal of Psychology.* 6:115–136; 1938.
14. A. Davis, B. B. Gardner, and M. R. Gardner, "The Class System of the White Caste," in T. M. Newcomb and E. L. Hartley, eds., *Readings in Social Psychology.* New York: Holt, 1947. Pp. 467–475.
15. G. Landtman, *The Origin of the Inequality of the Social Classes.* Chicago: Chicago University Press, 1938.
16. Max Levin, "Status Anxiety and Occupational Choice," *Educational and Psychological Measurements.* 9:29–37; 1949.
17. W. L. Warner and P. S. Lunt, *The Social Life of a Modern Community.* New Haven: Yale University Press, 1941. Table reprinted by permission of Yale University Press.
18. J. H. S. Bossard, *The Sociology of Child Development.* New York: Harper, 1948. Pp. 287–289.
19. A. Davis, *Social-Class Influences upon Learning.* Cambridge: Harvard University Press, 1948. Pp. 22–37.
20. H. P. Fairchild, ed., *Dictionary of Sociology.* New York: Philosophical Library, 1944. P. 193. Reprinted by permission of the Philosophical Library.
21. C. M. Harsh and H. G. Schrickel, *Personality: Development and Assessment.* New York: Ronald, 1950. Pp. 195–196.
22. A. Davis, *Social-Class Influences upon Learning.* Cambridge: Harvard University Press, 1948. Pp. 22–34.
23. A. Davis, "What Happens to Students from Lower Socio-Economic Groups," in H. C. Lindgren, ed., *Proceedings of the Northern California Regional Conference on Counseling, Guidance, and Student Personnel Services, July 5–7, 1950.* San Francisco: San Francisco State College. Pp. 12–21.
24. A. B. Hollingshead, *Elmtown's Youth.* New York: Wiley, 1949. Chapter 13.

SUGGESTED READINGS

G. Wilson and G. Ryland, *Social Group Work Practice.* Boston: Houghton Mifflin, 1949. Pp. 147–150.
T. M. Newcomb, *Social Psychology.* New York: Dryden, 1950. Pp. 555–571.
S. S. Sargent, *Social Psychology.* New York: Ronald, 1950. Pp. 109–127.
A. Davis, "Child Training and Social Class," in R. G. Barker, *et al.*, eds., *Child Behavior and Development.* New York: McGraw-Hill, 1943. Pp. 607–619.
K. Davis, "Mental Hygiene and the Class Structure," in P. Mullahy, ed., *A Study of Interpersonal Relations.* New York: Hermitage, 1949. Pp. 364–385.

X... *What Happens in Groups*

Awareness of Interpersonal Actions and Reactions. Poets, writers, and philosophers have made much of the psychological fact that "no man is an island," * emphasizing the essential truth that without others we lose many of the qualities that make us "human." It is something of a discovery when we find this out, because looking at ourselves "from the inside in," so to speak, we tend to evaluate what we see in terms of our individual development patterns and experiences, rather than in terms of our relationships to others.

Yet it is impossible for a person to achieve a good psychological understanding of himself without becoming aware of the cause and effect of the *interpersonal forces* that affect his life and mold his personality. This aspect of our lives is something that we have difficulty in perceiving. It takes an alert, sensitive, and psychologically mature person to be aware of *what he does to others and what others do to him.* Usually we are so absorbed in playing our life roles and reacting to the roles of others that it does not occur to us to try to observe these processes objectively. At other times, it is in keeping with our more or less neurotic needs to ignore or distort what we do to others and what others do to us.

Let us consider the case of Joe Spellman, who goes to ask his boss for a raise.

JOE: Good morning, Mr. Barnes.
MR. B.: Good morning, Joe.
JOE: Do you have a couple of minutes, Mr. Barnes?
MR. B.: We-e-e-ll, yes, I suppose so.
JOE: Mr. Barnes, there is a little matter that I wanted to talk to you about . . . As a matter of fact, the wife and I were discussing it last night. We were going over the monthly bills, and it seemed to us that . . .

* John Donne, "Devotions upon Emergent Occasions," Meditation No. 17.

203

MR. B.: Joe, I'm glad that you stopped in this morning to see me, because there is something that *I* have had on my mind for some time. Been meaning to speak to you about it. It has to do with the lunch hour. Now I don't want to be unreasonable about this, but for the general morale of the office, I think it would be better if you would stick to the one-hour time allotment.

JOE: Oh, if you mean last week, there was a piece of curtain material that my wife . . .

MR. B.: It's not just last week. This has happened several times to my knowledge. Now I don't mind your taking company time on special occasions for some personal errand, providing you speak to me or your supervisor first. Is this unreasonable?

JOE: Well, no. But I sorta hate to bother you or Mr. Kringle. You're both so busy, and sometimes . . .

MR. B.: Never too busy to talk to an employee, Joe. Now, was there something you wanted to ask me about?

JOE: Er, yes. . . . (*Pause*) The fact is, Mr. Barnes, I was wondering whether I wasn't about due for a raise.

(*Long period of silence, while Mr. Barnes looks out the window and Joe fidgets. Finally, Mr. Barnes turns to Joe.*)

MR. B.: Well, Joe, with business conditions the way they are now, it doesn't seem too likely. Furthermore, the Board of Directors has tied my hands by taking over complete power to grant raises. The best I can do is to place your case before them at the next meeting. But I can't promise anything. Anything else?

JOE: No, I guess not. Thank you, Mr. Barnes.

MR. B.: Not at all, Joe.

The following conversation took place over the supper dishes at the Spellmans' that night:

MRS. S.: Did you ask the boss for a raise, Joe?

JOE: Yes. Not much luck, I'm afraid.

MRS. S.: Didn't you tell him that you were fed up with him and the whole company and were going to look for another job?

JOE: Well, no, I guess I didn't.

MRS. S.: You *guess* you didn't! Look, Joe, didn't we decide last night that unless you got a $10-a-week raise, you couldn't stand to work for Barnes another minute!

JOE: Yes, I know, honey, but Barnes isn't so bad. He has a lot of good points.

MRS. S.: Humph! Well, what *did* you tell him?

Joe: Well, I *started* to tell him how we . . . gosh, honey, I don't know for sure *what* all I said.

Mrs. S.: (*sarcastically*) Well, that's fine! And what did *he* say when you told him whatever it was that you can't remember?

Joe: Well, he got off the track and started talking about . . . gosh, honey, why do you pick on me? *You* don't have to face old Barnes and talk him out of a raise. . . .

The fact is, Joe Spellman's memory of his interview with Mr. Barnes is somewhat blurred. He not only is unsure of the details of his conversation with Mr. Barnes, but, what is more important, he does not know what Mr. Barnes *did* to him and what he *did* to Mr. Barnes. In other words, he does not know what he did or said to cause Mr. Barnes to react in the way that he did, and he does not know what it was that Mr. Barnes said or did that caused him (Joe) to react in the way *he* did. Joe is not aware of the following sequence of interpersonal events — what *really* happened during his interview:

Joe's Behavior	Mr. Barnes' Behavior
Background. In some ways he wonders whether he really deserves a raise; on the other hand he feels that he is as entitled to it as some of his friends who work for other companies and who make more than he does. Yet he probably would not have made this request if his wife had not egged him on.	*Background.* His self-concept is that of a kindly and paternalistic individual who knows what is best for his employees. He does not look favorably on requests for raises. He likes to feel that *he* will decide what is just and proper without suggestions or promptings from his subordinates. Thus it is difficult for employees to communicate with him; he is distant and detached. He expects his employees to be afraid of him, yet he rather despises them for their fear. In contradiction to this, he *also* sees himself as ready and eager to talk to his employees about their problems.
1. His uneasiness is apparent; he hates to ask for a raise; he is afraid of Mr. Barnes and shows it.	1. He is aware from Joe's manner that Joe is going to ask for some sort of favor, probably a raise.

2. He couches his opening in halting phrases, saying, in effect, "Do you, so busy and important, have time for such an unimportant fellow like me?"

3. Joe stumbles around looking for an opening, much awed by Mr. Barnes' power and majesty.

4. Joe goes on the defensive, even though he had felt at the time that he had a right to the extra fifteen minutes of the lunch hour.

5. Joe says, in effect: (a) "It is humiliating to ask for minor favors." (b) "My superiors do not make themselves easily accessible."

6. Joe hesitates, tries in vain to recall his strategy (to threaten to quit), and blurts out his request.

2. Mr. Barnes accepts the implications that he is important and that Joe is unimportant. However, as a noble gesture, he finds that he can spare a few minutes.

3. He takes advantage of Joe's low opinion of himself by seizing the initiative; he puts Joe in his place by calling his attention to a minor infraction of the rules. This is a way of punishing Joe for daring to ask for a raise.

4. Mr. Barnes emphasizes the status system in the office, which requires that lower ranking people seek approval of their superiors for deviations from accepted practice.

5. Mr. Barnes waves Joe's objections aside with platitudes that reflect his opinion of himself as a person eager to talk to employees. He then permits Joe to make his request.

6. He scuttles Joe's request with another platitude. However, he recognizes that Joe's plea may have merit and promises to take this up with a higher authority. If Joe doesn't get his raise, it is because of a socially distant group, who, in turn, may very likely "pass the buck" on to "business conditions." If Joe *does* get his raise, it will be because Mr. Barnes magnanimously pleaded Joe's case. In any event, the decision will not be determined on the basis of Joe's merits but on the basis of the favor or disfavor of the persons in authority.

Joe Spellman's difficulties with Mr. Barnes demonstrate a lack of awareness that we all experience where the really important undercurrents of our lives are concerned. Part of this unawareness is because of our tendency to focus on the things that we believe are causing us the most anxiety. Thus Joe was very much concerned with (a) the social distance that separated him from Mr. Barnes, (b) the fact that his wife expected him to come home with a raise, and (c) anxieties and guilt feelings regarding his competency as an employee. As a result, he was unable to perceive the underlying causes of either his behavior or that of Mr. Barnes. Mr. Barnes, on the other hand, was concerned primarily with playing his role as a person of status and power and with maintaining what he considered to be the proper employer-employee relationship between Joe and himself. Because each was largely concerned with himself, neither would be able to give an accurate and objective account of the incident, particularly of the unspoken parts of the interview.

There is another way of describing what happened between Joe and Mr. Barnes. In social situations, the behavior of one individual evokes the behavior of another. Each is aware of the *behavior* but is unaware of the *motivation*, or the reason for the behavior. If we were to ask Mr. Barnes what occurred during the interview, he might say, "Joe asked me for a raise, and I told him that there was not much chance of his getting one." But Mr. Barnes would not be aware of Joe's motives, nor would Joe be aware of Mr. Barnes's motives, since each was concerned with reacting to the behavior (but not the motives) of the other.

In these respects, neither Joe Spellman nor Mr. Barnes differs markedly from the rest of us. The ability to be objective and perceptive where interpersonal relations are concerned is a skill that is acquired with difficulty. Yet it is a kind of skill worth acquiring if we seriously intend to improve our understanding of ourselves and our relations with others.

The Role of Interpersonal Relations. Interpersonal relations play such an intimate function in our lives that they may be regarded as a kind of barometer of our level of adjustment to life in general. The more we are plagued by guilt and neurotic anxiety, the more our relations with others suffer. In turn, guilt and neurotic anxiety are both caused and aggravated by friction developed in our relations with others.

The experiences of infancy and childhood that make us what we are today are essentially interpersonal in nature. The feelings and reactions that our parents and the other members of our family develop toward us form the foundations of our self-structure, and the expectations that we come to have for ourselves are more or less faithful facsimiles of the expectations others have for us. These concepts are, in turn, expressed through the roles we play. As we go through life, both our self-concepts and our roles may be modified by each new group with which we become intimately involved.

Larry Jones, who was five years old, played the role of a very proper little boy — one who spoke precisely, was neat and clean, and who seemed "old for his age." He was the only child of upper-middle-class parents, who spent much time with him. He occasionally played with other children in the neighborhood, but these experiences usually led to difficulties. Larry found the other children rough and noisy, and he was disturbed when they took his toys or tried to "roughhouse" with him. Larry played the role of a proper little boy, because this was what his parents expected of him and what he expected of himself. Other children rejected him because he did not participate easily in their kind of play, and they were unable to get along easily and comfortably with a child who was "old for his age."

Today, four years later, Larry is quite a different boy. His clothes are rumpled and dirty, and his room, once so neat, is a jumble of clothing, toys, and books. He is constantly in trouble at home for climbing over the furniture and running through the house. Most of his free time is spent with other boys in the neighborhood climbing trees, playing baseball, or riding bicycles.

Several factors have caused the change in Larry, not the least of which is the enforced association with a large number of boys at school. When Larry first went to school, he continued to play his role of the child "old for his age." At first he did not mind being snubbed by other boys; he either played by himself or with girls. After a while, he began to find this a lonely way of life, and within a few months he was playing with the boys in his class. They poked fun at his use of "fancy words" and made it clear that people who kept their clothes neat and clean and who knew all the answers in class were "sissies." When he learned this, Larry was eager to prove that he was no sissy.

The change in Larry's self-concept and role was largely brought about by his becoming intimately involved in a group whose expectations for its members were different from those of the group (his family) whose standards he had accepted until then. As it became important for him to adjust to the new group, he modified his expectations of himself; and this, in turn, resulted in the changes in his self-structure and his pattern of behavior, or role.

Larry was fortunate in that he was able to adjust to the demands of the group in which he sought membership. However, if he had continued to meet with rebuffs and rejection from them, the resulting anxiety would have appeared in some form of symptom. For example, he might have become moody and withdrawn, or he might have attempted to play the role of "smart aleck" in class as a way of attracting attention and showing that he did not want to be a sissy, or he might have become unruly at home. These are a few of the ways in which children express the anxieties that grow out of difficulties in interpersonal relations. The emotional health of adults is equally dependent on the state of their interpersonal relations. Many an employee has lost sleep because the boss neglected to say "Good morning"; and our outlook on life is often made brighter just because someone drops a word of praise about our appearance or the quality of our work.

Needs Are Met through Association with Others.   Since interpersonal relations are so important to us, it is not surprising that much of our activity is concerned with seeking the company and the approval of others. Even most of our basic needs are directly or indirectly satisfied through association with others. For example, the need for food can be met more effectively through the co-operative action of the group than by the individual foraging alone. The need for love, which is so important for the maintenance of physical and emotional health, can be satisfied only through a group arrangement of some sort. The most common of these arrangements is the family, which exists largely to provide emotional support and love to its members.

The higher level needs, those of status, respect, self-expression and creativity, are equally involved in group processes. An individual may assign himself status and value, but he does so largely in terms of what he has learned from his associates. A creative project, like a painting or an essay or a well-laid brick wall, may be carried out alone, but chief among the resulting satisfactions are those arising from the praise and appreciation of others. And communication itself, which is the commonest form of self-expression, requires an audience.

Communication is, in fact, the cement that holds groups together. People associate with one another in order to communicate feelings and ideas, and one of the criteria for a well-knit, satisfying (cohesive) group is that its members express themselves freely without fear of unjust criticism or rejection. One of the crucial tests of the group relationship we call friendship consists of the extent to which friends can speak to one another honestly, without risk of severing the relationship.

Groups also help us to learn more about our environment. By associating with others, we have the advantage of drawing on their experiences. In fact, we are so in the habit of using the eyes, ears, and memories of others that we often accept their statements at face value, without checking on their accuracy. We get along as well as we do because a sufficient amount of what we are told is both useful and true.

In addition to giving us the opportunity for widening the scope of our knowledge of our environment, groups also provide the means of carrying on various sorts of activities. Some groups are organized largely for friendly social contact — for example, bridge clubs, fraternities, picnics, tea parties, and bull sessions. Other groups have specialized activities as their purpose — athletic teams, professional societies, hobby clubs, churches, and unions. Still other groups are organized to attack, defend, or preserve — police squads, armies, the Women's Christian Temperance Union, lynching parties, and the Civil Liberties Union. Some groups are informal and relatively simple in structure, like the students who gather in clusters between classes to smoke cigarettes and talk about their last class. Other groups are more highly organized and complex, with well-defined status systems — occupational groups, schools, military organizations, and the government civil service. Few groups can be classified as "pure types"; most of them combine several functions. For example, a professional society may exist for the avowed purpose of encouraging research, but it can also provide its members with status and social contact, and may, on occasion, be used to attack or defend some right or privilege.

For most of us, the chief values of group life are highly personal ones. Often the special functions of groups are less important to

In the relaxed atmosphere of a small, friendly group, it is easy to discuss anything from the latest in make-up and hair-dos to the serious problems of getting along with husbands and boy friends.

us than their ability to provide us with emotionally sustaining experiences. If we are successful in our group relations, we find that we are better able to bear life's burdens. Through discussing our problems with others, we find ourselves moving closer to solutions. Difficult tasks seem lighter after we have shared our anxieties. Similarly, by listening to the difficulties of others, we help them — and then discover that we feel better about our own immediate problems. Thus, through group experiences of this kind, we renew our faith in each other and in ourselves.

The Dynamics of the Group

Goals and Purposes of the Group. The individuals who make up groups join them, as we have indicated above, in order to meet certain needs. However, once groups are formed, they often develop characteristics that are not identical with the characteristics of the individuals who compose them. In some ways, a group is like a person. It has a life span; it has stages of immaturity, maturity, and decay. When the group is "healthy," it is characterized by cohesiveness and high morale; the "unhealthy" group is marked by poor morale, dissension, and disintegrative tendencies.

When a group is functioning well (is "healthy"), it is moving in the direction of achieving its aims or goals. These goals may not be the ones for which the group was formed in the first place, or they may not even be the avowed goals of the members.

A group of high school girls formed a society called the Aidettes, for the purpose of assisting needy students in some vague, undetermined way. After they had been in existence a short time, they found that it was hard to determine who was a needy student and that, whoever needy students were, they never asked for help. So the Aidettes realized that they needed some other function for their group. They then decided that their purpose would be to "promote the American way of life." When they visited the high school principal to tell him of their plans and ask him how they might achieve their goal, he said that he was not sure, but that his biggest problem was to find some way of completing a special statistical survey that the superintendent wanted. Since no funds were available for hiring extra clerical help, he was being forced to spend week ends and evenings doing it himself. The Aidettes volunteered to do the work and completed it quite successfully, even though it took much of their spare time over a period of several weeks.

We would say that this is an example of a healthy group. This group attacked the solution of a problem with enthusiasm and success, although it was originally formed for a purpose different from the final goal.

The example we have given is that of a group which organized itself, which selected its own goals, and which voluntarily accepted responsibility for a problem and worked out the solution largely within the confines of the group. The morale of this kind of group — a group that starts spontaneously — is usually quite high, because it is free to select its own goals.

A more common example of spontaneous group formation is that which appears when individuals become aware of a threatening situation and form an organization to protect themselves and their interests. It does not matter whether the threat is real or imagined; as long as the members *feel* that the threat is real and present, they will postpone the gratifications of individual and personal needs and will submerge tendencies that are in conflict with the purposes of the group. This singleness of purpose will persist as long as threat is perceived as real and immediate. However, when group members no longer perceive threat in this way, there is a tendency for the group to disintegrate, unless some other force holds it together. Morale studies conducted by the Army during World War II showed that the solidarity of a fighting unit increased under actual combat conditions, and that hostility toward superiors decreased and favorable attitudes increased (up to a point) with exposure to danger (1).

Groups that are convened and directed by an external authority often find morale a difficult problem, particularly if the leaders pay little attention to the needs of the group and if group members are not permitted to participate in the making of decisions that affect them. Ronald Lippitt and Robert K. White observed this phenomenon in their celebrated study of autocratic, democratic, and laissez-faire leadership. Lippitt and White found that boys' clubs under autocratic leadership acted in less mature ways — they displayed overdependency, were easily frustrated, and sometimes showed aggression toward weaker members — than did groups under democratic leadership. At the opposite extreme, when the leader displayed little responsibility or interest in the activities of the group, morale again decreased and signs of immaturity increased (2). When we analyze this study, it seems apparent that the morale of the groups was high when the members felt that they were achieving the aims of the group and that it was low when they felt that the leader was imposing his aims and ignoring theirs, or was detached and uninterested and thus did not give them the help or the emotional support they needed.

Cohesiveness in Groups. In order for a group to achieve its goals and to satisfy the needs of its members, it must be cohesive. That is, it must possess qualities that will cause its members to come together in a tightly knit group organized for the purpose of meeting common goals. If the group is cohesive, its members will be willing to by-pass individual needs in conflict with the group goals. Since such decisions, whether conscious or unconscious, involve some sacrifice, it is obvious that either the goals of the group or the needs that can be met through the group must be felt by the members to be highly important.

For example, during the recent war, persons who otherwise would not have consented to donate blood did so because they wanted their office or their shop to have a 100 per cent record. They did this in spite of considerable fear and anxiety, because it was important to them to maintain status with their group and because they felt that such a sacrifice would aid the winning of the war. And the more cohesive the group, the easier it was for the members to make this sacrifice.

The satisfactions individuals find in group life are enhanced by the cohesiveness of the group. D. G. Marquis and others, in making a survey of conferences in which decisions were made, found that the satisfactions of the participants increased in accordance with the cohesiveness of the group and decreased according to the lack of cohesiveness — that is, they decreased when members were concerned with their individual needs, rather than with the needs of the group (3).

Productivity of groups is also related to cohesiveness. A study by K. W. Back shows that members of groups that rate high in cohesion make more efforts to reach agreement and are more effective in reaching agreement than are members of groups that rate low in cohesion. He noted that in groups where cohesion was low, members acted independently and with little consideration for each other. There was no attempt in such groups for members to accommodate the opinions of others; they were, instead, concerned with their own needs for self-expression (4).

When individuals form groups, they generate strong forces that produce the cohesiveness needed for satisfactory operation of the group. These forces express themselves through inducing a certain uniformity or unanimity of attitude, action, or opinion with regard to matters of importance to the group. As Leon Festinger and others have found, the more individuals deviate from the standards set by the group, the more the other members of the group try to get them to conform (5). Naturally, if this process does not succeed and if a sufficient number of members refuse to conform, the group does not become cohesive and its effectiveness is impaired.

The Importance of Norms. Groups that have some permanence usually develop norms or standards of attitudes and behavior to which members are expected to conform. The norm becomes the "test of membership." If an individual is interested in maintaining his membership in the group, he will conform to its norms; otherwise, he will be subjected to pressures either to conform or to leave the group. If we are vitally interested in a group, we usually have little difficulty in conforming; and, in actual practice, we are largely unaware that we are conforming at all and even come to believe that the standards we have taken over from the group are actually ones that we developed ourselves.

S. E. Asch conducted an experiment that demonstrates this principle. He asked students to judge the proportionate lengths of various pairs of lines. When students were placed in groups that had been previously instructed to give the wrong answers, a large percentage of their judgments erred in the direction of the answers of the majority. Error increased as the differences between the two lines became less. Some persons always yielded to the majority, no matter how obvious the error was (6). Well-established group norms have more effect on the thoughts and activities of individuals than do directives of leaders. For instance, R. W. Berenda found that children were more influenced by the alleged opinions of other children than they were by teachers' opinions (7).

The chief functions of norms are to help groups to become cohesive and to provide bases for achieving unanimity. In accepting the norms of the group, the member gives up some of his individuality in exchange for the advantages of membership.

The Function of Roles. Roles divide themselves roughly into two classes: those we learn in childhood, which persist in some form throughout our lives, and those we learn at any age. Sometimes the latter are in conflict with roles learned in childhood.

The family is the first group with which the child comes in contact. It is within this setting that he learns some of the roles he will play, with major or minor variations, throughout life.

Frank Levy was an oldest child and thus received the full effect, for a while, of parental love, hopes, expectations, and anxieties. As other siblings appeared in the home, he lost his "place in the sun." He tried to compensate for this in part by imitating his father — by dominating the behavior of his brothers and sisters. In this role he was a sort of "junior father," who competed, in effect, with his own father. As an adult, Frank attempted to dominate his associates much as he had his brothers and sisters. He often found himself attempting to compete with established leaders in certain subtle ways, somewhat as he had tried to compete with his own father. His tendencies to act like an older brother were brought home to him in a particularly effective manner when those he tried to dominate proved "unco-operative," just as his brothers and sisters had proved "unco-operative." Because Frank was able to realize the effect his behavior had on others, he was able to modify it to some degree and thus avoid some of his difficulties.

Not all of the roles we play in groups are "made-over" roles we have inherited from our childhood. Often they are dictated by the immediate situation or the needs of the groups in which we find ourselves. The story of Larry Watts will serve as an example of the latter kind of role.

Larry Watts went to work as a junior copy writer in a small advertising agency after he was graduated from college. Mr. Simpkins, the owner and manager of the agency, was disliked by his staff for a number of reasons. He was inconsiderate, autocratic, and dictatorial. His employees often said that if advertising jobs were easy to get they wouldn't work another day for Mr. Simpkins. They cordially hated him and despised themselves for not having the courage to quit.

For reasons unknown to Larry, Mr. Simpkins took a liking to him. He always took occasion during the weekly staff meetings to praise Larry's work, and he admonished the others to do as well as Larry did. The effect of this was to erect a barrier between Larry and the other employees. They took to playing practical jokes on Larry; and, when things went wrong, it somehow turned out to be Larry's fault. Thus, through no fault of his own, Larry found himself cast in the role of the office scapegoat, and as such was the recipient of much of the bad feelings generated by his boss.

An interesting discussion of roles is presented by Kenneth D. Benne and Paul Sheats as their contribution to a symposium entitled "The Dynamics of the Discussion Group (8)." Benne and Sheats observe that there are roles that aid groups in selecting, defining, and solving problems common to the members of the group — those of the initiator-contributor, the information seeker, the opinion seeker, the information giver, the elaborator, the co-ordinator, the orienter, the evaluator-critic, the energizer, the procedural technician, and the recorder. Although these roles are primarily identified with the discussion group, they may be observed in other kinds of groups attempting to solve problems. Of course, one person may play any combination of these roles over a period of time, although there is a tendency for individuals to "specialize" in certain roles. Some of the other roles which Benne and Sheats identify and which may be found in all kinds of groups are the encourager, the harmonizer, the compromiser, the standard setter, the commentator, and the follower.

The roles listed so far have to do with building and maintaining the group and aiding it to carry on its work. But there are roles which persons play in response to their individual self-centered needs, roles which do not further the welfare of the group. Benne and Sheats classify such roles as follows: the aggressor, the blocker, the recognition seeker, the self-confessor, the playboy, the dominator, the help seeker, and the special-interest pleader. When we play these roles, it is because we are unable to suppress our self-seeking needs in the interest of the group. Roles of this sort reduce the cohesiveness and the effectiveness of the group. By way of illustration, when D. Rosenthal and C. N. Cofer "planted" an individual in a group and instructed him not to participate, they found that the entire group became less willing to co-operate (9).

Disruptive Roles. Some of the individualistic roles listed above may be merged into a single role, such as that of the "saboteur." John Hellman usually plays this type of role in the groups with which he associates.

When John was a child, his parents were never sure of how to handle him; they tried to compromise by alternating between firmness and indulgence. This policy was unsuccessful, because John learned at an early age that he could control his parents through temper tantrums. As he grew older, he continued this behavior in modified form. Although screaming and shouting did not enable him to have his way at school, this behavior did get attention from his teachers and even a certain amount of admiration from his schoolmates because of his willingness to defy adults. By the time John became an adolescent, he had learned not to scream and shout, because his friends did not tolerate such behavior. Instead, he learned that he could express his hostile feelings by objecting to proposals made by the leaders of the group and by encouraging noncooperation. He became active in stimulating opposition to the leadership by gossiping, "griping," and criticizing. So effective was his opposition that groups with which he associated were noted for their inability to complete and carry out plans. After a while, his fraternity brothers learned that if they planned to go fishing, they had to keep it from John, because if he were included in their plans, he would find fault with all the fishing places they suggested or would raise irrelevant objections, with the result that they would usually have to give up the idea. When the fraternity planned to give a dance, those members most interested in the project had difficulty in maintaining the support of the other members of the fraternity, because John would go out of his way to persuade them that the plans were defective.

The role of the "exhibitionist" is sometimes as distracting as that of the saboteur. Exhibitionists glow, scintillate, and dramatize themselves in their never-ending search for attention and approval. Sometimes they depreciate themselves and sometimes they are comical. But the goal is always the same: an attentive and appreciative audience.

Jane Semple was a second child. She was pretty and people tended to make comparisons between her and her older sister. Her older sister dealt with this competition by becoming a model child and excelling in school. Their childhood was marked by periodic skirmishes, each using her favorite technique to attract parental approval. Jane turned out to be a reasonably attractive girl, and she made the most of her assets by dramatizing herself. The groups she joined liked her initially, but found that she tended to monopolize their time and attention with trivial, inconsequential matters. Leaders and more serious members of groups resented the necessity of competing with her for the attention of the group, with the result that Jane frequently felt rejected in groups that took their purposes seriously. On the other hand, she was tolerated and appreciated in groups whose chief purpose was social enjoyment.

The Role of the Leader. According to the dictates of "common sense," there are certain persons who possess the qualities of leadership and who will be the ones to emerge as leaders in any given situation. Some psychologists, however, see leadership as a product of the social situation. Irving Knickerbocker, for example, sees leadership as "the functional relationship which . . . exists when a leader is perceived by a group as controlling the means for the satisfaction of their needs (10)." Thus he sees the leader as someone who is endowed with leadership by the group rather than as someone who happens to possess an attractive combination of personal qualities. On the other hand, R. M. Stogdill points out that the *organization* of a group may have much to do with the kind of leader it produces (11). A group organized along democratic lines would thus tend to produce a democratic leader, whereas an authoritarian structure would result in an authoritarian leader. Some support is found for the "common sense" position in the study by Graham B. Bell and Robert L. French of the consistency with which the same persons play leadership roles in different groups. As a result of their research, the experimenters concluded that leadership may not be entirely the result of the psychological situation (12).

J. K. Hemphill conducted a survey in which 500 respondents described what they felt were the things that characterized leaders of all types of groups:

1. The ability of the leader to advance the purposes of the group.
2. Administrative competence.
3. Pace-setting and motivating activity.
4. Contribution to the member's feeling of security about his place in the group.
5. Freedom from activities serving only his own interests (13).

Although this survey serves to confirm the "common sense" belief of the man in the street, who sees leadership largely as a matter of personal qualities, both the situational and the organizational aspects of leadership are also implicit in the above list of characteristics. In all probability, leaders are persons who possess certain personal qualities, who are perceived by their groups as leaders, and who are able to provide the kind of leadership consistent with the organization of their group.

Appointed and Elected Leaders. There are, roughly speaking, two kinds of leaders, those who are designated by some higher authority and those who are selected by the group. In the former category are teachers, scoutmasters, army officers, and various kinds of supervisory personnel; in the latter category are leaders who serve through the tacit agreement of group members or as the result of formal elections.

The appointed leader starts with an initial disadvantage, particularly when the group feels, unconsciously or otherwise, that it has played no part in his choice and thus is more or less free to decide whether it will co-operate with him. This situation exists even in military situations, where individuals are technically not supposed to have freedom of choice as to whether they will obey. Yet, in actuality, some military leaders are highly successful in obtaining the co-operation and obedience of their subordinates, and others are not.

The group that elects its own leader feels, at least initially, under some obligation to co-operate. Hence the elected leader begins with a backlog of good will, which gives him an advantage over the leader selected by an external authority. Whether or not he uses this advantage effectively will depend on a number of factors, not the least of which is his way of using his leadership.

The importance of the latter factor is demonstrated by an experiment conducted by Malcolm G. Preston and Roy K. Heintz. These experimenters split a group of eighty-three students into subgroups of four or five, and asked each subgroup to elect a leader. Half the leaders so selected were instructed to participate with their subgroups in solving an assigned problem, and the other half were instructed to supervise their group but not to participate in solving an assigned problem. Preston and Heintz found that the participating leaders were more effective in bringing about necessary changes in the attitudes of the subgroup members. Subgroups operating under the leadership of supervising leaders tended to resist the formation of a strong subgroup opinion. Furthermore, subgroups under participating leadership were more satisfied with the results of their work, were more likely to find the task interesting and meaningful, and were more likely to look upon themselves as efficient and productive (14). Similar conclusions were reached by Norman R. F. Maier, who found that leaders untrained in democratic processes were unable to get discussion groups to accept certain solutions to the problems under discussion, even when the proposed solutions were superior to those developed in the course of group discussion. On the other hand, leaders trained in democratic methods were much more successful in helping groups reach superior solutions to the same problems (15).

Although much depends on the personal qualities and skill of the appointed leader, as well as on the circumstances of his appointment and the prevailing climate of the organization at large, he usually tends to be more or less authoritarian. The more authoritarian the leader, the greater the difficulty in communication, and this holds true whether we refer to communication among group members or to communication between groups and leaders. And the more difficulty the group experiences in communication, the more difficulty it has in maintaining morale and cohesion.

When, however, the security and welfare of the group are threatened, morale and cohesion may be quickly restored. Some authoritarian leaders therefore see to it that the situation is always threatening. Hitler was able to maintain his control over a large segment of the German people partly through the expedient of painting word pictures of a Germany threatened from without by the rest of the world and from within by the Jews.

The democratic leader serves only at the sufferance of his group and is thus much closer socially and emotionally to the members. He *participates* in the making of group decisions, instead of retaining this function for himself. He is acquainted with the needs and goals of the group, for he has kept the lines of communication open between the group members and himself. Under such leadership, groups maintain their morale at a high level; they are effective and productive; and the individuals who constitute such groups find their membership satisfying and rewarding.

SUMMARY

Although interpersonal forces play an essential function in our lives, we are usually unaware of them. For example, we are usually unaware of what we *really* do to others and what they *really* do to us.

The story of Joe Spellman and Mr. Barnes illustrates how two people can interact and still be unaware of the real bases of their interaction.

The way we get along with others constitutes a key to our general level of emotional adjustment. Our personality patterns were formed by the interpersonal relations of childhood. Many of our basic needs are met directly or indirectly through association with others, and the emotionally mature individual needs association with others to maintain mental health.

Groups have psychological lives of their own. They have stages of maturity and immaturity; they may be "healthy" or "unhealthy." When they are healthy, or functioning efficiently, they are meeting the needs of the individuals who compose them. Under such conditions morale is high and groups are cohesive. The more cohesive a group, the more productive it is likely to be, and the easier it is for its constituent members to reach unanimity of opinion. On the other hand, the perception of a threatening situation also may result in an increase in morale and cohesiveness. At such times, there is a banding together against the common danger.

Groups develop norms or standards of behavior and belief as a way of encouraging solidarity or as a test of membership. The norms developed in this way have such a powerful effect on the thinking of group members that perception frequently may be distorted if reality conflicts with the group norm. The individual who conforms to the norm symbolizes his acceptance of the group, for by doing so he gives up some of his individuality in exchange for group membership.

Individuals in groups sometimes play roles that they have learned in childhood. However, the group itself may assign roles to individuals. Some roles grow out of functions necessary in maintaining the group and in aiding it toward its goals. An example of such a role is that of the leader. Other roles are more disruptive and are played by individuals unable to accept the group. Among the latter are the roles of the saboteur and the exhibitionist.

Leadership is a quality that is in part a product of the group situation — that is, leaders are people who derive their power from the willingness of others to follow them. However, some persons tend to become leaders because they have the personal qualities considered characteristic of leadership and because the organizational pattern of the group permits leadership to be assigned to such persons.

Leaders who are appointed by external authorities usually have different problems from those who are elected by the group. Appointed leaders often have greater difficulty in developing morale and cohesion because the groups they are appointed to lead may have reservations about accepting them. The leader who is selected by the group and who participates in the group processes has a better chance for success.

REFERENCES

1. E. A. Shils, "Primary Groups in the American Army," in R. K. Merton and P. F. Lazarsfeld, eds., *Continuities in Social Research.* Glencoe, Illinois: Free Press, 1950. Pp. 16–39.
2. R. Lippitt and R. K. White, "An Experimental Study of Leadership and Group Life," in T. M. Newcomb and E. L. Hartley, eds., *Readings in Social Psychology.* New York: Holt, 1947. Pp. 315–330.
3. D. G. Marquis, *et al.*, "A Social Psychological Study of the Decision-Making Conference," in H. Guetzkow, ed., *Groups, Leadership, and Men.* New Brunswick, N. J.: Rutgers University Press, 1951. Pp. 55–67.
4. K. W. Back, "Influence through Social Communication," *Journal of Abnormal and Social Psychology.* 46:9–23; 1951.
5. L. Festinger, *et al.*, *Theory and Experiment in Social Communication.* Ann Arbor: Research Center for Group Dynamics, 1950.
6. S. E. Asch, "Effects of Group Pressure upon the Modification and Distortion of Judgments," in H. Guetzkow, ed., *Groups, Leadership, and Men.* New Brunswick, N. J.: Rutgers University Press, 1951. Pp. 177–190.
7. R. W. Berenda, *The Influence of the Group on the Judgments of Children.* New York: King's Crown Press, 1950.
8. K. D. Benne and P. Sheats, "Functional Roles of Group Members," *Journal of Social Issues.* 4(2):4–49; 1948.
9. D. Rosenthal and C. N. Cofer, "The Effect on Group Performance of an Indifferent and Neglectful Attitude Shown by One Group Member," *Journal of Experimental Psychology.* 38:568–577; 1948.
10. I. Knickerbocker, "Leadership: A Conception and Some Implications," *Journal of Social Issues.* 4(3):23–40; 1948.
11. R. M. Stogdill, "Leadership, Membership, and Organization," *Psychological Bulletin.* 47:1–14; 1950.
12. G. B. Bell and R. L. French, "Consistency of Individual Leadership Position in Small Groups of Varying Membership," *Journal of Abnormal and Social Psychology.* 45:764–767; 1950.
13. J. K. Hemphill, *Situational Factors in Leadership.* Ohio State University Studies, Bureau of Education, Research Monograph, No. 32; 1949.

14. M. G. Preston and R. K. Heintz, "Effects of Participatory versus Supervisory Leadership on Group Judgment," *Journal of Abnormal and Social Psychology.* 44:345–355; 1949.

15. N. R. F. Maier, "The Quality of Group Decisions as Influenced by the Discussion Leader," *Human Relations.* 3:155–174; 1950.

SUGGESTED READINGS

T. M. Newcomb, *Social Psychology.* New York: Dryden, 1950. Although the entire book is pertinent to the subject of this chapter, Section III, dealing with social norms and roles, and Section V, dealing with group membership, are especially worth reading.

T. M. Newcomb and E. L. Hartley, eds., *Readings in Social Psychology.* New York: Holt, 1947. See sections on group situations, role and status, and leadership.

S. S. Sargent, *Social Psychology.* New York: Ronald, 1950. See Section III.

S. H. Britt, *Selected Readings in Social Psychology.* New York, Rinehart, 1950. See selections on group differences, group functioning, crowd behavior, critical social situations, social norms, fads and fashions, leadership, and morale.

S. H. Britt, *Social Psychology of Modern Life,* Rev. edition. New York: Rinehart, 1949. Most of this book deals directly or indirectly with the phenomena of group behavior. Sections IV and V deal with behavior in the presence of others and the social psychology of institutions.

H. Cantril, *The Psychology of Social Movements.* New York: Wiley, 1941. A lucid discussion of the forces that motivate individuals to seek groups precedes a description of such social movements as the lynching party, the Townsend Plan, and the Nazi party.

D. Krech and R. S. Crutchfield, *Theory and Problems of Social Psychology.* New York: McGraw-Hill, 1948. Chapter 11 deals with theories relating to group morale and leadership.

M. Sherif, *An Outline of Social Psychology.* New York: Harper, 1948. Sherif is a recognized authority on the formation of social norms and "reference groups."

J. H. Rohrer and M. Sherif, eds., *Social Psychology at the Crossroads.* New York: Harper, 1951. A series of papers on various aspects of social psychology. See section on group structures and individual roles.

G. C. Homans, *The Human Group.* New York: Harcourt, Brace, 1950. A sociologist comments on some basic studies of various types of groups: informal, occupational, primitive, etc.

H. Guetzkow, ed., *Groups, Leadership, and Men.* New Brunswick, N. J.: Rutgers University Press, 1951. A series of papers and experiments covering research in the field of human relations.

F. J. Roethlisberger, *Management and Morale,* Cambridge: Harvard University Press, 1941. A discussion of principles of leadership and group behavior in the setting of business and industry.

H. H. Jennings, *Leadership and Isolation,* 2d edition. New York: Longmans, 1950. A study, using the method of sociometry, of interpersonal choices made by girls at a correctional institution.

H. C. Lindgren, *The Art of Human Relations*. New York: Hermitage, 1953. See Chapters 9, 10, and 11 for a discussion of some of the problems and conflicts that arise when people associate with each other and form groups. The chapter headings give clues to the nature of these problems: "Why Other People Are Important to Us," "The Problem of Freedom," and "Why We Strive for Power and Status."

D. Cartwright, "Emotional Dimensions of Group Life," in M. L. Reymert, ed., *Feelings and Emotions*. New York: McGraw-Hill, 1950. Pp. 439–447.

R. M. Wittenberg, *So You Want to Help People*. New York: Association Press, 1947. Although written as a handbook for leaders of youth groups, this text contains much of interest and value for the student who is interested in the practical side of how groups function.

J. H. S. Bossard, *The Sociology of Child Development*. New York: Harper, 1948. The life of the child in family and non-family groups.

M. Sherif and H. Cantril, *The Psychology of Ego-Involvements*. New York: Wiley, 1947. See particularly the chapters on group situations and social situations.

F. H. Allen, "Dynamics of Roles as Determined in the Structure of the Family," *American Journal of Orthopsychiatry*. 12:127–134; 1942.

B. Bettelheim and E. Sylvester, "Therapeutic Influence of the Group on the Individual," *American Journal of Orthopsychiatry*. 17:684–692; 1947.

E. W. Bovard, "Social Norms and the Individual," *Journal of Abnormal and Social Psychology*. 43:62–69; 1948.

J. F. Brown, "Individual, Group, and Social Field," *American Journal of Sociology*. 44:858–867; 1939.

J. W. Powell, "The Dynamics of Group Formation," *Psychiatry*. 11:117–124; 1948.

F. Znaniecki, "Social Groups as Products of Participating Individuals," *American Journal of Sociology*. 44:799–811; 1939.

XI...*Communication: The Process of Social Interaction*

Communication as a Basis for Getting Along with Others. Communication is a process so basic to everyday life that we tend to take it for granted — like breathing or digestion. It is only when it breaks down or when we get into trouble because of its misuse that we become aware of its importance. We can see its importance dramatically displayed on a large scale in the international scene. One of the best instances of effective international communication is the relationship existing between the United States and Canada. The fact that the peoples of the two nations speak a common language aids communication, as does their adherence to similar patterns of values, culture, attitudes, etc. But the chief reason for good communication is that the two countries *want to understand each other.*

Let us contrast this situation with that existing between the United States and Japan before World War II. The two countries were drifting further apart in their relations and in their ability to communicate amicably. The contributing causes of the war were complex — our disapproval of the Japanese, their fear of us, the lack of common values, the suspicious air with which the two nations eyed each other, the lack of a common or even a similar culture, the differences in language — yet they all may be seen as factors that aggravated a situation that eventually developed from one of poor communication to one of virtually no communication, total war. During the war, communication was carried on with great difficulty through third parties (the Swedish government, for example) and by propaganda. The attempts of the Japanese to negotiate a peace were dependent in part on their success in re-establishing communication, and the present peaceful relations reflect both the ability and the intent to communicate.

Communication is as important for the welfare of the individual as it is for the welfare of states, because it provides the means whereby he establishes relationships with others, relationships that are essential to the meeting of basic needs. Disturbance in the individual's relations with others will result in or rather will express itself in a disturbance in communication. The reverse is also true: if communication is difficult, relations with others are also difficult. Indeed it is difficult or impossible to distinguish or separate what is interpersonal or social relationship from what is communication.

It should be noted that when we use the term "communication" in this book, we are referring not only to verbal or linguistic modes of expression and social intercourse but also to such important means of communication as signs, gestures, symbols, and symbolic behavior. One example of a nonlinguistic (or at least a semilinguistic) form of communication is money. Money symbolizes "value" and/or "economic power" and can be used to communicate demands on others for goods and services. Another form of communication that is of great importance, psychologically, is empathic communication. Inasmuch as we discussed this mode of communication at length in Chapter 3, we shall not give it extended treatment here. However, we should note that empathic awareness is of vital importance in determining our attitudes, feelings, and actions in any situation involving others. Empathy is one of the components of normal anxiety, particularly when it is associated with or results from concern for the feelings of others. Many persons who are troubled with neurotic anxiety are less able to empathize than those of normal adjustment, whereas persons who have strong neurotic needs are unusually empathic — too sensitive for their own good, so to speak. Persons who lack normal anxiety tend to be deficient in empathy, because they are unconcerned about the feelings of others. And as for the rest of us — those who have the usual amounts of both normal and neurotic anxiety — our empathic communication can be either impaired or heightened during periods of stress, depending on the situation, as well as on our characteristic ways of dealing with disturbances.

Readers of this book will find much emphasis on the importance of communication in the shape of reminders that such apparently

Harold M. Lambert, from Frederic Lewis

These children are communicating some of their feelings through the medium of painting.

unrelated phenomena as strikes, divorces, and psychoses are, in effect, "breakdowns in communication." The writer has taken this approach for two reasons.

The first reason for this emphasis is to remind the reader that we must probe beneath the surface of any sort of human difficulty if we are to gain better understanding of it, and that the examination of problems from the standpoint of communication enables us to see phenomena and relationships not apparent before.

Let us, for example, look at the problem of Alice McIntosh, who is having trouble with her seventh grade classes in English. Miss McIntosh feels that her difficulties are due principally to the fact that the students in her classes are indulged by their parents and given too much freedom by the other teachers in the school. Furthermore, she has examined the personnel folders of her students and has found that those who create the most disturbance have been "problem cases" since the third or fourth grade. As long as Miss McIntosh looks upon her problem as one of discipline and control, it is very likely that she will make little headway with it. On the other hand, it may help her to look at her problem as one in communication. She might ask herself such questions as: Do I know how my students feel about school? About English? About me? Do I know when they do not understand me? Am I able to convey my enthusiasm for literature to them? In what ways is my failure with this class due to my inability to understand my students and their inability to understand me?

If Miss McIntosh asks herself these questions in all sincerity and humility and searches earnestly and objectively for the answers, the chances are good that she will improve the situation in her classroom. To be sure, she must sincerely *want* to improve the situation, even to the extent that she is willing to change herself if necessary; and, furthermore, she must have sufficient insight and objectivity to recognize the social processes at work in her classes. However, even assuming that she is sincere, insightful, and objective, she may still be unable to make progress with her problem unless she knows where to start. And communication provides a good starting place for such understanding.

The need for understanding, particularly self-understanding, provides the second reason for the emphasis on communication in this textbook. Its ever recurring theme of "understanding, acceptance, tolerance, and respect for self and others" is based on "understanding." One of the ways in which we can begin to gain some understanding and insight in interpersonal relations is to become aware of the effect we have on others and they on us. These effects are both the causes and results of communication. By being alert to the cues and clues that reveal how others react to us and how others interact among themselves, we may begin to acquire some understanding of the communicative processes that make us what we are and others what they are.

The preceding chapters have been concerned more with the causes and effects of communication (for example, anxiety, social class, and status), rather than with the process as such. The present chapter focuses on communication as a process.

Social Maturity and Linguistic Maturity. Observations of children reveal that growth in linguistic ability roughly parallels growth in the ability to socialize. Communication first develops as an attempt to establish some kind of relationship with others. Initially, a child uses sounds and gestures in an attempt to communicate his feelings: pain, fear, anger, pleasure, etc. Then he may learn words like "mama" and "dada," which are associated with significant adults. Calling these adults by name helps to establish their relationship to him. Then he may learn words used to make demands on others. He says "baw" to indicate that he wants someone to give him his ball, and he says "no" when he does not want to give back grandfather's gold watch.

This is all rudimentary when contrasted with the verbal give-and-take of a small group of four-year-olds who are testing each other by taunts and "bathroom language," who are working cooperatively at playing house one minute and are embroiled in a shoving contest the next. For a while they use their language as a way of asserting themselves; then they use it as a way of building a friendly group; and then they use it as a way of temporarily destroying the group. Some individuals leave the group for long periods, but others find that they cannot live without it. Eventually they all find that group membership of some sort is necessary for satisfactory human existence, and that communication is the tool enabling individuals to form groups and maintain membership therein.

Meeting the Need for Human Relationships. A freshman psychology class meets for the first time. Perhaps all the members are strangers in a new school. In the few minutes elapsing before and after class, a few of the class members find that they have common interests or mutual friends. This incipient friendship is continued over coffee and cigarettes in the cafeteria, and a small group is formed that serves the social and self-expressive needs of its members. Another member of the class draws his chair up to the group. He listens to the conversation for a while, sees an opening, and comments. A well-knit, intimate group might object to a stranger attempting to seek acceptance as a member, but a loosely organized, informal group of coffee drinkers tends to be more permissive with would-be members; they are happy to share their social warmth with others.

Harry Roland had just moved to a small town as the local representative of a large oil company. He knew no one in the town at first, but gradually developed a small circle of acquaintances through his business contacts. However, even after three months, he still felt very much the outsider. Most of the social life of his acquaintances was centered in a lodge known as the Biped Lodge. Harry felt that he had much in common with those Bipeds he knew and would like to be associated with them. So he made application for membership. The membership committee interviewed him and, finding that he had a background similar to theirs, recommended him for membership. On the appointed night, he was inducted as a member of the Bipeds with appropriate ceremonies.

As a Biped, Harry's activities involve visiting and chatting with other Bipeds at the meeting hall, on street corners, in bars, over coffee, in their homes, in their places of business; participating in the ritual of the Biped Lodge; participating in the Lodge's business meetings; and co-operating in the organized activities of the Lodge.

Harry established and now maintains his membership through communicative behavior: through conversation he learned of the Biped Lodge and discovered that he had much in common with its members; he communicated his intention to be a member on an application blank; the membership committee communicated with him in the course of an interview; the ritual of the Lodge, if not entirely verbal, had symbolic meaning that served to draw members together. Since Harry has become a member, the circle of persons with whom he can communicate and to whom he has access has widened. He is accepted because he can demonstrate symbolically (through membership in the Lodge) his similar background and interests; communication with other Bipeds proceeds on a formalized basis during the meetings; and Harry finds that he can express himself further through aiding the Lodge in promoting its outside activities.

Communication and Family Relations.   On a more intimate level, family relationships are also maintained through the medium of communication.   Parents make children aware of their love symbolically by providing care and protection and by expressing warmth and affection, both verbally and nonverbally.   Discipline and punishment are usually effective because of their symbolic nature — that is, the invoking of limits and the infliction of pain symbolize both the anxiety felt by the parents and their temporary rejection of the child.   The child who feels that his siblings are receiving love that should be bestowed upon him may symbolically act out his feeling of deprivation by taking toys from others, or he may make a bid for attention by throwing a tantrum.   Unfortunately, we are all too often more concerned with the symbol itself than with the message it is supposed to convey.   The child is of no help to us in this matter, because he does not have the verbal tools either to analyze the situation or to tell us of his feelings.

Parents communicate with each other, too.   They reaffirm their mutual love and confidence, they solve the large and small problems that each family must meet, they engage in those warm disagreements that are normal in most families, or they devote themselves to verbal duels that literally blast the family relationship apart.   For communication can be used both as a tool and as a weapon — as a means of building better and more mature human relationships or as a means of implementing immature or neurotic needs.

Communication as a Means of Manipulating Others.   The discussion of communication and group membership has so far largely been concerned with the therapeutic or emotionally sustaining aspects. There is another aspect of communicative behavior that involves the individual and his attempts to control and direct others.

The discussion here is not of leadership in the democratic sense, where the leader aids the group in coming to decisions and in carrying them out, but of leadership in the authoritarian sense, where the leader attempts to induce the group to behave in a predetermined manner.   Very frequently attempts to control and direct do not express themselves directly as attempts to lead but rather as attempts to manipulate and maneuver situations and individuals in order to achieve certain prescribed ends.

Much directive communication is highly self-centered or ego-centric. We see it in the baby who cries for his bottle and in the boy who suggests a game of baseball because he likes to pitch. But directive communication may also be based on group decision. When the gang elects Leo captain of the ball team and he assigns Fred to play shortstop, he is acting on behalf of the total group.

The distinction between ego-centric verbal manipulation, on the one hand, and social control with the approval of society, on the other, is frequently a difficult one to make. It is very difficult to determine whether Mr. Klein, the policeman, Mr. Spencer, the dean of the law school, and Dr. Garrett, the superintendent of the hospital (who are described in the following "thumbnail sketches"), enjoy their work because it enables them to be of service to mankind or because the exercise of their official functions satisfies their thirst for power. Probably both needs are satisfied.

The kinds of difficulties developed or encountered by Mr. Klein, Mr. Spencer, and Dr. Garrett in the course of the day are due partly to their misuse of communication as an instrument of direction and control. People in positions of authority are frequently inclined to take themselves and their positions very seriously and to deal harshly with breaches of discipline. This is particularly true if they are appointed leaders rather than elected by the group.

Dr. Garrett tries to run his hospital as efficiently as possible. He lies awake nights thinking of changes in procedure that will eliminate waste. He issues these orders in the form of mimeographed memoranda. Yet the cost of operating the hospital remains as high as ever. Dr. Garrett is trying to communicate, but no one is really listening. When he does obtain results, it is through fear and coercion. In some ways, he is aware of this, and it disturbs him, because he is a kindly, sensitive man. But he has not learned that communication, in order to be effective, must operate on a two-way channel. He has not learned that it is as important for his staff to communicate with him as it is for him to communicate with them.

Mr. Spencer, the dean of the law school, has a somewhat different communication problem. He is too clever to try to run a staff of highly individualistic law scholars by issuing orders. He runs his school the way he plays poker. He has analyzed each staff member and his role in the group and plans his strategy and tactics accordingly. He is not above playing off one staff member against another or nominating a scapegoat when his staff is in a rebellious mood. By one means or another he has been able to control his group and promote his programs. His law school has an excellent reputation, but the morale of his staff is poor. His staff hate him not only because he knows their weaknesses so well but also because he is able to render them powerless to oppose any of his plans or to promote any of their own. Dean Spencer would probably defend himself by stating that he is better prepared, in his position as head of the law school, to make plans and decisions. However, to the objective observer it appears that he is using the tools of communication in a way that is detrimental to the mental health of his staff. Even though the results seem to justify the means, he is heading for trouble.

Mr. Klein, the policeman, has twice been reprimanded by the chief of police because of complaints made by citizens that he has used strong language in citing them for traffic offenses. Although Mr. Klein is performing a socially valuable function in controlling traffic and arresting violators, he sometimes is carried away by a feeling of power. When he communicates this feeling to traffic violators by his choice of words or his tone of voice, the result is irritation and resentment.

Communication as a Means of Attack and Defense. In the individual's relations with others he occasionally feels called upon to attack others or defend himself. Presumably primitive man was more likely to express this feeling directly, by striking or killing his opponents. Children and immature adults also are likely to use physical means of expressing fear and anger. The use of language appears to be an improvement over physical attack. Once one has learned the techniques of invective, it seems to be even more satisfying than the direct methods of physical aggression; and one who is skillful in the art of verbal defense can protect himself more effectively against the attack of a large group than would be possible in the case of hand-to-hand combat. Defense and offense can be conducted more efficiently and with less bodily danger through the use of language. There is, of course, always the possibility that hostilities expressed linguistically may develop stronger emotions, which in turn may lead to violent aggression. This phenomenon can be observed on an international scale when nations goad one another with charges and recriminations that eventually lead to war. For example,

Bismarck was able to touch off the Franco-Prussian War by sending an insulting telegram to the French government.

Because the middle-class pattern of behavior stresses peaceful relations and does not condone the open expression of hostile feelings, members of the middle-class cultural group are expected to suppress and repress these feelings. If they express them at all, they do so as indirectly as possible. Thus, what would lead to physical attack on the part of primitive man leads instead to sarcasm, malicious gossip, and competition on the part of the modern middle-class adult. Not only is invective watered down, but it is more usually expressed to some other person than the offending one. If Joe the Worker feels exploited by his boss, he is not likely to tell him so to his face, but is likely to complain to his fellow workers and his wife about his mistreatment. If he finds that other workers feel the way he does, the feeling of hostility and resentment may become too strong to be expressed by griping and may call for stronger action. Even then the workers do not take the direct action of killing the boss or burning the plant — they take the indirect and symbolic action of going on strike. On the other hand, if channels of communication to the boss are open, the matter may be taken up with him directly or through a workers' representative, and the grievance may be adjusted. In either event, the hostility is expressed symbolically rather than directly. Only the very immature, emotionally disturbed, or psychotic individual is likely to take direct physical action.

Although communication, when used for purposes of defense and offense, represents an advance over more direct methods of physical attack, it is likely to serve as a means of worsening human relations rather than bettering them. This is due to no fault in the medium of expression but rather to our lack of emotional maturity, particularly during periods of stress and tension. The lack of emotional maturity is one of the reasons it takes so long to negotiate even minor issues during some industrial strikes. The representatives of labor and management meet in an atmosphere charged with tension. Especially during the first sessions there is a tendency for negotiators to argue the merits of their cases and to attack the opposition. When they are at this stage, they are using communication to express hostilities and to act defensively. It is only when members of the negotiating group agree that they have more to gain by working together than by attacking each other that any progress toward a settlement can be made. Even then, progress may be impeded by sporadic expressions of distrust and resentment.

This is not to say that satisfactory human relations cannot be maintained if feelings are expressed. Joe the Worker would be a happier person if he could express his feelings of being exploited directly to the boss. Perhaps it is to the boss's discredit that he cannot. Generally speaking, it is "good therapy" for feelings to be expressed, and frustrating and emotionally blighting for them to be repressed. However, the free expression of feelings is possible only in special circumstances, such as when we are among bosom friends; the free expression of feelings in most instances results variously in alarm, hostility, or scornful amusement on the part of listeners. It appears that general emotional health would be improved if our culture would permit greater tolerance and acceptance of the free expression of feelings.

Communication as a Way of Maintaining the Group

Helping Group Members to Find a Common Identity. So far we have discussed the role played by communication in enabling the individual to express his individuality and to maintain relationships with others. The third major function communication performs in interpersonal relations is to aid the group to maintain itself.

As we stated in Chapter 10, groups resemble individuals in many ways. Even as the individual has a need to feel that he *is* an individual, different from others, so do groups need to feel that in some ways they are different from other groups and from people in general. They need to develop some common bond, something which helps to identify them, which serves to express the feeling of the members that they are a part of a special group. As the skilled and objective observer records the behavior of groups, he notices that their members follow certain routines that serve to identify them both to outsiders and to the members themselves. Thus the informal group meeting over coffee in the student union may limit conversation to certain prescribed areas. International and national politics, art, music, literature, philosophy, psychology, and the characteristics of courses and instructors may be on the approved list, but the group must never discuss sports, local politics, and radio programs. Perhaps the group may take a very "advanced" point of view; perhaps it is conservative. In any event, if the group achieves continuity and stability, certain characteristics will appear that serve to identify it. This is true of large and small groups alike. Even to be a member of a college student body is to submit oneself to the pressure to conform to certain behavioral and attitudinal patterns.

To remain a member of the student body, one must practice a certain minimum of self-discipline in attending classes and completing assignments. One cannot indulge repeatedly in "long week ends" or undertake duties that would prevent the maintenance of a satisfactory scholastic average. If one has been hitherto indifferent or hostile to learning, this attitude must be changed. Before Nancy Hawkins came to college she read sparingly. Now she finds herself reading constantly. In colleges where students can communicate among themselves and with members of the teaching staff, certain attitudes toward life and certain patterns of belief tend to emerge. If the teaching staff has a highly developed sensitivity to art and music, this attitude will very likely permeate the student body. The assumption is, of course, that communication between staff and students is two-way.

Communication and Group Norms. The function of norms in bringing about cohesiveness in groups was discussed in some detail in Chapter 10. By way of review, the general principle involved was that each group tends to develop standards or norms of attitude and conduct that serve as guideposts for the thinking and the behavior of its members. The typical group member modifies his attitudes and behavior to conform to the norm that has been developed by the group. The atypical or deviant member either withdraws from the group or remains on its fringes, conforming as little as possible. When the latter behavior occurs, the deviant member is likely to be subjected to much pressure either to conform or to withdraw. By developing and maintaining norms, the group gives itself identity and differentiates itself from other groups and people in general. The important aspects of this process are twofold: (a) the development of norms, and (b) the feeling of the group members that they should adapt their behavior to these norms. Two examples may serve to illustrate these principles.

Bill Louis was twelve years old. He had just moved from the country to an industrial area of a large city. Other boys in the neighborhood belonged to a gang known as the Purple Devils, composed mostly of boys eleven to fourteen years of age. At first Bill was an outsider, but as he made friends with a few of the members and proved himself with his fists and in sand-lot baseball, he was accepted. After a few months the character of the gang changed; it became dominated by a few older boys who had delinquency records, and the activities of the gang changed from baseball and touch football to inter-gang warfare and stealing. Although Bill had been law-abiding up till this time, he found himself increasingly tolerant of the delinquent behavior of the other members of the gang. Before long, he, too, was involved in their antisocial activities.

One of the members of the Purple Devils was Gary Strauss, the only child of a widow. Mrs. Strauss married a railway clerk, and the family moved to another part of the city. Gary's stepfather made a wholehearted attempt to be friendly with his stepson and was successful in developing a good relationship. He encouraged Gary to join the junior section of a hiking and mountain-climbing club in which he himself held membership. Spending his week ends camping with the new group, Gary came under the influence of a group norm quite different from that of the Purple Devils, and he found himself developing new interests and a different pattern of behavior. His spare time was now spent with the other members of the hiking group in trip planning, rock climbing, and camping.

Sometimes groups develop *rituals* as a means of formalizing symbolically (a) the existence of group consciousness, (b) the acceptance of the individual by the group and the group by the individual, and (c) the goals, behavior, and attitudes common to the group. Sometimes the rituals are deeply symbolic, such as the ceremonies that open and close each meeting of the Biped Lodge. Sometimes the rituals are developed as a means of conducting business more efficiently, as, for example, the rules of order under which most formally organized bodies conduct their business. Sometimes ritual grows spontaneously, such as the order of service in a church. Church members follow the service easily, perhaps unconscious of its ritualistic importance, but visitors fumble with hymnbooks and prayer books in an attempt to keep in step. Thus, the ritual of church service serves not only to provide the church members with a common, unifying experience, but it serves to differentiate members from strangers.

Communication as a Means of Differentiation. The need to differentiate between members and nonmembers is basic to the development of group norms and standards. Sometimes this factor may overshadow the other functions of a group. Some groups are organized largely as an expression of the need for prestige and status — for their "snob appeal." Among such groups are college and high school fraternities and sororities, and social clubs whose membership is limited to persons with specific qualifications. Other groups are formed in an attempt to recognize and identify characteristics that help some people "feel different" from others.

To be a member of the Indigenous Society, you must have been born in this country; to be a member of the Acme Club, you must be a member of the "first families" of the town; to be a member of Garibaldi Lodge, you must be of Italian-American extraction; to be a member of the Deutscher Verein, you must speak German; to be a member of the Forward America group you must be a veteran of World War II.

Although these standards of membership operate to aid persons who can qualify in finding common characteristics that can serve to draw them together, they also serve as a means of erecting a barrier of exclusiveness between the group and the rest of society. Members of each of these groups hope thereby to make membership in their organization a desirable thing. The more difficult it is to qualify for membership in a given organization and the higher the social status of those who can qualify, the more the organization takes on the quality of a select group. Thus the group serves both to express and to emphasize the social distance between the group members and the rest of society. This feeling of exclusiveness is communicated to others through publicity which appears to deal with the activities of the group, but which actually serves to advertise its exclusiveness and the selectivity of its membership standards.

"Correct Grammar" as a Social Norm. Group norms, exclusiveness, and social distance operate jointly on a large scale in another area of communication — the aspect of "correct" and "incorrect" language. It would be more accurate if we were to speak of "acceptable" and "unacceptable" or "appropriate" and "inappropriate" language, because essentially a linguistic form is "correct" if it conveys the speaker's meaning without distorting or obscuring it. If a person mentions "dese and dose tings," we understand what he means, but we understand something more — either he is a foreigner or is a member of the lower class who comes from an area where

his class pronounces "th" as "t" or "d." When we say that his speech is "incorrect," we are saying in effect that it does not conform to middle-class standards.

When we receive letters from persons whose spelling does not conform to dictionary standards, we react not only to what they say, but also to their evident membership in a lower class or their lack of education or "culture." If such a letter is an application for a job, we must consider whether the job requires the services of a person who conforms to middle-class norms and standards and who has reached a certain level of education. Incidentally we may not be correct in our conclusions, because a minority of middle-class persons are poor spellers, and a minority of lower-class persons are good spellers. Nevertheless, "spelling accuracy," like other linguistic standards, has some validity as a rule-of-thumb method for assigning class status.

Our ideas regarding the correctness and incorrectness of linguistic expression have their origin in the public school. Most school-teachers are members of the middle class, and one of the purposes of the school, unconscious or otherwise, is to teach children middle-class standards of behavior. When children from lower classes speak the English language as they learned it at home, teachers put them under considerable pressure to change their speech habits to conform to middle-class norms. Any deviation is termed "wrong," whereas middle-class speech patterns are termed "correct." Actually, the lower-class pattern is not "wrong" but is merely inappropriate to a middle-class setting, just as middle-class intonations and patterns of speech would appear inappropriate in a lower-class setting.* Possibly in a few decades these language-level differences will disappear under the impact of the movies, radio, and television, which operate to keep middle-class norms of speech constantly before persons of all classes.

Even within the framework of standard middle-class speech there are acceptable differences, depending on the occasion and the role being played by the speaker. Words and phrases appropriate to the smoking car are not used at the afternoon tea; the language of the business letter is different from that of the political speech; a minister giving his sermon uses different speech forms from the ones he uses in discussing a picnic with his family; a doctor, in describing

* This is truer in some parts of the United States than in others.

a case to a colleague, uses different language from that used in teaching his wife how to drive the family car. In other words, just as speech is varied with the psychological role played by the individual, even so is it varied with the social role.

Problem-solving by Groups. Communication is the tool by which groups conduct planning and other problem-solving activities related to their purposes and goals. Their use of communication for these purposes resembles the use of symbols by the individual in his problem-solving activities, except that the group provides a wider range of information and experience, which should make for better solutions than those by group members operating individually. However, as we stated in Chapter 10, the effectiveness of the group as a problem-solving body is limited by its cohesion; by the extent to which it permits and facilitates communication on all levels by its members; by the presence of tensions outside and inside the group; by the tendency of individual group members to dominate, impede, or delay normal group processes; and by the lack of awareness of the group either of its purposes or of the extent to which it is achieving its goal.

Propaganda

The Need to Be Objective about Propaganda. One kind of communication that merits attention, partly because it is so thoroughly misunderstood, is propaganda. Because we tend to have such pronounced prejudices regarding the nature of propaganda, it might be well to cite the definition of a social psychologist who has studied this area of communication: "Propaganda is a systematic attempt by an interested individual (or group) to control the attitudes of groups of individuals through the use of suggestion and, consequently, to control their actions (1)."

A careful examination of this definition will reveal that there is nothing indicating that propaganda is by nature "bad" or "evil" or "underhanded" or "untrue." These are popular misconceptions of the propagandist's technique. Seen in the light of the above definition, much of what happens in the following activities can be classified as "propaganda": advertising, friendly discussion, political speeches, education, religious activities, public relations, and morale-building activities. Probably every information-giving program carried on by any organization, whether for selfish or for altruistic reasons, is propagandistic in some way. If we can learn to examine propaganda in an objective, unemotional manner, perhaps we shall be able to use or resist it more effectively.

If we were to ask the man in the street to define "propaganda," he would probably characterize it as "lies like those the opposition (the Reds, or the British, or the Socialists, or the Republicans, or the Democrats) are spreading in such an underhanded manner." He would say this because most of us have a preconception of propaganda as "untruthful" or "deceptive." However, if we persist in this point of view, we are placing ourselves in a position where we cannot communicate with or even understand the opposition, because we are prone to believe that everything it says is false and intended to deceive us. We tend to react emotionally to attempts to influence us, rather than to analyze them rationally. We thus make ourselves vulnerable, because, in our emotionalized state, we may act impulsively and do just what the opposition wants us to do. In addition, we are placing ourselves in a position in which we are unable to evaluate attempts of our proponents, allies, and associates to influence us, for we are unaware that they, too, can propagandize. Then, too, we may be denying ourselves the use of an effective tool of communication merely because someone has labelled it "propaganda."

Actually, propaganda can aid as well as impede communication.

Richard McGee decided to run for city councilman because he is convinced that there is corruption in the city hall. He is backed by the Association for Decency in Government. His speeches and campaign literature are propaganda in that they suggest that citizens cast their votes for McGee. Yet because of his campaign and its propaganda, citizens will learn more about affairs in the city hall, will discuss these matters among themselves, and will hear what the incumbents have to say in their defense. Through hearing Mr. McGee speak, citizens will be enabled to become acquainted with him as a person while they learn his views. Because of this background, they will be aided in discussing civic matters with him when they meet him individually.

Thus propaganda may serve a useful purpose in bringing public issues to the attention of the people, even though it is used with intent to persuade and influence.

Yet people who are alert to the real dangers of propaganda, who ask themselves: What are they trying to make us do? Who is trying to influence us? Why are they telling us this? What techniques are they using on us? — these are the people who are in a position to exercise greater freedom of thought, action, and belief, because they are much better prepared to cope with their own tendencies to accept or reject the message of the propagandist uncritically.

Finding the Susceptibilities of the Audience. The skilled propagandist operates by analyzing the audience to determine what existing attitudes may serve as a basis for the new attitudes and subsequent behavior he desires to have the audience develop. The cigarette manufacturer learns that American women are class-conscious and are likely to follow the lead of women representing the upper social classes. His propaganda will therefore depict socialites smoking cigarettes and will quote their endorsements of his product. In this way, women are led to develop favorable attitudes toward cigarettes because of their existing favorable attitudes toward leaders of society.

Some propagandists waste their time and money because they attempt to promote attitudes on barren ground. During World War II, the Germans were unable to convince Americans that the conquered peoples of Europe were happy under their domination, in spite of the thousands of radio broadcasts and the tons of literature distributed. The American atmosphere was unfriendly to these claims and remained so. On the other hand, the Germans were able to score some small successes in their appeal to the American spirit of fair play by urging us to stop bombing helpless civilians. Because of this appeal, a number of speeches were made and letters were written to newspaper editors condemning this method of warfare. There is no evidence, however, that this appeal had any effect on the conduct of the war. The Germans scored another minor success in their attempt to discredit American leaders and public figures by claiming that they "really" were Jewish — for example, that Roosevelt's name was really Rosenfeld. These "facts" were cited in an attempt to attribute the responsibility for the war to "the Jewish capitalists of Wall Street," who were trying to subjugate "the Aryan race." A small group of Americans already dominated by an existing prejudice toward Jews accepted these interpretations. Again, evidence is lacking of the extent to which their defection affected the conduct of the war.

Devices Used by the Exploiting Propagandist. During the late 1930's, the Institute for Propaganda Analysis was organized for the purpose of providing the public with the means of protecting itself against the more sinister forms of propaganda, particularly propaganda that had as its purpose inciting war, riot, or revolution. Even though the Institute operated more or less on the basis of the "common sense" assumption that "all propaganda is bad," their research is of considerable value in understanding propaganda techniques. The researchers of the Institute were able to identify seven devices used by propagandists of the sinister variety.

1. *Name-calling.* A device used for discrediting or "smearing." Examples of name-calling are "pinko," "fascist," "Communist Jew," "Cossack," and "besmircher of the sanctity of the home." This technique has strong emotional appeal in that it identifies the opposition with symbols that are perceived by the audience as unsavory.

2. *Glittering Generality.* A vague, indefinite, noble-sounding abstraction used to enlist emotional support for a cause by stifling or allaying criticism: "That honest, God-fearing, farsighted, and patriotic supporter of our cause . . ."; ". . . pausing in his daily duties to shed a tear of sympathy and compassion on behalf of the vicious exploitation of the downtrodden and bleeding workers of the world . . ."

3. *Transfer.* Setting up a wave of positive emotion, whereupon the focus is rapidly shifted to the cause or candidate in the hope that some of this attitude will "transfer." For example, a political meeting may start with the national anthem and a presentation of colors with drums and flourishes, whereupon the leader may appear, hoping to pick up some of the feeling of loyalty and enthusiasm aroused by the display of patriotic symbols. Or a leader may strongly espouse some popular cause, like "bring the boys home, now that the war's over," not because he believes in it, but because he hopes that its popularity will attract followers for his cause.

4. *Testimonial.* For example, quoting well-known national figures in support of a cause or issue, or listing their names on the letterhead of an organization.

5. *Plain Folks.* For example, pictures of the leader at home with his family, or pitching hay, or milking cows, or shaping a rivet with an air hammer, the message being, "I am a regular fellow, a modest, hardworking perfectly ordinary person — just like you."

6. *Card-stacking.* The clever selection and display of facts and falsehoods, distortions and distractions, all arranged in a logical or quasi-logical fashion in order to give the best or the worst possible case for a person or a cause.

7. *Band Wagon.* For example, "Our cause is growing. Three years ago, a pitiful handful of 10,000 members. A year ago, 1,000,000 members. Six weeks ago, 4,000,000 members. Today, 6,000,000. Six million honest, loyal, and sincere workers for the cause! At this rate, 90 per cent of the people will be with us within eighteen months! Why not join up now?" (2)

The theme running through these techniques is consistent. The propagandist is attempting to influence opinion and action by appealing to already existing attitudes, by high lighting certain attitudes as group norms, and by enlisting the confidence of the people by making them think that he is one of them. When he is successful, it is because he has blocked or impaired some of the individual's capacity to perceive the realities of life. It is as though he had anesthetized the ability of his audience to be sensitive to differences between truth and fiction.

Propaganda Exploits the Passive Individual. The propagandist is able to achieve his successes partly because so many of us have a neurotic need to be "told the answers." Working out a problem in international politics for oneself is likely to be a trying and difficult job. It is not easy to wait for the appearance of sufficient data on which to base even a tentative conclusion, and even at best the issues are seldom, if ever, all black or all white. Many of us cannot tolerate an ambiguous situation; we would like to be told what to believe by persons of power, prestige, and authority. There are plenty of easy solutions available — newspaper columnists, editors, senators, radio commentators, governors, and generals will make pronouncements on any conceivable issue. One needs only to take his choice. One of the difficulties is that we are so surfeited with communicated opinion that we are likely to accept uncritically rather than to evaluate, test, and judge. This situation is akin to "spectatoritis," which we see in sports — a few persons playing the game, and the rest sitting on the side lines, participating passively, while the game is won or lost *for* them, but not *by* them. Similarly, the man in the street participates passively in the give and take of political life, sitting on the side lines and permitting others to make up his mind for him. As he casts his occasional vote, he is involved only minimally in the struggle.

One of the reasons we are so vulnerable to propaganda is that we tolerate so much one-way communication. The propagandist speaks to the group; the group does not talk back, does not evaluate, but reacts. This situation is very similar to that of the group dominated by the autocratic leader in that in both there is insufficient communication. When communication is impaired, it is difficult for either the group or the individual to make a realistic and accurate analysis of the subject discussed.

Distortions in Communication

Communication Reveals Disorientation.   A person who is under great emotional tension will reveal his anxiety by his strained tones, by his difficulty in finding words to express himself, by his misuse of words. When he writes a letter, his writing may be less legible, he may misspell more words than usual, and he may make grammatical errors. Perhaps he will not display all these symptoms, but if he is emotionally upset, he will display some of them.

Inasmuch as the interpersonal relations of individuals who suffer from psychoses or psychoneuroses are markedly affected, we should also expect their speech to be affected. Some persons who are psychically ill reveal their illness by the use of peculiar words and expressions they have invented — for example, a pair of eyeglasses may be referred to as a "seeing tool" or a sidewalk may become a "cement pathway" or a fence may be called a "boundary barrier." Other seriously disturbed persons are unable to concentrate on one idea for any length of time and may switch to three or four different subjects in the course of a single sentence. Still others may be unable to talk recognizable sense and will converse in a kind of "word-salad" consisting of allusions, nonsense, plays on words, and garbled phrases. Speech behavior of this type deviates widely from the norm and reflects the extent to which these individuals are disoriented from the world of everyday reality.

Jurgen Ruesch and Gregory Bateson have made much of this concept and have proposed that neurosis and psychosis are essentially stages of difficulty in communication, in that neurotic and psychotic persons are unable to express their thoughts and feelings adequately and are unable to make reasonable and accurate interpretations of the statements and behavior of others. Thus psychotherapy is seen by these researchers as a means of restoring communication (3).

Stuttering and Stammering.   Stuttering is a good example of a speech distortion due to an emotional disturbance. It is significant to note that stuttering or stammering is much more frequent among boys than among girls (4). This may be because girls tend to have greater facility with words than boys, a fact for which there is as yet no satisfactory explanation, although it may be due to the tendency in our culture to overreject boys and to overaccept girls, a condition that would tend to make boys more emotionally disturbed. Wendell Johnson says that some stammering or repetition of sound appears normally in the speech of many small children. If parents and teachers are overconcerned about this "normal stammering," if they insist that children conform to adult standards in their speech, there is a strong likelihood, according to Johnson, that they will encourage permanent stuttering or stammering. He says further:

> The more anxious the parents become, the more they hound the child to "go slowly," to "stop and start over," to "make up his mind," to "breathe more deeply," etc., the more fearful and disheartened the child becomes, and the more hesitantly, frantically, and laboriously he speaks — so that the parents, teachers, and others become more worried, appeal more insistently to the child to "talk better," with the result that the child's own evaluations become still more disturbed and his outward speech behavior becomes more and more disordered. It is a vicious spiral, and all the factors involved in it are closely related (5).

Defensive Behavior. Stuttering is only one form of speech distortion caused by anxiety. Another symptom of anxiety is that displayed by intellectuals who use abstract and involved language as a defense mechanism. In what seems to be an attempt to explain themselves more precisely, these individuals use language that is involved, technical, and highly abstract. The net effect of such maneuvers, of course, is to confuse the listener. It is as though the speaker were taking refuge behind a verbal fog.

Shy persons who are forced to speak to strange groups or to make reports in class are seldom as effective and as intellectually efficient in these situations as they are when talking with a small informal group of their peers. Their ability to communicate in the more formal situation is seriously impaired by their feelings of inadequacy. (See Chapter 6, particularly the case of John Malloy.)

Bilingualism. The difficulties experienced by children from the lower classes who are put under pressure to modify their language in accordance with middle-class norms have been touched upon earlier in this chapter. This situation is an example of the problem produced by a conflict in cultures. Another example of cultural conflict is that of the child who comes from a bilingual background. A child who has learned to speak both Spanish and English before entering a school where English is spoken usually has more difficulty with the school curriculum than the child who can speak only English. His problem is: Which language shall I think with? Another possible explanation is that the child actually has to master two vocabularies. His vocabulary span as measured by his knowledge of the two languages is actually greater than that of the child who knows only one language. Yet his vocabulary in English is smaller than that of the child who has learned only English.

In a study of children of non-American parentage in Hawaii, M. E. Smith found that children coming from a bilingual background were, on entering school, retarded by three years in their ability to use English, as compared to children coming from monolingual families (6, 7). However, it is difficult to make generalizations regarding the effect of bilingualism from these data, because the issue is clouded by such factors as the low socio-economic status of bilingual children and the common use in Hawaii of a form of pidgin English.

Spelling Difficulties. The phenomenon of the above-average student who reads and writes well but has much difficulty in spelling is quite common in high school and college. Although students who are more intelligent tend to have less trouble with spelling, the relationship between measured intelligence and spelling is lower than the relationship between intelligence and ability in other subjects found in the standard high school curriculum (8). Published research regarding the relationship between spelling deficiency and personality factors is scanty, but clinical observations by the author indicate that college students who are poor spellers are usually persons who resist conformity, particularly the kinds of conformity enforced or required by figures of authority, like parents or teachers. Their inability or refusal to develop acceptable spelling habits has all the earmarks of a defiant gesture against the forces of conformity. However, like so many other defiant gestures, the refusal to learn spelling is an immature pattern of behavior, which harms the doer more than the individuals in authority toward which it is directed. Thus, the person who consciously or unconsciously elects poor spelling as his behavior mechanism will find that it impedes his progress in school, in business, and in the professional world.   Many a valuable report containing sound and thoughtful recommendations has been rejected or discarded because its author was unable to conform to the conventional standards of spelling.

Group Contagion.   Distortions in communication typical of groups are in many ways similar to distortions by individuals in that they are usually due to emotional immaturity on the part of some or all of the individuals composing the group, or are due to the presence of environmental factors producing emotional tensions, or both.

Contagion is one form of neurotic communication appearing in groups.   Fritz Redl and William W. Wattenberg describe how disruptive behavior spreads in a classroom:

If some child breaks a pencil point and noisily resharpens it, a class which is bored or has been kept immobile too long may be seized by an epidemic of the same kind of noisemaking.   The reason for the epidemic is that the children have built up the need to move around and to be relieved of their tension by a chance to manipulate something.   However, they have hitherto kept to their seats because their consciences somehow insisted that they stay within the limits of teacher-approved behavior, no matter how unpleasant a duty that might become.   The openly demonstrated courage of the child who "broke the ice" by seeking release for himself acted as a stimulant for similar behavior in all the others (9).*

Another example of communication by emotional contagion is panic.   The death toll in many a theater fire would have been negligible if the audiences had filed out slowly, if each person had waited his turn in line.   Evidently the audiences were already in a state of tension produced by the discovery of the fire, and the panic was touched off by a few persons exhibiting terror and rushing the entrances.   This terror, communicated to other persons in the crowd, spread in a contagious manner.   Other manifestations of crowd behavior — riots, lynchings, and military routs — appear to be the product of similar emotional contagion.†

Rumor.   Rumor is another form of communication by contagion.

* Reprinted from Fritz Redl and W. W. Wattenberg, *Mental Hygiene in Teaching*, by permission of Harcourt, Brace and Company, Inc.

† A description and analysis of the panic precipitated on October 30, 1938, by a broadcast purporting to describe an invasion of the earth by Martians may be found in H. Cantril, "The Invasion from Mars," in T. M. Newcomb and E. L. Hartley, eds., *Readings in Social Psychology.*   New York: Holt, 1947.   Pp. 619–628.   This article is a partial summary of H. Cantril, *et al.*, *The Invasion from Mars.*   Princeton: Princeton University Press, 1940.

Rumors gain currency and acceptance because they meet a need. For example, a premature peace celebration in World War I was touched off by a rumor that peace had been declared. This rumor gained acceptance because the people hoped the war would end without further bloodshed. Another example is the rumor circulating during World War II to the effect that there was actually plenty of gasoline and that persons in high places were hoarding it. This rumor met the neurotic needs of people who were buying gasoline on the black market. If they could believe that rationing was unnecessary and that its administration was corrupt, they would not have to feel guilty about buying black-market gasoline. The rumor that President Roosevelt was insane and required the supervision of a psychiatrist had particular appeal for persons who had a need to justify their hatred and distrust of him as a leader. The rumor that President Hoover promised the voters "two chickens in every pot and two cars in every garage" met a special need for those persons who thought of him as an inept, impractical leader.

We are often inclined to give some credence to rumors on the "common sense" basis of "Where there's smoke, there's fire." However, such reasoning is a way of rationalizing our desires to believe the rumor. Allport and Postman, in their investigation of rumors current during World War II, were unable to find any that had basis in fact, and therefore concluded that a rumor "is never under any circumstances a valid guide for belief or conduct (10)."

Communication and Education

Communication and the Student. Although communication is important to the psychological existence of everyone, the student has certain special problems of communication that do not figure as largely in the lives of other individuals. Indeed, the question of what the student learns, how he learns, or whether he learns at all depends on the kinds of communication that develop in his relations with his fellow learners and his instructors.

For purposes of analysis, the goals of education may be divided into four areas:

1. The learning of skills and techniques
2. The acquiring of information
3. The growth of familiarity with new ideas or concepts
4. The development of attitudes

In relation to the effectiveness of learning, these areas are arranged in order (a) from the least important to the most important, (b) from those activities most usually associated with learning by the man in the street to those of which he is least aware, (c) from the most conscious learning activities to those most deeply rooted in unconscious processes, and (d) from those activities most concerned with intellectual processes to those most concerned with emotions or feelings.

Skills and Information. When most persons think of education, they are likely to think of it in terms of the acquisition of skills and information — learning the three R's and the facts of geography, civics, literature, history, etc. To the average person, education in the secondary schools and in college is an extension of these activities — largely the acquisition of more complicated skills and the learning of more abstract information.

Concepts. Although the point of view that the aim of education is the accumulation of facts and skills is popular, it is essentially sterile. In order for facts and skills to be remembered, they must be perceived by the student in relationship to a conceptual framework. In other words, they must "make sense." Otherwise such skills as those involved in the multiplication of fractions are remembered only for the purpose of placating the teacher and passing a test — they simply have no meaning for the student. The result is that most adults cannot multiply fractions, although they were able to do so in a ritualistic fashion when they were in grammar school.

Importance of Attitudes. Attitudes deserve primary consideration. *Learning cannot take place at all unless students want to learn;* no one can learn for them and no one can force them to learn if they are set against learning. Furthermore, attitudes figure very prominently in the goals of education; both the public at large and the educators feel strongly that students should develop positive attitudes toward solving problems through reason rather than through violence, toward the use of democratic principles, toward the respect for law and order.

A Challenge to the Teacher. It is in the development of concepts and attitudes that the communicative skills of the teacher are put to the test. If the educator is to succeed in the area of attitude formation (and he must succeed if students are to learn), he should become the skillful propagandist, using this term in its positive sense, because he may find it necessary to persuade students to learn, to give up their past prejudices and their neurotic defenses against learning.

Inasmuch as these concepts will be treated more extensively in Chapter 16, "Getting an Education: Learning," this discussion will not be prolonged. However, it should be emphasized that the basic skills, including the three R's, are communication skills, as are, in part, all skills based on them and all skills taught in schools. Facts and information constitute important media of communication, because, through a common store of facts, we are enabled to communicate with one another and to find common grounds for agreement. Through the assimilation of facts and information, we become a part of our own social environment. Concepts and ideas form the organizational structure into which facts and ideas are fitted, whereas attitudes are basic to what one wishes to communicate or to whether one wishes to communicate at all.

Classroom Communication Not One-way. If the student thinks of education as a communicative process, he tends to think of it as a one-way process — that is, a process in which the instructor imparts his knowledge, information, concepts, attitudes, and skills to the student. This is not surprising, inasmuch as many instructors regard education in much the same light. Actually, in order for education to become effective, it must provide for two-way communication. It must be possible for the student to formulate tentative concepts and ideas, to fit together some of the facts he has learned, and to try out new skills. Most important, the channels of communication must be open for him to communicate the results of these trial efforts to the instructor. As a matter of fact, two-way communication does occur in good educational practice. It appears in nearly ideal form in the primary grades, where the teachers are able to follow the progress of each pupil as he struggles in his attempts to master new skills. In the well-run primary class, the pupil has little difficulty in communicating with his teacher, and there is much interaction between teacher and pupil as he masters the basic skills.

Such communication is more difficult on the secondary and college levels. The subject matter of learning is more complex, more abstract, and, compared with the primary grades, there are fewer instances where "right" and "wrong" can be easily demonstrated. Furthermore, the relationship between the teacher and the student is less intimate: the teacher at the high school or college level is less intimately involved in his students' lives. This detachment comes about partly because the teacher is usually a subject-matter specialist, who must give most of his attention to keeping abreast in his field. Furthermore, he has several times as many students under his supervision as has the primary teacher. The student's means of communicating with the instructor are more formal than in the primary grades; this is particularly true where classes are large. However, techniques for communicating with the instructor do exist, and it is the student who must use them if any learning is to take place.

Communicating with the Instructor. If the lecture sections are not too large, and if the instructor permits, asking questions in class is one method of improving the communication. An even more effective method, in some instances, is that of speaking to the instructor in person before or after class or by appointment. If the instructor uses the class discussion method, the student has an added advantage. Not only can he communicate with the instructor, but he can communicate with other students and, through verbalizing, can clarify his own thinking. Class discussions offer an excellent opportunity for students to become involved in a subject; this, in turn, increases motivation, a necessary prerequisite of learning. Informal discussions with other students outside of class are also useful.

Probably the commonest means of communicating with the instructor is the quiz, or examination. This is a highly structured, formalized method of communication, which is unfortunately regarded by many students as an ordeal prepared by a sadistic instructor, rather than as an opportunity to communicate knowledge.*

Other means of communication are the papers and projects that are prepared as part of the course requirements. These generally offer more scope and freedom for the student to communicate with the instructor than do tests. However, the very element of freedom that makes them desirable sometimes proves threatening to the insecure student, who is not able to rely on his own ability to organize ideas and express them in written form, or who has formed the habit

---

* For a more extended discussion of this subject, see H. C. Lindgren, "Anxiety in Examinations," *School and Society.* 76:231–232; 1952.

of relying on specific directions as to what he should write and how he should write it. Such students are often thoroughly frightened at the prospect of having to do even a partially original piece of work. Sometimes they feel so inadequate that they rely on the help of fellow students or copy long passages from standard texts, changing a word here and there in a futile attempt to give the work some flavor of originality. Students who feel compelled to use such tactics in the preparation of term papers are "more to be pitied than scorned," inasmuch as they are influenced by their experiences with education which has been treated as a pattern of one-way communication (from the instructor to the student) and which has been concentrated on the "mastering" of skills and information, to the detriment of the learning of concepts and attitudes.

This essentially autocratic concept of education is one of the major blocks to communication plaguing both instructor and student. But there are other obstacles to communication. One of these is the social distance between instructor and student, which sometimes prevents each from feeling at ease with the other and from communicating freely and naturally. Frequently the barrier of social distance prevents students from speaking to instructors at all. It is probably inevitable that there be some social distance between instructor and student as long as the instructor is the more expert, and as long as we have a tradition of one-way communication between the expert and the beginner. However, if learning is to take root, it is the responsibility of the student to learn to communicate in spite of this barrier, rather than to use it as a rationalization for noncommunication; just as it is the responsibility for the instructor to minimize the effect of the barrier as much as possible — to make it easier for students to talk to him.

Related to the autocratic pattern of education is the concept of intellectual sterility, which is sometimes injected into the learning situation by anxious, insecure persons (both students and teachers) as a way of protecting themselves from having to tolerate or even consider ideas that are original or "different." When education is thought of as a rigidly structured, stereotyped process, communication and spontaneity are reduced to levels below the minimum necessary for intellectual growth.

Technical Terms. Another barrier to communication is the unfamiliarity with technical terms that plagues the student when he enters a new field. The progress of each field of science is marked by the invention of terms and phrases needed to describe new concepts and discoveries. The student frequently reacts to unfamiliar terminology with irritation and resentment, as if to say that learning is difficult enough, without having to struggle with a new vocabulary. However, since the new ideas that find expression in the advance of science are so closely related to the symbols expressing them, it is doubtful whether they could be separated very long, even for ease in learning. In other words, to learn a science is also to learn its language, and if one can understand the language of a science, one of the major obstacles to understanding the science itself is already overcome. Having mastered the terminology and other symbolic aspects of science (including its mathematics, if it has any), the student is in a position to use the "language of science" in reading, listening, and communicating with intelligence and comprehension.

In short, if he can communicate, the student can learn; if he is unable or unwilling to communicate, he cannot learn.

SUMMARY

Communication is the very essence of human relationships; it is the means whereby social interaction takes place. Disturbances in communication will result in disturbances in interpersonal relationships, and vice versa. Communication consists not only of linguistic interchange but also in the use of other symbols, of gestures, of signs, and of symbolic behavior. Communication is an important area of activity for the student of mental health. It is suggested that the understanding of oneself and others begin with observing the phenomena of social intercourse from the standpoint of communication.

Communication is used by the group as a means of maintaining itself and achieving its goals. The group exerts power over its members through the formulation of codes of conduct and belief, or norms, to which members must conform if they are to continue to be accepted as members. By conforming to norms, individuals recognize and accept the power of the group to prescribe behavior. Conformity to norms further aids in identifying group membership, and the norm itself serves as a kind of focal point that helps to unify the group. Rituals and ceremonies serve much the same purpose in a more formalized manner. Conformity to norms also serves to increase the social distance that exists between a group and the rest of society. A good example of conformity to norms is the stress placed by the middle class on "correct English," which is not necessarily correct but which seems so to most of us because it is the middle-class norm.

Propaganda is a special form of communication by which an individual or a group attempts to influence the attitudes and behavior of others through suggestion. Inherently, propaganda is neither "good" nor "bad"; such evaluations should be made on the basis of its purpose and the methods actually used. By understanding and recognizing propaganda, the individual is enabled to use it where appropriate and to protect himself against it when necessary. Propagandists use a variety of methods to arouse prejudice and to incite wars, riots, and other forms of violence.

Distortions in communication include stuttering and stammering, the use of abstract language, chronic misspelling, and ineffective communication resulting from shyness, bilingualism, emotional contagion, and rumor.

The student encounters special problems of communication in his attempts to become educated. Education involves four kinds of goals: skills, information, concepts, and attitudes. Many of the student's difficulties arise because only the first two types of goals are commonly recognized and stressed, and because the autocratic nature of many educational situations limits communication to a one-way relationship — from the instructor to the student. The most serious deficiencies in the educational situation are the lack of emphasis on motivation and the discouragement of communication among students or between students and instructors. However, even in the most autocratic situations, there is much that the student can do to improve conditions of communication, thus increasing the rate and the amount of learning.

REFERENCES

1. L. W. Doob, *Propaganda: Its Psychology and Technique*. New York: Holt, 1935. Pp. 75–76.
2. A. M. Lee and E. B. Lee, *The Fine Art of Propaganda*. New York: Harcourt, Brace, 1939.

3. J. Ruesch and G. Bateson, *Communication: The Social Matrix of Psychiatry.* New York: Norton, 1951.

4. D. McCarthy, "Language Development in Children," in L. Carmichael, ed., *Manual of Child Psychology.* New York: Wiley, 1946. Pp. 554–555.

5. W. Johnson, *People in Quandaries*, New York: Harper, 1946. Pp. 443–447. Reprinted by permission of Harper & Brothers.

6. M. E. Smith, "Some Light on the Problem of Bilingualism as Found from a Study of Progress in Mastery of English among Preschool Children of Non-American Ancestry in Hawaii," *Genetic Psychology Monographs.* 21:121–284; 1939.

7. M. E. Smith, "A Comparison of the English Vocabulary Used by Children of Non-American Ancestry in Hawaii before They Reach the Age of Seven Years with That of Kindergarten Children in Continental United States," *Journal of Experimental Education.* 9:121–132; 1940.

8. E. A. Bond, *Tenth-grade Abilities and Achievements.* New York: Teachers College Bureau of Publications, 1940.

9. F. Redl and W. W. Wattenberg, *Mental Hygiene in Teaching.* New York: Harcourt, Brace, 1951. P. 225.

10. G. W. Allport and L. J. Postman, "The Basic Psychology of Rumor," in T. M. Newcomb and E. L. Hartley, eds., *Readings in Social Psychology.* New York: Holt, 1947. Pp. 547–558.

SUGGESTED READINGS

W. Johnson, *People in Quandaries.* New York: Harper, 1946. A stimulating discussion of the semantics of maladjustment.

S. I. Hayakawa, *Language in Thought and Action.* New York: Harcourt, Brace, 1949. This is a highly readable book that presents an interesting, almost popularized analysis of communication from the standpoint of semantics. This writer would list it as the best in its field from the standpoint of readability, humor, and good sense. This is a revision of an earlier book, *Language in Action*, also very good, which may be available in some libraries.

S. Chase, *The Tyranny of Words.* New York: Harcourt, Brace, 1938. One of the first books to popularize the semantics movement. Interesting and readable, even though most of Mr. Chase's examples seem "dated."

S. Chase, *Roads to Agreement.* New York: Harper, 1951. An excellent and readable account of the progress made in the improvement of interpersonal relations through communication, and the hope for the world stemming from the newer developments in this field.

I. J. Lee, *Language Habits in Human Affairs.* New York: Harper, 1941. An introduction to semantics; contains much illustrative material.

H. C. Lindgren, *The Art of Human Relations.* New York: Hermitage, 1953. Chapters 6 and 7 deal with communication.

R. H. Thouless, *How to Think Straight: The Technique of Applying Logic Instead of Emotion.* New York: Simon and Schuster, 1939. A well-written approach to the logic of communication. A revision of an earlier book entitled *Straight and Crooked Thinking*.

J. E. Anderson, *The Psychology of Development and Personal Adjustment*. New York: Holt, 1949. Chapter 7 of this elementary text in psychology deals with the development of language and symbolic skill.

S. H. Britt, *Social Psychology of Modern Life*. New York: Rinehart, 1949. See particularly Chapter 8, "Social Psychology of Language," and Chapter 23, "Prejudices against Minority Groups."

S. S. Sargent, *Social Psychology*. New York: Ronald, 1950. See particularly, Chapter 9, "Communicating and Symbolizing"; Chapter 10, "Social Interaction and Social Groups"; Chapter 15, "Propaganda"; and Chapter 18, "Group Differences and Prejudice."

T. M. Newcomb and E. L. Hartley, eds., *Readings in Social Psychology*. New York: Holt, 1947. See Section IV, "Language"; Section V, "Suggestion, Imitation, and Sympathy"; Section XII, "Prejudice"; and Section XIII, "Mass Communication and Propaganda."

T. M. Newcomb, *Social Psychology*. New York: Dryden, 1950. Chapter 8 deals with group norms and their effect on individual and group behavior.

S. H. Britt, *Selected Readings in Social Psychology*. New York: Rinehart, 1950. The following articles are provocative: Albig, "Language and Public Opinion"; Allport and Postman, "Why Rumors Circulate"; Farnsworth, "Stereotypes"; Cantril, "Conditions of Suggestibility"; Sherif, "The Formation of a Norm in a Group Situation"; Murphy, Murphy, and Newcomb, "Attitudes of White Children toward Negroes"; Spitzer, "Presenting America in American Propaganda"; and Linebarger, "The British-German Radio War."

W. F. Vaughan, *Social Psychology*. New York: Odyssey, 1948. See chapters entitled "Rumor-Mongering," "Propaganda," and "Prejudice."

H. Cantril, *The Psychology of Social Movements*. New York: Wiley, 1941. Reveals, among other things, the role played by various forms of communication in the formation and conduct of the lynching mob, the Kingdom of Father Divine, the Oxford Group, the Townsend Plan, and the Nazi party.

H. W. Hepner, *Psychology Applied to Life and Work*, 2d edition. New York: Prentice-Hall, 1950. Chapters 25 and 26 deal with the effectiveness of advertising — a form of propaganda.

I. J. Lee, *How Do You Talk about People?* New York: The Anti-Defamation League of B'nai B'rith, 1950. A discussion of how the structure of our language leads to prejudice.

N. Cameron, *The Psychology of Behavior Disorders*. Boston: Houghton Mifflin, 1947. See Chapter 4, "Language, Thought, and Role-Taking in Behavior Disorder."

F. J. Roethlisberger, *Management and Morale*. Cambridge: Harvard University Press, 1941. See Chapter 6, "Of Words and Men," which deals with the importance of communication to the executive.

XII... *Adjustment Factors in*

Employment

Interrelationship of Adjustment Problems on and off the Job. The most obvious fact about the interrelationship of emotional adjustment and job adjustment is that there is a tendency for off-the-job problems to affect on-the-job adjustment and for on-the-job frustrations to affect off-the-job relationships. This is equally true of the unskilled laborer, the teacher, the salesman, the lawyer, and the grocer — of white-collar and blue-collar workers alike.

Employment problems affect even those persons who are not gainfully employed. For example, as the student proceeds through the adolescent period, problems involving vocational plans meet him at every turn. Relations between members of the family, employed or otherwise, are affected by the joys and tribulations experienced by the working members of the household in their daily employment. Life is very tense if the breadwinner did not get the raise or the promotion he expected, or if the housewife had to do the washing by hand because the washing machine broke down; but life can also be very pleasant if the boss praised the work of the breadwinner, or if the housewife was able to pick up some attractive curtains for the kitchen at one-third what she expected to pay. During periods of financial depression, reactions of the breadwinner to his failure to find employment have a profound effect on the emotional climate of the family. Furthermore, during periods of employment, the breadwinner's attitude toward his work affects his relations with the other members of the family.

The Place of Work in Our System of Values. In our culture, work is not something to be taken lightly or incidentally. It is much more than merely the activity whereby we obtain food, shelter, and clothing. Work is "good." According to Kingsley Davis, the values of work permeate the middle-class structure of values that is the basis of our outlook on life. Davis sees our basic philosophy as *worldly*, in that it stresses such earthly values as the pursuit of a calling. He also sees it as *ascetic* in its emphasis on thrift and industry; and as *individualistic*, in that it places responsibility on the individual for his own economic destiny and it stresses *personal* ambition, *self*-reliance, *private* enterprise, and entrepreneural ability. The "normal" person in our society is one who selects an occupation and strives to achieve success in it (1).

Although our system of moral values gives work a high rating, we nevertheless have some conflicts about it, for in some ways idleness is more attractive than work. It is as though our "official position" is that we should all work, whereas really we wish for lack of work — for idleness and leisure. A common compromise for this conflict is to say that leisure is a reward for work. Actually, this has the effect of placing idleness and leisure higher than work in our scale of values.

This conflict is presented symbolically in the first book of the Old Testament, where we read that because man committed the sin of learning to distinguish good and evil, he was cursed by having to support himself by toil. On the other hand, we have the doctrine of original sin, which says, in effect, that man can avoid the ultimate penalty of his sin by devoting his life to serving penance through good deeds, suffering, and hard work. In essence, these two ideas, though somewhat opposed, underlie our attitudes toward work even today. Work is a curse, but it is also a means of attaining eventual salvation. Although this conflict permeates our feelings about work in the modern world, it does not account for all the problems of adjustment that have their source or their expression in the employment situation.

Work as a Barrier. Reduced to its starkest terms, work is an economic device that has as its end purpose the maintenance of life itself. It is the means of our supplying ourselves with food, shelter, and clothing. Perhaps man should therefore have a more accepting attitude toward work than he does. But the complications of life today make it difficult to see the direct and logical connection between subsistence and work. There are a number of intermediary processes and at least one intermediate economic device — money.

"Money is what provides subsistence," says the man in the street, "not work. Work is something I must suffer in order to get *money*."

Work thus serves as a frustrating barrier between the individual and something he needs. He sees no direct connection between digging a ditch and eating ham and eggs for breakfast, but if he is a laborer, he must dig his ditch before society will permit him to have his ham and eggs. The work does not "produce" the ham and eggs — they were in existence all the time; and the money that purchased them was in existence. The individual therefore sees the work as an inconvenience that must be borne before he is permitted to possess the money that can be used to purchase food.

Applying this principle to the man in the street, we see that he feels or anticipates the need for food. He has learned that economic power (money) is necessary to acquire food. His immediate goal is to acquire economic power, but between him and economic power is a barrier. He must attack this barrier directly by seeking and engaging in work, work being a process of translating his muscle power and his intellectual power into economic power (money). Thus there is a tendency for the man in the street to see work as the barrier that separates him from the things he really wants. His position, as he sees it, is illustrated on page 262. He sees his needs as frustrated by the barrier of work, which must be surmounted before he can have access to the highways of economic power leading to the goals that will satisfy his needs. Because the barrier prevents his immediate access to goals, he feels frustrated and hostile. He may direct his hostility toward work itself, or he may direct it toward his employers who, he feels, force him to work in exchange for economic power. Or he may attempt to by-pass the work barrier by securing money dishonestly. The latter method also serves the additional purpose of rebellion against the society that, he feels, erected this barrier for the purpose of thwarting his personal convenience.

One by-product of this orientation is the feeling that if work is bad, its opposite, idleness, must be good. Therefore, we work so that we will not have to work — so that we may be idle. As was noted in Chapter 7, "The Struggle to Become Independent and Self-reliant," we have a tendency to admire the "idle rich." We admire them not only because they have been able to combine dependence with social respectability, but because they are suc-

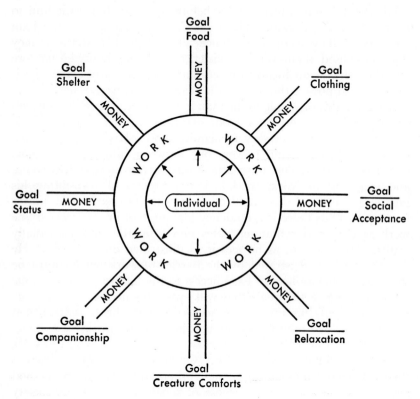

Work seen as a barrier.

cessful in achieving that much desired state — irresponsible, care-free idleness. This attitude toward idleness is what makes high-status positions attractive to the uninformed, who say, in effect, "If I were a bank president (or running my own business, or a lawyer, or a movie star, or a senator), I could take off and go fishing any time I wanted to. And I *would*, too. I wouldn't care if school kept or not!"

Probably all of us have had such feelings. At such times, idleness seems most attractive and work seems to be an evil designed for our personal inconvenience. However, for most of us this feeling is occasional and wistful, whereas those who suffer from vocational maladjustment tend to have such feelings with greater frequency and intensity.

Work as a Means of Acquiring Money. Sometimes the man in the street sees the accumulation of wealth as the chief object of work. Persons obsessed by this orientation are motivated by a profound sense of insecurity, which is basically psychological, but which is, they feel, entirely economic. The person of this persuasion feels that if he could earn "only a little more money" his economic problems would be solved. However, when such persons *do* earn "a little more money," they automatically adjust their rates of spending to this increased income. They find that they can even *double* their income for short periods of time without effecting a no-ticeable change in their standard of living. The fact is that families with incomes of $25,000 and $30,000 a year have much the same budgetary problems as families whose incomes are $8,000, $5,000, and even $3,000 per year (2).

Money is not the cure-all for feelings of insecurity. The idea that increased income will solve our problems is not only fallacious and unrealistic, but it serves the purpose of diverting attention away from the real issue — why we live beyond our incomes, what the *real* reasons are for our worry about the future, etc. The chief shortcoming in these attitudes toward work is that they lead us to see work as a source of frustration rather than as a normal, natural, and healthy means of meeting our basic needs.

It should be noted that not everyone regards work either as a barrier to need-satisfaction or as a means of making money, although these two concepts are very widespread. Many people look upon work as the *means* to attain satisfaction of their needs, rather than as a barrier. Looking upon work as an opportunity rather than as an obstruction is, of course, a more positive approach, but even in such cases it is possible to lose or to ignore some of the more desirable psychological values, because the individual is still more interested in what he will receive because of his work than he is in the work itself.

Other persons see work as an end in itself. As we say, "They live for their work." Sometimes this occurs because the individual is using work as an escape from or a defense against anxiety, and sometimes it is because the individual sees his work as an opportunity to express his individual talents and to serve others.

Factors in Employment That Tend to Produce Frustration

The Disassociation of the Individual from the Total Productive Process. The inventive geniuses who helped to bring about the industrial revolution were operating to break down the "work barrier" (see illustration on page 262) that separates man from his goals. Ideally, technology attempts to free man from the necessity of spending his days in a brutish struggle for existence. Presumably by the reduction of the amount of time required for work, man is released for more worth-while activities. But while the industrial revolution has produced goods, services, and leisure beyond the dreams of those who started it on its way, we are not so free to engage in worthwhile activities as we should like, partly because we are deeply involved in coping with the social and psychological problems created by the very technological changes that took brute force out of the production process.

One of the basic needs, which were mentioned in Chapter 2, is the need to be creative and productive. During the period in world history when the master craftsman was dominant, it was relatively easy for the individual to meet this need through his daily work. A worker was able to express a portion of his personality in his product. Now, with mechanization and mass production, most of the opportunities for creativity and becoming "ego-involved" in one's work are gone (3). Formerly the cobbler satisfied his creative urges in part by creating shoes. Often the shoes were intended for someone he knew personally, and the cobbler felt a sense of responsibility and importance — responsibility to create a good fit and a stylish appearance, and importance because he knew that he was fulfilling a known person's need for shoes. He may even have had the chance to fit the shoes himself and keep them in good repair. Thus he was able to identify himself closely with his work and his customer's needs.

But consider the man who works all day long at a machine buffing the soles of shoes. Perhaps this job was a challenge to his skill during the first few weeks, until he reached the production norm. But now it is the same thing day after day. It is easy for him to feel that his work is monotonous and unimportant. Because he is isolated from the end product and the consumer, he may feel no particular urge to do a good job. If he leaves his work for a day or a week, production will go on. If he leaves his job, the company can easily fill his place — another man can be trained to the same level of skill in a short time. His job gives him no opportunity to feel creative, responsible, or important. He is easily maneuvered into the "work or starve" orientation, whereby he regards his work merely as a barrier between himself and what he wants. With such an attitude, it is easy for him to develop feelings of frustration, resentment, and discontent.

The Loss of Identity. Another need, even more basic than the need for creativity, is the need to enjoy self-respect and self-esteem, as reflected in the respect and esteem of others. In other words, a sense of importance is basic to a feeling of well-being. As an indirect result of the industrial revolution, the worker has been deprived of some of the sense of importance he had when he was a craftsman. The usual policy followed by management minimizes the importance of the worker by denying him a share in making decisions. If decision-making is shared at all, it is usually shared grudgingly. What often happens is that management makes changes that ought to result in savings and lower costs without consulting the worker; the worker feels resentful of the fact that management has the power to make changes without consulting him; he worries because these changes may affect his status and earning capacity; and he expresses his anxiety by blocking any benefits that might result. On one occasion, during the Depression, the management of a factory decided that the pay should be reduced 20 per cent in order to place the company in a better competitive situation. The workers were incensed, agreed among themselves to limit production accordingly, and actually succeeded in reducing the production of the plant approximately 20 per cent. If they had participated in the decision that led to the wage cut, they might have accepted it willingly or might have produced more efficiently. However, management in general is reluctant to share its power to make decisions.

Progress as a Virtue. One of the central values in the middle-class pattern is the feeling that everyone should strive to improve himself economically and socially. A man is expected to be working constantly to better his own status and, in any event, is expected to attain a higher position than that attained by his father. If the worker has any middle-class aspirations, and most workers do, he is almost forced into a kind of dissatisfaction with his job. If he works on an assembly line, then he should become an inspector; if he is an inspector, he should become a foreman; if he is a foreman, he should become a supervisor. Furthermore, he is under pressure from advertising and the general "feeling of the times" that he should buy more and more consumer goods. He should trade in his secondhand car on a new car; he should trade in his low-priced car on a bigger, more powerful car. Life cannot be complete unless his home resembles an interior decorator's dream, and it should be outfitted with a deep-freeze, an electric ironer, air conditioning, an electric dishwasher, television, and so on and on. To acquire these symbols of life made more beautiful, he must make more money, he must be promoted, and perhaps when he gets to be plant manager, he will have all these desirable things.

From a realistic point of view, the chances are that he will be frustrated if he actually expects to attain these goals. Only a minority of workers are promoted, and even those who are promoted eventually find levels beyond which they cannot rise.

Resentment of Workers Expressed toward Management. Because the employment conditions today tend to frustrate the worker's needs for status, self-expression, and creativity, and because he feels compelled to work for goals he cannot attain, he may become aware of a feeling of frustration and futility, which, in turn, may express itself in acts of aggression directed toward management. Sometimes hostility may be expressed through strikes and slowdowns, but usually it appears in the form of general complaints or through any of the wide variety of behavior mechanisms (rationalization, projection, etc.).

Because some workers expect or want more from life than they are receiving, because they can make unfavorable comparisons between their kind of life and the kind of life they believe is lived by "the bosses," they feel exploited. They feel that through their power and skill they have given raw materials value in the form of a manufactured product, and that this value is being skimmed off by management, while they, the workers, must struggle along on a pittance. In order to get their share of this "surplus value," they feel they must deal with their employers directly and aggressively, sometimes over the council tables and sometimes by striking. If they are unsuccessful in these attempts, they can rob the employer of the fruits of victory by slowdowns, carelessness, inattention, and by taking time off. Very often the worker has been led by his own problems of emotional adjustment to magnify the difficulties of his work and the shortcomings of management. The emotionally mature person is more likely to look for ways to improve his situation, rather than to dissipate his energies in useless gestures of rebellion against his employer.

Workmen's Skill Considered a Commodity. The attitudes of some employers are colored by their conviction that a workman's skill is a commodity to be bought and sold like any other commodity on the market. This viewpoint implies that the employer has no more responsibility to his laboring force than he does to the coal, iron, or natural gas that is going into the manufacture of the product.

An employer who operates by these principles can close his plant without warning and throw hundreds out of work. When laborers are plentiful, he bids the price down as cheap as he can. If possible, he hires youths and women to do his work, because their skills may be obtained more cheaply. Fortunately, the employers who operate in this manner are a diminishing group, thanks to the vigilance of unions, the government, and the public. An important cause of this change in employer attitude, however, has been the desire of management to find more effective ways of working with employees. This desire has led to the realization that employees resent being treated as commodities. Despite this change in attitude on the part of management, many workers are quick to suspect that employers are taking advantage of them, and this suspiciousness is readily exploited by labor organizers.

Emotional Climates that Produce Maladjustment

The kinds of psychological atmospheres likely to produce tensions in employment situations may be divided into two broad and somewhat overlapping types: *authoritarian* and *competitive*. There are usually some elements of authoritarianism and competition in most work situations — this is unavoidable in a patriarchal culture like ours, which encourages hostility to be expressed as competition. But in some situations the authoritarian aspects are stressed; in others, the competitive element dominates; and of course there are situations where these elements are relatively absent or are stressed to only a slight degree.

The Authoritarian Climate. Any enterprise needs to be regulated, and a hierarchy of leaders is needed to carry out the regulations for the good of all. Any organization in which there is good communication from top to bottom, in which decisions are evolved by the total group or through their representatives, in which the aim of management is to develop employees who are responsible and self-disciplined, in which employees are helped to meet their basic needs through programs promoting interest in their work, and in which employees have an opportunity to discuss grievances and personal problems with professional counselors, may be characterized as *least* authoritarian.

An organization that operates on authoritarian principles displays the following characteristics:

Communication is difficult: Workers do not obtain prompt hearing for their grievances. Management communicates to the workers only through the chain of command. Relations between supervisors and workers are "dehumanized." The worker who desires to make suggestions for the improvement of the product or its processing has trouble in getting his idea considered. If any communication takes place between management and labor, it occurs only at the "top level" — that is, between union representatives and company officials.

Regulations are drawn up by management and are published in bulletins or communicated through the supervisory staff. Sweeping changes in hours and working conditions are ordered without advance notice. Punishments for infractions are impersonal and severe. The names of violators may be published. Great stress is laid upon conformity; failing to conform is regarded with suspicion. Suspicion also characterizes most of the relations among employees on the same level. Supervisors serve primarily as inspectors or "snoopers." Job functions are very specifically and rigidly laid down, and nothing is left to individual discretion — manuals that contain all the answers are provided.

The net effect of the authoritarian climate is to discourage individual initiative, to prevent the worker from identifying himself with his work, and to stifle normal sources of job satisfaction. The employees who can give up individuality and become submissive are the ones who make the best adjustment to the authoritarian climate. However, in such instances there is a tendency to displace hostility on more vulnerable folk: members of the family, minority groups, or subordinates. The employee who has strong needs to express his individuality suffers in the authoritarian situation; he would be happier in the competitive atmosphere.

The Competitive Climate. Although the authoritarian atmosphere creates hostilities and anxieties, it is, in its best form, a stable situation, and as such it tends to conserve, rather than to overexploit, the energies of the employee. The competitive situation, on the other hand, encourages the employee to pour forth as much energy and time as he can. The individual who can exceed the record of other employees and can then repeatedly exceed his own record is the employee who is rewarded. Whereas the authoritarian situation emphasizes tightly organized, efficient activity, the competitive situation is tense, dynamic, and sometimes dramatic. The retiring, submissive individual who fits well into the authoritarian situation would have grave difficulties of adjustment in the competitive climate. Whereas hostility is internalized or "driven underground" by the authoritarian climate, it tends to be expressed more openly in the competitive situation. This hostility is not usually expressed verbally or physically but appears in the form of such direct action as price-cutting, the discreet depreciation of a competitor's product, the aggressive approach to a customer, persistence, and high-pressure selling.

There is a tendency, too, for employees living in the two different psychological atmospheres to have different kinds of occupational goals: the employee in the authoritarian situation is more interested in security and working conditions, whereas the employee in the competitive situation tends to be more interested in large sums of money as represented by commissions or bonuses. The fact that in most instances the individual cannot consistently maintain a high earning level means that a chart of his earnings would be marked by dramatic "peaks and valleys" characteristic of a "feast-or-famine" type of existence.

Adjustment Problems Arising from Authoritarian and Competitive Climates. Psychological atmospheres that are overcompetitive or overauthoritarian in nature produce in the workers frustrations, anxieties, and tensions that are carried over into other aspects of their lives. The drop-hammer operator in an authoritarian plant, for example, may feel resentful because he finds his fellow workers unfriendly, because he cannot communicate his grievances to the management, because he feels his work is not appreciated, or because he feels that he has an idea which would help production, but which he cannot discuss with anyone who counts. He may work out some of this resentment on his family by playing the same authoritarian role at home he has observed in his supervisors, or he may sublimate some of his feelings of inferiority and rejection by joining a lodge and becoming elected to a position of importance in order to obtain a feeling of status.

The employee in the competitive situation who generates more hostility than he can express (he has learned that it does not pay to be too aggressive with customers), who loses almost as often as he wins in the struggle for customers, who feels somewhat exploited carrying on so fierce a fight for somebody else's product, may attempt to compensate for his sense of failure by urging his children to get the best marks in school, or he may sublimate some of his hostility by playing poker with "the gang" on Monday nights.

Factors in Employment that Foster Good Adjustment

Employment Situations Are Unique. Perhaps it appears that we have overstressed the negative aspects of employment by depicting those factors in the work situation that tend to produce frustration, anxiety, and insecurity. Actually, of course, the attitudes and emotional states that result from any employment situation are compounded partly from the factors which may be recognized by the unbiased observer and partly from the personality characteristics of the employee which affect his attitudes toward his work, his fellow employees, and his employer. The morale of a worker depends not so much on what happens on the job as it does on how he interprets what happens. The following case may serve as an illustration.

Vera McCarthy was three years old when her sister was born. She had been idolized and overprotected, and now this attention was lavished on her baby sister. Her attempts to regain favor were rebuffed, and she took refuge in jealousy and self-pity. As the girls grew older, Vera was the plainer of the two, and the praise directed toward her sister helped to increase her bitterness and her sense of having been deprived and cheated by life.

By the time Vera became an adult, she had learned to suppress the open expression of her feelings of bitterness; she nonetheless came to see threat and deprivation in everything that occurred around her. When the office manager hired a new typist, she "knew" it was because he was preparing someone to replace her. Any change in the office procedure was interpreted as a move to take away some of her duties. Although her annual efficiency ratings were high, the fact that someone in the office received a higher rating was an indication to her that the manager was prejudiced. Since the employment situation in which Vera worked contained some elements of authoritarianism and competition, as is usually the case, each occasion when management acted in an authoritarian manner or when competitive elements were prominent was a signal for renewed bitterness and anxiety on Vera's part. For example, when management decided to move all the desks in the office without consulting the office force, it was inevitable that Vera's desk should be moved to a less desirable location; and when a senior stenographer's position became vacant, Vera did not even apply, because she "knew" that the final choice would be determined by favoritism.

Vera's position is better than it might be. Her office manager is a sympathetic person, who understands his subordinates and knows how to deal with them effectively. He acts as a buffer between top management and his office force and is often able to reinterpret and to soften the more authoritarian aspects of the work situation and to minimize some of the competitive elements. However, because Vera's orientation toward life is so rigid, so suspicious, and so neurotic, neither he nor any other person is able to give her the emotional support and reassurance she would like to have. Her demands are so excessive and unrealistic that they can never be satisfied. On the other hand, if Vera were to work in an atmosphere that was overauthoritarian or competitive, her troubles would be greatly aggravated. An emotionally secure person would be much more able to withstand authoritarian and competitive pressures.

Employment Helps in Giving a Feeling of Identity. As Everett C. Hughes says, "Man's work is one of the more important parts of his social identity (4)." In addition to its function of aiding the individual to sustain life, work has certain cultural functions, particularly with regard to role and status. In our culture, work enables an individual to develop his identity — that is, it helps him to determine "who he is." If an adult is given three chances to say who he is, it is very likely that he will name his occupation in one attempt to identify himself.

One of the signs of adult maturity in our culture is the ability to be able to prepare oneself for an occupation and perform it successfully. In working, the individual knows that he is doing something that is culturally approved; and this knowledge helps him to feel at peace with society. When he cannot obtain employment, he feels ashamed. His unemployment may be due to circumstances beyond his control, but he feels he has failed the expectations of society, he feels outside of society, marginal, a "fringer." Conversely, when he is employed, he feels a certain satisfaction in being able to get and hold a job, particularly if it is a job consistent with his self-concept. Because he is doing something that society approves, he feels that he "belongs." As an employed person, he feels identified with a group, and this in turn gives *him* identity.

An accountant feels something in common with other accountants; there is a bond that connects them. When accountants get together, they talk the same language, even though they work for different kinds of firms. They may further emphasize this feeling of camaraderie by joining a national professional association; this tends to give them additional status as professional accountants. The accountant also feels a bond between himself and workers in other departments at his place of employment: they, too, have a common experience; they, too, can "talk shop" when they get together.

Thus, belonging to an occupational group and being employed are ways in which individuals meet the need for belongingness and the need to be accepted. The accountant is accepted by other accountants as a brother accountant; he is accepted by the world at large as an accountant; and he is accepted by other employees in his place of business as a fellow worker.

Work as a Means of Meeting the Need for Self-expression. If employment is psychologically satisfying, it thereby aids the employee in meeting his needs for achievement, self-expression, and accomplishment. This works both ways. His ability to express himself through his work is dependent on his level of emotional maturity, and his attainment of emotional maturity is partly dependent on his ability to meet his needs for self-expression. An additional factor in the latter case is the general suitability of the work performed. An individual who must work at tasks which require skills and talents he possesses to a low degree and which do not provide expression for skills and talents he does possess will find life frustrating and difficult. These frustrations, in turn, may affect his general level of emotional maturity. However, emotionally mature persons who are forced by circumstances to do work unsuited to their talents can usually "make the best of it" and often derive some sense of satisfaction in spite of their difficulties. Evidence of this may be found in the experiences of persons who had to accept jobs below their level of competence during the Depression of the 1930's or, because of military necessity, during World War II.

Work of some kind is usually necessary for a good psychological adjustment — otherwise the individual may lack opportunity to express himself. Satisfactory work experiences are as important to good adjustment as are satisfactory experiences in other interpersonal relations.

Forms of Substitute Activity. But what of the person whose work is routine, whose work apparently gives little opportunity for creativity? Unfortunately, the advances of the industrial revolution have not made much progress in eliminating this source of frustration. Intelligent employers carry on vigorous campaigns aimed at heightening employee morale through providing information about the company and the job, providing opportunities for employees to meet together in friendly fashion (bowling teams, picnics, etc.), providing counseling programs, and the like. However, while these campaigns aid the general adjustment of the employee, nothing helps so much as his taking some responsibility for meeting his own needs. Some individuals engage in creative and artistic hobbies like photography, ceramics, and wood carving. Others develop interests in social work and become Boy Scout or Girl Reserve leaders. Still others become involved in civic affairs and political reform. Each person should choose his hobby according to the kind of talents he has and the needs that should be met.

We have referred to the ways in which tensions and anxieties generated on the job find expression in off-the-job situations. The converse is also true. Frequently tensions and anxieties generated off the job find expression in the job situation. Sometimes this expression is positive (for example, sublimation) and sometimes negative (for example, displaced hostility).

Persons who experience sexual frustrations frequently find that pouring their energy into creative work aids in relieving the sense of frustration. Hostilities, too, can be made to melt away through vigorous physical activity. Unrelieved tensions find expression in the job situation: relationships on the job suffer when the foreman who cannot have his way at home because of a domineering wife develops into a dogmatic dictator whom nothing will satisfy; or a mimeograph operator who is unable to make an impression on a certain girl may experience a falling off in the quality of his work because of a general feeling of inferiority and discouragement.

Indications that work is a crucial area in the individual's over-all psychological adjustment are found in the evaluations that psychological workers make of individuals who come under their scrutiny. *Individuals whose adjustment to life is something short of successful usually have some kind of difficulty in their work, and individuals who have some kind of difficulty with their work usually have some personality problems that are giving them trouble.*

These findings, as well as the other conclusions reported in this chapter, have serious implications for students, because most of what has been said about the function of work as an aid or as a deterrent to adjustment also applies to the student as he participates in educational activities. For example, an otherwise competent student who is having difficulties with his studies usually finds that immature patterns of behavior are interfering with his success; and such common complaints as "the inability to concentrate" are, like "the inability to produce on the job," very likely to be related to repressed hostility or the inability to identify himself with the subject (job), or are due to distracting and tension-producing situations involving his personal life.

How Employers Can Facilitate Adjustment

The Hawthorne Study. One of the important studies made to learn how to improve the psychological climate of the work situation was conducted at the Hawthorne plant of the Western Electric Company in the late 1920's (5, 6). The study consisted of three parts: (a) a study by interview of workers' attitudes toward their work, (b) the close observation of the work habits and interpersonal relationships of a group of workers engaged in "connecting banks of terminals with color-coded wires," and (c) a study of the work behavior and interpersonal relations of a group of five women assembling small electrical relays under special conditions.

Twenty thousand employees were interviewed as a part of the first portion of the study, and careful accounts were kept of their statements on a wide variety of matters that seemed to have a bearing on their work. It was discovered by the researchers that the assumptions of management and its engineering and technical consultants bore little relationship to the actual operating conditions of the plant. For example, management assumed that workers were interested only in their wages and would therefore produce to the utmost in order to obtain the special rewards for extra production. In actuality, the researchers found that workmen banded together to limit production because they were afraid that if they produced more the rate would be cut. This feeling was part of a larger attitude — a fear that changes instituted by engineers and technological experts were aimed at depriving workers of status or at breaking up the chains of social interaction that were well-established among the workers. The interviewers also discovered that the relationship between workers and their *immediate* supervisors was of utmost importance in determining morale.

The observations in the bank-wiring room tended to bear out the findings of the interviewers. The workers here co-operated to keep the rate of production at a minimum. This was done in spite of the extra pay management had provided for production beyond this minimum, on the assumption that workers would always operate in their best — that is, financial — interest and produce more. Inspectors who acted in ways the workers felt were too haughty, authoritarian, and superior aroused so much antagonism that it was necessary to transfer them. Here again relations between workers and their immediate superiors were shown to be crucial.

The third portion of the study consisted of a four-and-one-half-year observation of a group of five women employees to determine what factors had the most influence on production. Some of the various conditions tried were pay on a piecework basis, rest pauses, differing hours of labor, and changes in rates of pay. During this period there was a gradual but regular increase in productivity, *regardless of the kind of working conditions imposed.* The most likely explanation is that this gain was the product of high morale among the group of workers. For the purpose of this experiment they had been freed from the constant and critical supervision of supervisors and minor executives, and there was opportunity for them to work out more natural relationships with one other and to develop their skills more efficiently. When the experiment was concluded, the rate of production dropped abruptly. Later, when one of the girls was asked why this had happened, she said, simply, "We lost our pride (7)."

The Hawthorne studies have not effected a revolution in management, but they have resulted in a small but growing group of employers who have "humanized" their employee relations with good results — freedom from strikes and slowdowns, increased production, lowered costs, and a vastly improved morale.

Improvement in Communication. One of the most important ways in which employers can improve worker morale is through improvement in communication — making it possible for management and the worker to discuss matters of common concern and to understand each other. Stuart Chase describes how communication was improved at the Calco Company, chemical manufacturers in New Jersey. Management at Calco was aware of a serious lack of co-operation not only between workers and management, but among the various levels in management itself. This problem was solved by setting up a round table with fifteen members, representing all levels of authority, which discussed the problems of the company in a relaxed, informal atmosphere. The result has been a vast improvement in communications between various levels and departments, which presumably has brought about an improvement in the emotional climate (8).

Taking the Worker into Partnership. Profit sharing alone does not appear to be a successful means of enlisting the support of the worker (9). This is probably because most of the plans are formulated by management without the advice, consent, and participation of the worker. Yet when workers are accepted as "partners in production" by management, as they are by the Hickey-Freeman Company and the Lapointe Machine Tool Company, the joint co-operation produces an increase in profits, which can be used for increased wages and bonuses (10). Workers who know the facts about their company will even voluntarily accept necessary pay cuts (11).

The principle here is that productive employment can and does give workers a sense of importance and self-reliance, which is basic to morale and efficient production. When this feeling is threatened or undermined, production suffers, and such difficulties as strikes and slowdowns may result. Those industries that grant workers a major voice in decisions are helping them to maintain the feeling of personal importance. As Edwin E. Ghiselli says in his review of research in the field of industrial psychology, "In general it appears that higher levels of production are not achieved by stress on production itself, but rather through procedures designed to stimulate ego motivations of self-determination, self-expression, and personal worth (12)."

Improved Conditions in Professional Fields. Although much of this discussion has been focused on business and industry, everything said here applies with equal force to other kinds of employment situations — government service, teaching, medical and social service, etc. No matter how much pride a teacher feels in her ability to help youngsters learn, if her morale is undermined by a punitive, critical, and authoritarian administration, her functioning as a teacher is almost certain to be impaired. On the other hand, a teacher who is unsure of herself can develop and improve if she has the support and guidance of a principal who awakens in her a feeling of personal worth and who helps her develop her best potentialities. The attitude of the administration of a school permeates every aspect of teacher-pupil, pupil-pupil, and even teacher-teacher relationships. The writer is acquainted with a substitute teacher who says that she knows what kind of day she will have in the classroom — that is, how many "discipline problems" she will have — when she meets the principal in the morning and sees what kind of person he or she is. If the principal is kindly, sympathetic, and understanding, her day will be enjoyable and pleasant, but if he is rigid, authoritarian, and defensive, she can count on her day being spoiled by skirmishes with aggressive children.

SUMMARY

In our culture, work occupies a central place in problems of adjustment. Frustrations that occur on the job affect one's total adjustment, while anxieties resulting from conflicts in one's life off the job can affect one's job adjustment.

We have mixed feelings about work in our culture, and our ambivalence is a potential source of conflict. The man in the street regards work as the barrier that separates him from fulfilling his needs, and he tends to resent it for that reason. Or he may look upon it solely as the means whereby one acquires money, power, and status. Each of these orientations is in part unrealistic, and contains the seeds of maladjustment.

There are a number of forces and conditions that make the employment situation a conflict-producing one. One of these is the disassociation of the individual from his work. Mechanization and mass production have resulted in a tendency for the individual to feel that he is only a cog in the wheel. At the same time, he feels the pressure of a cultural pattern that stresses progress, advancement, self-improvement, and competition in the face of a general employment situation that provides for successively fewer opportunities for advancement as one progresses. Because of these frustrations, workers often feel resentful toward management. Sometimes this resentment results in individual adjustment problems, sometimes it results in low production and inefficiency, and sometimes it finds open expression in strikes and slowdowns.

Employers at times aggravate the tensions of the employment situations by taking the attitude that the workman's skill is a commodity like any other component of the industrial product, something that can be bought and sold irrespective of the human element.

There are two kinds of emotional climates that can cause maladjustment on the job: authoritarian and competitive. Under authoritarian conditions, communication between management and the workers is at a minimum. Workers are expected to obey the dictates of management without question. The emphasis is on regulation and conformity and not on individual expression and originality.

Under competitive conditions, the stress is placed on the worker's ability to defeat other workers who are striving for the same objectives. This makes for a situation which is less secure than that provided by authoritarian controls, but which makes more provision for individual incentive and initiative.

Employment can make a positive contribution to adjustment by giving the worker an occupational role and affording him an opportunity to feel identified with a group. Furthermore, work is the chief means of self-expression available to most of the individuals in our culture. Employers can provide more of a mental hygiene atmosphere in work situations by working with, rather than against, the social systems that workers have organized on their own level, and by recognizing that the incentives that cause workers to work are for the most part emotional and psychological, rather than wholly economic. Morale and production can be improved by taking the worker into partnership (permitting him to participate in decisions that affect working conditions and his welfare) and by improving the communication existing between him and the management.

The general principles laid down in this chapter apply to the employed professional worker as well as to the industrial employee. The work of professional people is just as susceptible to poor morale as is the work of employees in business and industry.

REFERENCES

1. K. Davis, "Mental Hygiene and the Class Structure," in P. Mullahy, ed., *A Study of Interpersonal Relations*. New York: Hermitage, 1949. P. 366.
2. "$25,000 a Year: A.D. 1948," *Fortune*. 37:66 ff.; January, 1948.
3. K. Young, *Personality and Problems of Adjustment*. New York: Appleton-Century-Crofts, 1940. P. 366.
4. E. C. Hughes, "Work and the Self," in J. H. Rohrer and M. Sherif, eds., *Social Psychology at the Crossroads*. New York: Harper, 1951. P. 314.
5. F. J. Roethlisberger, *Management and Morale*. Cambridge: Harvard University Press, 1941.
6. F. J. Roethlisberger and W. J. Dickson, *Management and the Worker*. Cambridge: Harvard University Press, 1939.
7. T. N. Whitehead, *Leadership in a Free Society*. Cambridge: Harvard University Press, 1936.

8. S. Chase, *Roads to Agreement.* New York: Harper, 1951. P. 151.

9. "Experience with Profit-Sharing," *The Conference Board Management Record.* New York: National Industrial Conference Board, Inc., 1946. Pp. 33–38.

10. S. Chase, *Roads to Agreement.* New York: Harper, 1951. Pp. 140–146.

11. S. Chase, *Roads to Agreement.* New York: Harper, 1951. P. 140.

12. E. E. Ghiselli, "New Ideas in Industrial Psychology," *Journal of Applied Psychology.* 35:229–235; 1951.

SUGGESTED READINGS

T. M. Newcomb and E. L. Hartley, eds., *Readings in Social Psychology.* New York: Holt, 1947. Section 10 contains articles dealing with industrial morale and worker productivity.

J. G. Friend and E. A. Haggard, *Work Adjustment in Relation to Family Background.* Applied Psychology Monograph No. 16; June, 1948. Stanford: Stanford University Press, 1948.

H. W. Hepner, *Psychology Applied to Life and Work,* 2d edition. New York: Prentice-Hall, 1950. See particularly Chapters 18–23.

E. Fromm, *Man for Himself.* New York: Rinehart, 1947. A concise exposition of a humanitarian approach to life and its problems growing out of the writer's psychoanalytic experience. Particularly useful for its description of the productive and nonproductive orientation to life and its comparison of the authoritarian conscience with the humanistic conscience.

H. C. Lindgren, *The Art of Human Relations.* New York: Hermitage, 1953. See Chapter 12, "Interpersonal Relations at Work."

R. K. Merton, "Bureaucratic Structure and Personality," in C. Kluckhohn and H. A. Murray, eds., *Personality in Nature, Society, and Culture.* New York: Knopf, 1948. Pp. 282–291. A sharply drawn portrait of the bureaucratic type of personality and the conditions and dynamics that produce and foster personality patterns of this type.

K. Young, *Personality and Problems of Adjustment.* New York: Appleton-Century-Crofts, 1940. See particularly Chapter 23, "The Relation of Occupation to Personality Adjustment."

T. Parsons, "Certain Primary Sources and Patterns of Aggression in the Social Structure of the Western World," in P. Mullahy, ed., *A Study of Interpersonal Relations.* New York: Hermitage, 1949. Pp. 269–296. An incisive description of the place of hostility and aggression in our occupational life.

R. Stagner, *Psychology of Personality,* 2d edition. New York: McGraw-Hill, 1948. Chapter 21, entitled "Economic Factors," reviews the stresses placed by employment and unemployment on the personality of the individual.

M. L. Blum, *Industrial Psychology and Its Social Foundations.* New York: Harper, 1949. The entire book is related to the subject of this chapter, but see particularly the chapters dealing with the Hawthorne studies, job satisfaction, industrial morale, incentives, fatigue, industrial warfare, and unemployment.

W. F. Vaughan, *Social Psychology.* New York: Odyssey, 1948. Chapter 18 deals with human relations in industry.

F. Redl and W. W. Wattenberg, *Mental Hygiene in Teaching.* New York: Harcourt, Brace, 1951. Chapter 16 deals with the kinds of adjustment problems teachers must face.

N. Fenton, *Mental Hygiene in School Practice.* Stanford: Stanford University Press, 1943. See Section 4, "Mental Hygiene and the Teacher," particularly the chapter entitled "Human Relations and School Morale."

S. A. Szurek, "Emotional Factors in the Use of Authority," in E. L. Ginsburg, *Public Health Is People.* New York: Commonwealth Fund, 1950.

Partners in Production: A Basis for Labor-Management Understandings. A report by the Labor Committee of the 20th Century Fund, 1949.

F. Deake and K. Deake, "Partners in Velvet," *Reader's Digest.* 59:56–60; August, 1951. A story of how the American Velvet Company pulled itself and its employees out of a financial mess by inviting employees to participate in the management of the business.

"More Dignity in the Job," a report by the Labor Committee of the 20th Century Fund, in S. H. Britt, ed., *Selected Readings in Social Psychology.* New York: Rinehart, 1950. Pp. 433–436.

D. Katz, "Morale and Motivation in Industry," in W. Dennis, *et al., Current Trends in Industrial Psychology.* Pittsburgh: University of Pittsburgh, 1949.

E. E. Ghiselli, "New Ideas in Industrial Psychology," *Journal of Applied Psychology.* 35:229–235; 1951. A review of current psychological approaches to problems of industrial morale, job satisfaction, and production.

F. J. Roethlisberger and W. J. Dickson, *Management and the Worker.* Cambridge: Harvard University Press, 1939. The story of the Hawthorne Study.

S. Chase, *Roads to Agreement.* New York: Harper, 1951. An easy-to-read discussion of the problems that face management and labor, with a description of some successful solutions.

XIII...*Choosing a Vocation:*

Self-Appraisal

Importance of Vocational Choice. In the broad, general areas of occupational adjustment, the problem of choosing an occupation plays a *minor but important* role. If the end goal is satisfaction in one's work, it is evident that not everyone achieves this goal. The question is: To what extent does poor occupational choice interfere with the attainment of job satisfaction? Evidence is lacking that would enable us to say with any certainty that persons who are dissatisfied with their jobs would attain job satisfaction merely if they were to change to other occupations. Indeed, from what we know from clinical and experimental studies, we can assume that occupational dissatisfaction, like other kinds of behavior, is frequently symptomatic of other psychological difficulties. Yet it is obvious that there must be those persons whose occupational adjustment is caused or is aggravated by conditions peculiar to their form of employment. The story of Otto Spiel, the bookkeeper of the Eldorado Packing Company, which was discussed in Chapter 3, is a case in point. Otto's adjustment to his job as a salesman is made difficult by his inability to "feel right" toward his potential customers. But this personality problem produced only minor difficulties of adjustment in his bookkeeping job. Although it might be said that Otto's problem would have been avoided by his having made the proper occupational choice (to have remained with bookkeeping), it should nevertheless be noted that Otto's *neurotic needs* were what prevented him from appraising his situation realistically and finding the obviously correct solution to his problems. Hence it may be said that the success of occupational choice, like that of other decisions we must make, is very much dependent on our general adjustment.

At the same time, in order for a decision to be realistic and sensible, it should be based on a careful appraisal of prevailing conditions. Thus, no student, however excellent his adjustment, is in a position to decide what course of action he should take vocationally unless he is sufficiently well acquainted with his needs, his potentials, and his deficiencies, on the one hand, and the occupational situation, on the other.

George Harlow was a friendly, easygoing chap of more than average academic ability, as demonstrated by his B+ average in high school. He had no severe problems of adjustment, he was well-liked by fellow students of both sexes, and he was active in extracurricular activities. By the time he graduated from high school, he had made no occupational plans and had done little exploration of a vocational nature. However, most of his friends had planned to continue their education at a small liberal arts college in a nearby town, and it seemed reasonable for him to go with them. During the first two years of college, George merely took the required courses, spending little thought on his vocational future. When he entered his junior year he asked his adviser to suggest a major. On learning that George had no particular field of interest, and had done equally well in all subjects, the adviser suggested that George major in business administration, stating that a background in business "would fit in anywhere." George completed the business administration program and graduated with good grades, although not with honors. The summer after graduation, George took a job with a local department store as a buyer trainee. Within a month he knew he had made a mistake. The thought of dealing with profit and loss for the rest of his life suddenly became repulsive to him. As long as he had to think about them in the abstract — in the classroom — the situation was tolerable, but dealing with them in a real-life situation was different. All at once, his hobbies began to take on new meaning. He began to look forward to the end of the day, when he could go home and work in his wood-working shop in the basement. He longed for the week ends, when he met with a couple of the fellows in a garage where they tinkered with, tore down, and reassembled speedboats. He thought of the summer he had enjoyed so much, working with a surveying crew as a rod-and-chain man. As he talked the problem over with his father, the subject of engineering came up again and again. Finally it was decided that George would go on to the university and take up mechanical engineering.

That fall George registered at the university. Inasmuch as none of his business administration courses fitted the engineering pattern, he matriculated as a junior and went on to complete work for the bachelor's degree in mechanical engineering. At this point George was drafted in the Army. The Army sent him to OCS, commissioned him as a second lieutenant, and then gave him a billet in ordnance engineering. As his period of military service drew to a close, George thought increasingly about what his work would mean in civil life, and he decided that mechanical engineering was not the field for him; it was too confining. Working all day with machinery in factories and laboratories made him miss the human contacts that had been so important to him in high school and college. At this point he made a wise move: he went to see a vocational counselor.

The tests that the vocational counselor gave him confirmed his interest in people, as well as his interest in machinery and handicraft. The occupation that seemed to offer the most satisfactory combination seemed to be that of manual arts teacher. However, preparation for such a job would require a year or two of additional training, and George already had received seven years of higher education, with nothing beyond a bachelor's degree to show for it. After further discussion with the counselor, George decided to look for another kind of work which would give him an opportunity to use his talents and experience and which would also enable him to receive satisfactions from human relationships. After a brief "trial flight" as the personnel manager for a small steel fabricating plant, George found the job he wanted: veterans' co-ordinator for a technical junior college, with a promise of an administrative job if he proved to be satisfactory. At last reports he was happier in this work than he had ever been before.

It is true of George Harlow as it is true of all of us — choice is not the only factor involved in job satisfaction. For George the choice factor was probably more crucial than it is for most of us, inasmuch as time and expense could have been saved if George had been given an opportunity, through vocational counseling during the earlier years of college, to study himself and the occupational field.

In many ways George's experience is typical. A high proportion of persons who have made satisfactory adjustments in the world of work have "found themselves" only after having tried a variety of jobs. Changing jobs is common practice. The writer was present at a conference of school guidance workers when the question was asked, "How many of those present planned, when they entered college, to be in the kind of work they are in today?" Only one person out of the hundred assembled was able to raise his hand. However, when the question was asked, "How many of you planned, on entering college, to go into education?" the proportion of hands raised was over 50 per cent. Thus the academic preparation and the subsequent occupational experiences of this majority might be considered excellent preparation for guidance work. And if an analysis could have been made of the minority who had not planned for a career in education, it would have been found that a large proportion had majored in fields closely allied to education, such as social science, psychology, and social welfare. It is the writer's experience that only a small percentage enter the field of guidance from such divergent areas as engineering, medicine, statistics, foreign languages, etc., and this situation holds true for other professions. In other words, occupational mobility tends to be *within* broad vocational areas rather than *between* vocational areas. In the skilled trades, for example, it is more common for a worker to go from one type of metalworking to another kind of metalworking than to transfer to an entirely different field, like cement-finishing or cleaning-and-dyeing.

Significant Factors in Vocational Choice. The following factors appear to be significant in vocational choice:

1. Choosing an occupational goal is not the most important factor in preparing for a good vocational adjustment, but it is one of the important factors.

2. The choice of a goal should be made in accordance with what one can find out about oneself and about the occupational areas under consideration.

3. Vocational plans should be made in terms of as broad occupational fields as possible in order to provide for the flexibility that may be needed later.

4. Making early vocational plans may forestall losses in time and money that may occur if one makes vocational decisions haphazardly and, as a result, is forced to try a series of different jobs in a random attempt to find "the right one."

The Process of Self-appraisal

Getting to Know Yourself. Perhaps the most important step in choosing an occupational field is the process of learning to know yourself vocationally. This is a many-sided, complicated problem, and there is a considerable range in the kinds of information that are helpful. There is information of a specific nature, such as the scores you make on a mechanical aptitude test, and information of a broad, general nature, such as the nature of your life goals. Inasmuch as the broader, general areas of information are the more significant, we shall start with them.

What kind of a person are you? There are three ways of finding out what kind of person you are: self-analysis, evaluation by others, and psychological tests. Each has its shortcomings and its advantages.

What Kind of Person Do You Want to Be? One way to analyze yourself vocationally is to think about the kind of person you want to be ten years, twenty years, thirty years hence. What would you be doing then if you had complete freedom of choice? Keeping your picture within the bounds of realistically possible attainment, what kind of life do you see yourself living to give yourself the greatest personal satisfaction?

What you plan to be in the future is closely related to your present needs, to the kind of person you are now. The problem, of course, is to determine which needs are unrealistic and neurotic and which are fundamental and basic to your personality. For example, if you see yourself twenty years hence as a traveler, possibly a diplomatic courier or a buyer for an export-import firm, perhaps it is because you now have a need to "get away from it all," to escape from the frustrations of life as you now live it. On the other hand, this projected picture of yourself may be the partial result of an active, intense curiosity, which represents you as a person finding out how others live, learning whether what the travel books say is true. More than likely, there is a little of both needs in your twenty-years-hence picture of yourself — a little of wanting to get away from everything, and a little of active curiosity. In any event, jot these phantasies down as they come to you; they may contain important clues to your vocational personality.

What Kind of Person Are You? Another approach to self-understanding is to look at yourself objectively. Ask yourself: What kind of person am I? How do I express my "need for creativity"? Creativity is a highly personal matter. It is expressed in a variety of ways. Here are a few of them, together with typical jobs that afford an opportunity for such expression:

SELF-EXPRESSION THROUGH:	CAN BE FOUND IN THE WORK DONE BY:
Helping others	Social workers
Creating order	File clerks
Organizing	Office managers
Verbalizing	Salesmen
Color	Painters
Persuasion	Public relations counselors
Growing plants	Nurserymen
Mothering	Kindergarten teachers
Music	Musicians
Precision	Machinists
Food	Housewives
Texture	Plasterers
Research	Plant biologists
Discovery	Petroleum geologists
Motion	Truck drivers
Profits	Brokers
Aggression	Professional hockey players

Although each of the occupations listed above provides a variety of creative expressions in the course of its activities, it favors one more than others. For example, kindergarten teaching offers opportunities for self-expression in creating order, in developing and adjusting human relationships, in color and texture, in music and rhythm, in verbalizing, in persuasion, and even in research. Yet if one were looking primarily for an opportunity to express oneself in research or in music or in texture, one would not select kindergarten teaching.

Furthermore, each person uses his job differently to achieve the various types of expression he seeks in his job. Mr. Strong, a social science teacher in high school, may derive his chief occupational pleasure from reading sociological literature in preparation for his lectures. Miss Levine, another social science teacher, may enjoy most helping students to work on committee projects. Mrs. Swenson, who also teaches social science, may enjoy reading sociological literature as well as helping student committees, but really gets her biggest creative thrill when she can use her warm personal qualities in transforming an unruly, disorganized class at the first of the semester into an efficient but friendly organization by the end of the fourth week.

Where Do You Prefer to Work? A third way of looking at yourself vocationally is to ask: What kind of environment do I prefer? Do I prefer the clatter of machinery or the chatter of typewriters? Or do I prefer quiet? Must I be out of doors? Or am I more comfortable inside near the radiator or air-conditioner? Here are a few kinds of environments, together with some occupations which are associated with them:

AMID THESE ENVIRONMENTS:	CAN BE FOUND PEOPLE WHO WORK IN THESE OCCUPATIONS:
The ocean	Fishermen
Children	Recreation workers
Hospitals	Nurses
The home	Housewives
Forests	Lumbermen
City streets	Policemen
Poles and high wires	Telephone linemen
Figures and ledgers	Accountants
Noise, dirt, and smoke	Foundrymen
Open fields	Farmers
Animals	Dairymen
Laboratories	Chemists
Kitchens	Culinary workers

As a general rule, environmental considerations are less important than are opportunities for creativity, because the former are not as often related to personal needs as are the latter. In other words, if an individual is enabled to find satisfactory expression for his creative drives, he will be less inclined to be concerned about his physical environment. If, however, his creative needs are not being met, annoyances arising from the environment may assume large proportions.

If James Murdock enjoys his work as a draftsman and finds that the Albert Steel Construction Company gives him full opportunity to demonstrate his skill on the drafting board, he will probably not mind working next door to a noisy boiler shop, even though he might at one time have expressed a preference for work in an architect's office, where it is quieter. On the other hand, if Mr. Murdock is unable to find creative outlets for his talents with the Albert Steel Construction Company, the fact of working next to the boiler shop will become very important and may even be his stated (conscious) reason for quitting.

Jane Chenoweth is an interior decorator with highly original ideas, who detests cold weather. She worked first for a medium-sized department store in a Southern town. She had little opportunity to demonstrate her ability, because the townsfolk were conservative and resisted new ideas. But opportunity came her way in the form of a position on the staff of a well-known firm in Chicago. Miss Chenoweth took the job and finds life much more enjoyable than it was formerly, because her ideas are accepted and her work is highly successful. This feeling of acceptance, status, and value compensates for any physical discomfort she may feel because of the long, cold Chicago winter.

What Vocational Successes Have You Had? A fourth way of learning to know yourself vocationally is to consider those life experiences in which you have been successful and in which you have found enjoyment. Ask yourself: Which hobbies give me the most satisfaction? What kinds of recreation are the most enjoyable? Least enjoyable? In what school subjects am I most successful? Least successful? And, most important of all, what can I learn about myself from my work experience?

Previous work experience can produce valuable clues to the kind of person you are vocationally. What did you like most about the job you held? What did you like least? Make your analysis precisely and objectively, for overgeneralization may be misleading.

Roy Folsom spent one summer selling magazine subscriptions from house to house. He thought that he was going to like this work, but he found it irksome and was glad when the summer was over. However, on looking back on the experience, he remembered the following things:

1. He disliked the supervisor, who seemed never satisfied with the day's sales and gave the team of salesmen a tongue-lashing each morning before they set out.

2. He disliked walking up to a strange house and ringing the doorbell.

3. He was angry and depressed when housewives refused even to listen to his sales "message."

4. He got a thrill of pleasure when he succeeded in selling a prospective customer; sometimes this feeling lasted for several hours, even when business was bad.

5. He took pride in his ability to make a quick analysis of the situation and to thread his way through customer resistance to the sale.

6. He was top man on the team in earnings for the summer.

7. He would have made more money working on the grease rack of his uncle's service station.

If Roy concludes that because he was not happy on a particular selling job, selling is not for him, he may be making a mistake. There is evidence to indicate that he enjoys practicing techniques of persuasion. On the other hand, it may well be that he would never enjoy selling that involves the "cold canvass" approach of the door-to-door salesman. He should not be concerned about disliking the supervisor; few people enjoy working for unappreciative and punitive supervisors. Such factors must be separated from the other aspects of his summer job and examined carefully and dispassionately.

Negative information may be the chief yield of a job experience:

June Jennings held a job for three months as the waitress in an ice-cream parlor. She took the job to earn money to buy a fur coat. She had thought in advance that she might like the job, because she would often see her friends who patronized the establishment, and the possibility of free milk shakes was rather attractive. However, June did not enjoy the job and wanted to quit at the end of the second day. Somehow, she continued until she had earned the price of her coat. As she looked back on the experience after a year had elapsed, the following facts appeared:

1. During the busy periods, she was rushed to the point of distraction; she thoroughly disliked being hurried — it made her tense and jittery.

2. During slack periods she was required to wash glasses and silverware, clean up the counter, and even sweep up under some of the booths; she had never liked jobs like these at home.

3. While the proprietor never said anything to her directly, it was clear he did not like to see her sitting down, even for short periods; he limited her to two free milk shakes a day, but by the end of a month, June no longer cared for milk shakes.

4. She was usually too busy to chat when her friends came in; in fact, she felt somewhat uncomfortable waiting on them.

5. She enjoyed her associations with the other employees; and her relations with customers, when she was not rushed, were friendly.

6. She was very proud of her ability to save money to buy her fur coat — "strictly on her own."

It is clear that June does not like conditions that require her to work under pressure. It is a question whether menial labor could ever be satisfying to her, though her attitude might be different if she were working in her own home as a housewife and mother. She has learned that places of business that are attractive to customers do not have the same attractions for employees. It is plain that it is important for her to be on an equal level with her friends. She is able to have friendly relations with fellow workers and customers, and she has the perseverance necessary to stay with a job she does not like until she has achieved her goal.

What Skills Do You Have? In these processes of self-examination we have tended to stress the attitudinal aspects — factors concerned with how we feel about working conditions and opportunities. It is also important to consider carefully the factor of skill. What kind of successes have you had? What things have you done well? What things have you done poorly? Why have you succeeded or failed — was it because of the presence or absence of skill, motivation, opportunity, training, or experience? Do your chief skills seem to be in the mechanical area? Did you get better grades in high school chemistry than in other subjects? Would your model planes never fly? Were you unable to wear any of the clothes you made in home economics? Were you elected to a number of class offices in high school? Were you particularly effective as the chairman of the arrangements committee for school dances?

Here, as in other areas of self-analysis, it is important to make a careful and objective appraisal of one's strong points as well as one's weaknesses, for both are important in considering the choice of a career. Realistically, everyone is "deficient" in some respects, and it is mistaken pride to ignore these deficiencies in one's self-appraisal.

Securing Help in Making an Appraisal. It is hardly likely that anyone could achieve a satisfactory level of objectivity without some outside help. Attempts at self-examination and appraisal always involve considerable distortion, and there are "blind spots" in our consciousness that prevent us from perceiving what may be crucial aptitudes and disabilities. Therefore, no attempt at vocational analysis can be completely satisfactory unless one consults with others.

Friends and relatives first suggest themselves as possible consultants because they are easily accessible and have had ample opportunity to know us during our lifetime. However, these individuals are so close to us, psychologically speaking, that they are usually unable to be very objective in their evaluation of our strengths and weaknesses. They are so ego-involved in our welfare that their evaluations are likely to be strongly colored with what they know we

would like to become, what they would like to see us become, or
what they themselves would like (or have liked) to become. Furthermore, they are likely to overstress strong points and to overlook or
minimize weaknesses. And, usually, none of these individuals has
had training in the rather specialized field of vocational guidance.

Nonetheless, if we are alert to these difficulties, it is possible to
obtain some valuable insights from persons close to us, because
usually their psychological picture of us is different from the one
we have of ourselves, and it is important to have a number of different appraisals. Subjective as they are, it is better to have the evaluations of friends and relatives than to depend entirely on one's own
resources.

Parents, of course, deserve special consideration. The American
middle-class pattern is that parents should aid their children in
obtaining higher education and professional training if the family
budget can support such expenses; and the pattern, furthermore,
specifies that sons and daughters be permitted to choose their own
careers without undue influence. To some young people this has
meant that they should completely reject parental wishes or suggestions in choosing a career. At the other extreme are the parents
who refuse to aid their children unless they can do so on their own
terms — for instance, they will pay for a college education only if the
son goes to law school. It is difficult for such parents and children
to find a common meeting ground for discussion. However, in
families where these tensions do not exist or are minimized, youth
find their parents to be sympathetic and sometimes, to their surprise,
highly objective counselors in certain vocational areas.

The Role of the Professional Counselor. Self-appraisal and consulta-
tion with friends and relatives are no substitute for the professional
counselor and his tools. A trained and experienced guidance worker
knows that his function is to *aid* students in self-appraisal, in making
decisions, and in becoming familiar with appropriate occupation
information. Contrary to the opinion frequently expressed by
students, a guidance worker's function is *not* that of telling an individual "what he is best fitted for." It is the unskilled, untrained
vocational adviser who says, "According to this test you should go
into selling," or "I'm sorry, but you are not intelligent enough to
go to college." A well-trained vocational counselor does not use
pressure tactics to force a preference for or against a certain voca-

tional field. (This situation is not to be confused with that in which a counselor advises a student *out* of a field because low grades or aptitude test scores necessitate his being dropped from or refused admittance to certain curricula or schools.)

It should be noted in passing that not all vocational counselors are as well-trained or as competent as they should be. Objectivity and competence are highly variable commodities even in this area. Many high schools and some colleges have in the past appointed vocational counselors who have had little training or experience in vocational guidance. Fortunately, this situation is improving. Colleges and universities have expanded their facilities for training guidance workers; and institutions that hire counselors usually specify that applicants for positions must meet certain standards of professional competence.

One of the chief contributions the well-trained vocational counselor makes is that of providing an objective evaluation of the student's capabilities and potentialities. He has learned to be objective through his extensive experience in counseling students with a variety of problems and backgrounds. He is aware that academic success in high school is related to academic success in college — that is, persons who get high grades in high school tend to succeed in college; but he is also aware that a large minority of those who receive average or even poor grades in high school successfully complete college.

To illustrate the work of the vocational counselor, let us consider the efforts of one counselor to help Alfred McGraw, who made only average grades in high school. The job of the counselor was to find out whether Alfred had the qualities that would make him a successful candidate for an elementary teaching credential in spite of this apparent academic handicap. The counselor gave him a rather careful interview, and had him fill out a detailed questionnaire, the purpose of which was to bring out important facts related to academic grades, work experience, success or failures in interpersonal relations, extracurricular activities, hobbies, interests, family background, socio-economic background — anything that might have a bearing on future vocational and educational success or failure. The counselor also looked over Alfred's test scores on the college entrance battery and selected tests to be administered that would provide additional information about Alfred's particular problem — the need for a decision relating to a career in elementary education.

One of the most important kinds of tests that Alfred took was an academic aptitude test. Scores on this test are related to success in college. Inasmuch as Alfred scored at the 50th percentile, which is "average" for a college student, the counselor thought that he might succeed in the elementary education sequence of courses. Alfred's score on a reading test was at the 30th percentile for college freshmen. The counselor related this "low-average" score to Alfred's C grades in high school and decided that there was probably a connection between the two. Inasmuch as reading is a skill essential for success in college, the counselor recommended that Alfred take a remedial course in reading. A test in the "effectiveness of expression in English" placed Alfred at the 15th percentile for college freshmen (in the lowest sixth of the group) and indicated that he had much difficulty with spelling. Taken together, the English test and the reading test showed Alfred's chief difficulties to be linguistic and indicated the kind of problems he was likely to experience in college.

The counselor did not have to depend on Alfred's own opinion of his interests, his likes, and his dislikes. He gave sympathetic and thoughtful attention to Alfred's discussion of himself, but also gave him one or more interest tests. From these tests the counselor gathered valuable clues as to the areas in which Alfred had greater or lesser potentialities for vocational satisfaction. The interest tests measured Alfred's interests by comparing his preferences for various kinds of activities with those preferences expressed by other persons who had taken the same test. Alfred seemed to prefer mechanical and outdoor activities more than others did. In fact, his preference for mechanical work was very high. He also had strong preferences for work in the social service area; he had little interest in clerical work, business, medicine, engineering, the arts, writing, and mathematics.

The counselor had other tests that he could give Alfred, tests that could be administered later if it seemed necessary. However, he felt that for the time being he had enough evidence to help Alfred toward his next step — occupational exploration.

Alfred and the counselor discussed the findings of the tests. The results were neither encouraging nor discouraging, as far as Alfred's initial objective was concerned. Apparently Alfred had the basic intelligence or academic aptitude necessary to complete college work, but his high school grades and his scores on the reading and English tests indicated that success would come with difficulty. Alfred had to determine whether his life experiences revealed a reserve of perseverance, persistence, and drive, for he would need these qualities to carry him forward in spite of handicaps.

His interest-test results pointed to interests in three areas: mechanical, outdoor, and social service. Teaching would seem to fit the social-service area, but how about the first two areas? A teacher with this pattern of interests might be happy if he had well-developed hobbies embracing the two fields that did not fit in with teaching, or he might be happy if he taught physical education or manual training. If it was important to Alfred that he teach, it was advisable that he consider the opportunities in and the requirements for teaching these two subjects. On the other hand, there were many other jobs that combined mechanical, outdoor, and social service activities.

At this point, Alfred's *background* was drawn into the picture. His father was a teacher, his mother was a teacher, his brother was an accountant, and his sister was a registered nurse. His family did not put any pressure on Alfred to select teaching as an occupation, but he felt close to them, respected their judgment, and listened with interest to the family conversation whenever matters pertaining to the teaching profession were discussed. Despite his interest in teaching and the desire to make a choice that would please his family, he decided that, to be safe, it might be wise to explore a few occupations outside the field of education. Of the dozen or so suggested by the counselor, he selected those of park ranger, county agricultural agent, policeman, and landscape architect, which he added to his original list of manual training teacher, physical education teacher, and elementary teacher. Alfred now had an approximate idea of his strengths and deficiencies, and he had a tentative list of potential occupational areas that might be suitable. He was ready for the next step — the study and exploration of the occupations themselves.

(*For Summary, References, and Suggested Readings, see the end of Chapter 14.*)

XIV...Choosing a Vocation: The
Study of an Occupation

Sources of Information. There are four main sources of information available to those who wish to learn significant facts concerning occupations: occupational literature, interviews with experts, first-hand observations of occupational processes, and actual experience on the job. Each source has its advantages and shortcomings.

Occupational literature is readily available in most schools and colleges. It is useful in providing a quick survey of vocational operations and activities, working conditions, and occupational requirements. Any study of an occupation should start with at least a brief survey of the literature. On the other hand, facts contained in occupational literature grow rapidly out of date; there is a tendency in some literature to overstress the advantages of the job in an apparent attempt to "sell" the occupation; and, most important, it is easy to obtain a distorted, unrealistic picture of an occupation if one merely reads about it.

Interviews with experts and other persons associated with a given occupation are highly important sources of information. Frequently it is desirable to consult these individuals for no other reason than to obtain an understandable interpretation of information presented in occupational literature. Information available from experts is less likely to be outdated, and frequently they can give hints and advice that cannot be included in books. Experts in the field are also usually very familiar with the local scene; this is important when local conditions are different from the national conditions, for the latter are usually the ones reported in the literature. On the other hand, even the best of experts tend to "personalize" their information. Subtly or obviously, unconsciously or consciously, they tend either to sell interviewees on their occupation or to discourage them unduly, depending partly on their own job satisfaction and partly on the extent to which they feel that their profession is undermanned or overmanned. Furthermore, no single expert can, in the course of an interview, give the breadth, detail, and scope of information that can be given in a printed occupational brief. Statements by experts also share one of the disadvantages of occupational literature — they are secondhand information.

Information gleaned from readings and interviews takes on new meaning when one visits a place of business and sees workers actually performing their functions. This method also has its shortcomings — during the usual field trip one sees only a limited scope of activities and that too rapidly.

There is no substitute for *actual experience on the job*, even if the experience lasts only a short time. The chief disadvantage of this source of occupational information is, of course, its general non-availability. The college student cannot usually secure actual working experience in all the fields he is considering, no matter how desirable this might be. Other disadvantages are that it is not easy to obtain a broad grasp of job information concerning a certain vocational area merely by working in one specialized job. Furthermore, jobs usually held by beginners are of a different level from those held by trained workers, and any generalizations made on the basis of the former should be considered in the light of that difference.

Nevertheless, there are some special advantages of part-time or short-term work experience that are well worth considering. Certain skills and attitudes are appropriate to most job situations and can be learned as well on one job as another. Among these are pride in one's work, appreciation of accuracy and promptness, practice in adjusting to the requirements of an employer, and the ability to get along with fellow workers. The temporary work experience is of particular value to adolescents and young adults who are in the process of dissolving home ties. For them, the temporary job is an opportunity to leave the home for short periods; it gives them a feeling of independence because they are earning their way like full-grown adults; it gives them an opportunity to try out skills and training in a real-life situation; and it gives them a chance to be of value to someone on their own merit. This latter value has

Adolescents and young adults can gain valuable vocational information and insight through part-time or temporary work. This girl is working as a camp counselor.

great attraction for many adolescents. Some of them feel that their parents tolerate and love them because they have to, that if they were not related, things would be different. Working on a job, being appreciated away from home, being praised, being paid off at the end of the work period — these are good antidotes for feelings of inferiority and overdependency.

The Social Value of an Occupation. Of considerable pride to many an employed worker is the feeling that his work is making a valuable contribution to society. To know that one's work is necessary or appreciated or useful helps to satisfy the needs for status, value, and acceptance. In many ways, it is easier for the professional worker than it is for other workers to have this feeling, for he operates under less supervision, has more direct contact with persons benefiting from his services, and is in a better position to see direct results of his efforts. For example, lawyers, who can deal directly with their clients and evaluate the results of their efforts, tend to have a higher degree of vocational satisfaction than do streetcar motormen or assembly-line workers. Furthermore, most professional work has a tradition of social value.

Indeed, it might be hypothesized that the greater tendency to strike displayed by workers outside the professional group may be due to a feeling that the public does not appreciate their importance. Hence they take steps to prove their importance to the public (and themselves) by striking. The flurry of activity that follows — indignation meetings, pleas on the part of high public officials to return to work, public inconvenience — is highly gratifying and serves as balm for the lacerated group ego, for even negative attention is better than no attention at all. A strike serves to punish employers and the general public for having held the services of a working group in low esteem, and it draws attention to the value of these services by the vivid demonstration of what life is like without them. Naturally, strikes are not usually called for the stated (conscious) reasons of drawing public attention and "negative appreciation"; their stated goals are usually pay raises and other benefits, which are psychologically of less intrinsic value than the feeling of status and personal worth. Yet when the strike is successful and pay raises or other benefits are won, they serve to symbolize to the union, the employer, and society in general, the public recognition of the status and value of the striking working group.

Some working groups, like those professionally employed, have come to feel that status and social value is theirs as a matter of course; whereas other groups, like skilled and unskilled craftsmen, have come to feel that status and social value are qualities that must be wrested from those in control or from society in general. In any event, the feeling that one's work is of importance to society is a basic factor in job satisfaction. As Hughes points out in his analysis "Work and the Self," people tend to ascribe value to their work no matter how lowly (1). It is doubtful whether any person can feel that his vocational contribution is worthless and still feel happy on his job, and those persons who have not attained job satisfaction frequently feel that their contributions are inferior or else they fail to see any social value in them.

Realistically, of course, all occupations are of value to someone, or they would not exist, and the happiest persons in any occupation are those who are aware of this value. Inasmuch as this feeling of being important to society is crucial to job satisfaction, it behooves the student to become aware of the social values that result from the contributions of the occupation he is studying. In interviewing representatives of an occupation, he might ask, "In what way is this occupation important to society?" "What value does society see in it?"

History and Traditions. Related to the status, importance, and social value of an occupation are its history and traditions. Many employed persons cherish the fact that the history of their occupation goes back hundreds and thousands of years and that the old traditions of their occupations are still followed today. Typical of such traditions are the Hippocratic oath taken by physicians, the striped barber pole, the autonomy of a ship's captain, and the rule embodied in typographical union contracts specifying that editorial workers will not handle or touch printer's type. One of the most widely followed of such traditions is the apprenticeship agreement, which usually specifies that before a person can become recognized as a skilled craftsman or journeyman, he must have served a stated number of years as a trainee, working under the supervision of skilled craftsmen. The existence of these traditions helps to give a feeling of cohesiveness and group identity to members of the old crafts and professions. They derive satisfaction from the feeling that not only are they rendering services of value to society but that they are also the heirs of an ancient and honorable tradition. Their spirit is illustrated by the high school vice-principal who entered the Navy in World War II. Whenever he was asked by his fellow reservists what he did as a civilian, he never mentioned his administrative responsibilities, but said simply, "I was a teacher."

Glamor. Many newer occupations have achieved considerable status during the short period they have been in existence. Sometimes their status is based in part on traditions derived from older occupations with which they are allied (for example, television and radio follow the traditions of the theater), and sometimes their status is based on the glamor and mystery with which society has endowed them. Typical of the latter type are occupations in the electronic field, which derive part of their glamor from the keen interest the public displays in the broad field of physical science, technology, and invention, an interest denied any of the social sciences, with the possible exception of psychology. Consequently the job of the electronics technician probably ranks higher in public estimation than that of the social worker, even though it would be difficult to justify assigning a higher social value to the former than to the latter. The person who is considering the occupation of electronics should be aware that this occupation has a glamorous appeal to the general public, and he should carefully consider the extent to which his interest in this occupation is stimulated by its glamor rather than by a familiarity with the operations and functions of persons who work with electronic apparatus. On the other hand, the person who studies the occupation of social worker should be aware that the public has little contact with social workers as such, is largely unaware of their contributions to public welfare, and thus may be inclined to assign this profession a relatively low rank in the occupational status hierarchy. In other words, the person who considers this occupation should be aware of the public's tendency to ignore the contributions of the social worker and should carefully consider the extent to which the public's attitude may have colored his own thinking.

Occupational Trends. Additional background information is included under the heading of occupational trends: Is the demand for workers growing? What are the predictions for the future? Is the occupation gaining or declining in importance, or is it holding its own?

Occupational trends are related to technological and social changes. Blacksmiths have declined in number, and the occupation of smithing is less important than it was fifty years ago because of the supplanting of the horse by the automobile and the introduction of improved methods in the manufacture of metal products. The increasing complexity of problems in government, management, and technology has led to an increase in the need for statisticians. In the last fifty years, the proportion of unskilled workers in the working force of the country has slowly declined, while the percentage of white-collar workers has slowly grown. There was unemployment in the ranks of teachers during the 1930's, but it appears that teachers will be in short supply for the next decade or more.

Certainly no decision as to the choice of a vocation should be based on occupational trends alone. Nevertheless, a knowledge of trends constitutes one facet of the occupational information on which vocational choice should be based, for it aids in forming a realistic picture of potential job opportunities.

One of the most valuable sources in this field is the *Occupational Outlook Handbook*, compiled and produced by the joint efforts of the Bureau of Labor Statistics of the United States Department of Labor and the Veterans Administration. Its pages contain brief and highly readable reviews of the trends in every occupational field. The volume also contains reports on agricultural occupations, classified by region (2).

Job Descriptions. When most of us think about a given occupation, we tend to judge it by what people do on the job: What tasks do they perform? With what tools and equipment do they work? What materials do they use? What products do they produce? What services do they provide?

The student will do well to begin his quest for information of this sort by referring to the *Dictionary of Occupational Titles. Volume I: Definitions of Titles* (commonly referred to as the *D.O.T.*), which contains brief yet comprehensive descriptions of virtually all kinds of jobs in the United States. This volume is the product of the efforts of hundreds of job analysts employed by the War Manpower Commission and, later, by the United States Department of Labor. The following definition will illustrate both the brevity and the scope of *D.O.T.* definitions:

DIETITIAN . . . . (profess. & kin.) 0–39.93 . . . .
Applies the principles of nutrition to the feeding of individuals and groups: plans menus and special diets with proper nutritional value for a hospital, institution, school, restaurant, or hotel. Determines dietetic value of foods and food products. Purchases food, equipment, and supplies. Supervises chefs and other food service employees. Maintains sanitary conditions. Prepares educational and nutrition materials (3).

The above definition commences with the title usually applied to the occupation in question, followed by alternate titles. The designation "profess. & kin." refers to the classification of this occupation under the heading of "professional and kindred" occupations, and "0-39.93" is the code number assigned to this occupation. *D.O.T.* code numbers are frequently used in various kinds of occupational literature to aid in identifying jobs, and they also serve as the basis for several systems of filing occupational literature. The description following the code number gives the processes, procedures, and techniques used by persons who are called dietitians. Note that the limits of responsibility are carefully defined. It is clear that their *chief* functions do not involve the handling of food; dietitians are primarily *supervisory* personnel. Apparently many dietitians are called upon to do some professional writing.

These facts are worth noting, because they are not usually known by persons outside the profession. Perhaps the usual idea is that a dietitian personally prepares special dishes for persons on diets. Certainly most of the lay public does not think of a dietitian as a professional writer.

The chief function of a *D.O.T.* definition is to provide a basic description of the functions and responsibilities of the job concerned. A *D.O.T.* definition does not reveal what kind of training an individual must have to perform a job, it tells nothing about wages and salaries, and it only hints at working conditions. Its chief function is to *describe* the job for the purpose of *identifying* the worker by what he does, how he does it, what he works with, what he works on, where he works, the limits of his responsibility, who supervises him, and whom he supervises. The *D.O.T.* is a useful starting point for a person who wants to study an occupation, although it contains only a fraction of the information needed in choosing one.

It should be further noted that there are regional differences in occupations, and duties assigned to persons with the same occupational titles differ from job to job. (The *D.O.T.* covers only those duties usually assigned.) Therefore, it is desirable for the student of an occupation to make one or more visits to the occupational scene in order to see for himself what duties are of primary importance and under what conditions they must be performed.

Classification of Jobs. Another contribution to occupational study made by the *D.O.T.* is that of providing a convenient system of classifying jobs by the level of skill, training, and experience required (4). The system of classification (found in *Volume II* of the *D.O.T.*), together with typical jobs, is as follows:

Professional occupations: minister, architect, physician, teacher, accountant, librarian, trained nurse.

Semiprofessional occupations: aviator, chiropractor, commercial artist, draftsman, photographer.

Managerial and official occupations: credit man, personnel manager, railroad conductor, purchasing agent.

Clerical and kindred occupations: bookkeeper, stenographer, office machine operator, telephone operator.

Sales and kindred occupations: salesperson, salesman, demonstrator, auctioneer, insurance broker, canvasser.

Service occupations: barber, janitor, waitress, cook, usher, policeman, guard, porter, maid, doorman.

Agricultural, Fishery, Forestry, and kindred occupations: farmer, fisherman, lumberman, gardener, hunter.

Skilled occupations: baker, cabinetmaker, lithographer, shoe repairman, machinist, dyer, electrician.

Semiskilled occupations: roofer, gateman, service station attendant, taxidriver, carpet layer.

Unskilled occupations: longshoreman, handyman, stock boy, tankcar cleaner, roustabout, gift wrapper.

A glance at the above list will reveal that the classifications range from jobs at the top of the list which involve a high level of skill and training, through descending levels of skill and training to jobs at the bottom of the list, which involve a minimum of skill and no training. Persons in occupations like those at the top of the list are expected to perform their duties with little or no supervision; they are expected to feel a high degree of responsibility for the quality of their work. Persons filling jobs at the bottom of the list perform their duties under close supervision, the chief responsibility for the quality of the product or service being borne by a supervisor or foreman.

Although the compilers of the *D.O.T.* disclaim any attempt to identify this system of classification with the existing hierarchy of social class or status, it will be noted that persons holding jobs near the top of the list tend to be identified with the middle and upper classes, whereas those holding jobs such as those near the bottom of the list tend to be identified with the lower-middle and lower classes. Furthermore, the total life income of persons in jobs near the top of the list will in general exceed the total life income of persons in jobs near the bottom of the list.

Working Conditions: Expected Income. Under this category are included a variety of environmental aspects of the job: pay, hours, regularity of employment, and typical places of employment.

It is important for the student of an occupation to know what his starting wage will be and what he can expect as maximum pay. He should also find the answers to questions like the following: What does the "typical" or "average" worker earn? What are typical earnings for the most competent, the most experienced worker? Is the worker paid on an hourly, weekly, monthly, or annual basis, or does his compensation come from clients' fees, or does it come from profits? What kind of deductions can one expect: income tax, social security, unemployment insurance, retirement, health plan? Are there special expenses and costs that must be paid by the worker: uniform, special working clothes, tools and equipment, professional books and other literature, dues to unions or professional societies? What take-home pay might be expected?

It is important to stress the need to form a "frame of reference" in evaluating the income received by workers in the occupation under consideration. Some occupational briefs or brochures contain statements to the effect that workers in X occupation tend to be "underpaid" or are "well paid." It is highly desirable that the student make his own decision as to whether X occupation is well or poorly paid. He might make this decision on the basis of reports of average earnings from local or state employment offices, the United States Bureau of the Census, or local groups like chambers of commerce. Or his information may come from what he knows

about the earnings of persons who live the style of life to which he
has been accustomed. Another way to pose the problem is to ask
oneself the question: How much income does it take for a man, a
wife, and two children to live in a three-bedroom house on Y Street
and buy a new Chevrolet every fourth year? Or: How much
income does it take for a woman to share a three-room apartment
in Z neighborhood and go abroad for a vacation every summer?
In other words: How much income is required to support the kind
of life I might reasonably expect to lead?

Working Conditions: Hours of Work. Most persons now think of a
work week as made up of forty working hours. Yet most professional
workers, even those employed ostensibly on a forty-hour week, spend
considerable time above and beyond this in professional duties.
Under this category can be included time spent in advanced study,
in learning new skills, in professional reading, in attending conferences of professional organizations, and in the completion of work
that for some reason is left unfinished at the end of the working day.
The work load for most professional persons ebbs and flows. There
may occasionally be times when twenty or thirty hours a week
suffice to meet the demand for production or services, and there
may be other times when sixty, seventy, or even eighty hours a week
are barely sufficient. It is partly for this reason that professional
persons have a tendency to be more informal about their hours than
other occupational groups. The attitude of the professional group
as a whole seems to be that their prime responsibility is to the job,
to perform it in a competent manner no matter what the time
involvement is; but when an immediate need is passed, relaxation
is in order. In other words, professional workers tend to take an
independent point of view in the way in which they allot the time
spent in performing their work, and they feel that the exercise of
this privilege is a partial reward for their devotion to their profession. A similar point of view is usually maintained by proprietors
and persons employed in managerial positions.

This individualistic approach to the matter of working hours is at
variance with the attitudes displayed by most other white-collar
workers and by workers who are employed at an hourly rate.
Their responsibilities begin and end with the workday. Their
leisure hours are protected by law, by contract, or by tradition, and
the trend is that hours worked over and above the standard work

week should be paid for by the employer in accordance with an overtime schedule.

It should be noted that teachers and other kinds of professional workers employed by government agencies are in a marginal position, in that they are subjected to two kinds of stresses. Though informality toward hours of employment is discouraged, these workers are frequently expected to contribute large amounts of time beyond the legal or standard work week. A number of partial solutions have been introduced in an attempt to adjust and to equalize the injustices inherent in this situation. For example, some school districts give teachers advances in salary if they complete additional professional training on their own time and at their own expense; some government agencies pay the expenses of professional employees who attend conferences; some governmental agencies categorically state that they neither expect nor require the performance of duties in hours outside the time limits of the standard work week; and some physical education teachers have been successful in obtaining overtime pay for performing activities related to coaching and supervising sports after school hours and on week ends.

Working Conditions: Regularity of Employment. Another variable of working conditions is the regularity of employment. There are a number of jobs that provide employment for relatively short periods of time. In the entertainment field, musicians, for example, may be employed on a night-to-night basis, on week ends, for a "season," or for several weeks. For construction workers who specialize in building tunnels, dams, bridges, large buildings, and the like, each job lasts only as long as it takes to complete a project. Sometimes these projects follow one another without interruption; sometimes they are interspersed with long periods of unemployment. These conditions affect most persons in the construction industry, although in general it may be stated that the higher the skill, experience, and training of the worker, the less difficulty he will have in finding further employment, although not necessarily in his specialty. For example, a civil engineer may have less difficulty in finding work than a bulldozer operator, whose experience and skill is limited to handling one piece of equipment. It is common practice for engineers to change specialties (for civil engineers to go into mining engineering, for example), and, if economic pressures are severe, a civil engineer can take a job at a lower level — as a surveyor, a draftsman, or an estimator.

Self-employed persons face special hazards in that their employment depends on national economic conditions, such as depressions and prosperity booms; local conditions, such as strikes, disasters, and local business booms; current demand for their goods and services; competition; and their ability to finance their undertakings.

Working Conditions: Places of Employment. Also of interest to the student of an occupation are the typical places of employment. Do the processes associated with the occupation take place indoors or outdoors? Does the job require much traveling? Is the work performed in a laboratory, an office, a classroom, a factory, a ship, in an open but protected area? Is one exposed to extremes of heat and cold? What hazards are present on the job?

The significance of working conditions as a factor in occupational choice is illustrated in the stories of Jack Logan, Claire Myers, and George Harper.

Jack Logan was always interested in astronomy. Even in high school, he ground his own lenses and built his own telescopes. He got A grades in science and mathematics courses in both high school and college and went on to a major in astronomy. Today he is employed in a large observatory, but what was attractive to him as a hobby and a school subject is distasteful to him as a life profession. He works all night and sleeps during the day — a difficult feat with two small children in the house. He sees his family only for brief intervals during the week. If he attempts to spend time with them on week ends, he can do so only by reversing his waking and sleeping schedule. His schedule of working hours is irregular; he must sometimes forego week ends with his family because certain observations must be made. Inasmuch as heating the working space would distort the calibration of astronomical instruments, observatories are unheated, and Jack's working hours during the winter are far from comfortable, in spite of heavy clothing and fur mittens. It is clear that Jack did not anticipate fully the *conditions under which he would have to work* as a professional astronomer, and he certainly was unaware of the possible effect of these working conditions on his private life.

Claire Myers is a quiet, retiring, studious person, who used to enjoy playing the piano. She was encouraged by her family and teachers, took additional training, and became a competent professional pianist, though not of concert stature. To maintain professional status as a musician and earn what she considers a living wage, she must entertain, she must attend parties given by others, she must travel, she must work long hours at inconvenient times, and she must associate with people whom she heartily detests. What Claire would really like to do would be to live a life well regulated as to hours; she would like to travel seldom and only when pleasure prompted her; she would like to maintain a small but select circle of friends; and she would like to spend much time alone with her books and her piano. When she entered the profession, she had not realized the demands that would be made on her; she thought the only requirement was that she be able to play the piano well. Now she wishes she had a profession that would not clash so violently with her personal needs; sometimes she wishes she were unable to play the piano. If she had been aware of the *working conditions* of the entertainment industry, she would have undertaken another profession or would have used her talents differently.

George Harper's outstanding performances in high school plays brought him to the attention not only of his dramatics teacher but of the leaders of the local little theater movement as well. His family was not able to send George to college, but a fund was raised locally to help put him through junior college and a year at a nationally recognized dramatics school. His coaches and his teachers praised his ability and encouraged him to prepare for a professional career. However, their warnings about the sacrifices necessary for success did not mean much to George until it was too late. Now, at twenty-five, he wonders whether he made a mistake. He is married and has a small son. In the six years he has been on Broadway he has been able to average only ten weeks of work in the theater per year. The rest of the time he looks for work, practices, and works "for free" in amateur productions. If it were not for his wife's working and the occasional odd jobs he finds, he would have to give up his acting career. George is the unfortunate victim of an employment field harassed by a chronic oversupply of capable job seekers. Perhaps if he had been aware of employment conditions in show business or if he had been more realistic in his life plan, he could have avoided his present dilemma.

Advancement and Related Occupations. Frequently people who are occupational misfits find it possible to use their skills and experience in allied fields or in an administrative capacity in their own field.

Dr. Carr was a successful dentist but found that he was temperamentally unsuited to the routine aspects of dental practice. He had excellent personal relations with his patients and would rather talk with them than work on their teeth. He also had a flair for research. He "found himself" when he got an opportunity to teach in a dental college, and, after an exploratory period, decided to make teaching dentistry his career.

Most persons probably consider opportunities for advancement from the standpoint of occupational rewards that will surely be theirs if they prove themselves competent on the job. This is a reasonable point of view, provided advancement involves higher levels of the skills required in subordinate positions. However, advancement to supervisory positions usually involves quite different skills. Furthermore, supervisory positions frequently call for the assumption of responsibilities out of all proportion to the increase in salary.

It is advisable to learn what advancement is available to the person who finds or who feels he has administrative talent. A striving, progressive person may find himself chronically frustrated if he enters a profession in which advancement comes slowly or not at all.

Characteristics of Workers. What kind of people work in this field? What qualifications must they have? What kinds of lives do they lead? What skills and attitudes are essential? What is the attitude of the occupation toward minority groups?

Under the heading of personal qualifications for an occupation are included a wide variety of characteristics that frequently defy objective classification and analysis. The usual list of traits necessary for success in *any* vocational field — teaching, law, salesmanship — look suspiciously alike: good moral character, good health, intelligence, the ability to get along with people, etc. Superficially, at least, it appears as though *any* paragon of virtue might succeed in *any* occupation. Yet we know that this is not true. Accountants appear to have quite different characteristics from mining engineers, and social workers' personal traits differ markedly from those of commercial artists. The question is: Is there any way we can separate potentially successful engineers from potentially successful carpenters on the basis of personality characteristics?

So far, the only objective method that has met with any success is the test developed by E. K. Strong, which is described in his *Vocational Interests of Men and Women* (5). Strong discovered that persons from different occupational groups who took his test tended to produce different response patterns and that these response patterns, in turn, were related to differences in basic patterns of life peculiar to people in different occupational groups. Chemists tend to live lives that differ, in many ways, from the lives lived by artists, teachers, purchasing agents, and journalists. And there are viewpoints that are typical of chemists but not so typical of persons in other walks of life. Because chemists differ in these respects from other workers, they also differ in their responses to the items on Strong's test. Their pattern of scores differs from the patterns produced by ministers, architects, and persons of other occupational groups. Strong has found, furthermore, that the patterns appearing in late adolescence tend to persist into adulthood. This is not true for every individual, but it tends to be true for adolescents taken as a group. This means that by taking the Strong test most older adolescents and young adults may discover what basic occupational groups they have the most in common with; thus, they can narrow their field of occupational choice considerably.

Although the Strong test is the best of its kind, it should not be used to deprive any person of the right to determine for himself which vocational area he should select as his first choice. Scores and profiles obtained on the Strong test are only *indications,* or straws in the wind. A person who scores high in the social-service occupations of the Strong test should not base his decision on that fact alone. He still needs to undertake the occupational research and self-analysis described in this chapter and Chapter 13. The stories of Jack Logan, Claire Myers, and George Harper constitute evidence of the kinds of difficulties that may result when young people have insufficient information about the kind of life lived by persons engaged in various occupations.

One more warning about the Strong test: It should be interpreted by a trained and experienced vocational counselor and not by the person taking the test.

Special Qualifications. In addition to the personal qualifications we have discussed, there are a number of special qualifications that are necessary for certain jobs. For example, teachers should be able to speak clearly. A few teachers are successful in spite of a mild speech impediment, but usually this is an obstacle to their success. Bus drivers should have excellent vision; the need to guard the safety of others precludes exceptions being made on this score.   A minimum level of academic ability is required before one can undertake professional training in colleges and universities. Where competition is extremely keen, professional schools may insist that applicants have superior grades in high school and college work.

One way to look at the problem of qualifications is to see it in terms of "tolerances."   Each occupation has its special hazards and strains that must be tolerated if an individual is to maintain a good level of adjustment.   If one plans to be a doctor, it is important to know whether he can tolerate interruptions of sleep and leisure at all hours, and whether he can tolerate the impossible and insistent demands some patients make on their physician.   If one plans to be a forest service man, it is important to know the extent to which he can tolerate loneliness, extremes of temperature, and the strain of severe physical exertion.   If one plans to be an accountant, it is wise to know the extent to which he can tolerate the responsibility of safeguarding someone else's funds, the strain involved in being correct to the penny, and the confusion that will exist in a new situation until a proper accounting system has been organized and installed.

Unions and Professional Societies.   Employed persons frequently express their vocational and social needs in the form of vocational organizations: unions and professional societies.   Sometimes these organizations are able to control the entry of new workers into the profession or occupation.   Unions sometimes set up apprenticeship agreements specifying that training programs shall be organized to train apprentices under the supervision of journeymen.   Such agreements usually specify the ratio of apprentices to journeymen, the length of the training period, the amount and kinds of related training that must be supplied, the sequence and variety of tasks that must be performed adequately by the apprentice, and the wages to be paid.   Agreements between the employer and the union may also prevent the hiring of persons who are not journeymen or who have not been accepted into the apprentice training program. Other agreements are not concerned with apprenticeship and journeymen status but provide that hiring shall be done from the union rolls on a seniority basis.

In some respects, medical and legal associations control the certification and entry into earning status of new workers in a manner similar to that of trade unions, except that the state rather than the employer is administrator of the agreement. Through licensing examinations, these professional societies act to protect themselves and the general public against the entry of untrained persons into the profession. Training schools are also certified and inspected, in an attempt to maintain certain minimum standards of competency agreed on by the profession.

All unions and professional societies are concerned with representing their occupational groups before the public. In this capacity they build public relations, initiate and influence legislation, and recruit new workers. Some professional societies, like the educational and scientific organizations, have no regulatory functions and are concerned only with intraprofessional problems, research, and public relations.

Probably most of the workers in the United States belong neither to a union nor to a professional organization. However, membership in these groups has much to recommend itself to the individual worker because it promotes the feeling of identity with a group of people who have one thing in common: their occupation. The feeling of having a common bond with other workers in the same occupation reaches its height in the professions, where it is not unusual to find a person who is a member of five or more professional societies, each devoted to a special interest.

Discriminatory Practices in Employment. Women, the handicapped, and members of minority groups need to pay special attention to employers' attitudes toward their members in the vocations being studied. The rule of thumb that may be followed is that where there is some prejudice, but not to the point of outright exclusion, it is usually necessary for the person against whom the prejudice is directed to be outstanding in order to be hired. For example, a woman endeavoring to enter the field of aeronautical engineering would probably have to be outstanding in order to compete with men on an equal basis. If she had an average academic record, the chances are that, if she were hired at all, she would be assigned a lower level job than would be given a male engineer of equal ability. Similar treatment would very likely be accorded a severely disabled person or a member of a minority group.

Persons who are the target of such prejudice have a difficult task when they decide to enter occupations where these attitudes are strong. For them it is particularly important to have objective appraisals of their ability by trained and competent guidance workers, because there is, perhaps, an unconscious tendency on the part of the public to overencourage or to overdiscourage their vocational plans. Some well-meaning persons will overencourage because they feel sorry for the victim of prejudice, and in this way they attempt to "make up" for society's wrongs. Others will over-discourage because they are afraid that the person who is an object of prejudice may complete his plans for a career, be unable to get a job, and will then feel frustrated and resentful. They are trying to protect the individual from being hurt at a later period, but in doing so they ignore the occasional successes that outstanding persons enjoy in spite of prejudice. Persons against whom prejudice is directed should be aware of the vocational fields in which prejudice is minimized and in which one may obtain success on one's merits; if they *still* have strong desires to enter fields where prejudices run high, they should have objective assurances that their talents are outstanding, and in any event must be prepared for setbacks and other discouragement whether or not they achieve the success and acceptance that should be theirs.

Preparing for and Entering an Occupation. There is probably more information available on this aspect of "occupationology" than on any other. Experts are understandably vague about the kinds of lives led by statisticians, about the kind of person who makes the best chiropodist, and about the kinds of skills most essential for success in newspaper reporting. But the student who seeks complete and accurate information on how to prepare for and enter these and other well-known occupations can find it in abundance. This is one area in which occupational literature excels. There are a number of reasons for this. In the first place, courses of study leading to professional status in a given vocation are usually pre-scribed by the profession or the educational institution, and they are listed in the catalogues of colleges and professional schools. Furthermore, vocational preparation takes place in a "laboratory situation" — a training institution — where the process can be observed and described more objectively than is possible with persons in the field, practicing a profession. Then, too, it is easier to measure the skills and traits required for success in training than it is to relate these same skills and traits to success on the job. Incidentally, one of the most difficult obstacles to the devising of techniques that would predict success on the job is the difficulty of deciding what success is and how it can be measured. Until this problem is solved, our more precise predictions will have to be confined to probabilities of success or failure in training. Thus, when the dean of the college of dentistry sends a letter of regret to the five-hundred-odd unsuccessful candidates for admission, he is saying, in effect, that on the basis of their grades, their general academic aptitude test scores, and their special aptitude test scores, he predicts that most of them would fail the dental curriculum. He cannot say whether they would be good dentists if they *were* to receive their D.D.S. degrees, because his criteria (grades, test scores, etc.) do not predict success in the profession but only predict success (or failure) in the dental curriculum.

In some respects this is wholly reasonable, inasmuch as the beginner cannot enter the occupation unless he has satisfactorily completed his training. Therefore, it is sensible for the vocational counselor to provide the student with information concerning himself, which he may then use as a means of deciding whether he should undertake training for a given occupation. However, the student should not assume that *merely* because he has completed the training program required for a given occupation he will therefore be successful and happy in his chosen occupation. There are skills and attitudes necessary for success on the job that are not a factor for success in training. However, it should be noted that representatives of the occupation concerned have analyzed it carefully and have organized the course of study on the basis of what they believe are the skills and knowledges essential for vocational success. Until better means of appraising vocational success are found, professional training courses and other existing vocational curricula will have to be accepted as reasonably valid predictors of occupational success.

An examination of professional and preprofessional requirements reveals the logic that has guided their evolution. High grades are required of applicants for medical school because researchers have found that there is a positive relationship between grades received in preprofessional courses and success in medical school. Inasmuch as far more people apply for medical school than can be accepted, the requirement of high grades in preprofessional work appears to be a sensible one. Engineering schools require applicants to have completed a rather broad curriculum in science. This requirement is justified by the considerable emphasis on science found in the engineering curriculum. Most schools of education require the applicant to have completed an introductory course in psychology. This course serves to provide a foundation for additional courses in psychology included in the teacher-training curriculum.

The student will do well to satisfy himself about these questions relating to training: How long will it take? How much does it cost? Where can it be obtained? What requirements must be met before applying for training? How much competition is involved in becoming accepted as a candidate for admission? What academic standards are required for admission? What courses are designated as prerequisites for admission?

Legal regulations and restrictions are also important to consider. In order to practice some occupations, it is necessary to secure a license from the state, and this sometimes involves passing an examination. Here, it should be noted that the completion of training is not synonymous with the attainment of a certificate to practice. Many people complete law training and receive their LL.B. degrees, but fail to pass the bar examination and are thus unable to qualify as practicing lawyers. Vexing problems also arise when a person obtains his training in one state and endeavors to practice in another. The second state frequently requires that additional training be secured locally in order to take its examination.

Occupational Placement. Many students postpone consideration of the problem of placement until graduation, feeling that it can best be dealt with at that time. However, anticipating problems that may appear in the course of getting a job may aid the student in solving or even in avoiding them. For example, if all students were aware of the stress placed by many employers on extracurricular activities, there would be more of such activity and fewer regrets after graduation. In this connection, it may be said that employers who seek potential administrators tend to be more interested in the person who has average grades and who shows leadership in a variety of extracurricular activities than they are in the person who has made high grades but who has not participated at all in such activities.

A student can plan his life more realistically if he knows what will be involved in getting a job after graduation. In the course of his professional activities, the writer has met several young psychologists who were much annoyed because they could not find jobs in metropolitan areas. There were a number of vacant positions in rural areas one or two hundred miles away, and experience obtained on these jobs would qualify them for positions in cities. But they had lived all their lives in large cities and were unprepared for any other kind of existence. What was most upsetting was the fact it had never occurred to them that they might have to work in the country; they had assumed as a matter of course that when employment came, it would be in a large city. Naturally, there are always disappointments and frustrations incident to starting a profession, but the earlier they can be anticipated, explored, and realistically evaluated, the easier the adjustment after graduation will be.

Another type of disappointment, even more common than that of the disappointed psychologists, is that of the person who graduates from college and finds that he must start at the same level as the high school graduate, or that his friends who did not go to college have positions that now pay better than his. At such times life seems very dark, and the preceding four or five years seem wasted. However, it should be noted that many business firms make it a practice to start *all* new applicants on the same level, regardless of their experience or training. This practice enables the firm to evaluate the new employee, to learn whether he is worth keeping, and to discover where he might best be used and whether he deserves promotion. Sometimes this trial period lasts for months or even years, during which time the individual concerned is certain that he has been forgotten.

Some firms place no premium on a college education and tend to make promotions on the basis of seniority, personal qualities, and evidences of supervisory ability. However, there is a steadily increasing trend to hire college-trained personnel for those positions that lead to managerial responsibilities or to limit promotions above a certain level (frequently that of foreman) to persons with some college education. This practice is justified by employers on several grounds. A person who has graduated from college has proved his ability to complete a program calling for perseverance, intellectual

ability, and the capacity to co-operate with persons in authority;
a college-educated person has more in common with a college-
educated management than a person of lesser educational attainment; a college-educated person is usually more competent in
speaking and in writing. Whether or not these are the chief reasons
for this practice, the fact remains that the number of executives with
college education continues to increase (6).

In any event, students planning to prepare for any occupation
should be aware of how one actually makes his vocational start. Is
it necessary to take a lower level job? Are most people in this field
placed by the college placement bureau? Is direct application the
best way? To what extent are private employment agencies used
by persons in this occupation?

Suitability. This is the crux of the job study. This is the point
where self-appraisal and occupational information are brought
together and compared. This is where the student sits down,
figuratively, with the data concerning himself on one side and the
data concerning the occupation on the other, and checks the items
relating to himself against the items relating to the job. Naturally,
we do not expect to find a one-to-one relationship between these
two sets of data. The question is: How important are the discrepancies?

The case of Michael Santos will serve to illustrate the process
necessary in deciding how important are the discrepancies between
one's capabilities and the demands of the occupation.

Michael Santos wants to be a psychologist so that he can help people
the way he was helped by his freshman counselor. Although his academic aptitude is above average, his grades in junior college have aver-
aged a B −. This would probably disqualify him for graduate work in
psychology. Furthermore, he is not at all certain that he could finance
the four years of graduate work required. His adviser suggested that
he explore the possibility of social welfare work, inasmuch as social
workers work with individuals in much the same kinds of relationships
enjoyed by psychologists, and he felt that Michael had many of the
personal qualities that help to make a successful social worker. Michael
did occupational studies of both social work and psychology. He confirmed the statements made by his counselor to the effect that he would
have difficulty in psychology, and he found that social work was not
only feasible, but would meet many of his needs. Yet he hesitates giving

up his original goal for a second choice, particularly one he did not think of himself. In Michael's case the discrepancies between his vocational aspirations and the possibilities presented by opportunities in social work are minor, but *if* he is objective and realistic, he will give up his dream in exchange for a practical vocational plan such as that leading to a career in social work, which offers real possibilities for fulfillment and eventual satisfaction.

In the early stages of a college career, it is seldom necessary to come to a final and irrevokable decision regarding the choice of a professional career. Much to be recommended are patterns of courses which postpone the necessity of final choice and which enable an individual to prepare for a *variety* of occupations. For instance, if Michael is completely unwilling to give up his dream of becoming a psychologist, he might take a combination of courses that would lead to graduate work in either social welfare or psychology. Even though the chances are much against his entering the field of psychology, he might derive much personal satisfaction out of taking psychology courses, he would have the chance of finding out for himself that a career in psychology is not for him, and courses in psychology would very likely help him in his sociological studies. Another such combination is the premedical curriculum, which may also be used as the basis for a teaching major in high school science, should the goal of medical school prove unattainable.

Vocational Tryout. There are two means whereby students may discover whether the tentative conclusions they reached as a result of their occupational studies are valid. One method is that of taking the academic courses preparing one for the occupation concerned. The other means has already been mentioned as one of the four main sources of occupational information: part-time or short-term work experience (including volunteer work). However, this type of experience is not always available to the student at the appropriate time. Often the job must be actively sought by the student, and it may even have to be created by a sympathetic employer.

Alfred Ross scores high on the advertising-man scale of the Strong test. His analysis of the field of advertising has helped him to develop much interest in this field, but he feels that he does not know enough about it to abandon his original choice of mechanical engineering. He has an opportunity to work in the timber country during the summer and make two dollars an hour. This money could be used to buy a car he has been planning on. While it is true that the lumbering job would give him practical experience in earning and saving money and in getting along with adults, his occupational future would be less tentative if he could get a job in the advertising field. *Any* job in this field, no matter what the level of work or the pay, would be valuable in giving him an opportunity to see the advertising industry *from the inside*. After this experience he would be in a much better position to decide whether he should include advertising in his plans or whether he should pass it by.

Pitfalls. A variety of generalities and stereotyped concepts sometimes prevent students from making realistic occupational choices.

The concept of the "ideal job" is a common one. It assumes that there is only one occupation for each individual. This resembles the fallacy that there is only one ideal mate for each person. (See Chapter 17, "Building Sound Relationships between the Sexes.) Actually any individual who can make a good adjustment in one occupation can probably be equally happy in a variety of allied occupations. Except for a few severely disabled persons, no one's needs and talents are so specific that he must say, "There is only one job that will suit me, and there is no point in my trying anything else."

Another concept worth noting is the tendency of the new or inexperienced worker to stress the economic factors — wages and security. In some ways this is inevitable, inasmuch as it is one of the stereotypes of our culture that the price of something is also its value. However, as individuals develop a fund of employment experience, other values — the opportunity for independent thinking, the willingness of management to discuss problems with employees, friendly relations with fellow employees — overshadow wages and security in relative importance.

Some individuals, because of shyness or false pride, avoid seeking the help of the vocational counselor. These persons are frequently more successful in avoiding the counselor than they are in solving their vocational problems. Consequently, their plans are usually developed and carried through on a trial-and-error basis, and the result is an undue amount of frustration and disillusionment. If competent professional help is readily available, it is wise to avail oneself of it before making an important decision like the choice of a career.

Another difficulty that frequently besets the student who endeavors to make a realistic vocational choice is the white-collar fetish. There is an unconscious tendency on the part of many of us to assume that anyone who has the opportunity will naturally prepare for professional or white-collar work, and that blue-collar or manual work is only for those unfortunates who are unable to become white-collar workers. In effect, this stereotyped concept serves to set up an artificial barrier between professional and clerical workers, on the one hand, and skilled and semiskilled craftsmen, on the other. It implies that only white-collar workers can achieve adequate job satisfaction and that blue-collar workers are certain to be dissatisfied, because any one of them would change his lot if he could. It is hard to estimate what damage these false standards have wrought. Undoubtedly many persons whose greatest potential for occupational satisfaction lies in some sort of creative handicraft have been persuaded to seek less satisfying careers of the white-collar variety. Furthermore, this concept has helped raise a barrier of prejudice and hostility between the two groups, so that it is difficult for them to communicate. The white-collar worker needs to be aware of the value of the contributions made by the blue-collar worker to the national economy and to society, and each ought to see the other *as a person* rather than as the representative of an envied or a despised class. It is to be hoped that students who undertake occupational studies, and who thereby find themselves sincerely interested in the skilled trades or the service occupations, will be enabled to minimize the effects of the all-too-persistent prejudice that only white-collar work is worth considering and that blue-collar work is degrading.

SUMMARY

Vocational choice plays a lesser but nonetheless important role in the problem of attaining satisfactory occupational adjustment. The choice should be based on an objective appraisal of one's strengths and weaknesses, as well as on a thorough analysis and understanding of the fields of work under consideration. Vocational plans should be laid as early as possible and should be made flexible.

The first important step in choosing a career is self-appraisal — learning to know oneself. On the basis of this self-knowledge, one should select a limited number of tentative occupational areas for exploration. These areas may be studied by reading about them in occupational literature, by interviewing experts or other persons in the field, by visiting places of employment, and by experiencing part-time or short-term work on the job. Those aspects of an occupation that may yield useful information on which to base a job choice include background, duties, working conditions, characteristics of workers, preparing for and entering the occupation, and suitability. On the basis of the information thus gathered and an objective self-appraisal, the student should be able to select one or more tentative occupational areas, which he may further explore academically or through part-time or short-term employment. The important thing is to select the most suitable and appropriate alternatives and to gather as much valid and realistic information about them as possible.

It is hoped that in making this analysis the student will not be misled by the popular beliefs that there is but one ideal job for each individual and that only white-collar work is worthy of serious consideration. If the skilled, professional help of a vocational counselor is readily available, the student will do well to avail himself of this service to aid him in his problem of vocational choice — to help him clarify his thinking about occupations, to confirm the choice he has already made, or to provide suggestions about additional vocational areas worth considering.

REFERENCES

1. E. C. Hughes, "Work and the Self," in J. H. Rohrer and M. Sherif, eds., *Social Psychology at the Crossroads*. New York: Harper, 1951. P. 316.
2. *Occupational Outlook Handbook*, United States Department of Labor, Bureau of Labor Statistics in Co-operation with the Veterans Administration, Washington, 1951.
3. *Dictionary of Occupational Titles. Volume I: Definitions of Titles*, 2d edition. Washington, D. C.: Federal Security Agency, 1949.
4. *Dictionary of Occupational Titles. Volume II: Occupational Classifications and Industry Index*, 2d edition. Washington, D. C.: Federal Security Agency, 1949.
5. E. K. Strong, *Vocational Interests of Men and Women*. Stanford: Stanford University Press, 1943.
6. F. W. Taussig and C. S. Joslyn, *American Business Leaders*. New York: Macmillan, 1932. P. 103.

SUGGESTED READINGS

C. L. Shartle, *Occupational Information*, 2d edition. New York: Prentice-Hall, 1952. A thorough-going analysis of the sources and types of occupational information by an authority in this field.

M. F. Baer and E. C. Roeber, *Occupational Information*. Chicago: Science Res., 1951. Like the book by Shartle, this text is written primarily for counselors and other personnel workers. It, too, lists and classifies occupational information and its sources.

D. E. Super, *The Dynamics of Vocational Adjustment*. New York: Harper, 1942. Discusses the necessity for self-appraisal in the light of factors required for adjustment to employment.

G. Forrester, *Occupational Pamphlets*. New York: H. W. Wilson, 1948. An annotated bibliography of occupational information materials.

H. W. Hepner, *Psychology Applied to Life and Work*, 2d edition. New York: Prentice-Hall, 1950. Chapters 11 and 12 deal with choosing an occupation and getting a job.

E. T. Prothro and P. T. Teska, *Psychology: A Biosocial Study of Behavior*. Boston: Ginn, 1950. Chapter 17 discusses vocational guidance.

J. E. Anderson, *The Psychology of Development and Personal Adjustment*. New York: Holt, 1949. Chapter 21 deals with adjustment to a vocation.

F. McKinney, *Psychology of Personal Adjustment*, 2d edition. New York: Wiley, 1949. Chapter 9 covers such areas as personality analysis, occupational analysis, and vocational choice.

L. C. Steckle, *Problems of Human Adjustment*. New York: Harper, 1949. See the chapter entitled "Happiness in Work."

J. G. Friend and E. A. Haggard, *Work Adjustment in Relation to Family Background*. Applied Psychology Monographs No. 16. Stanford: Stanford University Press, 1948. A study of individuals counseled during the Depression by the Family Society of Greater Boston. Comparison of persons who made good occupational adjustment and those who made poor adjustment.

M. L. Blum, *Industrial Psychology and Its Social Foundations*. New York: Harper, 1949. See Chapter 4, "Job Satisfaction."

M. E. Hahn and A. H. Brayfield, *Job Exploration Workbook*. Chicago: Science Res., 1945. Helpful suggestions on how to study an occupation.

P. W. Boynton, *Six Ways to Get a Job*. New York: Harper, 1945. How to sell yourself to a prospective employer.

J. M. Brewer and E. Landy, *Occupations Today*. Boston: Ginn, 1949. A description of the occupations in the world today.

H. D. Kitson, *How to Find the Right Vocation*. New York: Harper, 1947. How to satisfy your prospective employer and yourself.

The following pamphlets, published by Science Research Associates, are well written and informative. Their titles are self-explanatory: M. Dreese, *How to Get the Job*, 1949; J. A. Humphreys, *Choosing Your Career*, 1949; J. C. Worthy, *What Employers Want*, 1950; P. W. Chapman, *Your Personality and Your Job*, 1944; T. E. Christensen, *Getting Job Experience*, 1949; A. H. Frankel, *Handbook of Job Facts*, 1948.

XV...*Getting an Education:*
Intelligence

Intelligence and Mental Health. This chapter and the one that follows are included in this book in order to help the student gain some understanding of the factors and processes that are important in getting an education. In this chapter we shall consider the relatively static factor of intelligence. Intelligence is of great importance to the student, for the amount and kind of intelligence he possesses helps to determine his success in school and, indirectly, his general level of adjustment, which is so intimately associated with success or failure in any undertaking.

There are further reasons for discussing intelligence in a textbook of this type. Many students worry about whether they are "intelligent enough" to succeed in college. Then there are students whose lower level of academic ability will make it difficult for them to complete courses required for graduation. They are perhaps unconcerned about this deficiency, because they do not know what frustrations and failures lie ahead of them. Each of these kinds of students has problems of adjustment related to intelligence.

It is further hoped that this chapter will help to clear up some popular misconceptions about intelligence. Many people believe, for example, that persons of high intelligence (those who are "smart" enough to have completed a college education, for instance) are not troubled with problems of emotional adjustment, as are persons of lesser intelligence, because high intelligence somehow carries with it the power to solve such problems. It is devoutly to be hoped that students who read this chapter will learn enough about intelligence to discover that this is not so and, furthermore, why it is not so.

324

Cultural Attitudes toward Intelligence. One of the highest compliments that can be paid in our middle-class culture is to call a person "intelligent." Conversely, one of the worst insults is to call a person "stupid." The feelings we have about intelligence and stupidity reflect the value system of a culture that sets great store by man's capacity to control and manipulate his social and physical environment. Some cultures stress the attainment of peace of mind, some cultures value creative effort, and still others feel that man's most important task is to live according to the role assigned him by the society in which he lives. The study of the history of our American middle-class culture reveals a people who see their triumph over the threats and dangers of their physical and social environment as a victory won by hard work and the application of intelligence and ingenuity. We tend to accept as worthy members of society those persons who demonstrate the capacity to act intelligently; and we reject, with a mixture of scorn, derision, and pity, those persons who do not appear to possess intellectual abilities that are at least as high as those of the "average person." Perhaps we are afraid that the latter will be unable to cope with life and may thus come to depend on us, or perhaps we are afraid that they will "get us into trouble." Perhaps they make us wonder, secretly, whether *we* are as intellectually competent as we represent ourselves to others. Perhaps we feel frustrated because we cannot seem to communicate with these persons — we cannot make them understand what we expect of them. Probably all these reasons are basic to our negative feelings about people whom we characterize as "just not very smart," or "stupid," or "dumb."

Anxiety regarding Intelligence. The great stress placed by our society on intelligent behavior is a major source of anxiety for many of us who are not sure of ourselves. This is particularly true of young people who are just beginning to make their way in the adult world. It is a commonplace for students to come up to the psychology instructor after class to ask if there is any way in which they can find out their IQ's. A conversation like the following frequently ensues:

STUDENT: Mr. Instructor, I'd like to find out my IQ.
INSTRUCTOR: Tell me, why do you want to know your IQ?
STUDENT: I don't know, but I certainly would like to find it out.

INSTRUCTOR: There are many tests that yield what we call IQ's; I have four of them in my office; if I gave them all to you we might have four different IQ's. Would that help you?

STUDENT: Well, don't you have a test that will give me my *real* IQ?

INSTRUCTOR: I think you mean that you want to know how intelligent you are. We can find that out without giving an intelligence test. What kind of grades are you getting?

STUDENT: I am making a B + average.

INSTRUCTOR: That is an indicator of a high level of one kind of intelligence. Do you get along well with people?

STUDENT: I have lots of friends. I must get along well, because I was just elected president of the freshman class.

INSTRUCTOR: That is further evidence of intelligence of a high order. Do you have any mechanical skills?

STUDENT: I am more interested in having bull sessions with the fellows now, but when I was in high school, I was able to tear down my car and put it back together as fast as any of the other guys on the block.

INSTRUCTOR: I'd say that you were a rather unusual person. You have above-average intelligence in at least three fields: academic, social, and mechanical. You should have no worries; your intellectual horsepower rating should be quite high!

STUDENT: That sounds swell, Mr. Instructor, but when can I take one of those IQ tests?

The anxiety displayed by the student in the above conversation is quite typical. He *must* know what his IQ is. In spite of his obvious successes in life, in spite of the objective evidence of a high level of intelligence, he must be reassured again and again that he is not stupid. It is questionable, of course, whether his feelings of inferiority would actually be dispelled by taking the test. Such feelings usually have a rather deep-seated origin, which gives them the strength to withstand the repeated impacts of objective data. The writer has had the experience several times of telling students of their high scores on intelligence tests, only to have them receive the news with polite comments that barely mask their skepticism and disappointment. It was fairly obvious that they expected the tests to confirm their own feelings that in reality they were quite stupid!

Overstress on Intelligence. There is no denying the importance of intelligence as a factor in man's attempt to control and manipulate his social and physical environment. Undoubtedly it has played the major role in the progress humanity has made to date. But we tend to overstress the function and the role of intelligence. Economic, social, and scientific progress can result only through the efforts of intelligent people, it is true, but they must be intelligent people of good will, and they must be able to work together harmoniously. In our overstress on intelligence and intellect, we have tended to ignore the roles of motivation, emotion, and feeling. Evidence of this attitude is found in the fact that words characterizing a person as lacking in emotional maturity ("irritable," "quick-tempered," "cold," "gloomy," "dour," "embittered," "cynical") are not nearly as insulting as words reflecting his lack of intellectual capacity ("stupid," "dumb," "moronic," "imbecilic," "foolish," "obtuse"). This overrating of intelligence and underrating of emotional factors is consistent with the middle-class pattern of attempting to deny, suppress, or repress the emotional side of life. In effect, it amounts to a distortion of reality, for motivation, if anything, is more fundamental to human behavior than is intellect. In other words, the desire or the readiness to act is a prerequisite to any act and takes precedence over intelligence or the capacity to act intelligently. Perhaps at least part of our anxiety concerning our intelligence is due to this blind spot in our perception: although we insist that intelligence (or the capacity for intelligent behavior) is the prime requisite for success and progress, we may sense that this does not fit the facts. We are disturbed by our unrealistic attempts to ignore the emotional basis for behavior.

Intelligence and Social Status. Another source of anxiety is our association of intelligence with status. We assume that persons of high status and prestige are more intelligent than persons of low status and prestige. Furthermore, we often assume that such persons have attained their positions as leaders through becoming "intelligent" (acquiring education), or because they already were intelligent. Some of us even go so far as to assume that *any* person of high intelligence will attain a position of prestige and status. Consider, then, the dilemma of the person whose intelligence, as demonstrated by successes in various areas of life, is of a relatively high order, but who feels lacking in status or prestige. He is likely to be disturbed by his gap between his expectations and his accomplishments. Because he is unable to live up to his aspirations, he feels anxious, and his anxiety may express itself in increased striving, in frustration and bitterness, in hostile aggression, in feelings of depression and inferiority, or in any of the other characteristic ways in which he tends to express his anxiety.

The "Anyone Can Be Intelligent" Myth.   Perhaps because of our "common sense" faith in the efficacy of will power, we also tend to feel that intelligent behavior is a matter of individual choice, that intelligence is the result of education or of "trying hard enough." We are likely to feel that students who fail, do so because they haven't studied hard enough.   The failing student himself believes this, too.   He may already be studying three hours outside of class for every hour in class (the recommended ratio is two hours of study for one in class), but when called to the dean's office because of his failing marks, he almost invariably says that he feels that he can bring up his grades by studying even harder and longer. Sometimes the failing student accounts for his lack of success by saying that he doesn't know *how* to study.   However, it is the writer's observation that reading books on how to study is helpful to only a small minority of failing students.

The fact is that people differ widely in their ability to achieve success in college, just as they differ widely in their abilities to succeed in other activities of life.   This is the result of the operation of the principle of individual differences, which is one of the important contributions psychology has made to our understanding of ourselves and our behavior.   It is on this principle of individual differences that most psychological testing is based.

The Measurement of Individual Differences.   The concept of individual differences dates back to 1796, when a laboratory assistant named Kinnebrook, at the Royal Observatory at Greenwich, was dismissed from his post because his reported observations of the transit of stars were consistently eight-tenths of a second later than those of the Astronomer Royal.   It was assumed, of course, that this difference was due to Kinnebrook's incompetence.   However, he was vindicated some twenty years later, when an investigation revealed that the differences between the observations made by different persons were to a large measure due to the differences in the amount of time they required to react rather than to the amount of skill.   The discovery of individual differences generally annoyed the scientific world, because it meant that scientific accuracy is compromised to the extent that the human element is

". . . And I say he could have a higher IQ if he just tried . . ."

George Lichty and the Chicago Sun-Times Syndicate

Psychologists and the lay public have differing concepts regarding intelligence.

involved. Only gradually was it recognized that the discovery of individual differences meant the opening up of a new scientific area: the study of human behavior, hitherto the realm of the philosopher and the theologian. In the second half of the nineteenth century, physiologists and psychologists became interested in measuring physical characteristics and abilities, and a start was made in psychological experimentation.

The father of intelligence testing, Alfred Binet, published a number of papers, between 1893 and 1911, devoted to the differences between bright and dull children. In 1904 the schools of Paris became concerned about the number of children who were incapable of learning and who were more likely to be helped in special schools where they would not be held to the regular curriculum. The school authorities wanted to be sure that children would be selected on an objective basis; they were afraid that if selection were left to individual teachers, they might reject as "dull" those bright children who were troublemakers and might retain in their classes dull children from prominent families or dull children who were pleasant and co-operative. Because of Binet's reputation, he was given the task of developing a scale that would classify children objectively into levels of intelligence. The scale as developed by Binet consisted of a series of thirty tasks ranged in order of difficulty. Binet and his collaborator, Simon, tried the scale out on groups of normal and mentally retarded children, and, on the basis of this experimentation, were able to set up norms or standards based on age levels. Thus the ninth test in the series marked the upper limit for three-year-olds, and the sixteenth item separated five- from seven-year-olds.

Binet's work was received with interest in this country. His scale was revised by L. M. Terman, who published in 1916 what is now known as the Stanford-Binet test. Terman carried Binet's age norms a step further and developed the concept of mental age, which was indicated by the ability of a child to complete the number of mental tasks typical of children of a given age, and the IQ, which he computed by dividing the mental age by the chronological age and multiplying the result by 100 $(IQ = \dfrac{MA}{CA} \times 100)$.

Within a period of ten years, the idea of the IQ, with its apparent ability to describe the intelligence of the individual in one convenient figure, had become so widely accepted that it had even entered the vocabulary of the man in the street. And although the mental-age concept becomes less useful in adolescence and virtually useless in adulthood, it has such a grip on the imagination of both the lay and the professional public that virtually every author of an intelligence test feels compelled to convert his scores into IQ's. Thus in popular parlance any test of intelligence is known as an "IQ test."

Percentage Distribution of IQ's in the Terman Merrill Standardization Group (1)

IQ	Per Cent of Cases	Per Cent of Population Falling in and Below Each Interval
150 and over	0.2	100.0
140–149	1.1	99.78
130–139	3.1	98.67
120–129	8.2	95.56
110–119	18.1	87.34
100–109	23.5	69.3
90–99	23.0	45.7
80–89	14.5	22.7
70–79	5.6	8.2
60–69	2.0	2.6
50–59	0.4	0.6
Below 50	0.2	0.2

Interpretation: The left-hand column contains IQ's as reported by Terman and Merrill in their standardization of the 1938 revision of the Stanford-Binet test. The figures in the second column represent the percentage of the population that falls into each IQ grouping. The right-hand column gives the cumulative percentage for each IQ grouping, going up the scale. For example, children with IQ's between 140 and 149 comprise 1.1 per cent of the total group, and their IQ's are higher than those obtained by 98.7 per cent of the total group.

World War I gave mental testing its greatest impetus. When it became necessary to expand the Army to several times its peace-time size, psychologists were requested to produce a *group* test of intelligence (the Binet scale and the Terman revision could be given to only one individual at a time) that could be used to select officer trainees, to reject those who were unfit, and to classify personnel generally. This test, termed the Army Alpha, proved to be such a convenient and efficient measure that it went through several editions and revisions as a test for civilians and thus became the prototype for hundreds of other group intelligence tests.

The success of the Army Alpha and the concept of the IQ gave impetus to the testing movement that swept through the schools in the 1920's and 1930's. Today psychologists are more sophisticated and more skeptical about tests, for reasons we shall discuss later in this chapter. The early enthusiasm was based partly on the fact that we thought we had discovered the formula for solving many of our educational problems. For example, it was felt that education could be made more "efficient" by distributing students into classes according to their IQ's, so that instruction could be modified according to their levels of aptitude. Although experience has indicated that this method creates as many problems as it solves, it is used in many school systems.*

Test makers have established beyond a reasonable doubt that the concept of individual differences applies to intellectual abilities as well as to physical abilities. It is just as reasonable to accept the fact that A can think more efficiently than B as it is to accept the fact that C can run faster than D. Thus, successes in school and in other activities of life are based on the intellectual capacities of the individual as well as on effort, persistence, and good fortune.

Theories regarding the Nature of Intelligence. Because intelligence tests have become a part of the program in most schools, society has tended to accept them at face value, with the tacit assumption that there is general agreement about what intelligence is and about the validity of intelligence tests in measuring it. However, the fact is that psychologists are not generally agreed as to the nature of intelligence, nor do all intelligence tests measure the same thing.

Binet thought of intelligence as comprising such capacities as comprehension, inventiveness, persistence, and critical analysis (2). In 1921, the outstanding psychologists working on the problem of intelligence offered their definitions in a widely quoted symposium. Terman defined intelligence as the capacity to do abstract thinking; Colvin defined it as the ability to learn to adjust to one's environment; while Thorndike thought it was the power of good response from the point of view of truth and fact (3). Thorndike had previously suggested that there were three main types of intelligence: mechanical, social, and abstract (4). The idea that

---

* For a brief but comprehensive discussion of "Ability Grouping," see W. S. Monroe, ed., *Encyclopedia of Educational Research*, Rev. edition. New York: Macmillan, 1950. Pp. 376-378.

intelligence is divisible into factors receives its chief support today from the work of L. L. Thurstone, who has identified nine primary factors or abilities (5). On the other hand, David Wechsler, the author of the Wechsler-Bellevue Scale of Intelligence, sees intelligence as "the aggregate or global capacity of the individual to act purposefully, to think rationally and to deal effectively with his environment (6)."

An examination of various tests of intelligence reveals the influence of the author's philosophies regarding intelligence. Terman's Stanford-Binet test yields a single score, which is presumably indicative of the individual's ability to perform the abstract thinking that might be expected of a person of his age. Thurstone's tests yield separate scores on six of the factors of intelligence he has identified. Wechsler's test samples a variety of mental capacities, reducible to a single score that, in turn, may be taken as an index to the individual's level of intellectual functioning.

Limitations of Intelligence Tests. Inasmuch as many group intelligence tests are prepared for the public school market, there is a tendency for educators to think of intelligence in terms of what it takes to succeed in school. If an intelligence test is constructed with this criterion in mind, it is actually an "academic aptitude test" rather than a "test of general intelligence." A test of this type that is properly constructed and validated can be expected to predict academic marks with a relatively high degree of efficiency. In other words, persons who get high scores on the test will also tend to make high marks in school, and those who obtain low scores on the test will tend to make low marks.

The question is whether intelligence tests can predict success in *nonacademic* activities as well. Most test makers have side-stepped this issue, and with reason. Before a test can be devised to predict success in nonacademic situations, these situations must be described in detail and general agreement must be reached as to the nature of success. For example, if the ability to teach successfully is accepted as a kind of practical intelligence, a test that would measure this ability should be able to predict success in teaching. But if success in teaching is selected as a criterion, we must ask ourselves: What kind of teaching — elementary, secondary, rural, urban, physical education, foreign languages, home economics? And, what shall we consider to be the evidence of success: amount of salary, ratings given by supervisors and principals, increase in pupil knowledge, ratings of teachers by fellow teachers, activity in the community? The difficulty of solving this problem is indicated by the fact that psychologists and educators have been working for several decades to find a device to measure success in teaching, but have been unable to produce a satisfactory measure (7). It is not surprising that intelligence-test makers have had difficulties in devising tests that do much more than predict success in academic areas.

A review of most of the tests in use in the schools indicates that makers of tests for general school usage have to a greater or lesser degree tried to measure the ability to do abstract thinking. The Stanford-Binet, as well as the many group tests in common use, stress the abstract, verbal approach to the measurement of intelligence. The result is that the person who is clever at manipulating words and symbols, who has a large vocabulary, who reads with ease and enjoyment, who can express himself easily in writing, is also the person who scores high on these tests. This person is also the one who does well in most of the courses of the standard school curriculum (English, social studies, foreign languages, science, mathematics). Since these tests measure those skills needed to succeed in school, it is not surprising that there is a high relationship between intelligence-test scores and school marks. If the courses that comprise the school curricula were less academic — that is, if they consisted largely of experiences in music, industrial arts, design, graphic arts, sports, drama, and practical human relations — there would be a lower relationship between intelligence-test scores and success in school.

The close relationship between the IQ and school success has been attacked in recent years by sociologists and psychologists such as Allison Davis. Davis and his group state that the traditional school curricula, the attitude of teachers and administrators, and the typical intelligence test are all biased in favor of the child who comes from the middle-class family, has a favorable attitude toward school, uses the kind of English at home that is used in school, has parents who are in sympathy with the aims of the school, is being prepared for college and a white-collar career, and has the behavior and appearance that meet with the approval of teachers and administrators (8, 9, 10). Davis states further that children from lower-class homes usually have less success with intelligence tests and school courses because they are not encouraged by their parents to be successful in school; they do not use the same sort of English at home that is used in school — that is, it is less "grammatical"; most of them have no real aspirations for a white-collar career; and they behave and dress in a manner that, although it is tolerated in lower-class surroundings, does not meet with the approval of teachers and administrators. Many lower-class children, according to Davis, could do much better on intelligence tests, but they are not motivated to try. Since there tends to be a mutual dislike between this group of children and the school, they are likely to drop out of school at the earliest possible age. Davis's recommendation is twofold: a more sympathetic and humane understanding on the part of teachers and administrators, and a type of intelligence test that measures some aspects of intelligence other than aptitude for the traditional school curriculum.

Intelligence Tests and the Mentally Retarded. It will be remembered that the earliest function of intelligence testing was to identify those children who could not benefit from the usual instruction of the public schools; and for many years we believed that existing tests performed the function of identifying the mentally retarded child rather successfully. However, there is a growing suspicion that there may be many individuals who obtain lower scores than they should because of special factors or conditions. Sometimes these factors are largely external, as with the child coming from a home in which a foreign language is spoken; and sometimes they are internal, as with the child who is emotionally disturbed. We are becoming increasingly aware of the child who, because of emotional difficulties, obtains an IQ in the 50–79 range and who is thus classified as mentally retarded, but who has an intellectual potential that is actually much higher. The work done by Virginia Axline in play therapy with emotionally disturbed children — in one instance, with a group of nonreaders— indicates that a reduction in the amount of maladjustment operates in a high proportion of cases to "free" children's intellectual capacities so that they can obtain markedly higher IQ's (11, 12).

This is not to say that we should find some other means of identifying those children who need special instruction because of their mental retardation; the individual intelligence test is still the best tool for this job. However, there is a tendency on the part of many of us to rely too heavily on the results of tests, particularly the group tests of intelligence given in schools, colleges, industry, and the armed forces. We are likely to feel that the person who scores high on these tests is able to do *all* things well and that the person who scores low does all things poorly and is a slow learner. In employment situations we are likely to place persons who score low on intelligence tests on unskilled jobs, and in schools we are likely to ignore them as long as they cause no problems in discipline.

Thus little Jean, who had an IQ of 80 on a group intelligence test, receives very little help from the teacher, because "with an IQ of 80, she couldn't learn anyhow." In Jean's case, the recording of an IQ score serves as a sort of intellectual short cut — the teacher doesn't have to think about Jean anymore, because she is "unteachable" — whereas it may be that her true IQ is much higher than 80. Perhaps she was kept awake the night before the test by a quarrel between her parents; perhaps she is a withdrawn child who is afraid of competitive situations and upset by tests; perhaps she is afflicted by visual or hearing defects; perhaps the whole testing situation is so frightening to her that she is unable to meet any demands on her intellectual capacities. If so, these facts could be uncovered by follow-up interviews and individual tests given by a trained psychological worker. Even if her true IQ is close to 80, the decision to ignore Jean can hardly be justified, because she undoubtedly has capacities and capabilities worthy of development. Furthermore, any child, merely by his rights as an individual, should be entitled to a share of the teacher's care and attention.

Intelligence Tests Can Be Helpful. Although the results of group intelligence tests are often misused by teachers and administrators desirous of "labeling" students, they may serve a very useful function for those who are intent on learning more about the children placed under their care. Very often students who have a high level of academic aptitude make very poor progress in school. Here, the difference between the school record and the results of the intelligence test serves to warn the teacher or the counselor that something is amiss. Sometimes the student can be helped by enrolling him in a more stimulating curriculum, one better

By using an individually administered test, a clinical psychologist is enabled to make a valid estimate of a child's level of intelligence.

suited to his needs and interests.   Sometimes the student needs special care and attention because of health problems or problems of emotional maladjustment.   Many students who were originally identified through a comparison of intelligence test scores and academic grades have been brought to the attention of teachers and have subsequently received specialized help.

Universities and colleges frequently use intelligence tests as a means of determining which applicants should be accepted for admission.   Students who are less likely to succeed are spared the trouble and expense of enrolling in a college where they would be unable to benefit from instruction or where they would be forced to compete with persons of higher academic aptitude than they possess.   By scores, colleges can markedly reduce the number of students who would otherwise fail.   Since failing students require more time and expense, as a rule, than successful students, the result is increased efficiency.

However, from the standpoint of the individual student, the case in favor of the college entrance test is not very clear-cut.   The IQ that one should have in order to succeed in college is difficult to estimate.   One study of 323 colleges, using a group intelligence test, indicated that in the colleges at the top of the list the "average student" had an IQ somewhere between 118 and 126; whereas in the colleges at the bottom of the list the "average student" had an IQ between 87 and 102 (13).   Another study indicated that while it is true that 80 per cent of college freshmen with IQ's of 126 and above became seniors, it is also true that 64 per cent of those with IQ's below 116 also became seniors (14).

One implication of these studies seems to be that IQ's have different meanings at different educational institutions — that is, an IQ of 110 may mean that a person has only one chance out of four of succeeding at one institution, whereas he may have nine chances out of ten of succeeding at another institution.   Another implication seems to be that, as important as test-measured academic aptitude is, there are other factors that may decide in the final analysis whether an individual will succeed or fail in college. Among these factors are his ability to finance himself while in college, his general attitude toward school, his ability to read, his ability to express himself in writing, the presence or absence of problems that might prove to be emotionally disturbing, his ability to take examinations and quizzes without becoming emotionally upset, the intensity of his desire to complete college and to attain middle-class status, and his ability to break away from home ties. In general, high school grades are even better indicators than test scores of probable success in college (15). Frequently these two measures are combined to produce a superior index of probable college success. However, even the combined use of these two measures is not infallible. Regardless of where the line is drawn, there are always some persons rejected who would succeed if admitted, and some persons admitted who eventually fail. The chief advantage of college admission requirements is that by their use colleges are able to improve their "batting averages" and cut down the percentage of potential failures.

Heredity versus Environment. Psychologists differ among themselves as to the effect of heredity and environment on intelligence. The position of the hereditarians is that intellectual capacity is inherited. To prove their case, they cite studies that indicate a relatively close relationship between the IQ's of parents and their children and among the children of one set of parents. The position of the environmentalists is that the level of intelligence is a product of the social and physical environment: if the environment is intellectually stimulating, IQ's will be higher; if the environment is stultifying, IQ's will be lower. They state that the close relationship among IQ's of members of the same family can be laid to the similarity of their intellectual environment.

Most educators and psychologists believe that some aspects of what we call intelligence may be encouraged or inhibited by the quality of the physical and social environment. One popular point of view is that the limits of intelligence are set by inheritance and that the level of intelligence attained by an individual within these limits depends on the extent to which his environment stimulates or discourages its growth.*

As we have indicated in this chapter, educators and psychologists have been mostly concerned with a kind of intelligence that may be variously described as "verbal intelligence" or "abstract intelligence" or "academic aptitude." However, a number of

* For a more detailed discussion of the respective influences of heredity and environment, see "The Nature-Nurture Problem" in F. S. Freeman, *Psychological Testing.* New York: Holt, 1950. Pp. 477-487.

psychologists have devised tests that endeavor to measure non-verbal abilities. In general, we know less about the meaning of test scores on nonverbal intelligence tests. We know that there is a fair relationship between nonverbal and verbal test scores in that there is a moderate tendency for persons who get high scores on nonverbal tests to get high scores on verbal tests, and vice versa, but we are not sure whether this relationship is due to motivation to get high test scores, to the ability to take tests, or to a common factor, which we might call "general intelligence." In any event, nonverbal intelligence test scores are not very closely related to success in school. In fact, we have not been able to correlate them consistently with success in any area of endeavor. In general, we feel that they do measure a form of intelligence whose function is largely an unknown quantity.

Effective Intelligence. At this point in our discussion it would be well to differentiate between two forms or aspects of intelligence: (a) the kind of intelligence we have described, which we shall term "test" intelligence (because it is measured by standardized tests, largely of the paper-and-pencil variety); and (b) the kind of intelligence we need to cope with real-life situations, which we shall call "effective intelligence." The latter kind of intelligence is much closer to what is considered intelligence by the man in the street. The person who has a high level of effective intelligence is one who is competent to deal effectively with a wide variety of life situations — problems of a social, business, mechanical, and practical nature, or those problems that must sometimes be coped with during periods of physical stress and emotional tension. Effective intelligence may be defined as the capacity to meet one's basic needs through a constantly improved understanding and mastery of oneself and one's physical and social environment.

An interesting account of an attempt to measure and evaluate effective intelligence may be found in the published report of the wartime activities of the Assessment Staff of the Office of Strategic Services (16). The OSS was faced by the necessity of selecting personnel who were not only good security risks — that is, who would not release secret information even if subjected to all sorts of pressures and inducements — but who could be depended upon to act intelligently under severe stresses and in the presence of great and immediate personal danger. The Assessment Staff early agreed that the typical intelligence test would not produce a usable index of effective intelligence and that what the staff really wanted was a clinical "picture" of an individual's effectivity rather than a single score, such as an IQ. For the purpose of their project, they classified the abilities they were interested in into the following types or phases: (a) collection of data, including perception and selection of significant facts; (b) diagnosis of the situation; (c) conception of a plan, including selection of most strategic goals, improvisation of means thereto, prediction of results, plans to meet contingencies, and communication of plans to others; and (d) execution of action, including dealing with things, animals, and people, managing and administering, and striving with perseverance until the goal was reached.

The Assessment Staff went about their task of evaluating candidates by subjecting them to three days of tests. These included some paper-and-pencil problems, such as writing propaganda that might be successful in undermining the morale of the guards on the Manchurian Railway. But the chief weight was placed on tests of the situation type. In one of these situation tests, the candidate was required to build a small structure with the "help" of two stooges who were directed to impede the work, to annoy him, and to test his tolerance for frustration at extreme limits. In another situation, candidates were asked to suppose that they had been caught in the secret files of the War Department at night without any form of identification; they were then given ten minutes to prepare a plausible explanation, which they had to defend before a committee who sought to confuse and upset them with rapid and merciless cross-examination. The candidates' participation in free discussion and debate also yielded valuable data with respect to the level of effective intelligence.

The OSS assessment differs markedly from previous attempts to measure intelligence. The makers of traditional intelligence tests had been and still are concentrating on measuring small, statistically pure, and often highly artificial samples of human behavior, whereupon the results of these measurements are combined into an IQ or a set of scores. However, test intelligence may at times be far removed from total ability to act intelligently in a given situation.

A case in point is that of Dr. Gruber. Dr. Gruber is a nationally recognized expert in plant chemistry. He is a painstaking, careful, brilliant person, who completed his work for the Ph.D. degree at the age of twenty-one with a straight A average. Recently he was heard to complain that it always takes him an hour to drive home from the university, a distance of three miles. On questioning, it appeared that he always takes a route which is geographically the most direct, but which leads right through the heart of the city, where the traffic is the thickest. He was unaware that there are several routes only a few blocks longer, which skirt the downtown area and would enable him to make his trip in ten or fifteen minutes. Dr. Gruber's test intelligence is phenomenal, but he would likely rate below average in a situation test designed to evaluate effective intelligence. Part of his difficulty is probably due to faulty perception — he does not see the selection of a better route from the university to his home as a problem at all. Thus his failure to achieve a high score in effective intelligence would probably be unrelated to his total intellectual capacity and would very likely be the result of insufficient motivation. On the other hand, perhaps insufficient motivation also serves to explain low scores made on paper-and-pencil tests by many grade school students. There are many boys in school who, though they do not know nouns from verbs, know the complicated rules of several kinds of mumbletypeg, as well as the batting averages of several dozen big-league ballplayers. There are also adults who would do poorly at multiplying fractions but who perform infinitely complicated computations in handicapping horses.

Kinds of Intelligence. Another way to look at intelligence is to break it down into broad aspects. One way to do this is to think of it in terms of the *objects* of intelligent activity. For the purposes of discussion, these areas do not need to be as fine and precise as the narrow functions selected by the test maker. The Assessment Staff classified mental functions into the following:

1. Ability to deal with things (for example, physical obstacles, machinery, weapons, radios, gadgets) — mechanical intelligence.
2. Ability to deal with people — social intelligence.
3. Ability to deal with ideas (for example, concepts, numbers, symbols, abstract formulations, ideologies) — conceptual intelligence.

Test intelligence is a variety of "conceptual intelligence." All three kinds of intelligence are important and necessary, and we all require a certain amount of each in order to meet our basic needs and to cope with the demands of our physical and social environment. Because conceptual intelligence is easier to measure and because it is more important than the other two kinds for success in school, we have allowed ourselves to overstress its importance and to mistake it for the broader aptitudes of effective intelligence. If it were more widely recognized and accepted that there are other kinds of intelligence as important as test intelligence, there would be less anxiety about IQ's, there would be more acceptance of persons whose better skills lie in the areas of social intelligence or mechanical intelligence, and perhaps schools would alter the curriculum so as to give equal stress to activities that involve all three kinds, instead of overstressing conceptual or test intelligence, as they do now.

SUMMARY

People in our middle-class society worry about intelligence; they wonder what their IQ's are, they overstress the importance of the intellectual aspect of modern life, and they link intelligence with status and prestige. Though they recognize intelligence as a force, they nevertheless tend to reject the idea of individual differences, because somehow they feel that intelligence should be achieved through education and hard work. The fact is that we all differ intellectually, just as we differ physically.

For the last sixty years, psychologists have been interested in measuring intellectual differences. The modern intelligence test is based on the pioneer work of Binet and Terman, who developed individual scales of behavior classified according to levels of intellectual maturity. Group intelligence tests were used successfully in World War I; this led to their adoption by educators and to wholesale testing in the 1920's and 1930's.

Most intelligence tests in common usage would be more accurately described as "tests of academic aptitude." Scores on these tests appear to be affected by motivation, social class and status, and problems of emotional adjustment. Although test scores were devised to help us understand people better, sometimes they are misused in that they provide an all-too-convenient label that serves to thwart further understanding rather than to help it. The example is given of the child who, classified by a group test as having an IQ of 80, thereupon gets no further help from the teacher because she is felt to be unable to learn. In the hands of competent persons, however, intelligence tests can be used to promote deeper understanding. Academic aptitude tests are useful devices for colleges, which cannot accept all applicants and must select those who can best profit from instruction.

The controversy over whether intelligence is the result of inherited qualities or of environmental forces is as yet unsettled. One commonly held point of view is that heredity sets the limits to intelligence and that environment determines the extent to which an individual will develop his intelligence within those limits.

One of the shortcomings of "test intelligence" is that it comprises only a narrow aspect of what most of us consider to be total intelligence. The totality of the individual's tendency to act intelligently has been described as "effective intelligence"; this is closer to the idea of intelligence held by the man in the street. Effective intelligence can be divided into three aspects: mechanical, social, and conceptual. Intelligence tests of the paper-and-pencil variety are largely tests of conceptual intelligence.

REFERENCES

1. M. A. Merrill, "The Significance of IQ's on the Revised Stanford Binet Scale," *Journal of Educational Psychology.* 29:641–651; 1938. Reprinted by permission of Warwick & York, Inc.
2. A. Binet, *Les Idées Modernes Sur Les Enfants.* Paris: E. Flammarion, 1909.
3. Symposium, "Intelligence and its Measurement," *Journal of Educational Psychology.* 12:123–147, 195–216, 271–275; 1921.
4. E. L. Thorndike, "Intelligence and Its Uses," *Harper's Magazine.* 140:227–235; 1920.
5. L. L. Thurstone, *Vectors of Mind.* Chicago: University of Chicago Press, 1935.
6. D. Wechsler, *The Measurement of Adult Intelligence,* 3d edition. Baltimore: Williams & Wilkins, 1944.
7. A. S. Barr, "Teaching Competencies," in W. S. Monroe, *Encyclopedia of Educational Research,* Rev. edition. New York: Macmillan, 1950. Pp. 1446–1454.
8. A. Davis, *Social-Class Influences upon Learning.* Cambridge: Harvard University Press, 1948.
9. A. Davis, "What Happens to Students in Lower Socio-Economic Groups?"

H. C. Lindgren, ed., *Proceedings of the Northern California Regional Conference on Counseling, Guidance, and Student Personnel Services, July 5–7, 1950.* San Francisco: San Francisco State College, 1950. Pp. 12–21.

10. K. Eells, *et al.*, *Intelligence and Cultural Differences.* Chicago: University of Chicago Press, 1951.

11. V. M. Axline, "Nondirective Therapy for Poor Readers," *Journal of Consulting Psychology.* 11:61–69; 1947.

12. V. M. Axline, "Mental Deficiency — Symptom or Disease?" *Journal of Consulting Psychology.* 13:313–327; 1949. (Also in E. L. Hartley, *et al.*, eds., *Outside Readings in Psychology.* New York: Crowell, 1950. Pp. 520–540.)

13. A. E. Traxler, "What Is a Satisfactory IQ for Admission to College?" *School and Society.* 51:462–464; 1940.

14. L. D. Hartson and A. J. Sprow, "The Value of Intelligence Quotients Obtained in Secondary Schools for Predicting College Scholarship," *Educational and Psychological Measurements.* 1:387–398; 1941.

15. D. Segel, *Prediction of Success in College.* United States Office of Education Bulletin No. 15, 1934.

16. Assessment Staff of the United States Office of Strategic Services, *Assessment of Men.* New York: Rinehart, 1948.

SUGGESTED READINGS

H. A. Garrett, *Psychology.* New York: American Book, 1950. See chapters on intelligence.

E. T. Prothro and P. T. Teska, *Psychology: A Biosocial Study of Behavior.* Boston: Ginn, 1950. See chapter on intelligence.

G. Murphy, *An Introduction to Psychology.* New York: Macmillan, 1951. See chapters on intelligence and its measurement, and the pattern of abilities.

J. E. Anderson, *The Psychology of Development and Personal Adjustment.* New York: Holt, 1949. Section 2 deals with learning skills, including intelligence.

F. L. Ruch, *Psychology and Life*, 3d edition. Chicago: Scott, 1948. See chapters on intelligence.

E. L. Hartley, *et al.*, eds., *Outside Readings in Psychology.* New York: Crowell, 1950. Section 12 deals with intelligence.

W. Dennis, *Readings in General Psychology.* New York: Prentice-Hall, 1949. Section VIII contains several articles on Terman's work.

W. L. Valentine, *Experimental Foundations of General Psychology*, Rev. edition. New York: Farrar, 1941. See chapters on intelligence and the meaning of intelligence test scores.

"Intelligence and Intelligence Tests," in W. S. Monroe, ed., *Encyclopedia of Educational Research*, Rev. edition. New York: Macmillan, 1950. Pp. 600–612.

A. I. Gates, *et al.*, *Educational Psychology*, 3d edition. New York: Macmillan, 1948. See the chapters on intelligence.

C. E. Skinner, ed., *Elementary Educational Psychology.* New York: Prentice-Hall, 1945. Part III deals with mental abilities and individual differences.

R. A. Davis, *Educational Psychology.* New York: McGraw-Hill, 1948. Chapter 2 is concerned with scholastic ability (academic aptitude).

L. E. Cole and W. F. Bruce, *Educational Psychology.* Yonkers, New York: World Book, 1950. See Chapter 5, "The Development of Effective Intelligence."

G. Murphy, *Historical Introduction to Modern Psychology*, Rev. edition. New York: Harcourt, Brace, 1949. See the chapter on the measurement of intelligence.

L. M. Terman and M. A. Merrill, *Measuring Intelligence.* Boston: Houghton Mifflin, 1937. A description of the construction and the standardization of the 1937 edition of the Stanford-Binet test. The second half of the volume constitutes the manual for the test.

D. Wechsler, *The Measurement of Adult Intelligence*, 3d edition. Baltimore: Williams & Wilkins, 1944. The first section describes Wechsler's theory of intelligence, the second deals with the standardization of the Wechsler-Bellevue Intelligence Tests (the most commonly used individual intelligence test for adults), and the third constitutes the manual for the tests.

F. S. Freeman, *Theory and Practice of Psychological Testing.* New York: Holt, 1950. Chapters 3–9 deal with the theories, development, and chief characteristics of mental ability tests of all varieties.

J. L. Mursell, *Psychological Testing*, 2d edition. New York: Longmans, 1949. See Chapters 3–6 and 9–11.

L. J. Cronbach, *Essentials of Psychological Testing.* New York: Harper, 1949. See Chapters 6–8.

E. B. Greene, *Measurements of Human Behavior*, Rev. edition. New York: Odyssey, 1952. See Chapters 5, 6, and 8 for a description of individual and group intelligence tests.

XVI... *Getting an Education:*

Learning

Learning and Mental Health. This is the second of two chapters concerned with helping the student to understand the factors and processes that are psychologically important in getting an education.

We usually think of learning more or less uncritically as the process that occurs obviously and automatically in school situations. We are rather sharply reminded that learning is not an automatic process when, as students, we meet baffling problems that our education should have prepared us to solve or when, as teachers, we discover that students who return in the fall are unable to remember the skills and the concepts taught them the previous spring. The fact that our everyday attitudes toward learning are so unrealistic is in itself a matter of concern for students of mental hygiene. Many of the disappointments and frustrations we experience in our pursuit of an education are directly attributable to our lack of information regarding learning conditions and processes and our consequent unrealistic expectations.

Learning, in its broadest and most positive sense, is the process of becoming mature emotionally, intellectually, and socially. Education is an arrangement that permits and encourages learning; in its broadest and most positive sense, it helps the individual to become more mature emotionally, intellectually, and socially.

The interrelationships of emotional maturity, learning, and education may be brought out more clearly by a brief discussion of the characteristics they have in common.

The person who is emotionally and intellectually mature is reasonably free from illusions and delusions regarding himself or his physical and social environment. His perceptual processes are in

347

good working order: he perceives and empathizes with a minimum of neurotic distortion. He tends to see life's frustrations as problems to be solved, rather than as threats. As problems, they challenge rather than repel him. Since he is less likely to be concerned with himself in neurotic ways (egocentric), he is more emotionally involved with his environment: he has an active curiosity, a desire to learn, and a drive to master his physical and social environment.

The person who is emotionally and intellectually mature has a strong need to learn, to grow toward ever higher levels of maturity, and he organizes and reorganizes his experience in order to attain this growth.

Since most of us are more or less beset by neurotic needs, we are often unable to learn as efficiently as we would like, and our learning is inhibited or facilitated to the extent that our neurotic needs are active or inactive. For example, most of us have little difficulty in applying ourselves to a subject taught by an instructor whom we like or to a subject that is interesting or important to us — that is, in which we are ego-involved. On the other hand, our learning is impeded if the instructor is an individual who "rubs us the wrong way" or if we are forced to take a subject for which we see no immediate or long-range value. In the latter instances, our feelings of hostility toward the instructor, or toward being forced to do something we do not want to do, interfere with the learning processes. Sometimes, indeed, these conditions serve to strengthen our neurotic defenses rather than to increase our capacities to act intelligently. Thus the greater the positive emotional investment we have in the learning situation, the more likely we are to learn; and the greater the negative emotional investment, the less likely we are to learn and the more likely we are to regress.

Theories of Learning: Conditioning. Ever since psychology attained the status of a science, psychologists have been concerned with the investigation of the nature of the learning process. The result of their experimentation and observation has been the development of a number of theories that attempt to explain various aspects of the learning process.

For centuries before I. P. Pavlov evolved his theories of the conditioned response, philosophers had been aware of the fact that learning is influenced by associations. However, Pavlov based his theories on physiological experiments. While studying the operation of the digestive system of the dog, Pavlov observed that digestive juices, which he had assumed were called forth by the presence of undigested food, actually began to flow when the dog heard the footsteps of the experimenter bringing the food. This led to his setting up an experiment in which he measured the flow of the dog's saliva in response to various stimuli. In his classic experiment, he placed meat powder in the dog's mouth, with the result that saliva flowed at an increased rate. Pavlov called this automatic response the "unconditioned reflex." The sounding of a bell in the presence of the dog caused no increase in the flow of saliva. However, when the bell was sounded a number of times just before the powdered meat was placed in the dog's mouth, the sound of the bell alone was sufficient to cause an increased saliva flow. Pavlov called this connection between the bell and the increased rate of salivation a "conditioned reflex" (termed a "conditioned response" by psychologists), and he called the sound of the bell a "conditioned stimulus."

The principle involved here is that when stimulus A produces response X and when stimulus B occurs with A, after a while stimulus B alone will be sufficient to produce response X.

This theory of learning has proved to be a fruitful formulation, for it has formed the basis of thousands of psychological experiments and studies with both humans and animals and has served as the foundation of the behaviorist school of psychologists. (See the writings of John B. Watson, E. L. Thorndike, E. R. Guthrie, Clark L. Hull, Edward C. Tolman, Walter S. Hunter, B. F. Skinner, Karl S. Lashley, Z. Y. Kuo, Max Meyer, and many others).

The conditioned-response principle of learning is essentially an elaborated restatement of our "common sense" theory of learning. We catch Junior playing with the sugar bowl and we spank him. We do this because we hope and expect that Junior will associate spanking with playing with the sugar bowl. If Junior stays away from the sugar bowl, we congratulate ourselves on our knowledge of practical psychology, but if he continues to play with the sugar, we wonder what has gone wrong. (In the meantime, we continue to spank him.)

Actually, the principle of conditioning is still operating; Junior's continuing to play with the sugar bowl merely demonstrates that the principle is much more complicated than it appears on the surface. There are a number of possible explanations for Junior's persistent antisocial behavior, all of them consistent with the conditioned-response principle. Perhaps Junior interprets the spanking as "attention" rather than as "pain" or "punishment." If he has a need for more attention than he is getting from his parents, spanking may even seem desirable. Or it may be that though he dislikes spanking, the attraction of the sugar bowl is stronger than his fear of punishment. Or it may be that Junior gets punished so often that he is unable to remember which acts are punishable and may take punishment as a matter of course, something that must be endured as a matter of routine. Perhaps Junior is so intellectually and emotionally immature that he is unable to make the association between punishment and the sugar bowl.

Mrs. Athos, a tense, nervous, panicky young woman, has a daughter, Marcella, aged two. In spite of many warnings (verbalizations do not have much effect on a child of two), Marcella wanders into the street. Her mother sees her, drags her back on the sidewalk, and thrashes her soundly. Every day Marcella wanders into the street, and every day she gets soundly spanked. Perhaps she will eventually learn to be afraid of going into the street, but in the meantime it is likely that she is learning only that her mother is someone who punishes. Thus, severe physical punishment may teach children to avoid undesirable activities, but it also teaches them to fear their parents.

The conditioned-response principle underlies most of the educational experiences we provide for the young. We attempt to "stack the cards" in favor of a desirable response by associating it with some kind of a reward, and against an undesirable response by associating it with some kind of penalty. Children in school are rewarded with high marks for completing their lessons according to instructions; they are penalized for incomplete or inferior lessons by being awarded low marks. Employees are rewarded for efficiency and high production by raises in pay, promotions, or continued employment. They are punished by the withholding of raises and promotions or by dismissal.

There is much that is useful in this theory of learning and much that is misleading. It is true that people tend to do things that have pleasant associations and that they tend to avoid doing things that are unpleasant. But the theory does not tell us *which* associations are the ones that will make people behave the way we want them to, and it does not tell us how to introduce these associations into the situation in such a way that they will be effective. Also, it ignores the fact that the associations perceived by the teacher are not necessarily the same ones perceived by the learner. Furthermore, this theory misleads us into thinking that all we need in order to manipulate people easily is to discover the proper combination of associations and the proper techniques of presenting them. In effect, this is the kind of solution sought by the parent who asks, "How can I get my Willie to eat his spinach?" or the teacher who asks, "How can I get an unco-operative child to co-operate?" or the plant foreman who asks, "How can I get workers to stay on the job, instead of leaving their work ten minutes early to get washed up?" We ask questions like these because we have placed our faith in the automatic operation of the laws of conditioned-response, reward-punishment learning. By our very requests for "the right techniques" we repudiate any solutions that would involve our studying the persons with whom we are dealing, any attempts to understand their needs and wants. In our roles as parents, teachers, or leaders, we tend to see ourselves as directors of activities and supervisors of other people rather than as persons who, through understanding and accepting our subordinates, can create emotional climates that stimulate and encourage learning and production.

Theories of Learning: Trial and Error. Another concept of learning is that it is a trial-and-error process. Suppose that a child's ball has rolled outside his play pen. His first reaction is to set up a clamor, but this produces no results because his mother is busy washing dishes and she cannot hear him. He then tries to reach the ball through the bars of the pen, but his arm is too short. He picks up a stick and starts to beat on the bars, but, being attracted again to the ball, he uses the stick to beat on the floor near it. Suddenly he happens to touch the ball, which causes it to roll within reach, and he picks it up. If the ball rolls out again, he may go through part of the routine of crying for it, reaching for it by hand, beating with the stick, and finally using the stick to get the ball. After this routine has been carried out several times, however, he will abandon the preliminaries and will immediately use the stick to bring the ball within reach. This is "learning by blundering," by accidentally happening upon the correct solution. Because the correct solution has a satisfying effect, the procedure used to reach it becomes associated with it and is therefore remembered. "Nothing succeeds like success."

Trial-and-error learning plays its greatest role when the learner has little or no previous experience to bring to the problem. This is the situation with the very young child — he has not had sufficient experience with other problems to use any approach but the accidental discovery of a solution. More mature persons attempt to use methods they have employed previously in solving other problems, and not until these methods fail do they resort to the less efficient trial-and-error learning.

Trial-and-error learning has been explored extensively by psychologists of the behaviorist school, particularly through experiments with cats and other infrahuman animals.*

Theories of Learning: Learning by Insight. The intelligent use of knowledge gained from previous experience is the principle of insight. This principle was proposed by psychologists of the Gestalt school (*Gestalt* means "configuration" or "pattern"), who discovered that learners tend to solve problems by "discovering" relationships rather than by accident, by blundering, or by random movement, as in trial-and-error learning. The Gestalt approach to learning conceives of the learner puzzling over a problem, suddenly perceiving a new relationship, and using this relationship to solve the problem at hand. An important implication of this concept is that the learner solves each problem as a complete unit, rather than piecemeal. Thus, a child learns a new word as an idea represented by a group of letters, rather than as one letter, then another and another, until there is formed a cluster of letters that turns out to have a meaning. Similarly, a student learning to write a theme starts out with an idea that he breaks down into sections, then into paragraphs, and finally into sentences and words. He does not start out writing sentences, which eventually add up to paragraphs, which eventually add up to a theme. Gestalt learning is opposed to the traditional approach to education, which

---

* See J. A. McGeoch, *The Psychology of Human Learning.* New York: Longmans, 1942. Or see E. R. Guthrie and G. P. Horton, *Cats in a Puzzle Box.* New York: Rinehart, 1946.

tends to view learning as a piece-by-piece process, involving the mastery of each bit of technique or information until a larger skill or concept is formed. The traditional approach is still firmly rooted in those schools that teach the individual steps used in multiplying fractions *before* teaching the general concept involved in the multiplication of fractions. Also contrary to Gestalt principles are tendencies to emphasize isolated facts by giving examinations that call for memorized, minute details rather than familiarity with broader areas of knowledge.*

Theories of Learning: Learning as Adjustment and Growth. Another concept that psychologists have found useful is the principle of learning as a form of adjustment or adaption (1). Seen in this light, learning is a process by which the self attempts to achieve a balance among the psychological forces produced by the needs of the individual and the demands of the physical and social environment. The development of the superego processes described in Chapter 2 is a good illustration of this kind of learning, for it demonstrates how the individual must frustrate, inhibit, and rechannel the expression of certain basic needs in order to live at peace with society. Learning to play the piano is another example: through learning to play the piano skillfully, we learn to meet our needs for creativity and self-expression, but in doing so, we must sometimes deny those needs that would lead us to spend an afternoon with "the gang," relax with a magazine, or go to a movie. We learn to drive an automobile partly as a concession to a society that expects all adolescents and adults to drive automobiles and partly because driving enables us to be more sociable, to go for long drives in an attempt to get away from ourselves, and to meet members of the opposite sex.

Mowrer sees learning somewhat as we have described it above — that is, as reinforcement or need-reduction — but he also regards some learning as an attempt to reduce anxiety (2). We learn to get along with others because if we do not they will reject us and cause us to feel anxious and guilty. By learning to do what is expected of us, we protect ourselves against the feelings of anxiety. Other psychologists see learning as a process of growth (3, 4).

A number of psychologists have recently been concerned with

---

* For further and more complete descriptions of the Gestalt school of psychology, see the writings of Wolfgang Köhler, Kurt Koffka, G. W. Hartmann, and W. D. Ellis.

attempting to bring divergent points of view in the field of learning closer together or, rather, to identify elements that are similar. One of the most lucid attempts to construct a "bridge" between two points of view is the review and analysis by John Dollard and Neal E. Miller of problems of adjustment and psychotherapy, particularly as seen in the light of laboratory experiments in learning. Dollard and Miller are convinced, as a result of their analysis, that neurotic behavior, like all other forms of behavior, is learned. Therefore they view psychotherapy as the process whereby the patient or client *un*learns his inappropriate behavior or, rather, relearns behavior in forms that are more effective, realistic, and appropriate (5).

The ability of the individual to grow and to adjust to the changing forces produced by his needs and the demands of the physical and social environment depends very largely on his emotional maturity. The less the psychological maturity of the individual, the more defensive and rigid he is, and the more difficult it is for him to adjust to new situations. Positive learning requires that the individual surrender older, more infantile ways of thinking and behaving in exchange for newer, more realistic ways of thinking and behaving. It requires that he take the chance that the newer ways of thinking and doing will yield greater happiness and satisfaction. It requires that he become interested, that he extend himself, that he "invest" some of himself in becoming involved in this new activity. An individual who neurotically perceives threats on all sides, who is frozen by fear and anxiety, who withdraws into the armor of his neurotic defenses, who regards all growth-producing factors in his environment as threats to his existence, which must be met through aggressive tactics — he is the individual who cannot learn. Like the Bourbon kings, he cannot learn anything and he cannot forget anything. Perhaps his old way of life is inconvenient, impractical, childish, and a producer of unhappiness, but he feels he must defend it vigorously because it is "all he has."

The deadliest weapon the immature person has is his sheer refusal to learn; no one can be forced to learn anything against his will. Armed with this weapon, immature persons of all ages make their way through life, warding off learning by various attitudes of apathy and boredom. If they learn at all, it is how to build bigger and stronger defenses against the perception of reality, the understanding and acceptance of others, and the attempts made to educate them.

There are many of us whose neurotic defenses are so impregnable that we are virtually unteachable. Most of us are not unteachable, but because we have some neurotic anxiety, we are plagued with blocks to our learning. We cannot learn as fast as we would like. We have difficulty in concentrating; we would like to be interested, but we are bored. We avoid active participation, because involvement will bring about change in us, and we are afraid of change. We would like to think of ourselves as self-contained, competent, and self-sufficient, with no further need to learn, for to admit we have something to learn would necessitate humbling ourselves. These are the reasons why learning is so difficult, so painful, and why we have to work so hard at it. In effect, we not only must grow emotionally and intellectually, but we must also fight off those neurotic forces within ourselves that are trying to stifle or defeat learning. In the end, each of our attempts at learning is resolved either by positive growth or by a further stiffening of our neurotic defenses.

Motivation. Given this background of emotional conflict, it is apparent that any movement in the direction of positive learning must be impelled and supported by some emotional investment, or it will be throttled by those anxieties that prevent learning and keep us just as we are. Motivation is thus prerequisite to the learning process (6). The nature of the individual's motivation will determine whether he will grow in the direction of greater psychological maturity or whether he will stiffen his neurotic defenses; it will determine *whether* he will learn and *what* he will learn. The person who is ready to learn and who wishes to learn is the one who *will* learn, provided he has sufficient intellectual capacity, emotional maturity, and opportunity. If motivation is lacking, the efforts of others to educate him are in vain. People will learn (a) if they want to learn, (b) if they are given the opportunity to learn, (c) if they have the capacity to learn, and (d) if they receive help and direction in their learning *when they need it.* Too often the last comes first — the help and direction are forced upon students long before they have developed any intention of learning. This is the point at which the frustrated teacher attempts to invoke the laws of conditioned-response learning in order to manipulate

the situation and the students to produce the desired result. He
promises rewards to those who learn and punishment to those who
refuse to do so.

Sometimes it appears that we work too hard at trying to get
people to learn. There are certain needs present in most of us
— the need to master our environment, the need for self-expression, the need for status, the need to identify ourselves with figures
of prestige and power, the need to be accepted by the group
— that can easily serve as bases for directed learning experiences.
As a matter of fact, these needs are the bases of much of the positive
learning that forms a major portion of our experience. The small
child normally comes to school with an active curiosity about his
environment and a tremendous urge to express himself and relate
himself to others. Too often his enthusiasm to learn is stifled and
thwarted in an attempt to have him conform to the accepted
pattern. Some of this frustration may be necessary in a system
of mass education, but when the desire to learn has been so thoroughly extinguished by the time the child reaches the upper grades,
one wonders whether the forces of conformity have not been too
thorough.

Three Approaches to Education and Learning

One of the ways in which we can organize our thinking about
learning is to examine the kinds of situations in which students
commonly find themselves. Perhaps we can more or less arbitrarily call these situations laissez-faire, authoritarian (or autocratic), and democratic, partly because there are certain aspects of
these political philosophies embodied in each approach and partly
because these terms are convenient labels.*

The Authoritarian Approach. The authoritarian approach to education assumes that children (and students in general — even
college students), if left to their own devices, would develop bad
habits — that is, they would engage in antisocial, immoral, or
illegal behavior. Therefore education is presumed to serve a corrective function, to be a means of "keeping them on the right
track," so to speak. In other words, people will develop bad habits
unless they are forced to develop good ones. Training in good

---

* The use of these terms here is prompted by the classic study by Lewin, Lippitt,
and White, discussed in Chapter 10.

habits and discouragement of bad habits is best carried on, according to this point of view, by rewarding good behavior and penalizing bad behavior. This approach encourages an either-or orientation — one is either rewarded or one is punished; there is no middle ground. The success or failure of this approach depends on the individual concerned. Some will feel that the withholding of the highest reward (an A) is a punishment, while others will feel that avoiding a failing grade (an F) is in itself a reward. Some will feel that not to get an A is a failure, while others will feel that even a few F's do not constitute failure, so long as one graduates or advances to the next grade. Under this reward-and-punishment system, students do not strive in order to enjoy the feeling of success involved in having learned something new, but they strive for the reward of a "good" grade to avoid the disgrace of a "poor" grade.

We might characterize this approach to education as the good-and-bad-habit approach, or the reward-punishment approach. Although it leans heavily on the "common sense" concept of conditioned-response learning, there is enough truth in it to make it plausible and attractive to those who follow it. Some groups of children become unmanageable if left to their own devices, sometimes rewards are useful incentives and sometimes punishment is necessary; the completely satisfactory substitute for the grading system is yet to be found. On the other hand, the possibilities and the dangers of anarchy and disorder among children's groups are much exaggerated. Furthermore, this approach depends too much on artificial incentives and not enough on the normal motivation of students for it to be even reasonably efficient (7). Many students who are cited as successful examples of this system of education have learned in spite of it rather than because of it.

The Laissez-faire Approach. The laissez-faire school of thought is diametrically opposed to the authoritarian school. It is based on the principle that students, if left to their own devices, will work out a satisfactory and mature adjustment to their environment.* It sees people as inherently good, incapable of developing "bad habits," providing they are allowed complete freedom for self-development. This attitude is based on the principle that there are strong forces

---

* Contrary to popular belief, the proportion of schools and classes that operate on laissez-faire principles is infinitesimal.

within all of us that push us in the direction of greater emotional maturity if we permit them to do so. Furthermore, many so-called behavior problems that children (particularly small children) display, disappear of their own accord as children pass into the next stage of development. The shortcomings of this point of view are as follows: 1. Such a system does not provide for the emotionally disturbed and disturbing individual who disrupts group activities. This kind of individual is not as common nor as dangerous as we would like to believe, but he *does* constitute a potential menace. 2. Such a system attempts to build a situation that is completely free from anxiety-producing influences. It is highly questionable whether such an arrangement is feasible or possible; furthermore, it is questionable whether such an arrangement is desirable, since students must learn to cope with anxiety-producing forces outside the school and the home, both while they are students and after they graduate. 3. Such a system assumes that it is possible for the leader (teacher or parent) to be physically present in the group and "not do anything." However, even an adult who "does nothing" actually does *something* to the group merely by being present — even standing in the background and speaking only when spoken to has some psychological effect on the group.

In some ways, the laissez-faire approach is an improvement, psychologically speaking, over the authoritarian system. It recognizes and respects the capacity of individuals to think, act, and choose for themselves; and it respects their right to learn at their own speed those matters of the greatest importance to them. However, this system tends to ignore the responsibility of the school and the family to society as a whole, and it is unrealistic in assuming that the individual in such a system is completely free. Sometimes all that happens in a laissez-faire system is that the benevolent autocracy of an adult leader is replaced by the despotic control of an individual student or group of students. Furthermore, no techniques are provided to eliminate forces that impede learning.

The Democratic Approach. The democratic approach is not a compromise between the preceding divergent points of view but a synthesis of their virtues. It endeavors to inspire learning by attempting to find out the needs of the student group and providing the facilities for meeting these needs. Students are accepted and respected as individuals who have a right to question and to disagree with

Education is much more informal and student-centered than it once was —
particularly in the lower grades.

leaders and to present their own opinions. The learning situation provided by the school or the family under this arrangement recognizes that the institution has responsibilities to the student, to society as a whole, and to the pursuit of truth and knowledge. Thus the student, society, and the teacher each has a part to play in setting the stage for the learning experiences and in deciding what type of learning experiences will be undertaken. The teacher must demonstrate a high degree of sensitivity to know how much guidance should be employed. The younger the group, usually the more guidance is required; but each group varies from time to time in the amount of guidance it requires, and some groups need more guidance than others.

The advantages of the democratic approach are as follows: 1. It is not committed to any one principle of learning. 2. It permits the individual to have some say about what he shall learn and when he shall learn it. This makes for better motivation and hence better learning. 3. It provides for controls (guidance) when they are needed but does not require that controls be exercised at all times. 4. Since it recognizes learning as a form of growth, it realizes that the teacher cannot learn for the student; the student must do his own learning.

Many people confuse the democratic approach to learning with the laissez-faire approach. They feel that either you have an authoritarian, reward-punishment learning situation or "kids run wild," as under the laissez-faire system. They cannot conceive of a system that is permissive but in which there is intelligent guidance. They feel that it is a question of complete and rigid control or no control at all. They cannot perceive the possibility of the *shared* control of the democratic classroom.

There are disadvantages to this approach to learning: 1. The paths are not as well marked as they are in authoritarian or laissez-faire learning. In the authoritarian, one directs; in the laissez-faire one is completely permissive; the democratic teacher must know when he should direct and when he should be permissive. 2. There are no techniques that guarantee one's becoming a good democratic leader. One must find out the principles through experience, experimentation, and sensitivity. 3. Being a democratic leader makes more demands on the intelligence and emotional maturity of the individual. He is often thrown on his own resources, whereas authoritarian and laissez-faire leaders have more precisely and rigidly defined patterns of behavior to follow.

These approaches to education and learning have been described in their relatively "pure" form. In actuality, most teachers, parents, leaders, and other authority figures employ an approach to learning that combines qualities of each of these schools of thought. Most individuals who undertake to help others learn have their share of successes and failures, regardless of which approach they use. Some of these successes and failures are due to the strengths or the flaws of the approaches they employ, some are due to the personalities of the leaders, and some depend on accidental or situational factors beyond the immediate control of the individuals concerned: the educational philosophy of the school in which they teach, the kind of neighborhood in which the students live, the kinds of relationships that exist among the students in the group, the expectations that students have for themselves and of the adult leader, and so on, in infinite variety.

Although most educators and educational psychologists today are led by their personal observations or their research (or both) to favor some form of the democratic approach to education and learning, they recognize that many teachers are successful in using systems predominantly authoritarian or laissez-faire. In general, their feeling is that teachers who are successful and "comfortable" in their methods should not be coerced into changing but that the new crop of teachers and parents should be familiar with the psychological advantages of the democratic system before they begin to exercise their educational functions.

The Learning Situation in School

This section will deal with a few of the dynamic factors that affect learning in most schools.

Perceptual Rigidity. No matter what approach to learning dominates the educational scene, students tend to regard the teacher or instructor with some of the same attitudes they have developed toward their own parents and toward authority figures in general. If they have come to look upon adults as lenient, they expect their teachers to be lenient; if their parents are punitive, they expect teachers to be punitive; if they are in the habit of challenging and arguing with their parents, they will challenge and argue with their teachers. This tendency was discussed in Chapter 5 under the heading of "perceptual rigidity," a psychological mechanism whereby attitudes developed in one situation are transferred virtually without change to another situation that appears similar. Teachers, too, are likely to be affected by perceptual rigidity, in that they tend to develop stereotypes whereby they classify students. For example, one teacher may feel that students are essentially "lazy," another may feel that students cannot be trusted, and another may assume that all students like him.

Because teachers and students in our society tend to adopt roles that are mutually exclusive — that is, they do not usually mingle and associate with each other on any kind of equal basis — it is difficult for them to communicate with each other except about the subject being studied; and even here the communication is usually one way, from the teacher to the student. Students seldom, if ever, get to know what kind of people teachers are; and teachers, unless they happen to serve as counselors, seldom get to know what kind of people their students are. This lack of communication between the two groups encourages perceptual rigidity, which thrives on lack of information.

The effect of perceptual rigidity is very marked in students who, for any number of psychological reasons, were unable to learn easily from their parents or from previous teachers. These are the students who have to find out things for themselves. Then there are the students who never have learned very much in school, but who are pleasant and agreeable, and who go through the motions of making an effort to learn. When they happen to enroll in classes taught by teachers who insist on rather rigorously defined "results," such students become frustrated and disappointed because their usual techniques for "getting by" are not appreciated. The perceptual rigidities of teachers, too, can interfere with learning. The teacher who is convinced that "young people today are silly, unstable, and senseless," will have difficulty creating a stimulating atmosphere in his classroom.

Identification. Probably any student who is successful at learning in the classroom identifies himself with the teacher to some extent. Because he is interested (ego-involved) in the subject, because he likes the teacher, or because he is in sympathy with the general idea of education, or for all three of these reasons, he finds himself attempting to see the subject from the instructor's point of view and to discover how the instructor feels about the subject and life in general. In other words, he empathizes with the instructor. He may even attempt to follow up some of his empathic hunches by checking them with the instructor after class.

The Maintenance of Order and Discipline. Order and discipline are problems that assume their greatest magnitude in the authoritarian educational situation. Ostensibly, order and discipline are considered necessary as aids or prerequisites to classroom learning ("The other children can't study if you keep whispering!"), but they frequently become an end in themselves. When this occurs, the teacher becomes a policeman instead of a "learning supervisor," and the motivation of the children, which might have been channeled in the direction of learning, is converted into trying to avoid trouble with the teacher, or, on occasion, into trying to start trouble. In either event, little learning results.

Seen objectively, the chief function of order and discipline is not to help students to learn, but to help the teacher control the class. The buzzing of committees, the movement, the occasional loud talking, and the laughter that are typical of the laissez-faire and the democratic systems of education are upsetting to the authoritarian teacher. He is upset not because of his belief that no learning is taking place (although he may give this as his reason), but rather because the group is "out of control" — that is, because the situation is being controlled wholly or in part by students, rather than by the teacher.

Competition. In the section of Chapter 4 dealing with hostility, we discussed the effect on personality of the competitive atmosphere at school. The competitive atmosphere acts as a deterrent to genuine learning in many instances. Joey gets a B in sixth grade geography. His father says that he should be able to do better than that, because he is certainly as smart as the kids who got A's. So Joey spends extra time preparing for the next geography examination, memorizing the names of the rivers, mountains, capitals, and chief products of Asian countries. He gets an A in the test. Both he and his father are pleased. Three months later, he has forgotten 80 per cent of what he learned for this test; a year later, he has forgotten all of it. Joey really didn't *learn* anything; he just memorized some facts to get a grade. Nothing of what he memorized made much sense to him; as far as he personally was concerned, it was *non*sense. Psychological experiments point to the same conclusion — we will forget nonsense before we forget what makes sense to us (8, 9). If Joey spends his time in school in developing routines and techniques merely to get better grades than other children, it is questionable whether his school experiences will aid him toward intellectual and emotional maturity. However, there is always the chance that he may become really interested in some area of learning; if he does, he may be able to learn, provided that not too much of his time and energy has been consumed in competing with others. Sometimes the spur of competition causes us to become involved in subjects we would otherwise shun, and we find ourselves interested in spite of the competitive atmosphere. After all, most normal individuals have an active curiosity and a strong desire to learn. It is in meeting these more basic needs that we do some of our best learning.

There is some virtue in the argument that inasmuch as the world outside school is competitive, the school should teach students how to maintain themselves in a competitive society. The truth is, however, that schools generally provide many opportunities and situations for learning competitive skills and techniques, and those students who fail to learn to compete do so for some individual reason or reasons. On the other hand, schools generally provide few opportunities for students to learn to co-operate in an atmosphere free from competition. Yet this type of skill, too, would seem necessary for survival.

Most of us are unaware of the competitive nature of education as it exists today. This lack of awareness is particularly characteristic of many college students who are unable for some reason to learn as fast as their fellow students. These students enter college expecting to find a learning situation similar to that which existed in high school. Unaware of the stiffened competition, they are amazed to find themselves becoming academic casualties. College standards of performance are set much higher than high-school standards, with the result that even the high-school honor student must put forth extra effort in order to maintain above-average grades. Since universities and colleges attract applicants largely from the upper half or upper third of high-school graduating

"Have you 1964?   He might skip 3-B."

Our culture places much stress on the competitive aspects of school.

classes, the "superior" student of high school becomes the "average" student in college. Most college students come to accept this phenomenon, but a large minority are chagrined, frustrated, and defeated by their inability to maintain the same standing in college they had in high school. Some of them leave college, convinced that they are unable to learn, whereas they have merely underestimated the competitive drive necessary to maintain their status as college students.

Transfer of Training. Some sixty years ago, J. M. Rice discovered that children who had studied spelling forty minutes a day for eight years were no better spellers than children who had studied ten minutes a day. Rice's study was soundly condemned by the educators of the day, not only because its findings were at variance with "common sense" but because they felt it was irrelevant. "After all," they said, "the chief argument in favor of the forty-minute spelling period is that it is *good training for the mind.*" In other words, they believed that habits of order, precision, and accuracy learned during spelling drill "transferred" to other life situations, and the more spelling drill, the more transfer.

In spite of the studies made by Rice and many other researchers, the doctrine of transfer of training has as many adherents today as it ever had. The supporters of this theory believe, in essence, that the "mind" can be trained and strengthened by hard mental work, in the same way that a muscle is trained and strengthened by hard physical work, and that mental skills learned in one subject will transfer to other subjects. Thus plane geometry maintains its place in the modern high-school curriculum because "it teaches you to think"; Latin is defended because "it helps you in English"; and the traditional sequences of college preparatory courses in high school are taken by would-be college applicants year after year because "these are the courses that will prepare you to do college work." The facts are that there is no evidence to prove that plane geometry "teaches one to think" any better than any other subject (10); that studies made of students taking high school English with or without Latin reveal that the study of Latin as usually taught has little effect on success in English (11); and that people who receive high grades in high school tend to be successful in college, regardless of what pattern of courses they have taken (12). The many studies that have been made of transfer of training come up with the same answer: that transfer, if it does operate, yields such slight advantages that it should not be used as a justification for the teaching of any subject. Yet we are so enmeshed in believing what "common sense" tells us to believe that we are unable to use the knowledge placed in our hands by this research. Most of us are like the English teachers who were shocked and repelled when they read of the research demonstrating the lack of relationship between knowledge of formal English grammar and the ability to write competently (13). When faced by evidence of this kind, they were unconvinced and regarded the findings as a personal affront. As a result, they were able to rally like-minded laymen (who are unacquainted with the facts brought out by the research) to their defense and so far have been able to maintain the position of traditional English grammar in the public and private schools.

The research in transfer of training contains some valuable lessons. In the first place, it reveals the large gap between *what we know* about education and learning and *what we do* about education and learning. In the second place, it reveals that most of us tend to be conservative of the wrong things; in deference to our neurotic needs, we would rather continue doing things in our old, inefficient way than to reorganize our way of life. And if pushed too hard on this, we become defensive and vindictive. In the third place, the research reveals that improvements could be made in education and learning if we were able to use the knowledge we now have; the horizons are unlimited. But, in the fourth place, we can see that research alone is not enough, that changes for the better in the established order are wrought by persons who feel a strong need within themselves for such a change. This need cannot be "given" to the general public by the professional educator or the psychologist, any more than the teacher can "give" learning to a student. In other words, psychologists and other research workers in the social sciences themselves have much to learn about teaching the general public. It is not enough to discover truths; ways must also be found whereby truths can be communicated. Thus the problem of education and learning is not limited to the family, the classroom, or the factory — it is global; it relates to communication and the sharing of knowledge everywhere.

The Role of the Student in Learning

As has been indicated previously in this chapter, the factors that make learning operate are largely emotional and attitudinal, while the techniques and methods of learning play an important, but secondary, role. Most college students have at their command sufficient skills and techniques to learn adequately. The problem of the poor student in college is one either of lack of academic aptitude or of neurotic conflicts that interfere with learning. It is seldom solely a problem of poor study techniques, or lack of study techniques. This does not mean that the typical college student could not improve his techniques, but it does mean that the basic problem in college success is one of attitudes rather than of methods. This section will therefore be concerned with those areas of emotional conflict that are likely to affect the student's ability to learn.

Aspirations. Aspirations are important ingredients in college success. The competitive forces in college quickly eliminate the student who does not care whether he succeeds, or the student who is not strongly motivated to graduate. However, aspirations can also interfere with learning and with the successful completion of a college career.

One such situation involves the student who aspires for a goal beyond his reach. For example, a student may be convinced that he should be an aeronautical engineer, though his academic record shows only average or poor grades. Plainly he does not have the aptitude to complete the course he has selected for himself. Another student may have an equally strong desire to complete college and go into teaching. His academic record shows many failing grades; he was twice placed on probation and has now been suspended. His high school grades are only average, and his entrance test scores are in the lowest one-tenth of the entering class. He, too, aspires to a goal beyond his reach. Each of these students is unrealistic if he persists in attempting to achieve the goal he has set for himself.

Aspirations also may interfere with learning if they are aimed at goals that are inappropriate to the personality pattern of the student. This problem is treated at greater length in Chapters 13 and 14, "Choosing a Vocation"; hence it will be mentioned only briefly here. In this instance, though the student has a high level of academic aptitude and presumably could complete most courses of study successfully, he has selected a goal at variance with his real interests. A student in such a situation was the one who felt his debt to his parents so keenly that when he discovered that his father wanted him to enter the field of law, he signed up for a prelegal curriculum in spite of the fact that he was really interested in bacteriology and did not care for law. He did well in his courses, even though he was not particularly interested in them. However, learning would have been more successful and more satisfying had he enrolled in courses that were more in harmony with his real interests.

Egocentrism. The self-centered person frequently causes difficulty in college by his nonconformist behavior. He has the feeling that he is above rules and regulations, that they are primarily for others and do not apply to him. If he gives full expression to his noncomformist tendencies by attending class and completing assignments only when the mood strikes him, he will not stay long in college. Some egocentric people are able to keep this tendency in check and conform in only the barest essentials. The egocentric person is a poor learner, because he is "fixated" at a more or less childish level of emotional maturity and seemingly cannot progress beyond this point.

Rebellion against Authority. Superficially, the rebel resembles the egocentric person, because he, too, may express his feelings by breaking regulations. However, whereas the egocentric person breaks regulations because he considers them inconsequential and annoying, the rebel breaks them because he has a grudge against authority figures and uses this means of attacking them. Persons who have an excessively strong need to rebel do not remain long in college. However, many college students are rebels in one way or another, and their attitude does not markedly hinder their learning unless rebelling against authority becomes more important than learning. Even so, some college students expend much time and energy in attempting to avoid regulations, with the result that their learning efficiency is reduced.

Overdependency. This, too, has been the subject of a previous chapter and will be mentioned but briefly here. The student who has been successful in developing his capacity for self-direction has less trouble than most college students. True, there are times when he resents being told how and what to do, but usually he is able to avoid many of the difficulties besetting the average student. For example, some students who enroll in courses too difficult for them remain in these courses, even though they know they are failing, because they are too proud to withdraw. The self-directive student in this situation discusses the matter with his advisor, the registrar, and the instructor. He finds that he can drop the course with a "Withdrawal" grade, which does not count against him, on paying a small fine. He decides that he would rather pay the fine than have a failing grade on the record and waste time staying in a class for which he has had no preparation. He thus retires from the situation gracefully, while the more dependent, passive student remains in the course, drifts along, and receives a failing grade.

Although most colleges have advising and counseling facilities, it is usually difficult or impossible for the student to consult with deans and counselors about every problem, large or small. The dependent person is thus doomed to be chronically frustrated, since he cannot get expert help on every minor problem. The self-directive person solves as many problems as he can without asking the advice of his busy counselor. When he happens on a problem that is too big for him, however, he does not hesitate to ask for help.

Verbal Deficiencies. The oral and written burden of college work, even in colleges of agricultural and mechanical arts, is very high. The ability to read with speed and comprehension, and the ability to express oneself in writing and in speech are highly essential. Lack of ability to read with speed and comprehension contributes more toward failure in college than any other single deficiency. On the other hand, the student who can read with speed and a high level of comprehension has a considerable advantage over his fellows. Some students who are admitted to college in spite of their poor reading ability can sometimes compensate for this deficiency by taking special laboratory courses in remedial reading.

The ability to express oneself in writing is of great importance. Written material (tests, themes, term papers, projects, quizzes) is the chief channel by which the student can communicate with the instructor. The student should use this means to tell the instructor what he has learned, to express his concepts of the subject, as well as to organize and clarify his own thinking about the subject. Thus writing is not only an essential means of communicating with the instructor, but is also an essential technique of learning. The student who expresses himself with difficulty in writing not only is unable to make use of this means of learning, but he loses in the competitive struggle with his classmates, because the instructor assumes that he knows no more of the subject than he can express.

Many classes depend on discussion as a learning tool. Here, too, the student who has not learned how to express himself in a group is at a disadvantage in both learning and competing. Although remedial speech laboratories sometimes help the individual in this situation, frequently the problem has deeper psychological implications, as described in Chapter 6, "The Struggle against Shyness and Feelings of Inferiority."

Lack of Drive and Aggression. As we have said elsewhere, learning does not take place unless people have enough "normal anxiety" to be motivated to learn. A passive individual is one who is satisfied with his lot and who has no desire to progress. The person who will learn in college is one who has a drive to grow intellectually and emotionally and who is willing to make some sacrifice, some investment of his time and himself in order to attain this growth. Such a person tends to move aggressively (used in the positive, not the hostile, sense of the word) against the obstacles in the way of his growth. He tends to see the obstacles as challenges rather than as blocks to further progress. Persons who lack this drive are less likely to succeed in college. They do not feel that the sacrifice is worth while.

Test Nerves. A relatively common phenomenon is the student who "blows up" in an examination or who is unable to do as well as he should. Like all other mechanisms, "test nerves" are the result of individual patterns of development — that is, one cannot say that they are due to any one kind of situation. However, here are some motivational patterns that commonly express themselves in "test nerves."

1. Many persons afflicted by "test nerves" are also individuals who are trying to prove something to themselves. Often they are persons who have come "from the wrong side of the tracks" or are members of minority groups who count more on the college degree to give them status than does the student who comes from a middle-class, white-

collar environment. For such a student there is almost too much at stake; every test, he feels, can break him, and he tends to magnify its threat. Furthermore, the test situation awakens guilt — perhaps he should never have aspired to rise above his class; perhaps he is deserting the people he grew up with; middle-class, white-collar people do not want to accept him anyhow. Thus the old attitudes of submission to and acceptance of his deprived status come into sharp conflict with his aspirations.

2. Most students who are bothered by active feelings of inferiority will probably be more or less troubled by tests. It is as though they have been "coasting" or "getting by." Now the "chips are down," and the instructor will find out that they know nothing about the subject. Their sins have caught up with them, and they will be found out. They feel that they "do not deserve to pass."

3. The self-punishing person may be afflicted by belief that he *ought* to fail, that failure is inevitable for such an unworthy person as he.

4. The student who is afraid that he will not perform up to his expectations of himself is frequently troubled by "test nerves." Sometimes he is under great pressure to make the honor roll. As a result, he may be haunted by an unreasonable fear of failure.

"Test nerves" therefore have their bases in the student's neurotic needs and defenses, but they are also stimulated by certain forces in the external environment.

In the typical school situation, the instructor is seen as a sort of "father figure," who dispenses reward and punishment in accordance with progress or lack of it. Almost anything that occurs in the classroom can be interpreted in this frame of reference, and tests are frequently regarded by students and faculty alike as a form of punishment. Tests are the necessary preliminaries to the assignment of academic grades; they frequently contain questions designed to trick or trip students; they have the effect of reminding the student how little he knows about the subject and how much the instructor knows; and, finally, they have come to be accepted by students and faculty alike as painful and anxiety-provoking affairs. Perhaps the competitive aspect of education has been submerged during the rest of the term; but during the test period, anxiety due to competition is at a fever pitch.

The solution seems to be a reorientation of attitudes toward tests, an attempt to see in them their best potentials. Tests form one of the few means available to the student whereby he can communicate with the instructor, and they provide one of the few opportunities the student has for evaluating his learning. Learning always is more successful if progress is known. Unfortunately, evaluation in our culture seems permanently yoked with status: we cannot accept the fact of failure merely as a point of information or as an indication of where we should direct future learning attempts. Unfortunately, failure also carries the connotation of disgrace, just as success carries the connotation of virtue. As long as the failure phobia dominates our thinking, probably little can be done about the anxiety-producing effects of tests in general. Our efforts must therefore be directed primarily at aiding individuals to withstand the stresses of the testing situation.

False Pride. Most students, at some time in their college career, get into academic or personal difficulties — misunderstandings with instructors, enrollments in the wrong courses, unhappy love affairs, loss of part-time jobs, home-sickness, etc. Any of these can interfere with learning or with academic success, regardless of how much ability a student has. Many students prefer to keep their troubles to themselves and brood over them, sometimes for weeks, with the result that studies suffer. Students would do well at such times to put aside false pride and to discuss their problems with a counselor or a sympathetic adviser. Problems are almost always easier to bear once they have been discussed. Talking to a sympathetic listener helps reduce the anxiety that might otherwise interfere with college success.

SUMMARY

In this chapter, learning was considered as the growth toward intellectual and emotional maturity, and education was described as any condition that tends to promote this growth. The tendency to learn is inborn; it is a drive that can be thwarted by neurotic conflicts and by a nonstimulating environment.

Psychologists have studied certain aspects of learning in order to determine how it actually occurs. Pavlov, one of the earliest of the experimenters, proposed the conditioned-response theory, a theory of learning based on association. This theory was acceptable to "common sense" thinking, could easily be studied in the psychological laboratory, and has proved to be very popular among educators, psychologists, and the lay public. However, it leaves many learning phenomena unexplained. Trial-and-error learning has also been the subject of much experimentation, particularly with infrahuman animals. Learning through "insight," as proposed by the Gestalt psychologists, and learning as adjustment and growth are theories that have had much attention recently. Motivation appears to have a certain priority: what an individual learns or whether he learns at all depends upon his motivation.

Approaches to education in the schools are of three broad types: authoritarian, laissez-faire, and democratic. Authoritarian and laissez-faire approaches are at opposite extremes; the democratic approach is a synthesis rather than a compromise of the two. The most popular is the authoritarian approach, which rests on conditioned-response, reward-punishment techniques of learning. Laissez-faire is completely permissive, depending on natural forces within the individual that will presumably lead him to greater maturity if freed. The democratic approach attempts to help individuals meet their own needs through providing a permissive atmosphere, with controls and guidance when and where they are required.

Some of the factors that affect the learning situation are perceptual rigidity, identification with the teacher, the maintenance of order and discipline, emphasis on competition, and the belief in "transfer of training." Factors with which the individual student must contend are aspirations that are inconsistent with aptitudes or interests, egocentricism, the tendency to rebel against authority, overdependency, verbal deficiencies, lack of drive and aggression, test nerves, and false pride, which prevents his seeking help when he needs it.

REFERENCES

1. G. L. Anderson and A. I. Gates, "The General Nature of Learning," in National Society for the Study of Education, *Learning and Instruction*, Forty-ninth Yearbook. Chicago: University of Chicago Press, 1950. Pp. 12–35.
2. O. H. Mowrer, *Learning Theory and Personality Dynamics*. New York: Ronald, 1950.
3. R. J. Havighurst, *Developmental Tasks and Education*. Chicago: University of Chicago Press, 1949.
4. H. Beaumont and F. G. Macomber, *Psychological Factors in Education*. New York: McGraw-Hill, 1949.

5. J. Dollard and N. E. Miller, *Personality and Psychotherapy*. New York: McGraw-Hill, 1950.
6. E. Hilgard and D. H. Russell, "Motivation in School Learning," in National Society for the Study of Education, *Learning and Instruction*, Forty-ninth Yearbook. Chicago: University of Chicago Press, 1950. Pp. 36–68.
7. W. A. Brownell and G. Hendrickson, "How Children Learn Information, Concepts, and Generalizations," in National Society for the Study of Education, *Learning and Instruction*, Forty-ninth Yearbook. Chicago: University of Chicago Press, 1950. Pp. 92–128.
8. E. B. Newman, "Forgetting of Meaningful Material during Sleep and Waking," *American Journal of Psychology*. 52:65–71; 1939.
9. J. A. McGeoch and W. T. McDonald, "Meaningful Relation and Retroactive Inhibition," *American Journal of Psychology*. 43:579–588; 1931.
10. E. L. Thorndike, "Mental Discipline in High School Studies," *Journal of Educational Psychology*. 15:1–22, 83–98; 1924.
11. A. A. Hamblen, *The Extent to Which the Effect of the Study of Latin upon a Knowledge of English Derivatives Can Be Increased*. Philadelphia: University of Pennsylvania, 1925.
12. W. M. Aikin, *The Story of the Eight-Year Study*. New York: Harper, 1942.
13. M. E. Shattuck and W. Barnes, "The Situation as Regards English," *Ninth Yearbook of the National Education Association*. Department of Supervisors and Directors of Instruction, 1936.

SUGGESTED READINGS

H. L. Kingsley, *The Nature and Conditions of Learning*. New York: Prentice-Hall, 1946.

National Society for the Study of Education, *Psychology of Learning*, Forty-first Yearbook, Part II. Bloomington, Ill.: Public-School, 1942.

F. McKinney, *Psychology of Personal Adjustment*, 2d edition. New York: Wiley, 1949. See Chapter 3, "Concentration, Learning, and Thinking."

H. A. Garrett, *Psychology*. New York: American Book, 1950.

E. T. Prothro and P. T. Teska, *Psychology: A Biosocial Study of Behavior*. Boston: Ginn, 1950. See Chapters 14 and 15.

G. Murphy, *An Introduction to Psychology*. New York: Harper, 1951. See Chapters 14–20, which deal with learning, remembering, imagining and dreaming, thinking, and creating.

J. E. Anderson, *The Psychology of Development and Personal Adjustment*. New York: Holt, 1949. Section 2 deals with learning skills.

F. L. Ruch, *Psychology and Life*, 3d edition. Chicago: Scott, 1948. See chapters on motivation, learning, and study methods.

H. W. Hepner, *Psychology Applied to Life and Work*, 2d edition. New York: Prentice-Hall, 1950. See Chapter 10 on study methods.

E. L. Hartley, *et al.*, eds., *Outside Readings in Psychology*. New York: Crowell, 1950. Section 8 deals with learning, and includes an article on Pavlov.

W. Dennis, *Readings in General Psychology*. New York: Prentice-Hall, 1949.

Section VI, which deals with learning and retention, contains papers by several of the early experimenters in this field.

R. S. Woodworth, *Contemporary Schools of Psychology*, Rev. edition. New York: Ronald, 1948. Most of the material in this book is pertinent; the core of each school of psychology is its theories of learning and behavior.

W. L. Valentine, *Experimental Foundations of General Psychology*, Rev. edition. New York: Farrar, 1941. See chapters on conditioning, learning, remembering, reasoning, and maturation and growth.

"Intelligence and Intelligence Tests," in W. S. Monroe, ed., *Encyclopedia of Educational Research*, Rev. edition. New York: Macmillan, 1950. Pp. 600–612. There is a good review of learning on pages 668–690, plus several dozen other citations on learning in various educational situations.

A. I. Gates, *et al.*, *Educational Psychology*, 3d edition. New York: Macmillan, 1948.

C. E. Skinner, ed., *Elementary Educational Psychology*. New York: Prentice-Hall, 1945. See Part IV, which deals with the learning process.

R. A. Davis, *Educational Psychology*. New York: McGraw-Hill, 1948. The second half of the book deals with learning.

L. E. Cole and W. F. Bruce, *Educational Psychology*. Yonkers, New York: World Book, 1950. A particularly readable treatment of the subject covered in this chapter. See particularly Part III, "The Psychology of Learning in a Free Society."

A. D. Woodruff, *The Psychology of Teaching*, 3d edition. New York: Longmans, 1951. See chapters on the learning process, types of end products of learning, learning and the nature of mental activity, factors that modify learning, and the learning process and maladjustment.

G. Murphy, *Historical Introduction to Modern Psychology*, Rev. edition. New York: Harcourt, Brace, 1949. See the chapters on behaviorism, modern conceptions of association, Gestalt, and field theory.

E. R. Hilgard, *Theories of Learning*. New York: Appleton-Century-Crofts, 1948. A classical review of the outstanding theories of learning.

J. Dollard and N. E. Miller, *Personality and Psychotherapy*. New York: McGraw-Hill, 1950. See Part II, "Basic Principles of Learning"; Part IV, "How Neurosis is Learned"; Part V, "The New Conditions of Therapeutic Learning." Approach to learning that is a synthesis of older theories and psychoanalysis.

C. Gerken, *Study Your Way through School*, Guidance Monograph of the American Job Series. Chicago: Science Res., 1947. Helpful hints on how to study.

S. N. Le Count, *How to Improve Your Study Habits*. Palo Alto, California: Pacific Books, 1948. More helpful hints.

XVII...*Building Sound Relation-*

ships between the Sexes

Preference for Girls. "We are trying to adopt a baby," a married couple told me recently, "but it isn't so easy." In the conversation that followed, they described how they had registered at the agency, and, on being interviewed, had stated their preference for a baby girl. At this point, the interviewer asked if they had definitely decided on adopting a girl — would they consider a boy? It seems that 90 per cent of the couples who plan to adopt babies want girls. Of this number, less than half will consider boys. This couple will have a long time to wait, because they, too, insist on adopting a girl.

This preference for little girls is not limited to people who want to adopt children. All over America, little girls are placed on a pedestal and admired for their virtues, while little boys are stood in the corner till they learn to behave better. Little girls are angelic, sweet, demure, and usually pretty; little boys are demoniac, rough, tough, and usually dirty. Girls are better behaved, more co-operative, and appear to learn faster than boys. The question is: Are boys and girls *born* this way, or are they *made to grow* this way?

Sex Differences: Native or Acquired? As we indicated in Chapter 8, "The Forces That Mold Us: Determinants of Personality," there is considerable evidence to indicate that the personality traits by which we differentiate and identify the two sexes are largely the result of cultural influences rather than of physiological factors. The study by Margaret Mead, which we cited, demonstrated that personality traits and behavior considered "masculine" in one culture may be considered "feminine" in another, and vice versa (1). On the other hand, perhaps we *can* expect little girls to surpass

377

little boys. There are those who state that women are "naturally" superior. M. F. Ashley-Montagu, the anthropologist, believes that men are inferior because, as he says, male chromosomes are crippled versions of female chromosomes. This deficiency, he maintains, renders men more vulnerable to physical and mental disease and incapable of bearing children. Women's superiority may also be related to their capacity, as he puts it, to be more humane, more loving, and more co-operative (2). Erich Fromm believes that women at one time were the dominant sex but that they lost this dominance to men in a triumph of intellect and aggression over love (3).

Sex Roles and Early Childhood Experiences. Although there is no clear-cut evidence that differences in personality between the two sexes in our culture are acquired or learned rather than inherent, it is very likely that the crucial differences, particularly those leading to difficulties in marital relationships, are based on the differing experiences boys and girls have in our culture.

Talcott Parsons points out that the middle-class pattern of American family life, as it has developed in urban areas, is for the father to be away from home most of the time and the mother to stay at home and take care of the children (4). The father is with his children only before and after work and on week ends. Moreover, he frequently has a number of nonvocational interests outside the home absorbing time that might otherwise be spent with the family. Activities of this sort are fishing, hunting, competitive and spectator sports, clubs and lodges, and vocational organizations. The interests he is likely to develop lead him away from home rather than keep him there.

Thus the parent who is home all or most of the time is the mother. Without attempting further psychological interpretations of the relations that develop between the mother and her children, it is readily apparent that only the girls have extended and intimate contact with life models appropriate to their sex roles. Since girls are encouraged to be like their mothers and since they are with their mothers all day long, they normally take on many of their mothers' modes of behavior, characteristic attitudes, and personality traits. Boys, however, are expected to be like their fathers, even though they lack adequate contact with their life models. As Parsons points out, their life models are constantly engaged in complicated, highly abstract activities at the office or plant. Even participation in the father's leisure-time activities is discouraged until the son is "old enough." Frequently, boys try to adopt the attitudes and behavior of their mother. However, such conduct, when it happens to cross sex lines, is discouraged or even punished. This is very confusing for the boy: "My mother is a good person, I like her, she does good things, but when I try to be like her and do the things she does, my father makes fun of me!" On the other hand, the boy is encouraged to engage in active, aggressive play; and his parents show their pleasure when he jumps, runs, rides his bicycle, and climbs on the jungle gym. He finds that active, aggressive behavior is tolerated and encouraged in him but not in his sister.

In another of his discussions of this problem, Parsons explains the "compulsive masculinity" of boys during the grammar school years as overcompensation for any feeling of identification they may have had with their mothers. He states further that as boys discover that women possess inferior status in our culture, they react by attempting to prove themselves masculine. Inasmuch as mothers focus within themselves the symbols of "good behavior" and conformity, "goodness" becomes "feminine" in the eyes of boys, and "badness" becomes "masculine (5)."

Another explanation for the negative behavior of boys is that it is an outgrowth of their feeling of isolation from adequate male models. It is as though they find rebellion a way of expressing their resentment against an arrangement that limits and punishes them, that does not provide them with an adequate pattern for behavior.

Still another possible explanation is that boys do use their fathers as models. Their feeling may run somewhat as follows: "My father really doesn't like home; he stays away most of the time. Maybe there is something wrong with home life. *I* can't leave home, but at least I can fight it!" If this hypothesis is valid, it too helps to account for much of the violently negative behavior typical of many small boys.

The models boys are permitted and encouraged to admire are strongly "masculine" types like cowboys, policemen, pirates, bandits, and other stereotyped characters who are presumed to lead violent but charmed lives. It is questionable whether the values and standards derived from phantasy models rather than from real people are of positive assistance in forming realistic social adjustments in later childhood and adult life. Of course nothing is more natural than for a boy to seek models of this sort to fill the vacuum in his life.

Girls tend to have far fewer difficulties of this kind. Following their mothers' lead, they develop a pattern of behavior that stresses sociability, conformity, co-operation, submission, effort, domestic activities, and verbal skills. (Note that the skills of co-operation and agreement are largely verbal skills.) In general, what girls do has a good chance of meeting with praise and approval; what boys do has a good chance of being criticized, punished, or ignored. It is possible that this difference may account for girls being intellectually, socially, and verbally advanced to a noticeable degree, as compared with boys, in most scholastic activities.

Sex Roles and Later Childhood Experiences. At school, the pattern begun in the home is continued and reinforced. The new model, the elementary-school teacher, is also female, and male models continue to be absent. "Feminine" behavior is rewarded; "masculine" behavior is punished. Girls capitalize on their initial intellectual advantage, and boys compensate for their handicap by developing skills in large-muscle activities, by engaging in aggressive play, by displaying behavior that disturbs the teacher and the class, and by attempting to avoid competition with girls in academic activities. As a result of the superiority of girls in academics, many boys develop real feelings of inferiority about their intellectual ability, feelings that remain with them throughout life.

When children enter school, there are many friendships between sexes; but as they go through the grades, they develop group norms that restrict friendships to children of their own sex. Boys take their cues from the dominant persons in their group and displace the hostility they feel toward adults (which for obvious reasons they cannot adequately express) by hostility toward girls, who they feel are to blame for their mistreatment. As girls come under attack by the boys, they rally to their own defense. However, because they have foresworn, in their adoption of "feminine" modes of behavior, the more violent forms of aggression, their reprisals are largely verbal, usually being limited to name-calling and talebearing. The authorities move in to protect the "weaker sex" and remind both groups that the mores do not permit males to be physically aggressive toward females. Thus an uneasy peace is eventually created, and during the prepubertal period the two sex groups limit hostilities for the most part to verbal expressions of their hatred for each other.

Sex Roles during Adolescence. This pattern undergoes a marked change with the onset of puberty. Boys and girls, after a number of false starts, begin to become companionable. While this is a manifestation of the awakening sex drive, it also may be the result of intellectual growth and a more intelligent awareness of the social environment. It may be that the increase in friendly relations with the other sex is due in part to the discovery that boys and girls have much in common — that they have more in common with each other than with adults. Furthermore, because of his increased size and the growth of his intellectual powers, the male adolescent has less fear of the adult, feels enabled to express his hostility toward adults more directly, and consequently has less need to displace this hostility by hating girls.

While adolescence brings with it greater acceptance of the opposite sex, the patterns of "masculine" and "feminine" behavior remain much the same. Although there are numerous individual exceptions, boys in general tend to reject the academic-intellectual pattern of life; and almost none of them will tolerate girls who too openly display their superiority in this field. They remember very well the humiliations and defeats suffered in the classroom; hence they avoid becoming involved in situations where they (unconsciously) fear they will be found inferior and stupid. Vestiges of the rebelliousness that marked boyhood behavior in the classroom linger. Even after boys go on to college, they attempt to avoid the patterns of diligence and conformity that are so helpful in grade-getting. The result is that more men than women fail in college, and women win more academic honors, particularly in the humanities and the social sciences.

Most women readily discover that men do not value them for their intellectual prowess; hence they rapidly learn to de-emphasize and depreciate their academic achievements and to stress those characteristics generally considered "feminine." As a result of this change in emphasis, many women are highly successful in forgetting their academic skills as their roles change from student to fiancée to housewife and mother. Many make use of their professional training only during the relatively brief period between graduation and marriage.

Courtship

Barriers to Communication. The social forces that produce the personality characteristics we have come to recognize as "masculine" and "feminine" also produce what amounts to a transparent wall between the sexes. We have indicated that the beginnings of this separation are in childhood. As a result of living in separate worlds, particularly during the prepubertal period, boys and girls may not only live in ignorance of what individuals of the other sex are "really" like, but they may also provide themselves with unrealistic and distorted mental pictures or expectations of the members of the opposite sex. These erroneous expectations are developed, of course, as a partial justification of the hate and resentment each sex feels for the other during the prepubertal period. Since real communication between the sexes is rendered difficult because of mutual emnity, there is no practical way in which either sex can correct the picture it has of the other. Potentially, therefore, courtship and marriage can be the means for discovering what individuals of the opposite sex are really like — processes, thus, for correcting and readjusting expectations. Marriages that are not favorable to this readjustment have the poorest chances for success and happiness.

Patterns of Exploitation. Because of their unrealistic or neurotic expectations, adolescent boys and girls are not inclined to be at ease with each other, at least initially. They do not trust each other; they are prone to be prejudiced and oversensitive. Therefore dating may frequently start as an attempt at mutual exploitation.

Joan Carson looks upon her dating partner, Geoffrey Curtis, largely as a source of amusement or entertainment. It gives her a feeling of status and importance to have someone attracted to her and to do her bidding.* In order to maintain and continue this relationship, she uses

---

* For a discussion of the relationship between social status and dating among teen-age girls, see W. Waller, "The Rating and Dating Complex," in T. M. Newcomb and E. L. Hartley, eds., *Reading in Social Psychology.* New York: Holt, 1947. Pp. 388–394.

her "feminine charm" as effectively as she can — sometimes too effectively. Joan denies the existence of sexual yearnings on her part. She expresses surprise and alarm at the attitudes and behavior displayed by Geoffrey, which he states are in direct response to her seductive behavior. She disclaims any attempt to make herself sexually attractive and concludes that "men are beasts" or, at least, that they are oversexed.

However, the evidence is difficult to ignore. There must be a reason for Joan's behaving as she does. One explanation is that she does have sexual yearnings but that since our culture so severely censures extramarital sexual intercourse and since we all learn as children that sexual matters are "bad," "dirty," or "will get you into trouble," she represses any such feeling and is unable to identify her behavior as expressive of the sex drive. Another explanation is that she has learned how to attract men by observing other women, from the movies, and from other sources of useful information, and that she is using these skills to get Geoffrey and other men to provide her entertainment, to achieve status, and to compete with other girls. Perhaps both explanations apply.

Geoffrey, too, has exploitation in mind. Dating Joan gives him status with his fellows and with other girls. Taking her out proves to himself and to others that he can attract a girl. He, too, is aware of the bans on extramarital sexual activity, but the penalties for violating the mores weigh less heavily on males in our culture. Further, as Alfred Kinsey and others have pointed out, Geoffrey's sex drive is strongest during late adolescence and is probably stronger than Joan's (6). The limits of his frustration tolerance are more severely threatened. Thus it appears that, consciously or unconsciously, one of the reasons why Geoffrey dates Joan is that in some ways he sees her as an opportunity for sexual exploitation. Probably he has no real sexual expectations, but the fact that she is sexually attractive and has an inviting manner has awakened his hopes.

It is to be noted that the patterns of expectation followed by Joan and Geoffrey are egocentric and narcissistic. Each person is thinking of his own pleasure and each is propelled toward the other by his selfish desires. Because neither has an accurate concept of the other as a person, their dating starts out as an attempt at mutual exploitation. The girl attempts to exploit the boy for the things he can give her that are important to her role as she sees it — good times, status, and attention; and the boy attempts to exploit the girl for those things she can give him that are important for his role — status, admiration, and sex.

Erich Fromm terms this kind of relationship the "marketing orientation." He says that much of what passes for love is actually a seeking for success or approval. He further notes that many of us appear to be under a compulsion to be the latest model and to fall in love with the latest model. A boy of eighteen described this feeling to Fromm by saying that his ambition was to own a Buick instead of a Ford, so that he could pick up a better class of girls. Although most of us would censure such a standard of values, actually his comment was a frank statement of the exploitative nature of our practices of courtship and dating (7).

If Joan and Geoffrey are "normal" — that is, are no more immature or neurotic than most of us — they will eventually veer away from their pattern of mutual exploitation and will enjoy their dating relationship for its more enduring values: the opportunity to learn to know someone as a person (rather than merely as a member of the opposite sex); the opportunity for companionship; the opportunity to like someone for his own sake and to be liked in return; and the opportunity to build the basis for warm, affectionate relations, if not in the present, then in the future. This is the *mature* aspect of dating — mature because it is appropriate to the age level of the participants and is based on mutual appreciation rather than mutual exploitation.

It should be noted, however, that the adolescent, because he is insecure and uneasy in his new roles, is frequently inconsistent in his dating behavior. For example, it is not unusual for him to enter into the mature kind of relationship described above, whereupon, because of such forces as the ridicule of his friends or his family or because of his own doubts and insecurities, he may question the genuineness of the values he has been receiving from the relationship and impulsively reduce it to the more stereotyped exploitative relationship. Some adolescent (and adult) affairs, in fact, shift from exploitation to appreciation and back again in the course of a few days or even in a single evening.

Love during Adolescence. Adolescents who have markedly distorted ideas of what individuals of the other sex are like or who have especially strong needs for affection, or both, sometimes react to the discovery that the dating partner is a potentially likable person by falling madly in love. Such love affairs are seldom based on realistic considerations, such as the probability that both partners would wait through an engagement that might last for years, or the impracticality of marrying at once, or the high divorce rate which attends and the unhappiness which often harasses the early marriage (8). They are based rather on a particularly strong need to be loved, and, perhaps, on the unexpected discovery that they have the capacity to love. Since, when emotions run high, the ability of the individual to be aware of the realities and to deal effectively with them is impaired or blocked, the participants in these affairs are unable to "act sensibly." Most of these affairs end unhappily: one partner's need for love is satiated before the other's, or one partner recovers his awareness of reality and sees the impracticability of continuing the affair.

Dating as a Learning Situation. The learning problem in first dates is an interesting one. Initially, boys and girls have some difficulty in communicating. There is a boy's world and a girl's world, each with its own concepts, symbols, and values, and communication is impeded at first by these differences. In some ways, dating is a process of discovering what is common to both worlds or in creating a new "boy-girl world," in which there are symbols, values, and concepts understood by and acceptable to both sexes. (See the illustrations on page 386.) Some persons never bridge the gap. They are so involved in the world of their own sex that they go through life unable to communicate and empathize with persons of the other sex. Being less verbally inclined, men tend to have more such difficulties than do women.

The more ease dating partners experience in communicating with each other, the less the likelihood of exploitation. The greater the gulf between the two worlds, the greater the likelihood of exploitation. Inasmuch as the culture tends to stress the differences, rather than the similarities, between the sexes, it becomes all too easy for boys and girls to see each other as *sex stereotypes*, rather than as *persons* with needs and problems much like their own. Thus, if we expect the adolescent male to be the "wolf" or "big-time operator" or the girl to be a "gold-digger" (exploitative stereotypes), these roles are assumed as a matter of course, even though they may be in opposition to normal needs for sympathetic companionship. While it is fortunate that so many adolescents

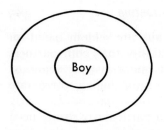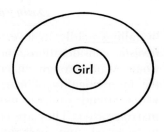

Separate worlds; no communication.

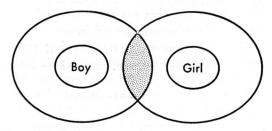

Finding areas common to both worlds;
communication possible.

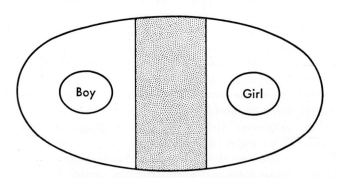

Creation of a common area of interest;
communication and empathy facilitated.

are able to find in dating a means of establishing friendly, companionable, and mature relationships, it is safe to say that they are able to do so in spite of the cultural stereotype of mutual exploitation, rather than because of it. On the other hand, many adolescents are unable, because of insecurities or other neurotic needs, to play any other role than the one they feel society has assigned them, and are therefore prevented from communicating effectively or making genuinely friendly contacts with members of the opposite sex. Unless they are able to shed these roles and to communicate successfully, they will, as adults, be among those persons who make the least successful marriages.

Adolescent Shyness and Dating. We have said little about the shy person, the one who is painfully self-conscious, who dates seldom, if at all. The existence of the exploitative stereotype probably acts as a deterrent to any dating tendencies shy persons might have. The shy person avoids aggressive behavior, perhaps because he has been too severely punished for early childhood aggressions, or has been overprotected in childhood against his own aggressive behavior or the aggressions of others, or has been hurt too deeply by real or threatened aggressive acts of others. The aggressive nature of the stereotyped dater (for exploitation *is* aggressive) causes shy persons to shun this avenue to the companionship they secretly long for. It is as though the shy person uses the stereotyped dater as a form of rationalization: "I certainly don't want to date if I have to be a gold-digger!" or "I think fellows who act like wolves are phonies. I don't want to be one of them!" or "I think fellows are all wolves. I wouldn't trust myself with one of them!" or "No point in trying to get a date; all girls are gold-diggers these days!"

One wonders what would be the result if our dating stereotypes were based on the assumptions (a) that all young people are more or less shy, (b) that dating based on mutual acceptance and respect provides necessary companionship with the opposite sex, and (c) that young people are in need of sympathetic adult help to get them over some of the hurdles involved in making contact with the opposite sex. Undoubtedly this sounds idealistic, but the proposed stereotype does contain the abstracted elements of the real situation. Most adolescents *are* more or less shy, the dating situation *does* provide companionship possibilities that help one become psychologically mature, and sympathetic and understanding adults (teachers, parents, group leaders) *can* do much to promote these relationships.

Multiple Dating. Many adolescents and young adults have themselves discovered a way to bridge the gap — multiple dating. The double or triple date offers an opportunity to learn more about the world of the opposite sex, to learn to know others as persons, and to learn to empathize and communicate with persons of the opposite sex in a sociable, less threatening atmosphere. Furthermore, it takes less courage to go on a multiple date. Nevertheless, the multiple date is no substitute for the companionship of two people, and if dating is to serve as a learning situation for such companionship, couples must eventually do some dating on their own.

From a psychological point of view, the mature individual can communicate and empathize with another individual, can appreciate the companionship of another, and can give as well as receive in companionship. Ideally, persons should have arrived at this point of maturity before they marry; yet most people marry before they have learned these important skills. Many must marry in order to learn them. Whenever such skills are learned, marriages can be said to be successful to the extent that both spouses can communicate and empathize, can appreciate companionship, and can become emotionally more mature because of the relationship. As for dating, its chief function is to give adolescents and young adults opportunities to develop these skills and appreciations.

The Problem of Adequate Sexual Adjustment

Folklore of Sex. Josephine Ball writes of the folklore of sex as follows:

There is in our culture a kind of legend about sex behavior that runs somewhat like this. Children are innocent until adolescence. They are unaware of sex organs and differences, except that they cannot help noting that there are two species of small human beings: those in pants who play baseball and those in skirts who play with dolls. And naturally they do these things with their own kind. Boys don't like girls and girls find boys too rough. Also, there are, of course, two species of large human beings, again differentiated, so far as the child knows or cares, entirely by clothes and behavior. At puberty, or a few years

From Eva Luoma Photos

Adolescents and young adults often learn that they can enjoy the companionship of persons of the opposite sex through the experience of multiple dating.

later, boys and girls suddenly like each other, start to pair off, and finally discover the one possible partner and marry this ideal mate. They do not touch each other before engagement. After becoming engaged they kiss and hold hands. The boy may kiss the girl's eyes, hands, forehead, and hair. The girl may think that these are sweet caresses to receive, but she never returns them. After they are married they "live happily ever after (9)." *

Probably there are very few of us today who believe this myth in its entirety; but many believe some of it, and nearly all of us have felt its influence.

There is another legend that is a continuation of the one recounted above. It tells us that romantic love is the only true basis of happy marriages, that marriages are happy and successful only when life is one long honeymoon, and that virtually the only thing men and women have in common is their ability to enjoy "romance." (It will be noted that this myth is closely related to the culturally stereotyped patterns, mentioned earlier in this chapter, which create artificial distinctions between men and women, placing them in different worlds.) The romantic-love stereotype is dangerous not only because it is untrue but also because its doctrine is propagated so effectively and persuasively by the movies, the radio, and popular fiction. We get it from all sides; we hear it from childhood on; and by the time we are ready for courtship and marriage, we are saturated with it.

There are two unfortunate results of this early indoctrination. One is that the romantic or sexual aspect of courtship and marriage is made to seem more important than it really is, and the other is that couples entering marriage entertain expectations that can only lead to disillusionment.

The Importance of Sex. There is no denying the importance of sex in the marriage relationship. The fallacy is that it is popularly stressed as the *most important* aspect of marriage. Yet sexual adjustment in marriage is largely symptomatic of the general adjustment of spouses to each other personally. Couples who enjoy or are working toward mutual admiration and respect tend also to have good sexual adjustment. Couples whose personal relationships with each other are hostile or exploitative, who would actually

---

* L. A. Pennington and I. A. Berg, editors, *An Introduction to Clinical Psychology.* Copyright 1948; The Ronald Press Company.

live happier lives apart, who are unable to understand, accept, or respect themselves or each other, are very likely to have unsatisfactory sexual relationships. Unhappy marriages are not usually the result of unsatisfactory sex relations, but unsatisfactory sex relations do result from unhappy marriages.

Our tendency to overstress the romantic component in marriage would seem to be our way of compensating for our denying sex its rightful place in life. It is as though we have tried to tell ourselves that children and adolescents know nothing about sexual processes, are not interested in sexual processes, and have no need for sex information. Having, in our minds, swept sex from the scene, at least for the period prior to marriage, we try to compensate for this deficiency by overstressing its importance in the marriage relationship.

Anxiety and Guilt regarding Sex. There is no question that we have made ourselves extremely anxious about sex, to the point that guilt feelings about sexual yearnings, sexual curiosity, or other sexual behavior, including masturbation, are a major source of neurotic conflict.

Most children of preschool ages appear to receive pleasure from touching or fondling their genitals. This manipulation is usually viewed by adults with a mixture of disgust and alarm; and through direct punishment, threats, or other means of disapproval, these feelings are transmitted to the child. Thus he learns early in life that genital matters call for anxiety and guilt.*

Western culture has also developed the concept that females have greater sex value than males — that males are attracted sexually to females, but not vice versa. Therefore, immature females must be protected from predatory males of all ages. As a result girls grow up in an atmosphere more charged with anxiety and tension about sexual matters than do boys. If girls learn their cultural lessons well, they learn to repress sexual feelings, stigmatizing sex as dirty, unworthy, disgusting, or boring. But when they grow into adolescence and womanhood, they learn that sexual activity is the norm in marriage, for this is "the price one must pay"

---

* In spite of these early experiences, most persons eventually come to use masturbation as one form of sexual outlet. Lester W. Dearborn, Director of the Boston Marriage Counseling Service, says that masturbation plays a part in the lives of 90 per cent of the men and 70 per cent of the women aged twenty-five or over (10).

for the support and companionship of the husband. They are told, furthermore, that no nice girl is interested in sex; hence, when husbands make sex advances, the role of wives should be a passive one.

Boys, too, are prevented from having "normal feelings" about sexual activity. Inasmuch as sexual matters arouse anxieties and fears, it is easy to see how boys learn to use sex as a form of aggression. Sometimes they express this hostility directly — through attempts at sexual intercourse; but more often they express it symbolically — through obscenity. This behavior often persists into adulthood. The person who enjoys telling dirty stories is probably using this means to express his hostile feelings toward authority in a symbolic manner. Since the culture teaches boys to be more aggressive than girls, it tacitly encourages them to develop aggressive feelings toward the opposite sex, and the doctrine is somehow spread among young men that the chief role of woman is to be sexually exploited by man. The male adolescent is thus faced by confusing and conflicting beliefs: (a) that he really ought to be sexually innocent and hence should treat every girl "as though she were his sister," (b) that women exist for man's exploitation and probably even enjoy this exploitation, and (c) that youths must engage in sexual intercourse before they can be considered "men." In addition, he is usually aware that sexual intercourse implies some responsibilities and may get him into trouble.

In view of the vast amount of contradictory misinformation, misdirection, and unadulterated folklore to which children, adolescents, and even adults are subjected, one is moved to comment on two minor miracles: (a) that we believe so much of it in the face of so much evidence to the contrary, and (b) that so many of us turn out so well in spite of what we believe.

The Need for a Balanced Approach to Sex. The net result of these indoctrination programs is that as a nation we are unable to adopt a balanced point of view toward sexual matters; *we are unable to accept sex as a matter of course.* If, on the one hand, we are traditional, ultraconventional, or strait-laced, we suppress and repress all sexual ideas; if, on the other hand, we rebel against conformity and restrictions or consider ourselves sophisticated and "enlightened," we overemphasize and overstress the role of sexual activity in relations between the sexes. Either point of view is an exaggeration and a distortion of the proper and most effective role of sex. In its proper perspective, sexual activity plays a *minor but important* role in marital relations.

Love covers a much broader area of human relations than sex and plays a *major* role in marital happiness. If we accept Sullivan's definition of love as a state in which "the satisfaction or security of another person becomes as significant as one's own satisfaction or security (11)," then it becomes apparent that a happy marriage relationship must be based on love.

On the other hand, a survey by J. T. Landis of some 450 married couples revealed that they considered sex relations a greater source of problems than spending the family income, social activities and recreation, relationships with in-laws, religious activities, and choosing and associating with mutual friends (12). However, this tendency to place sex high on the list as a source of problems may merely illustrate the fact that we are "vulnerable" when it comes to sex. Since our early experiences render us sensitive and anxious where sex is concerned, it is likely that any unconscious conflict of an interpersonal nature may result in difficulties of sexual adjustment. Furthermore, like occupational adjustment, sexual adjustment is a very sensitive barometer of the general adequacy of our emotional life.

As Frieda Fromm-Reichman says, "A person who is reasonably free from anxiety, greed, envy, and jealousy and who is able to experience interpersonal intimacy will be capable of expressing this in terms of satisfactory sexual activity (13)." It seems very likely that the opposite of this statement also holds true.

Erich Fromm states that sexual adjustment is more symptomatic than basic. He says "All that glitters isn't sex," by which he means that there are many motivations for sexual expression that are basically not sexual (14). Examples of this are the youths mentioned above, who employ sex as a means of expressing hostility. And sexual activity, like other forms of pleasure-seeking behavior, can be used as an escape from anxiety.

Obstacles to Courtship and Marriage

The Loneliness of Urban Living. There are other forces in our culture that interfere with the development of sound relationships

in courtship and marriage.   One of these is the breaking down
of social ties in urban living.   City dwellers as a rule live highly
compartmentalized lives;   privacy is stressed and respected far
more than is the case in small towns and rural areas.   It is quite
common for people to live a few feet apart, as in an apartment
house, and never know one another's names or faces.   If one is
unable to secure companionship with the opposite sex where one
works, it is necessary to take some initiative in seeking it in social
groups like churches, adult education classes, civic organizations,
professional societies, and the like.   In any event, the scope of
acquaintanceship with the opposite sex is extremely limited, particularly for the newcomer to the city.   In these days of shifting
populations there are many lonely people of both sexes who have
been unable to become acquainted with many of the other sex.

Marriage or a Career?   Many girls attend college because they
expect to find there the kind of man they would like to marry.   On
the other hand, reports indicate that the proportion of unmarried
women is higher among college graduates than in any other group
(15).   It should be noted, of course, that college also attracts the
career girl, who is less likely to be interested in marriage.   If the
number of careerists were deducted from the total, it would be
interesting to see whether the proportion of unmarried women
among college graduates would be much different from that among
the general female population.   Nevertheless, one would expect to
find some difference because of the tendency of men to avoid
marrying women with a level of education higher than their own.
On the other hand, there is a tendency for college-educated persons
to marry spouses who also have some college education.   In a study
of 330 students who attended Washington State College, Paul H.
Landis and Katherine Day discovered that 71.5 per cent of them
married individuals with some schooling beyond high school (16).

Obstacles to a Happy Marriage

Selfishness.   If one were to name the most important underlying
causes of unhappy marriage, most of them could be included under
the heading of selfishness: egocentricity; narcissism; rigidity; unwillingness to change, adjust, or compromise; and the belief that
the other partner should be the one to make changes, adjustments,
or compromises.

The self-centered person goes into marriage with the intention of satisfying his own needs, without recognizing or realizing that his partner, too, has needs that require satisfaction. Inasmuch as most of us are egocentric to some degree, this means that, for many of us, marriage will be an uphill struggle of learning to readjust our needs and expectations out of consideration for the needs and expectations of our spouses.

The story of Floyd and Marie Dewey is an example of the effects of egocentricity.

Floyd and Marie Dewey married while they were working as senior and junior accountants, respectively, in the same office. Floyd's father was a stern, silent man, who was strict with his children. Floyd idolized him, and, as an adult, was much like him. His mother was a compliant, talkative woman, who could always be dissuaded or persuaded, as the necessity arose. Relations were good between her and Floyd. Marie's father was much dominated by her mother, an outspoken, positive woman, who had a good head for business, meant well, but was likely to offend others by her brusque manner.

Both Floyd and Marie were new to the city. They were thrown together on the job and started going to lunch together. First they found that they had common interests — dogs, stamp collecting, and the theater. Then they decided that they were in love and married after a three-month engagement.

Their first difficulty arose over Marie's insisting that she work until they had enough to live a "comfortable life." Their next major quarrel arose over money — who should control it, who should spend it, and how much each should be permitted to spend on himself. Floyd gave in to Marie on both these occasions, but not until some bitterness had been expressed. After these two concessions, Floyd continued to yield on a number of issues, but each time with greater reluctance and diminishing good will. Finally he would give in no longer, and, since Marie found herself unable to compromise, they were at an impasse. From this point on, all their quarrels ended in a stalemate, with neither one giving ground. They separated after they had been married nine months, when they were unable to agree who should pay a fine levied for overparking.

Floyd and Marie were unable to achieve a satisfactory marital relationship because they were unwilling to change themselves or their expectations of each other. Floyd's gestures of yielding to Marie were hardly sincere or genuine — they were patronizing.

Yet they could have been the basis for further compromise if Marie had not been so determined that this relationship should be like that of her parents. Floyd and Marie probably feel that their marriage failed because they could not agree on money; they are unaware that they failed because each was unable to adjust himself and his expectations. It never occurred to them to discuss their marriage problems on this basis.

Some marriages are relatively satisfactory not because the partners are emotionally mature or flexible or particularly willing to adjust, but rather because their more or less neurotic needs are not in conflict, but instead supplement each other. If Marie had been pliable and dependent, or if she had needed a "strong man," their marriage would have had a much better chance for success. Or, if Floyd had been the pliable one, with a strong need to be dependent, their chances for working out a satisfactory marriage would have been much improved. As it was, their personal needs were predestined to crash head-on.

Most of us cannot gamble on meeting spouses who are direct complements to our neurotic needs and who do not have to change to meet our expectations. Realistically, therefore, we should plan on marriage to be a give-and-take affair. However, it is wise to be aware of some of the more obvious differences in personality, interests, and background that may lead to later difficulties and maladjustment.

Free-spending versus frugality. James Murphy's family had lived up to the limit of their incomes and a little beyond. They were always in debt. This did not interfere with their enjoyment of life; in fact, it helped make things more interesting. His wife, Sarah, came from a New England family, who put a little aside for a rainy day out of every pay check, even when times were difficult and putting money into the savings account meant self-denial. James and Sarah are so far apart in their points of view on money that they give each other much unhappiness.

Outdoor versus indoor. Lincoln McClure likes nothing better than to curl up with a book and a pipe in front of the fire. His most exciting pastime is chess. He likes to say that when he feels the urge to exercise, he lies down and closes his eyes until the idea passes away. Margaret, his wife, teaches physical education in junior high school. She is very much an outdoor girl and thoroughly enjoys swimming, golf, horseback riding, and skiing. The ways of life of Lincoln and Margaret are so violently opposed that each would have to change his life radically even to effect a compromise.

Work versus play. Thomas Hamilton is so interested in plant pathology that he spends many of his waking hours reading scientific journals, puttering with his collection of plants, and discussing professional problems with his colleagues. He has even attempted to convert his wife, Patricia, to this way of life, but her interests are elsewhere. She is more concerned with enjoying life as she sees it, and she sees it as action and movement. She would like to go out every night in the week — to the movies, to bridge parties, to the theater, to dances. It is only with the greatest difficulty that Thomas is persuaded to drop his parasites and accompany her to the neighbors for an evening of cards. Thomas is bored by social contact and Patricia is bored by staying at home. One wonders how such diverse types of people found enough in common to marry.

These couples represent but three of the common divergences in life roles that help to make it difficult for two people to adjust to each other. Adjustment and compromise are possible in all cases, but not without sacrifice. Each must give up so much of his way of life that it may be a matter of years before a happy relationship is established. If it is established, it is because the partners decide that it is more important to make their marriage a success than it is for them to continue being the kinds of persons they are. It means giving up activities and patterns of behavior near and dear to them. Many attempt this and succeed, but like many other worth-while things, attaining marital success in spite of difficulties taxes powers of self-denial and tolerance.

Other Differences. There are other types of differences that also are potentially dangerous to the success of marriage. Couples who differ widely in age tend to have less successful marriages than those whose ages are closer. A major difference in religion increases the hazards by some 200 per cent (17, 18). Persons coming from different social classes and markedly different educational levels have more than their share of difficulties when they marry.

On the other hand, there are many instances in which diverse backgrounds do not seem to interfere with good marital adjustment. For example, John Biesanz and Luke M. Smith found that marriages in the Canal Zone between United States citizens and

Panamanians turned out as well as marriages between United States citizens in the United States (19).

Perhaps it would make good sense for people not to marry if the probable obstacles to their marital success are many or great. But people do not marry because they are sensible, but because they are lonely, because they need companionship, and because they need to love and be loved. When these needs are strong, people marry in spite of inauspicious circumstances. And often these needs are so strong that couples overcome great difficulties in an effort to make the relationship work.

Some persons, however, are driven into marriage by a feeling of desperation that leads them to ignore the difficulties ahead. Perhaps there is the feeling, "This is my only chance (or my last chance). It's now or never." This attitude is neurotic and immature, because it is based on the feeling of personal unworthiness ("I am so inferior that no one will look at me"), or doubt of one's capacity for love, or a certain stubbornness — an unwillingness to admit that one has made a mistake in having been attracted to the other person in the first place.

Sociological Factors

Urban Living. Thus far we have considered internal factors, forces within the personalities and backgrounds of individuals, that prevent them from attaining success in marriage. There are also a number of cultural patterns that hinder the development of satisfactory marital adjustment.

One such pattern is urbanization, mentioned previously as a force preventing individuals from becoming acquainted. If married couples live in a large city, and particularly if they are strangers in a large city, the compartmentalization of urban life may cause them to live too much by themselves. They are unable to develop normal relations with others because they do not have the facilities for making social contacts. If marriages drift along in this manner, they may become ingrown, sterile, and unhappy affairs.

War Marriages. Another common pattern is the war marriage. When war marriages are made in haste, as they frequently are, the partners have not had sufficient time to become acquainted, to find out whether their love will survive a reasonably long engagement. The mortality of these marriages is high (20, 21).

The nomadic life that many couples find themselves living in times of national crisis also puts strains on marriage. Couples find it difficult to "put their roots down" and build enduring social relations with other married people in the community. The insecurities produced by a life that involves moving to a different locality every year or so sometimes become focused on the marriage relationship itself, with unfortunate results.

The Working Wife. The working wife comes in for considerable comment when problems of marriages are discussed. The fact that the wife works is not in itself a threat to marriage, but the way in which the husband views her working is most significant. Many a husband regards a wife's desire to work as a reflection on his ability to support the family, or he looks on it as a covert attempt to compete with him as the breadwinner and head of the family. In either event, he regards it as a threat; it arouses in him feelings of inferiority and inadequacy. Although marriage experts agree that the size of income, as such, is unrelated to happiness (22), the fact is that many middle-class families are caught in an inflationary spiral that threatens to reduce their buying power markedly. The choice in some families is whether the standard of living is to be drastically revised or whether the wife is to work. The choice that these families are making is reflected in the fact that there are eight to ten million married women working today. They outnumber unmarried women workers about seven to five.

There is no conclusive evidence to indicate that working wives are less satisfactory wives and mothers. The ability to fill both roles is highly individual and is related to the kind of person one is. Actually, the question may well be whether a woman who wishes to work should be denied the satisfactions to be gained from working. On the other hand, most women are able to get these satisfactions from the enactment of their traditional role as wives and mothers. Perhaps the best solution of the problem of what to do about the working wife is to leave it in the hands of the individuals concerned — that is to say, perhaps it is best solved in the light of the relationships peculiar to each family. If the wife *does* work, it is certain to mean readjustments at home. It may mean, for example, that more housekeeping duties have to be assumed by the husband, so that he, in turn, has to give up some of his activities away from home. Giving up things is always difficult.

Marriage and Emotional Maturity

Marriage as a "State of Normality." Most people marry at some time during their lives; hence, statistically speaking, marriage is a "normal state" for adults in our culture. Individuals are expected to marry. Persons who do not marry are, in effect, deviating from the social norm; and, as with other persons who deviate from the norm, we tend to look upon them somewhat askance, as though there were something a shade peculiar about them. This feeling applies even more strongly to persons who break marriage ties through divorce or desertion. Undoubtedly there are many persons who would prefer to remain single but who marry because they feel it is expected of them, just as there are many who would like to dissolve their marriages but who continue the relationship because they fear the disapproval of society.

There is probably some justification for our feeling that marriage is a symptom of normality, in that it does take a certain amount of emotional maturity to maintain a marriage partnership. Furthermore, mortality tables show shorter life spans for single and divorced individuals, and admissions of this group to mental hospitals are proportionately higher. However, it is a mistake to say that the poorer health of the single or divorced person is *caused* by the fact that he is not married. Both situations — unmarried status and poor health — are probably due to the same cause. In other words, the factors that make them poor marriage risks also affect their health adversely. Thus, we cannot say with any certainty that entering or returning to the marriage state would raise their level of physical or emotional health. Sometimes it might actually lower it.

Our critical attitude toward unmarried persons also ignores the fact that many single persons are living happy, well-adjusted, and useful lives, and that many married persons would actually be better off if their marriages were dissolved.

Effects of Marriage on Emotional Maturity. Probably most persons who enter the state of marriage are unprepared for the changes that will take place in their personality structure. Actually, any major change of situation will effect changes in personality, in that there are new demands and responsibilities, new roles to play, and new goals to achieve. Marriage causes great changes in personality because of its intimacy, a relationship that affects the very core of the self; whereas in other situations — change of job, for example — only the "outer layers" of the personality are directly involved. In other words, the marital situation is very much a part of the individual, sometimes even as much a part as the individual's own childhood experiences.

Employers are beginning to realize more and more how much marriage is a part of their employees' lives and personalities. According to a survey made by the magazine *Fortune*, some 50 per cent of American corporations now include the wives of applicants for executive positions, as well as the applicants themselves, in their personnel-screening procedures. One large corporation is said to have turned down 25 per cent of executive trainee applicants because of the unsuitability of their wives. Employers are increasingly aware of the fact that the general effectiveness and productivity of an employee is conditioned by the attitudes and feelings of his wife. A potentially effective executive, for example, may be rendered inefficient because his wife is unable to accept the goals of the employing corporation or her husband's assigned roles and responsibilities (23).

Although employers are interested in special competencies and skills and are thus only indirectly concerned about the marital happiness of their employees, psychologists have been interested in discovering the conditions that lead to happy marriages. As a result of his study of 792 couples, Terman came to the following conclusions: 1. The happiness of the couple is directly related to the happiness of their parents. 2. The happiness of childhood is related to happiness in marriage. 3. The more conflicts the partners experience with their own parents, the more the likelihood of unhappiness in marriage. 4. Chances for marital success are best if the discipline spouses received as children was firm but not too frequent nor too harsh. 5. Spouses who have good relationships with their parents are likely to have happy marriages. 6. Parental frankness toward sex aids marital success. 7. Premarital attitudes toward sex that are free from disgust or aversion are desirable (24).

E. W. Burgess and L. S. Cottrell, in their study of 526 couples, came to similar conclusions. In addition, they stressed the fact that the degree to which the marriage partner has achieved a satisfactory social adjustment is significantly related to marriage success (25).

Attaining Emotional Maturity through Marriage. Robert Louis Stevenson once said, "Marriage is one long conversation," which is a literary way of recognizing the importance of communication between spouses. If a marriage is successful in aiding individuals to attain higher levels of emotional maturity, it does so, in part, through providing opportunities for communication. Inasmuch as the marriage partnership, unlike most of our interpersonal relationships, can be accepted easily by us as a love relationship, it provides a better opportunity to communicate deeper emotions — a process that is important to personality growth. As marriage partners use communication to learn to know each other better, they are thereby enabled to understand, accept, and respect each other as persons.

R. S. Ort discovered in a study of marital relationships that 83 per cent of the marriage partners who experienced the least internal conflict resolved their differences through discussion; whereas only 29 per cent of those who had the most conflict used this method. On the other hand, arguing was used by 20 per cent of the individuals who had the least conflict and by 73 per cent of those with the most conflict (26). (Discussion is a form of communication that may improve interpersonal relations, whereas argument is a form of verbal aggression in which little real communication is likely to occur.)

The happiness of a family may often be enhanced or maintained through the development of areas of common interest that are outlets for creativity and self-expression. The usual interest of this type is the rearing of children, which can become particularly rewarding, especially if responsibilities are shared by both spouses. Homemaking is another area that often becomes a creative and rewarding interest when shared by both spouses. However, besides these everyday activities, there are hobbies like gardening, photography, and woodworking that can be shared by spouses to help them broaden the scope of their creative expression and thus facilitate the process of becoming emotionally mature.

Couples who are prepared to compromise and to adjust to each other's demands, even to the point of making personality changes and surrendering certain ways of life, have a good chance of building mutually satisfactory marriage relationships. Maslow found that a strong desire to dominate, on the part of either the husband or the wife, leads to difficulties in social and sexual adjustment (27). F. L. Kelly discovered that compatibility in marriage is favored by a willingness on the part of each spouse to believe in the superiority of the other partner (28). Thus it would appear that the persons who are good marriage risks are those who have reached a level of maturity and humility wherein they do not feel that their status or their emotional security is threatened by their spouses. Since, as we have indicated previously, many who marry are emotionally immature in many ways, it means that the marriage relationship has to be used as a means of attaining the maturity they were unable to attain before marriage. In actual practice, the marriage relationship has something to offer any person who is interested in becoming more mature — in learning to understand, accept, tolerate, and respect himself and others.

SUMMARY

Because our culture creates and emphasizes personality differences between the sexes, boys and girls of school age live in different psychological worlds and thus do not share many viewpoints and areas of common experience. By the onset of puberty there is considerable hostility and little real communication between the sexes. With adolescence, boys and girls become interested in each other, and much of the hostility disappears. However, because of the lack of areas of common interest and because of the difficulty of communication, early attempts to establish emotionally satisfying relationships are often unsuccessful. Because of these difficulties, courtship often becomes an occasion for mutual exploitation, in which each person is selfishly concerned with satisfying his own needs, without consideration for the feelings and needs of the other person. However, most adolescents learn, through dating, to communicate with members of the other sex and thus to meet some of their needs for companionship.

Relations between the sexes, both in adolescence and in adulthood, are complicated by our attitudes toward sex. The guilt and anxiety we feel about sexual matters lead us either to overemphasize or to underemphasize their importance in our lives. Thus we tend to look upon sexual compatibility as the basis for a happy marriage, whereas it is more likely true that sexual compatibility is symptomatic of happy marriages rather than the cause of them.

Another factor that may cause problems in courtship and marriage is the pattern of living in cities, which makes it difficult for lonely people to become acquainted. Furthermore, some women may have difficulty in finding mates because of their college education, as is indicated by the fact that the percentage of unmarried women is the highest in the college-educated group.

Building a happy marriage is hardest for self-centered persons, because they are able to think only of themselves and are unable to adjust to the needs of their mates. Maintaining satisfactory relationships may also be difficult for persons whose backgrounds and interests differ widely. There are many, however, who marry and are successful in spite of these differences.

Other factors that make marriages difficult are the lack of friendly social contacts in urban living, wars and periods of social stress, and nomadic patterns of life that make it difficult to "put down roots." Sometimes the fact that the wife needs or wants to work may cause difficulties, but this is a kind of situation to which mature people can adjust, if they really want to make their marriages successful.

Marriage is the "normal state" for adults in our culture, and we accept this fact so implicitly that we tend to look askance at persons who do not marry, ignoring the fact that many of them live happy and useful lives. Persons who marry find that being married changes one and that the experiences of marriage markedly affect patterns of personality. There are a number of conditions that can be used for predicting success in marriage. Relations with one's parents appear to be a particularly important factor in marital happiness.

Marriage is a challenge to personal development. If marriage partners are willing to communicate with each other and if they can use the trials of marriage to help them become emotionally more mature, they improve their chances of building happy marriages.

REFERENCES

1. M. Mead, *Sex and Temperament in Three Primitive Tribes*. New York: Morrow, 1935.
2. M. F. Ashley-Montagu, "The Natural Superiority of Women," *The Saturday Review*. 35:8–9, 27–29; March 1, 1952.

3. E. Fromm, "Man-Woman" in M. M. Hughes, ed., *The People in Your Life*. New York: Knopf, 1951. Pp. 3–27.

4. T. Parsons, "Age and Sex in the Social Structure of the United States," *American Sociological Review*. 7:604–616; 1942.

5. T. Parsons, "Certain Primary Sources and Patterns of Aggression in the Social Pattern of the Western World," in P. Mullahy, ed., *A Study of Interpersonal Relations*. New York: Hermitage, 1949. Pp. 269–296.

6. A. C. Kinsey, *et al.*, *Sexual Behavior in the Human Male*. Philadelphia: Saunders, 1948.

7. E. Fromm, "Man-Woman" in M. M. Hughes, ed., *The People in Your Life*. New York: Knopf, 1951. Pp. 3–27.

8. L. M. Terman and P. Buttenweiser, "Personality Factors in Marital Compatibility," *Journal of Social Psychology*. 6:143–171, 267–289; 1935.

9. J. Ball, "Psychosexual Behavior," in L. A. Pennington and I. A. Berg, eds., *An Introduction to Clinical Psychology*. New York: Ronald, 1948. Pp. 200–217.

10. L. W. Dearborn, "Masturbation," in M. Fishbein and E. W. Burgess, eds., *Successful Marriage*. New York: Doubleday, 1947. P. 361.

11. H. S. Sullivan, *Conceptions of Modern Psychiatry*. Washington, D.C.: William Alanson White Psychiatric Foundation, 1947. P. 20.

12. J. T. Landis, "Adjustments after Marriage," *Marriage and Family Living*. 9:32–34; 1947.

13. F. Fromm-Reichmann, *Principles of Intensive Psychotherapy*. Chicago: University of Chicago Press, 1950. P. 35.

14. E. Fromm, "Man-Woman," in M. M. Hughes, ed., *The People in Your Life*. New York: Knopf, 1951. Pp. 3–27.

15. Metropolitan Life Insurance Company, "Marriage and Educational Attainment," *Statistical Bulletin*, August, 1946. Pp. 4–6.

16. P. H. Landis and K. Day, "Education as a Factor in Mate Selection," *American Sociological Review*. 10:558–560; 1945.

17. J. T. Landis, "Marriages of Mixed and Nonmixed Religious Faith," *American Sociological Review*. 14:401–407; 1949.

18. H. M. Bell, *Youth Tell Their Story*. Washington, D.C.: American Council on Education, 1938. P. 21.

19. J. Biesanz and L. M. Smith, "Adjustment of Interethnic Marriages on the Isthmus of Panama," *American Sociological Review*. 16:819–822; 1951.

20. C. Hall, "The Instability of Post-War Marriages," *Journal of Social Psychology*. 5:523–530; 1934.

21. G. V. Hamilton and K. Macgowan, *What Is Wrong with Marriage?* New York: Boni, 1929.

22. E. M. Duvall and R. Hill, *When You Marry*. Boston: Heath, 1945. P. 220.

23. W. H. Whyte, Jr., "The Corporation and the Wife," *Fortune*. 44:109–111, 150–152, 155–156, 158; October, 1951. "Wives of Management," *Fortune*. 44:86–88, 204–206, 208–210, 212–213; November, 1951.

24. L. M. Terman, *et al.*, *Psychological Factors in Marital Happiness*. New York: McGraw-Hill, 1938.

25. E. W. Burgess and L. S. Cottrell, *Predicting Success or Failure in Marriage*. New York: Prentice-Hall, 1939.

26. R. S. Ort, "A Study of Role Conflicts as Related to Happiness in Marriage," *Journal of Abnormal and Social Psychology.* 45:691–699; 1950.
27. A. H. Maslow, "Self-Esteem (Dominance-Feeling) and Sexuality in Women," *Journal of Social Psychology.* 16:259–294; 1942.
28. E. L. Kelly, "Marital Compatibility as Related to Personality Traits of Husbands and Wives as Rated by Self and Spouse," *Journal of Social Psychology.* 13:193–198; 1941.

SUGGESTED READINGS

E. M. Duvall, *Building Your Marriage.* New York: Public Affairs Committee, Inc., 1948. Pamphlet No. 113. A brief, informal discussion of the road to marital happiness.

J. Levy and R. Monroe, *The Happy Family.* New York: Knopf, 1938. In this writer's opinion the best book on marital adjustment. Its thesis: How to have a happy marriage with partners who are not perfect — just normal.

H. A. Bowman, *Marriage for Moderns,* 2d edition. New York: McGraw-Hill, 1948. A well-known text; a broad survey of marriage problems.

H. T. Christensen, *Marriage Analysis: Foundations for Successful Family Life.* New York: Ronald, 1950. Another good text of the survey type.

J. T. Landis and M. G. Landis, *Building a Successful Marriage.* New York: Prentice-Hall, 1948. A very popular survey text.

E. W. Burgess and H. J. Locke, *The Family: From Institution to Companionship.* New York: American Book, 1945. Still another good survey.

M. F. Nimkoff, *Marriage and the Family.* Boston: Houghton Mifflin, 1947. Sociological treatment; well worth reading.

J. H. S. Bossard, *The Sociology of Child Development.* New York: Harper, 1948. Family relationships and their effect on children's personalities.

W. L. Warner, *et al., Who Shall Be Educated?* New York: Harper, 1944. Chapters 3 and 7 deal with social mobility through marriage.

A. B. Hollingshead, *Elmtown's Youth.* New York: Wiley, 1949. Chapter 16 deals with sex and marriage for the out-of-school adolescent of "Elmtown."

O. S. English and G. H. J. Pearson, *Emotional Problems of Living.* New York: Norton, 1945. Chapters 10, 11, and 12 discuss personality and emotional disturbances that occur in adolescence, and the place of work and marriage in emotional satisfaction. Heavy Freudian emphasis.

M. L. Ernst and D. G. Loth, *American Sexual Behavior and the Kinsey Report.* New York: Greystone, 1948. An excellent survey of sexual behavior in the light of the findings of the Kinsey group.

D. P. Geddes and E. Curie, *About the Kinsey Report.* New York: The New American Library of World Literature (Signet Books), 1948. A well-organized symposium of outstanding contributions by leaders in the field of medicine, psychology, law, and religion on the implications of male sexual behavior.

P. Mullahy, ed., *A Study of Interpersonal Relations.* New York: Hermitage, 1949. A number of the contributions are well worth reading for an understanding of the human relations involved in marriage. See particularly the articles on the psychology of women by C. Thompson.

H. W. Hepner, *Psychology Applied to Life and Work*, 2d edition. New York: Prentice-Hall, 1950. Chapter 13 deals with adjustments in courtship and marriage.

J. Warters, *Achieving Maturity*. New York: McGraw-Hill, 1949. Chapter 4 is particularly pertinent with regard to dating; other chapters contain valuable information regarding sexual development.

H. Sorenson and M. Malm, *Psychology for Living*. New York: McGraw-Hill, 1948. Most of Section VI deals with courtship and marriage; this book is written primarily for adolescents and young adults.

F. McKinney, *Psychology of Personal Adjustment*, 2d edition. New York: Wiley, 1949. Chapter 12 deals with problems of love and sex as experienced by young people; Chapter 13 deals with marital adjustment.

H. C. Lindgren, *The Art of Human Relations*. New York: Hermitage, 1953. See Chapter 13 for a discussion of interpersonal relations in courtship, marriage, and family living.

XVIII...*Patterns of Deviation:*

Antisocial and Abnormal

"Abnormal" Defined. In this chapter we shall consider a variety of behavior patterns that are classified as "abnormal." They are so classified for the following reasons: 1. They serve to set people apart from the general (so-called "normal") population. 2. They prevent people from participating normally in the everyday life situations. 3. They prevent people from leading reasonably happy, productive, and peaceful lives. 4. They are often symptoms of neurotic, immature, or unrealistic needs. These behavior patterns are further characterized by what we do to persons who display them. Individuals whose behavior is abnormal in the direction of being antisocial are locked up in jails; and individuals whose abnormal behavior may be characterized as "mental disease" are treated in clinics and by private practitioners, if the symptoms are relatively mild, or in mental institutions, if they are severe. The usual criteria used as a basis for institutionalization are the extent to which an individual may be considered a menace to himself and/or to society, and the extent to which his behavior is a threat to public morals. In actuality, we do not differentiate sharply between these two kinds of behavior. If a psychotic person commits a crime, he may be sent to prison or he may be sent to a mental institution, depending on the law, the judge, the local policy, and the attitude of the community. Sometimes alcoholics are treated in clinics, sometimes they are jailed, and sometimes they are sent to institutions. Sometimes an attempt is made to rehabilitate sex offenders; sometimes they are merely jailed. There is no really clear-cut public policy on the treatment of persons displaying behavior that society considers abnormal and antisocial.

408

We shall discuss these forms of behavior under three main headings: (a) delinquency and crime; (b) addiction to alcohol, drugs, and gambling; (c) neurosis and psychosis. Though these three groupings are markedly different in the superficial aspects of the kind of behavior involved, they have many characteristics in common.

Deviants and Normals. The persons who display behavior of the three types specified above may be termed "deviants," because their behavior deviates markedly from the group norm. We shall use this term in referring to them in this discussion. The persons whose behavior deviates only moderately, or not at all, we shall term "normals."

The difference between deviants and normals is one of degree rather than of kind. All of us possess to a greater or lesser degree the tendencies that cause humans to deviate — to develop abnormal and antisocial behavior. The normal differs from the deviant in that he is able to control these tendencies or does not possess them to as great a degree.

In general, deviant behavior tends to be more "neurotic" — that is, less realistic and more immature — than normal behavior. The deviant is less able to perceive, evaluate, and act in accordance with the facts of the physical and social environment. He is less able to see himself as he "really is" or as he appears to others. The deviant is less able than the normal to understand and to accept himself and others; he is less able to direct his conduct to his own real advantage. As compared with the normal, the deviant is more egocentric, more self-concerned, less involved in the welfare of others, and less able to involve himself in the problems of his environment. Because of his unrealistic expectations, the deviant's behavior pattern is more likely to be permeated with feelings of anxiety, guilt, and hostility. One of the most common characteristics of deviants is their seeming inability to learn from experience. Instead of using their intelligence to solve their problems, they use whatever deviant behavior dominates them to fight or flee from their problems.

Types of Individuals Who Are Usually Classified as Criminals or Delinquents

The Immature Personality. Our jails, prisons, courts, and reform schools today are full of persons whose deviant behavior is an expression of their psychological immaturity.   Childish behavior is expected from and tolerated in children, but is inappropriate when it appears in adults and older adolescents in the form of antisocial acts.   The psychologically immature person is one who is intensely selfish and egocentric, who can consider only his own needs and wants, who cannot tolerate even mild frustration, who lives only "for the moment," who takes what he wants when he wants it. Characteristic of this person is the feeling of omnipotence.   (See Chapter 7.)   When tempted to steal a watch or to practice target shooting with a .22 rifle near a busy intersection, he does so without hesitation, without the slightest thought of being caught and punished.   If he is caught and punished, he reacts with an attitude of surprise and resentment.   Sometimes his resentment on being caught turns into a desire for revenge, which in turn may lead him to commit additional crimes in an attempt to "get even" with society.   Unless he is guided to maturity, he may continue in his unrealistic, neurotic feeling of omnipotence and invulnerability, in spite of being caught and punished again and again.   Persons who feel omnipotent sometimes feel impelled to "try out" their fancied invulnerability, and committing crimes is one way of testing it.   When such people are not too emotionally ill, it may come as a relief to them that they can be caught and punished; others feel betrayed or just unlucky — next time things will be different.

The immature person follows a pleasure-and-thrill-seeking way of life to the practical exclusion of all other goals.   His pattern of life is to exploit his body, his associates, and his social and physical environment in his search for pleasure and thrills.   In general, the immature person is less likely to have feelings of guilt and anxiety than other deviant persons.   He so swaddles himself in his feeling of omnipotence that the possibility of his being wrong or immoral or misguided or in any way inadequate does not occur to him. His anxieties, if any, tend to be deeply buried in his unconscious processes.

It would actually be healthier if he were able to have conscious feelings of anxiety, guilt, or normal fear, for they would act as deterrents to his antisocial behavior and might serve as the bases for insight and maturity.   In fact, the immature persons who eventually are helped to become more mature are those who develop normal feelings of guilt and anxiety.

Esther Bubley and Children's Bureau

Occasional scraps and fist fights are a normal part of youngsters' everyday life; an adult who displays this pattern is emotionally immature.

Probably few delinquents or criminals of the immature type display *all* the characteristics listed above. Orville Holmes does not.

Orville Holmes's father was a traveling salesman who had an aggressive, easy charm and liked to have "a good time." He met Orville's mother in a night club, where she was a strip-tease artist. She continued to work in this capacity after they were married, taking time out to bear three sons, the youngest of whom was Orville. Her husband regarded the children as nuisances who, he felt, distracted his wife's attention from him when he was home. She, on her part, neither liked nor disliked her children. She gave them the minimum care, and left them to shift for themselves around the house as soon as they were able. The older boy was expected to take care of the younger ones, to get their breakfast, dress them, see that they stayed out of trouble, get their dinners, put them to bed, and do the housework. Orville's mother slept till noon each day and spent the afternoon listening to the radio and reading magazines. The two younger boys resented the sometimes autocratic control of the older brother and ran away whenever possible, returning late at night.

Orville first got into trouble when he decided not to go to school. This led to repeated visits from the truant officer, each of which was followed by whippings by his father or older brother. This punishment had no effect; he continued to play hooky whenever the mood struck him. When he was ten, he and his next older brother were adopted by a gang of adolescent boys who made a practice of stripping cars. He was arrested four times for stealing and malicious mischief before he was fourteen. When he was fifteen, he and his next older brother stole a car and tried to take it to Mexico. They were arrested and sent to reform school. He had been out of reform school only six weeks when he was arrested for attempted rape and sentenced to another term at reform school. He left reform school for the second time when he was nineteen and stayed out a year while he worked as a merchant seaman on a tanker running the German submarine blockade. Even this work, with its war-zone bonuses, could not keep him in spending money. On his twentieth birthday he was arrested while trying to hold up a teller in a bank. This time he was given a ten-year sentence.

Orville is certainly not a successful criminal. He repeatedly gets into trouble that most normal persons would avoid. He cannot resist the urge to steal; he seems to have no awareness of the possibility that he will be caught; he is not even clever about his crimes. His life is a loveless one; no one has ever been emotionally attached to him, and he has never been attached to anyone. His strongest emotion is to gratify his desires, the sooner the better. It is doubtful whether he will ever learn to act differently, inasmuch as his capacity to love and to be loved is badly impaired.

The Rebellious Personality. In some ways, the rebellious person is also an immature person. He is, however, more likely to be capable of warm feelings than is the immature person. The person whose behavior pattern is one of rebellion is frequently one who has been reared in an authoritarian atmosphere and who has learned somehow to react to restriction and frustration by direct, aggressive, and hostile attack. When frustrated, he feels *compelled* to express his hostility and express it directly; he is unable to contain it. The rebellious deviant expresses his feeling of resentment against authority, society, and restrictions in general by stealing, destructive acts, sexual assault, murder, and the like.

Although one cannot draw a sharp dividing line between the essentially immature person and the rebel, the latter is more likely to indulge in his particular form of aggression because he feels threatened. Sometimes this is because he "projects" his own hostile impulses to others. He feels he must attack others before they can attack him. When deviants of this type attempt to avenge themselves on society for some real or fancied wrong, they are doubly resentful when caught. They often feel that the scales of justice are again out of balance and that they must commit some new crime in order to bring them back into balance. They do not see punishment as the attempt of society to discipline them and to prevent further crimes; they see it only as a system that exists to persecute the underdog.

Fred O'Connor grew up in an orphanage where the discipline was strict and severe. He was popular with boys of his own age, although he got into many fights. He was punished often, sometimes by the authorities of the orphanage and sometimes by the older boys. He usually would fight back, sometimes until he was knocked unconscious. As he grew older, he was punished less because he became more skillful in expressing his hostility. However, when he was fourteen, he stole the purse of a teacher who, he felt, had humiliated him publicly. The theft was traced to him through fingerprints, and he was sent to reform school. He was discharged after two years and placed on probation. During the next two years he worked as a carpenter's helper, using the skills he had learned at reform school. Although he was liked by his fellow workers, he did not get along with foremen and was fired from several jobs. At the age of eighteen he joined the Army and distinguished himself on the battlefield by his reckless and aggressive bravery.

His Army career was marked by several instances of insubordination; on one occasion he was demoted from corporal to private, and on another he was demoted from the rank of sergeant. His inability to co-operate with persons in authority culminated in an incident high-lighted by his hitting a second lieutenant who had dressed him down publicly for failing to salute. Because of the sympathetic understanding of his commanding officer, he was transferred to a hospital for psychiatric observation and given an undesirable (not dishonorable) discharge. Fred went into civil life feeling that he had received a "raw deal" and filled with bitterness toward the Army and society in general. However, he returned to carpentry in an attempt to lead a normal life. Before he had been on his first job a week, he became involved in a violent argument with a foreman, and attacked him with a chisel. He was sent to the county jail for a year and a day.

Fred is apparently unable to learn that he cannot solve his problems by fighting those who supervise him. He carries far more than the normal burden of resentment and brooding hostility. He is aware that he has had more than his share of life's problems and vicissitudes, and he blames society for having made him its victim. The only method he knows is to attack directly. If he could undergo a kind of treatment that would help him to understand and accept his hostility and suspiciousness, he might have a chance for recovery. Realistically, the chances of his receiving this kind of treatment in jail are rather poor. Very few counties have rehabilitation programs of a genuinely therapeutic nature for their prisoners.

Antisocial behavior is not confined to deviants. It also appears in milder, modified form in normals. As we indicated in the previous chapter, rebelliousness frequently appears in normal males, both adolescents and adults, as a sort of compulsive masculinity. They feel that conformity is a feminine trait, and so they adopt a rebellious, nonconformist mode of behavior to compensate for any feminine tendencies they suspect in themselves.

The fear of femininity in an exaggerated form may very likely motivate the behavior of the deviant. Edward A. Shils, in his discussion and interpretation of data gathered by S. A. Stouffer and others in their study of the personnel of the American Army (1), reports as follows:

AWOL's tended to have been more isolated in childhood, and less inclined "to go around with a bunch" than any except psychoneurotic soldiers; as children they had been far more disposed to truancy than any other army group. They claim to have "really liked fighting" as children more than any other group and also to have had "dates with girls" more frequently.

This picture of the AWOL might be interpreted as that of a person with inferiority feelings, fearful of giving or receiving affection and yet desirous of doing so, concerned to overcome his image of inadequacy by demonstrating his masculinity and at the same time reluctant to undergo any test which would reveal the defects which he feels. It is the picture of a late adolescent worried about his capacity to "prove" his masculinity in an environment which would surely put it to test both by its composition and by the tasks which it would have to perform. Hypothetically this may be related to the feeling of uncertainty about heterosexual capacity and the fear of falling into a strictly male society which would reactivate latent homosexual tendencies and thus accentuate internal conflict about heterosexual capacity (2).*

Meeting Neurotic Needs. Crime and delinquency may also serve as means of meeting certain neurotic or unnatural needs. One such is the need for punishment. A person who is afflicted by this need may commit a crime for which he knows he will be arrested because he wishes to atone for another real or fancied crime. For example, an adolescent who feels guilty about masturbating may smoke in the boys' toilet at high school at a time when the janitor is likely to make an inspection. His behavior may be completely inexplicable to the school authorities, his family, his friends, and even to himself, because he may have been a model student before this time. His behavior seems quite logical if we see it as a way of meeting an unconscious need for punishment.

A neurotic need for affection may also lead individuals into deviant behavior. Persons who are afflicted with a need of this sort sometimes use deviant behavior in an attempt to gain attention. It is as though, feeling themselves unable to receive love, they settle for attention as a substitute. The negative attention of arrest, censure, notoriety, and punishment is better, they feel, than no

---

* Copyright 1950 by the Free Press Corporation.

attention at all.   In fact, the publicity that frequently attends crimes committed for this neurotic purpose is interpreted as an aid to status.

Status is accepted as a substitute for love by the youth who co-operates with his gang in criminal activities. He is attracted to the gang because it fills his needs for acceptance and status and because he does not feel that these needs are met at home.   Furthermore, as a member of an organized group, he is able to wreak revenge on the adult world whose representatives (his parents) are rejecting him.   Success in his attack on authority figures will gain him much status with the group.   If he is not successful and is caught and punished, he does not necessarily lose face, but instead may gain it.   After all, one usually expects adults to win — they are bigger and more powerful, and it is no credit to adults that they are able to defeat and punish a boy.   Thus he gains the sympathy to which the underdog is traditionally entitled.

Predisposing Causes of Delinquency.   The importance of psychological factors in the delinquent tendencies of youth is revealed in a study recently completed by Sheldon and Eleanor Glueck.   The Gluecks and their assistants made careful investigations into the physiological, sociological, and psychological characteristics and backgrounds of 500 "matched pairs" of delinquent and nondelinquent boys in Boston.

The Gluecks found that delinquents tended to be more aggressive than nondelinquents.   They lacked even a reasonable fear of failure, and were thus less inhibited in their attacks on society.   They were less concerned with the demands of authority figures and about conforming to social expectations.   Whereas the nondelinquent boys were able to express themselves symbolically, or through behavior mechanisms that were less deviant or antisocial, the delinquents tended to express themselves directly.   Thus when a nondelinquent was frustrated, he tended to displace, sublimate, or repress this feeling; whereas the delinquent expressed his frustration through direct and aggressive action (3).

Inasmuch as the delinquents and the nondelinquents in this study were matched as to the area of the city in which they lived, the factor of socio-economic status was more or less controlled; thus the study is not concerned with presenting evidence indicating the influence of socio-economic deprivation on delinquency.   However, a study of delinquency in Chicago does indicate that the most congested areas of the city produce the most delinquency (4).

Reading, writing, and arithmetic are symbolic forms of behavior. Because of the inability of delinquents to cope with life symbolically, it is not surprising to learn that the Gluecks found that delinquents could not adjust to school. The delinquents presented a picture of restless energy; they refused to conform to the rules. Because of their difficulty with the symbolic aspects of life, they were unable to interpret for themselves the demands of a complicated culture. Partly because they were unable to interpret the culture, they were unable to adjust themselves to it. When society made demands upon them, they had but one characteristic reaction — hostile aggression. They were unable to develop a flexible approach to life.

The study made by the Gluecks further shows that the family life of delinquents was inferior to that of nondelinquents. There was a higher proportion of unhappy marriages and broken homes. More lived with parent-substitutes rather than with their own parents. There was a marked tendency toward alcoholism, mental retardation, criminality, and emotional disturbance in the families of the grandparents. Discipline for delinquents was extremely harsh or extremely lax. Families tended to be disorganized, hostile, and noncohesive. Delinquent boys did not tend to admire their fathers and were not inclined to use them as models. Because of these family relationships, their superego development was defective, and they were unable to control their deviant, antisocial impulses.

Adolescence is a particularly fertile field for delinquency, because it is a stage of development usually marked in our culture by a build-up of hostile feelings toward adults and adult control. The adolescent is particularly vulnerable to the "temptations" of antisocial behavior, for he is caught in the cross fire between his needs to be free and independent and his parents' desires to maintain controls. (See Chapter 7.) Adolescents who are unable to resolve these problems satisfactorily, who express their hostile feelings too directly, who seek acceptance and status within groups of delinquent youth — these are the lost youth whose arrests and convictions make up the statistical reports that point to an increasing number of arrests among persons under twenty-one years of age.

Many of the so-called delinquent acts of adolescents are the result of attempts to find recreation in an urban environment that allows

little opportunity for play.   This is true even for preadolescents.
Howard Jones reports on a similar problem in postwar England:

> It is unfortunately true that modern urban life does not provide
> nearly enough scope for the spirit of adventure and the abounding energy
> of the younger group of children.   There are few open spaces, and such as
> exist are often enough only available for polite summer evening per-
> ambulations, or "properly organized" cricket and football matches.
> Where is the opportunity for adventure in a society which treats tree-
> climbing, playing in bombed buildings, or riding "two on a bike" as
> delinquencies?   Unless it is in being a delinquent (5).

Cultural Norms and Delinquency.   Then there are the persons who
display deviant behavior because they grew up in the midst of
cultures that differ from the accepted middle-class pattern.   Some
of these cultural groups are formed of first- and second-generation
Americans who have not assimilated the American middle-class
pattern.   Others are comprised of members from lower-class groups
that in some respects have markedly different standards of behavior
from the middle-class norm.   Their attitudes toward sexual behavior,
property, aggression, rights, and law and order differ from accepted
middle-class norms.   (The behavior pattern of the lower socio-
economic groups is discussed at length in Chapter 9.)   It is the
standard practice in our culture to hold the individual responsible
for wrongdoing; yet it is often true that the persons concerned know
no other way of life.   Jones raises the question of whether we are
dealing with a delinquent individual or with an entire subcultural
group whose standards are different from ours:

> When a child gets into trouble with the police no real attempt is made
> to deal with . . . [the] problem of the local community.   His parents
> are interviewed and are expected to raise their standards, but entirely
> without reference to the standards of the district in which they live.   No
> one seems to realize how impossible it is for any person with a normal
> share of social sensibility to swim against the stream of public opinion
> in this way (5).

Children who come from lower-class families find that their
behavior makes them unwelcome in school.   Middle-class teachers
punish them and withhold rewards because they do not conform
to middle-class norms — they swear, they fight, and they are not
much interested in learning.   However, as far as the children them-

selves are concerned, they feel that they are being rejected and punished for *being themselves*, for following the models set by their families and neighbors. Partly because school offers them nothing that meets their needs and partly because their culture demands that they become self-supporting as soon as possible, they drop out of school at the earliest legal age — and sometimes before (6). Even as adults, their way of life continues to clash with middle-class patterns; they are frequently arrested and punished for living according to the dictates of their own culture, which condones assault and battery, extramarital sexual intercourse, wife-beating, hunting and fishing out of season, bookmaking, bootlegging, and vagrancy (7, 8).

Then there are the children who are reared in families of professional criminals. Probably the man in the street feels that most delinquents have this sort of background, but this is not true. Like all other forms of behavior, deviant or normal, what we term crime and delinquency are *learned* methods of dealing with life's problems; deviant behavior is not inborn or inherited.

However, professional criminals do constitute a small, relatively well-knit subgroup in our larger culture (9). Like skilled workers, they take a professional pride in their work and may actually live a life that, at least in its superficial aspects, appears to be normal except for the antisocial aspects of their vocation. Professional criminals have a hierarchy and status system all their own, ranging from the pickpockets and shoplifters at the bottom to the confidence men at the top. Often their children grow up to be like them, unable to limit and control their predatory tendencies because they have learned a way of life that encourages rather than frustrates antisocial behavior.

Addiction to Alcohol, Drugs, and Gambling

The deviants discussed so far have one characteristic in common — aggressive, antisocial behavior. There is another group of deviants who solve their emotional problems in a quite different way. Theirs is a solution by flight, instead of by attack. These are the individuals who are so obsessed by their inadequacies that they seek refuge in alcohol and drugs. This neurotic means of solving problems is both a panacea and an anesthesia — something that helps temporarily by enabling these persons to forget the acute psychological pain that accompanies deep feelings of inferiority and inadequacy.

There may well be physiological or inherited traits that cause an individual to choose addiction to drugs or alcohol in preference to other forms of deviant behavior. Little is known on this score. More is known about the psychological background for addiction, although each case must be studied separately in order to determine its motivation.

The clinical picture of the drug addict is much the same as that of the alcoholic, in that the addicted person suffers from a strong feeling of discomfort, which he can relieve only by the use of drugs. One addict described this feeling as follows:

I was always getting into trouble before I got on drugs — never could seem to get comfortable; I had to go somewhere and do something all the time. I was always in trouble with the law. Some fellows told me about drugs and how good they made you feel, and I tried them. From then on I was content as long as I had my drugs — I didn't care to do anything but sit around, talk to my friends occasionally, listen to the radio, and only be concerned with the problem of getting money for drugs. This I usually did by picking pockets or other such petty stuff (10).

Drug addiction, like addiction to alcohol, is in essence a means of coping with life whereby emotionally immature persons try to reduce the pain and tensions that are the normal accompaniment of everyday living. Unfortunately, the use of drugs impairs the individual's ability to make normal adjustments to his problems. According to Victor Vogel and his associates:

Persons who have never been able to make a satisfactory adjustment to life, whose adaptive patterns of behavior have been inadequate, frequently find in morphine, much as the tired businessman finds in the . . . [before-dinner] cocktail, a means of return to "normal." This is a false situation which may be recognized by the tired businessman but is not recognized by the drug addict. Our studies indicate that patients who have made a marginal degree of emotional adjustment to life, and then have begun to use drugs, lose some of their normal adaptive patterns of adjustment. This regression in personality represents the greatest danger of drug addiction (10).

Gambling is a form of behavior that also has its share of addicts. Gambling becomes the most important activity of life to its addicts, just as drugs and alcohol dominate the life of their addicts. The habitual gambler rationalizes his behavior by the belief that he is playing to win. In doing so, he deliberately or unconsciously ignores the realities, which are that gamblers eventually lose more than they win. One might therefore hypothesize that habitual gamblers gamble because they (unconsciously) expect to lose; therefore they gamble because they have a neurotic need to punish themselves. Another hypothesis is that they are obsessed by a belief in their own omnipotence, which they must constantly put to the test. One cannot underestimate the powerful hold that gambling has upon those addicted to it. In its worst form it is as socially and emotionally disintegrating as addiction to alcohol and drugs.

Inasmuch as addiction is mainly a problem of personality adjustment and is not the result of occasional indulgence as such, the most effective form of treatment is that of psychotherapy, supplemented (in the case of alcohol or drug addiction) by medical treatment. The society of Alcoholics Anonymous has had the best success in its field, and a similar organization has been formed to aid in the rehabilitation of narcotic addicts. Forms of group psychotherapy also appear to have some promise in treating alcohol and narcotic addiction (11, 12).

Neurosis and Psychosis

Perhaps the largest group of individuals displaying abnormal, deviant behavior are those who suffer from emotional disorders — psychoneurotics, psychotics, and sexual deviates.

For the purpose of this discussion, distinction is made between persons who merely have some neurotic needs (normals), and persons whose lives are saturated with neurotic feeling to the extent that their ability to play satisfactory and effective roles as employees, spouses, parents, friends, and social companions is seriously impaired. Not only are their interpersonal relations defective, but they also tend to be more unhappy and depressed than normals.

Psychotics display symptoms somewhat similar to those of psychoneurotics, but the difference between psychotic and normal behavior is much more pronounced than that between psychoneurotic and normal. Not only are psychotics less effective in interpersonal relations, but they have to a large extent lost contact with reality, their behavior is disoriented, and they are a present or potential menace to themselves and to society. Psychoneurotics, on the other hand, have not lost contact with reality, although they may distort it for their own (neurotic) purposes, and they may possess some insight into their own motivation, whereas psychotics possess much less insight, if any. The usual treatment for psychotics involves hospitalization and institutionalization for purposes of observation and therapy; psychoneurotics usually remain at large and receive therapy in an out-patient status from clinics and hospitals or from private practitioners. (See Chapter 5 for discussion of neurosis and psychosis.)

Sexual deviates are grouped with the psychoneurotics and psychotics because their problems, too, are essentially emotional disorders and because they, like the psychoneurotics and the psychotics, can trace their deviations from the norm to childhood patterns. It should be noted, however, that what are considered deviations in sexual behavior in our middle-class culture are not regarded as deviations in some other cultures. For example, in many cultures homosexual behavior is not considered abnormal or morally reprehensible. Kinsey and his associates discovered that even in the United States the accepted standards of sexual conduct differ between social levels. For example, there is a tendency for petting to be considered abnormal and deviant by males with a grade school education, whereas it is conventional conduct for males with a high school education (13). The report shows also that extra-marital sexual relations are seven times more common among laborers with a grade school education than among males with a college education.

Thus the culture determines which kinds of sexual behavior are "normal" and acceptable, and which are "abnormal," "deviant," and reprehensible. This means that what we term "the sexual perversions" are not abnormal in and of themselves but have been endowed with the "quality" of abnormality by our culture. This method of classification does not differ from that used for kinds of nonsexual behavior which our culture, for reasons of its own, classifies as "abnormal."

Inasmuch as our culture *does* label certain kinds of sexual behavior as abnormal and deviant, this fact alone enables us to raise a question regarding the over-all emotional adjustment of persons who habitually engage in such behavior. We can hypothesize that the normal, well-adjusted person in our society patterns his sexual behavior according to the norm. Therefore, persons who follow deviant patterns of sexual behavior usually do so for neurotic reasons. Some individuals adopt this kind of behavior as a kind of rebellion against life as they see it; others take on the role of the sexual pervert in an attempt to flee from facing other (and to them more threatening) problems of adjustment; still others, for their own individual and neurotic reasons, are fixated at immature levels of behavior, sexually and otherwise.

Nathan Blackman, a psychiatrist, describes the dynamics of homosexuality as follows:

> The homosexual, a threatened, isolated, insecure individual, is encouraged to maintain homosexual ties by the reason that such an existence is actually shunted, suppressed, unreal, and socially disapproved. Being pushed into the byways or underpasses of everyday existence may be the essential need that these homosexual relationships require.
>
> Greater understanding, greater sympathy for the origin, needs, and gratifications that a homosexual relationship represents might also hasten the homosexual's ability to become freed from a mode of existence which is perpetuated by its temporary, unreal, make-believe quality. A more understanding grasp of the solitariness and aloofness within the homosexual might often mean the difference in helping these individuals to bridge the gap toward an adult life . . . [and to develop the feeling] of a relatedness toward life (14).

The Dynamics of Deviant Behavior

Persons who follow deviant paths of behavior have a number of factors in common. Except for those who deviate because of differences in cultural origin, they are neurotic to the point of being psychically ill and are characterized by histories of disturbed interpersonal relations. Defective relations with others are both a cause and a result of their problem. In each case the amount and kind of deviation depend on a constellation of factors: emotional temperament; the emotional climate of childhood; the interpersonal relations of childhood and later life; and, in some cases, certain events that had a powerful effect on the adjustment of the individual.

Some persons emerge from childhood with resilient, flexible self-structures. Others develop personalities which are immature, rigid, and "brittle," which adjust with difficulty, if at all. Whether or not one becomes emotionally disturbed depends on the amounts and kinds of pressures that life events place on one. The person with the flexible personality will probably be able to withstand severe pressures but may become emotionally disorganized if the pressure is too severe or too prolonged. The person with the immature, rigid personality may go through life relatively painlessly if he is fortunate enough to be able to live a sheltered existence and thus to avoid strains and pressures; however, a relatively mild amount of pressure of the wrong kind may precipitate emotional disorganization.

Deviant and immature people tend to be unable to make rational adjustments to the stresses of life. As they continue fixedly on their immature, rebellious, and neurotic way, they are brought into inevitable conflict with the correctional forces of society.

Rehabilitation and Recovery

Punishment. If abnormal and antisocial behavior is the expression of emotional difficulties and defective interpersonal relations, the correction for such behavior is obviously some form of therapy. Traditionally, however, our approach has not been that of therapy, but of punishment. Even psychotics at one time were beaten and tortured in an attempt to force them to see the error of their ways. We rationalize our use of punishment by our belief that it will eliminate crime. Although punishment can in some instances serve as a deterrent to some expressions of deviant behavior, its popularity can be explained, in part, by its ability to meet certain needs on the part of the punisher.

The first of these needs is a desire for revenge and retaliation. Here is an individual — a criminal — who has committed a crime or who has lived in a manner different from the prescribed norm. He has, we feel, deliberately affronted us with his conduct — he has injured someone, or taken something, or acted in an unseemly manner. He has wronged society; society should injure him in return.

A second need relates to our own antisocial tendencies and impulses. We normals have paid the price. As small children we had to give up what we considered was our right to do as we pleased in conformity to the demands of our parents. We learned that deviant behavior was followed by punishment. Now we see individuals doing things which we have foresworn, which we do not permit ourselves to do. We are afraid that if this deviant behavior goes unpunished, we will be unable to control our own antisocial tendencies any longer. When a deviant is apprehended and punished, we breathe a sigh of relief, so to speak, because our own antisocial impulses are again under control — they have no "excuse" for escaping.

A third need relates to the guilt feelings we all have to a greater or lesser degree. Perhaps we feel that we have not been as good as we should have been. Perhaps we feel that we have not lived up to our parents' expectations, or even our own. Perhaps we have secretly deviated from our own standards at times. Perhaps we feel guilty about our suppressed or repressed antisocial impulses. In any event there is, with many of us, a tendency to project these feelings of guilt on someone who has obviously and openly deviated from the norm, someone who can be labeled a delinquent or a criminal or a pervert. If he can be disgraced and punished, we feel somewhat relieved, as though, symbolically, through identification with him, we ourselves are punished for *our* deviations. Furthermore, through attacking him punitively, we have the feeling of attacking vicariously the same trait in ourselves of which we do not approve. Thus the judge who himself drives faster than the law allows is frequently harsh with speeders, or the person whose adolescence was marked by sexual deviation is frequently the one who proposes extreme punishment for sexual deviants.

Punishment as such, however, usually proves to be unsatisfactory as a rehabilitational technique. Individuals who do not perceive why they are being punished feel victimized. They develop a grudge against the society that has punished them, and they retaliate by adding to their crimes when freed. Although it may seem obvious to the normal that deviant behavior should be punished, it is not always obvious to the deviant. He sees his behavior as normal under the circumstances, as completely logical from his point of view. Even if he sees his behavior as deviant, he does not see what he can do about it — he simply feels that he lacks the ability to control it. Punishment does not help him: it does not give him any new ways to control his behavior, and it does not give him any real bases for developing needs that could be met by more acceptable kinds of behavior.

Persons who are locked up in a jail or a mental hospital are, in effect, rejected by society. The feeling of rejection is one of the most painful experiences man must bear. Combined with loss of status, it is a heavy burden for emotionally disoriented and disturbed persons, one that increases their fear and distrust of the world. Persons who are in the grip of fear and distrust cannot be changed for the better, for these emotions operate to make the personality rigid and inflexible.

Frightened, hostile, guilt-ridden, and anxious people are not amenable to rehabilitation. They are in no condition to gain insight into the causes of their behavior, to appraise the world of reality, to build sound interpersonal relationships, to become genuinely self-directive. Instead they struggle to maintain unchanged their distorted outlook on life, even though this attitude is the immediate cause of their deviant behavior.

Discipline. Discipline is a much broader concept than punishment. To many these terms are synonymous; to them, disciplining a child means punishing him. The larger idea of discipline is that of guidance, of helping the individual to grow up, to become psychologically more mature, and to take the responsibilities that are rightfully his. Thus, discipline in its larger sense means helping the individual to discipline *himself*, to become self-directive.

An important aspect of discipline is the principle of "setting the limits," which means helping the individual to become aware of the socially acceptable limitations to behavior and correcting him when these limits are exceeded. Sometimes it is necessary to use punishment or other corrective action to enforce limits, but the emphasis in discipline is on guidance, not punishment. It must be remembered that most individuals who habitually display deviant behavior have progressed so far with their neurotic pattern that they cannot be reached through correction, but must be dealt with primarily through an approach emphasizing acceptance and understanding — the approach of rehabilitation.

Rehabilitation. The philosophy of rehabilitation differs from that of punishment in that, when properly conceived and carried out, it helps to strengthen the individual's ability to deal competently

and effectively with life situations. A deviant who has been rehabilitated has been helped in his ability to understand, accept, tolerate,
and respect himself and others, and he has been aided in becoming
self-directive. The rehabilitation process must begin with an understanding and an acceptance of the deviant by society. This is
accomplished in two ways: by the understanding and acceptance
of the deviating individual by the rehabilitation agency itself, and
by the education of the general public in the causes of and cures for
abnormal and antisocial behavior.

Alexander has written as follows about the relative value of
rehabilitation and punishment:

> At present, we must be satisfied by a change in our attitude toward
> treatment of prisoners . . . . The therapeutic needs of inmates can best
> be served by the management of the inmate's life in a manner that is
> conducive to change and rehabilitation . . . . Punishment is not conducive
> to ridding society of crime, and . . . rehabilitation of the criminal, no
> matter how difficult a task, is the only effective method of dealing with
> those who are already engaged in a criminal career. We must realize
> that we cannot successfully apply . . . retaliation, intimidation, and
> rehabilitation at the same time, . . . [although] this [is what] is done
> in our institutions at present (15).

The rehabilitation agency accomplishes its purpose by employing
people trained in those psychological and sociological techniques
that are helpful in understanding individuals: interviews, tests,
case histories, and the like. Furthermore, it promotes and develops
attitudes which will enable its staff to be both objective and empathic, which will change their attitude from the traditional one of
rejection to one of acceptance and understanding. The rehabilitation staff provides the deviant individual with experiences which
enable him to understand and accept himself and which will give
him some feeling of competence and status. In the most completely
staffed and equipped prisons and hospitals, prisoners and patients
receive individual and/or group therapy as may be indicated;
occupational therapy, recreation, and vocational training are
available; and, most important, the institutional administration
reflects in its policies a humane and therapeutic viewpoint.

One theory of human behavior that accounts for the success of
rehabilitation workers concerns the existence of a "drive toward
health" in all individuals, which, if nurtured and permitted to

develop, helps to restore mental health. (See Chapter 19 for a full discussion of "drive toward health.") This theory, followed by Rogers and others, maintains, in effect, that there is in each of us a strong force working to maintain health and happiness (16). However, this force can be thwarted or rendered temporarily or permanently ineffective by neurotic or other abnormal patterns developed by the individual in his attempts to protect himself against real or fancied threats from within or without. Given an opportunity to recuperate in a permissive, accepting, and non-threatening atmosphere, the deviant is more likely to take the necessary steps of tearing down his old neurotic defenses and building his personality anew along more realistic and productive lines. Because the workers in the field of rehabilitation believe in their ability to release forces within deviants that will help them to help themselves, they continue their work despite many discouragements and frustrations.

In typical prisons and mental hospitals, however, the emphasis still tends to be on incarceration rather than on rehabilitation. The primary concern is that prisoners and patients are locked up; rehabilitation, cure, and reformation are of secondary importance. Fortunately, legislatures and governmental agencies are slowly coming to accept their responsibilities for curing, rather than merely locking up, the criminal or patient. Radio programs, newspaper stories, public addresses, and articles in popular magazines are all being used to enlist public support of the expenditure of funds for rehabilitation purposes and for educating the public to accept rehabilitated deviants as normal citizens.

This is not to say that rehabilitation is merely a matter of spending more money in the right places or that it is always successful or even that it is usually completely successful. Persons displaying deviant behavior are reacting to personality patterns that have taken a lifetime to develop. These patterns cannot be changed in a few months. Sometimes the process takes years; sometimes it fails. Some patterns, like that of the psychopathic deviant, are particularly resistant to rehabilitation. Some individuals are so firmly entrenched in neurotic patterns of life that they do not want to "get better," and no deviant can be rehabilitated who does not want to be cured. Hence, the safest, most efficient, most appropriate way of reducing the incidence of deviant behavior is to *prevent* it.

Prevention of Deviant Behavior. The discussion in this chapter has stressed the similar origins of most abnormal and antisocial behavior. Such behavior is the expression of neurotic personality patterns that had their origin in family backgrounds characterized by such factors as overprotection, extreme harshness, extreme laxity, lack of love, lack of family cohesiveness, undercurrents of family dissension and disunity, alcoholism, and the loss of one or both parents. It therefore appears that whatever promotes family unity and harmony, whatever promotes understanding, acceptance and love on the part of parents — in short, whatever promotes emotional maturity on the part of parents — will help to eliminate at the source the formation of personality patterns that eventually lead to abnormal and antisocial behavior.

Similar suggestions may be made concerning the school, which is the second great influence on the child. As it exists today, the school probably creates or aggravates as much emotional maladjustment as it cures. This would not be so if school personnel were helped to understand, accept, and respect children, to aid them in becoming self-directive, and to provide them with experiences that produce intellectual, physical, and emotional growth and maturity, instead of continuing the present pattern of stressing the memorization of facts, the learning of isolated skills, and the development of submissive and competitive attitudes.

So far the task appears to be twofold: parent education and the education of educators. To this must be added the general education of the public. The education of the public is a long-range job that will proceed slowly, if at all, because the changing of firmly rooted public attitudes can only come gradually. Probably any changes that are instituted in our present system of penal and mental institutions will also come slowly, for if the public is to provide financial support for the installation of rehabilitation programs in jails, prisons, mental hygiene clinics, and mental hospitals, it will do so only if convinced of the necessity for such expenditure. In the meantime, the man in the street prefers to spend his tax money for the alleviation of frustrations he can experience directly; this explains the huge expenditures for better highways rather than for improved and expanded facilities for mental hygiene services.

Much can be done for children and adolescents by providing recreational facilities that would enable them to have healthy experiences in group settings.   Playgrounds enable children to work off aggressive tendencies that otherwise might find their expression in antisocial and deviant behavior.   The adventuresome spirit that plagues youth who have been shut up in cities and towns can find its expression in Scouts, Campfire Girls, city-sponsored camps, and other forms of organized and supervised "vagabondage (17)." Some school systems even maintain camps that classes occupy in rotation (18).

But the basic need is for friendlier, happier families, for it is in the family that deviant behavior, both antisocial and abnormal, begins.

SUMMARY

The type of deviant behavior we term "delinquent" or "criminal" occurs as the expression of emotional adjustment problems of persons who are psychologically immature or overrebellious, or who have certain patterns of neurotic needs that are satisfied through antisocial behavior.   Other individuals come into conflict with society because they grow up in cultures that have different norms from those of the dominant culture;   while still others engage in criminal behavior because they know no other kind of life.   Some individuals attempt to solve their conflicts by taking refuge in drugs, alcohol, and gambling;   and others attempt to find solutions in psychoneurosis, psychosis, and sexual perversion.

The personality traits leading to these deviant patterns of behavior are present in all of us to a greater or lesser degree;   the difference between "normals" and "deviants" is one of degree rather than of kind.   Abnormal and antisocial behavior patterns represent unsuccessful attempts to solve life problems.   These patterns have a common element: they have their origin in prolonged, unhappy, and disturbing interpersonal relations during childhood.

The problems of rehabilitating the several types of deviants are basically similar.   Their solution involves creating a permissive and accepting atmosphere and providing deviant individuals with opportunities to grow into psychological maturity, to become more responsible and self-directive, and to gain in the understanding and acceptance of themselves and others.

The prevention of abnormal and antisocial behavior is essentially the problem of educating parents, educators, and the general public, in the hope that the causes of deviant behavior may be better understood and in the belief that such behavior may be reduced or eliminated through improved understanding of children and their problems and through the promotion of friendlier, happier family life.

REFERENCES

1. S. A. Stouffer, *et al.*, *The American Soldier*. Princeton: Princeton University Press, 1949.
2. E. A. Shils, "Primary Groups in the American Army," in R. K. Merton and P. F. Lazarsfeld, eds., *Continuities in Social Research*. Glencoe, Ill.: Free Press, 1950. Pp. 16–39.
3. S. Glueck and E. Glueck, *Unraveling Juvenile Delinquency*. New York: Commonwealth Fund, 1950.
4. C. Shaw and H. D. McKay, *Juvenile Delinquency and Urban Areas*. Chicago: University of Chicago Press, 1942.
5. H. Jones, "Group Sentiment and Delinquency," *Mental Health* (London). 8:41–44; 1948. Reprinted by permission of The National Association for Mental Health.
6. A. B. Hollingshead, *Elmtown's Youth*. New York: Wiley, 1949.
7. W. L. Warner and P. S. Lunt, *The Social Life of a Modern Community*. New Haven: Yale University Press, 1941.
8. A. Davis, *Social-Class Influences upon Learning*. Cambridge: Harvard University Press, 1948.
9. Chic Conwell, *The Professional Thief*, annotated and interpreted by E. H. Sutherland. Chicago: University of Chicago Press, 1937.
10. V. H. Vogel, *et al.*, "Present Status of Narcotic Addiction," *Journal of the American Medical Association*. 138:1019–1026; 1948. Reprinted by permission of the American Medical Association.
11. R. G. McCarthy, "Group Therapy in Alcoholism," *Quarterly Journal of Studies in Alcohol*. 10:63–108, 217–250, 479–500; 1949. 11:119–140, 309–330, 630–653; 1950. 12:103–117, 273–296; 1951.
12. M. Johnston, "An Experiment in Group Therapy with the Narcotic Addict," *American Journal of Psychotherapy*. 5:24–31; 1951.
13. A. C. Kinsey, *et al.*, *Sexual Behavior in the Human Male*. Philadelphia: Saunders, 1948.
14. N. Blackman, "The Genesis of Homosexuality," *Journal of the Missouri State Medical Association*. 47:814–817; 1950. Reprinted by permission of Nathan Blackman and the Missouri State Medical Association.
15. F. Alexander, *Why Men Punish*. Paper read at American Friends Service Committee Conference on Punishment, San Francisco, November 17, 1950. Reprinted by permission of Franz Alexander.
16. C. R. Rogers, *Client-Centered Therapy*. Boston: Houghton Mifflin, 1951. Pp. 487–491.

17. M. M. Levy, "Outdoor Group Therapy with Preadolescent Boys," *Psychiatry*. 13:333–347; 1950.

18. E. E. Pumala, "Secondary School Camping," *California Journal of Secondary Education*. 25:281–284; 1950.

SUGGESTED READINGS

L. J. Saul, *Emotional Maturity*. Philadelphia: Lippincott, 1947. Chapter 6 consists of a discussion of hostility and violence from the psychoanalytic point of view.

J. R. Cavanaugh, "Group Psychotherapy in a Naval Disciplinary Barracks," *U. S. Naval Medical Bulletin*. 49:645–654; 1949.

S. H. Britt, *Social Psychology of Modern Life*, Rev. edition. New York: Rinehart, 1949. Chapter 21 deals with patterns of delinquency.

W. F. Vaughan, *Social Psychology*. New York: Odyssey, 1948. Pages 181–202 review current material on delinquency from the public press and interpret it in the light of social psychology.

S. S. Sargent, *Social Psychology*. New York: Ronald, 1950. Chapter 4 deals with social influences on personality, including the influence of the family, parent-child relationships, and the school and neighborhood.

M. L. Ernst and D. G. Loth, *American Sexual Behavior and the Kinsey Report*. New York: Greystone, 1948. See particularly the chapter on normal and abnormal behavior.

J. McV. Hunt, ed., *Personality and the Behavior Disorders*. New York: Ronald, 1944. Part VI (Volume II) includes "Behavior Disorders in Childhood," "Delinquent and Criminal Personalities," "Unfit Personalities in the Military Services," "The Psychoneuroses," "The Functional Psychoses," "The Concept of the Psychopathic Personality," and "Seizure States."

K. Young, *Personality and Problems of Adjustment*. New York: Appleton-Century-Crofts, 1940. See Chapters 14, 15, 17, and 18.

H. Cleckley, "Antisocial Personalities," in L. A. Pennington and I. A. Berg, eds., *An Introduction to Clinical Psychology*. New York: Ronald, 1948. Chapter 12 is a discussion of the delinquent, the criminal, and the psychopathic personality.

H. Cleckley, *The Mask of Sanity*. St. Louis: Mosby, 1941. An outstanding book on the psychopathic personality.

R. G. Kuhlen, *The Psychology of Adolescent Development*. New York: Harper, 1952. Chapter 8 deals with the causes of delinquency.

J. C. Coleman, *Abnormal Psychology and Modern Life*. Chicago: Scott, 1950. See chapters entitled "Character and Behavior Disorders" and "Alcoholism and Drug Addiction."

C. Landis and M. M. Bolles, *Textbook of Abnormal Psychology*, Rev. edition. New York: Macmillan, 1950. See chapters on alcoholism and the psychopathic personality.

XIX ... *Integrative and Disintegrative Factors in Mental Health*

The purpose of the two final chapters of this book is threefold: to describe those forces in our everyday life that aid us in improving or maintaining mental health; to describe those forces in everyday life that have disintegrative effects on mental health; and to suggest some of the steps that may be taken by the individual to aid himself in particular and society in general toward a betterment of mental health conditions. Much of what is said in this chapter is in the nature of a review of concepts presented and discussed elsewhere in this book, but new material and concepts are introduced as appropriate in order to focus on the improvement of mental health and the promotion of a state of emotional maturity.

Integrative Factors in Mental Health

Homeostasis — the Drive toward Recovery, Survival, and "Self-actualization." In the last chapter we mentioned the existence of a "drive toward health," which can be utilized by rehabilitation workers in helping deviant and abnormal individuals to recover. We see this drive operate physically in the person who, ill with wound or fever, lies at death's door for a while, and, when he recovers, is himself again. We see it in the persons who are institutionalized as "hopelessly insane" and who recover spontaneously or through therapy and are themselves again. Or we see it in people who go into a severe depression at the death of a spouse or a parent and who actually lose interest in living for a time, but who eventually recover and resume their normal functions of living.

Man has a tendency to go on living, to meet his basic needs to the best of his ability, to "be himself" — as Kurt Goldstein says, "to actualize" his best potentialities — in spite of obstacles (1). We do not have to learn persistence in meeting our needs; most of the time we persevere at this task without knowing it. We may not be aware that we are seeking and finding sources of need-satisfaction, but this process goes on, nonetheless, or we would not be functioning normally.

"Homeostasis" is a term borrowed from the physical sciences. It refers, in part, to the tendency of a solid to return to its original shape and to maintain its original characteristics, once pressures that produce temporary change are removed. It is a homeostatic-like resiliency and elasticity that characterizes the human organism.

Man's homeostaticlike qualities may of course be impaired by prolonged fear and anxiety or by the disintegrative action of an unfavorable environment. Sometimes the drive toward health and self-actualization is virtually destroyed, as in the individual who becomes permanently psychotic; and sometimes it is partially impaired, as in those who never entirely recover from brutal experiences of their childhood or from the years spent in Nazi concentration camps. Individuals vary widely in their ability to recover from traumatic experiences; some recover, seemingly untouched by their experiences, and others bear psychological scars for life. In some, the will to live and express their individuality is very strong and persistent; in others it appears to be weaker, more hesitant, and more easily blocked.

All psychotherapists and counselors depend on the drive toward health and self-actualization to aid their patients and clients in attaining better mental health and emotional maturity. Some feel that this drive must be set in action by the skillful direction and interpretation of the therapist; while others, particularly the members of the nondirective or client-centered school of psychotherapy, feel that the "drive toward growth, health, and adjustment" (2) is so strong that it needs only to be freed. Whereas therapists of the first type often lean heavily on interpretation or on advice-giving, nondirective therapists endeavor to provide a situation in which the individual will not feel threatened, in which his drive toward better mental health may express itself fully. They feel that when this is permitted to occur, the individual will attempt the understanding and acceptance of himself, as well as of his physical and social environment, with renewed vigor and interest. Although these principles have been used to a greater or lesser extent by other therapists, members of the nondirective school appear to rely more heavily on the individual's ability and will to solve his own problem (3, 4).

If we can accept the principle that there are strong forces within individuals that tend to impel them in the direction of better mental health, the problem that faces all of us, how to promote better mental health, changes from one of trying to interest people in sounder mental health to one of helping people to attain a goal that they consciously or unconsciously already want for themselves. In other words, we can assume that everyone basically wants to be happier and better adjusted emotionally. Therefore our problem is: How can we create situations which will help them to become aware of this motivation and which will provide the freedom they need to move in the direction of their real goals?

If it were not for the existence of this drive toward health and self-actualization, the efforts of therapists and other workers in the field of mental health would be futile. No one can "give" another person a drive or a motive he does not already possess. Thus the existence of such a strong, basic drive lends much that is encouraging to the task of promoting better human adjustment.

Communication. Man not only possesses a drive toward better mental health, he also possesses the tool of communication. Although communication is a two-edged tool, one that can have a disintegrative as well as an integrative effect, we have not begun to exploit its therapeutic potentialities.

From the therapeutic point of view, communication plays an important role. As has been indicated in Chapter 5, "Emotions: Patterns of Defense and Escape," psychotherapy is based in the final analysis on communication. In many respects, the improvement of emotional adjustment through psychotherapy is a process of learning how to communicate or of re-establishing relationships with oneself and others. A well-adjusted, emotionally mature person is one who is able to find the real meaning of his own actions and the actions of others. He is also able to interpret himself to others. Interpretation is a communicative skill.

Of great importance to mental health is the therapy of everyday life, which will be discussed in the next section. Here again communication comes to the fore. It is through communicating with others that we are enabled to clarify our feelings, to achieve insight into ourselves and others, to express our acceptance and respect for others, and to receive their acceptance and respect in turn. The therapeutic aspects of marriage, which were presented in Chapter 17, depend largely on the ability of two people to communicate with each other, rather than merely on the facts of their living together and sharing the same quarters.

Techniques of Agreement. So far, we have not developed much skill in using communication to meet the real threats of the physical environment and the sometimes real, but usually fancied, threats of the social environment. The great contribution that communication can make is in the area of learning to live and work together in co-operation and peace. Techniques of disagreement have been brought to a high level of efficiency; the greatest need is for improved techniques of agreement. According to S. I. Hayakawa, there are three areas of communication that appear to bear much promise for the development of techniques of agreement (5). All three of these areas have been opened in the last quarter of a century, and it is only in the last decade that they have received much attention from psychologists.

The newest of these fields is the nondirective or client-centered psychotherapy of Rogers, which was mentioned above in connection with its use of the concept of homeostasis. Rogers' chief contribution to the field of communication is his discovery of the importance of intelligent and sympathetic listening. Though listening is an essential part of communication, it is overlooked in most discussions, marked as they are by aggressive and competitive attempts of individual group members to express themselves, to present their points of view, and to persuade others. We are so intent on expressing ourselves and convincing others that we often listen only in order to collect ammunition for our rebuttal. The Rogerian method of intelligent listening tells the client better than any merely verbal reassurances that he is accepted and understood. Thus he is relieved of the burden of trying to convince the therapist and defend himself at the same time. This leaves him free to grapple with his real problems and to achieve understanding and insight.

The contributions of general semantics (commonly called "se-

"This will teach you not to hit people."

The Saturday Review

Many of the problems and difficulties we face are due to certain basic inconsistencies in our culture.

mantics") also bear much promise for the development of techniques of agreement. Founded by the late Alfred Korzybski, this field emphasizes the need to become aware of the pitfalls and traps of language (6, 7). General semanticists are interested in bringing greater precision to language, so that the individual will be enabled to become more aware of what it is he is trying to say, what it is he is actually saying, and what it is others are trying to say to him. The general semanticists argue that (a) the fact that we speak "the same language" does not guarantee we will understand each other, (b) many of our difficulties in getting along with others result from the fact that language often obscures meaning rather than revealing it, and (c) unwarranted assumptions that we really understand one another frequently lead us into disappointments, if not into grave difficulties. Thus the general semanticists would have us become more aware of how we use language, so that we may come to use it more effectively as a communicative tool.

Probably the most promising development within recent years has been the discoveries in the field of the dynamics of group behavior (sometimes called "group dynamics" or "group processes"). This research owes its start to the late Kurt Lewin, who was able to demonstrate that the field of human relationships can be studied as scientifically as the areas of physical science (8). Researchers have discovered much that is of great potential use in the improvement of human relationships. They have discovered, for instance, that the apparent causes of human disagreement are seldom the true causes, that solutions to problems developed through the group process are more workable (for the particular groups that developed them) than those developed by individuals working alone (even by those individuals in positions of authority), and that leaders who do the least directing tend to be the most effective leaders. (See Chapter 10.) What is so hopeful about research in group behavior is the possibility that it may be used to help us eliminate some of the more violent phenomena of the social scene — wars, riots, lynchings, strikes, and acts of oppression. Furthermore, if we are ever to live together in an atmosphere of peace and co-operation, it will be because we have come to understand and to use the principles of group behavior.

Therapeutic Experiences in Everyday Life. It is the function of a culture to enable the members of its social group to meet their individual, basic needs. Otherwise, we would have little to gain from living together. Every society provides opportunities that enable its members to meet their needs in one way or another, but in this some cultures are more efficient than others. To the extent that they help people meet their needs, social arrangements are integrative and therapeutic; to the extent that they frustrate needs, they are disintegrative and a threat to mental health. The problem of the individual is thus to seek out and to take advantage of those situations in his everyday life that meet his needs and are therapeutic. If he can utilize these therapeutic experiences, he will not only be enabled to "actualize" himself but will be aided in meeting the frustrations and threats of life more easily.

The everyday process of living is full of situations that are potentially therapeutic. You go into the drugstore for a magazine. The clerk behind the counter recognizes you, addresses you by name, and cashes your check without question. You are happy that you can match this friendly gesture by calling him by name. To be sure, it is "good business" for him to be pleasant, but he does it in a voluntary way, and it helps him to humanize his job. Because he can call forth this friendly interchange, he is more than a mere clerk; he is someone who enjoys rendering a service to those who appreciate his help. This experience is potentially therapeutic for you, because being called by name and being able to cash a check on sight give you a feeling of status and importance. The fact that someone enjoys seeing you and greeting you sets up a wave of pleasant feelings. The incident is potentially therapeutic for the clerk, too, for it enables him to use his job as a means of meeting his needs for creativity and self-expression.

Or you spend an afternoon developing your backhand stroke in tennis. The following week end, this practice pays off, because you are able to hold your own with the school champion, who had always taken advantage of your weak backhand to beat you soundly. Both your friends and your opponent remark on your improvement, and this gives you the added lift of having status and being appreciated.

These are only two of the inconsequential incidents of everyday living that are potentially therapeutic for their participants. We can reap this therapeutic benefit if we are not too anxiously involved in ourselves, if we are not too busy repressing our hostilities and projecting our guilt feelings. It is true that our mechanized, urban culture restricts our freedom of thought, expression, and action.

This lack of freedom can aggravate anxieties and neurotic tendencies, particularly if we try to express our individualistic tendencies in those situations where only conformity is possible or if we look in vain for human values in situations that simply do not contain them. We can persist in nonrewarding, frustrating behavior, or we can intelligently seek out and appreciate those modes of behavior, those avenues of communication, and those homely little situations like the ones described above, which are available to us and which are potentially therapeutic.

Though there is no logical reason why an individual should lack social contact with his fellows, there are many lonely people in our society, particularly in large cities, where the possibility of social contact is theoretically increased. What makes these people lonely is not the lack of social facilities or the dearth of persons with similar interests but the existence of self-centered patterns of behavior, and feelings of inferiority or inadequacy that prevent the establishment of communicative channels with strangers. Thus the cause of loneliness lies largely within individuals rather than in the physical and social environment.

The lonely individual who will brave the pain of his anxiety and set out to seek the company of others will find that many facilities for socialization are available to him in a large city — churches, centers like the Y.M.C.A. and the Y.W.C.A., lodges, civic betterment organizations, and adult education classes and forums. Colleges in particular provide many opportunities for students to meet and communicate with one another: the student cafeteria, the coffee shop, or the student union; clubs devoted to special subject-matter interest, like geology clubs and foreign language societies; clubs dealing with international relations; clubs sponsored by religious groups; social fraternities and sororities; and intramural sports. In fact, it can almost be said that one must work very hard at being lonely if one wishes to go through college without having had therapeutic contact with others.

Opportunities for learning and growth both inside and outside the academic framework can also be therapeutic. As implied in Chapters 15 and 16, which deal with intelligence and learning, learning in its deepest sense involves change, growth, or progress in the direction of greater intellectual or emotional maturity, and the inability to learn is in itself a sign of emotional immaturity.

The activities provided by gainful employment are a source of therapeutic experiences. Not only does such employment enable us to meet our basic needs for food, shelter, and clothing, but it provides companionship, status, and an opportunity for self-expression and creative activity. The therapeutic outcome depends at least in part on the extent to which an individual is well placed vocationally — the extent to which his work is in harmony with his personality pattern, his skills, and his interests — and in part on the presence or absence of such disintegrative factors in the employment situation as stress on authoritarian control or emphasis on competition. However, even persons who are poorly placed or who must work in psychological climates unfavorable to sound working relationships can usually find satisfaction in their work, unless they are so emotionally upset by the negative aspects of their employment that they can concern themselves with little else.

It is often said that our culture overstresses the values of hard work and understresses the values of play. This is brought out in the fact that many of us feel a twinge of guilt when we are enjoying ourselves, for we are unable to avoid thinking of all the things we have left undone. Yet the emotionally mature person is the one who can separate himself on occasion from his responsibilities and can completely immerse himself in some pleasurable activity that he enjoys for its own sake. In order to be most effective, to help us achieve maximal involvement, it would seem that recreation should encourage active rather than passive participation. Again our culture appears to block the seeking of therapeutic experiences, because it stresses such passive recreations as spectator sports, movies, radio, and television. There is no question that passive participation has some value as sheer relaxation, but when it is the only form of leisure-time indulgence, it encourages a dependent, noncreative approach to life that is superficial, sterile, and stereotyped. Thus it tends to be nonproductive and does not stimulate growth, because it does not affect the individual deeply enough to result in any change.

Virtually all of us become at some time in our lives involved in some part of the courtship-marriage-child-rearing sequence. Not all of us find the experience rewarding or therapeutic, but probably the majority of us do, at least part of the time. The various relationships of dating, mating, and child rearing are potentially therapeutic, because they provide us with opportunities to love and to be loved, to be valued as individuals, to be creative, and to become involved in the welfare of others. Marriage is a relationship that probably creates as many problems as it solves, but this is true of all learning situations or of any situation that offers opportunities for learning and growth toward greater emotional maturity. For some, marriage and its problems provide needed opportunities to work toward greater maturity, and they thrive on the difficulties that must be overcome in building a lasting and satisfying relationship. For others, marriage is a series of frustrations and failures, and they emerge from the relationship with their neurotic defenses stronger than ever, more determined than ever that the freedom of the unmarried is worth its price of loneliness.

Religion. The psychoanalyst C. G. Jung stated that the problems of all his patients in the second half of life (over thirty-five years of age) were in essence the results of their inability to formulate a religious outlook on life, and that every one of them whom he was able to help through psychoanalysis was enabled to acquire a religious outlook. Naturally, Jung was thinking of religion broadly, not of a particular creed or a particular church (9). Although there has been little research in the value of religion in the attainment of emotional maturity, there are some bits of evidence to show that religion may constitute a stabilizing influence. For example, a study of 13,000 young people in Maryland revealed the following percentages of homes broken by divorce, desertion, or separation: Jewish, 4.6; Catholic, 6.4; Protestant, 6.8; mixed religions, 15.2; and no religion, 16.7 (10). If we eliminate the high percentage of broken homes occurring among young people from divergent religions as a natural consequence of a situation likely to cause abnormal conflict and disagreement, it becomes apparent that persons participating in some religion tended to have more stable homes than persons who had no religion. The question might be raised as to whether the stability of the home was produced by religion or whether it was produced by the kind of person who is likely to be religious. The contribution of religion to emotional adjustment is a matter that requires more study psychologically before precise conclusions can be drawn. If one approaches the matter from the standpoint of personality theory, however, it would appear that the mature person is one who has been able to surrender some of his original childish dream of omnipotence in exchange for the ability to be humble on appropriate occasions. Undoubtedly some immature persons cannot express the humility and respect manifested by religious persons toward their deity because they are unable to surrender their false sense of omnipotence.

In its best sense, religion offers the individual the opportunity to enter a nonthreatening environment, where such qualities as self-sacrifice, humility, and altruism are understood and expected. It is an environment quite different from the workaday world, with its emphasis on economic and social power and competition. Religion can thus be a therapeutic experience that permits the individual to satisfy certain of his basic needs. However, the religious situation must be selected with care, inasmuch as there are many differences among churches, ministers, priests, and rabbis (even within the same sect) as regards the freedom permitted the individual church member to realize his best potentialities. Some churches are rigid, authoritarian, and stifling, whereas others are friendly, accepting, and inspiring. Some ministers are excellent therapists, who can easily play the role of the accepting, friendly, nonthreatening, sympathetic listener, while other ministers are easily upset or shocked, or overwhelm one with rebuke or advice, or are grim and forbidding, or simply cannot be talked to. Again, these differences appear to be related to the personal qualities of the clergymen, rather than to the religious sect, although there may be sects that rather consistently select certain personality types to serve as their leaders.

Selection of a Therapeutic Environment. Some situations tend to produce more than their share of anxiety. Occupationally, this is true of the autocratic, overrigid, or highly competitive environments, and it also may be true of other situations too highly individualized to be classified. Basically, there are three ways in which an individual may cope with anxiety-producing pressures: 1. He can attempt to change the situation in order to make it less threatening. 2. He can remain in the situation and cope with it, to the best of his ability, by sublimating anxiety and hostility as much as possible. 3. He can leave the situation and seek another that is less threatening and more friendly. No one of these solutions is intrinsically and inherently "better" than the others. Their desirability depends on the personality of the individual concerned and the nature of the situation. The following examples illustrate how individuals use these methods in ways appropriate to the solution of their problems.

Jim Hicks is the foreman of the machine shop in a small shipyard. He is a kindly, generous, democratic person, who would like to do "the right thing" and not hurt anyone's feelings. Yet he finds himself caught in the cross fire between top management and labor. Virtually every month he is asked by management to issue orders that he feels are unreasonable and unenforceable. For example, he is charged with seeing that no time is wasted in unnecessary trips to the washroom. This means that several times a day he must interrupt his work and inspect the washroom to make sure that no one is loitering over a cigarette. When he finds a violator, he tries to explain the regulation in as kindly a manner as possible and is usually successful in handling the matter in an agreeable way, but he feels that the management is trying to make a policeman out of him and that this tends to break down his relations with his men. His method of coping with his problems involves his eating lunch with various groups of men in the shop and asking them for suggestions that might improve working conditions or production. Frequently his request is greeted with cynicism or silence, but most of the men realize that his interest is genuine, and this approach usually produces friendly conversations that do much to smooth the relations in the shop. Mr. Hicks writes down these suggestions in a notebook in the presence of his men, and he takes the notebook with him to the weekly foremen's meeting. So far only a small fraction of the suggestions have borne fruit, but his willingness to carry his men's ideas to management has improved his relations with his men. Furthermore, Mr. Hicks is building a reputation with management as a foreman who has his men behind him. Eventually he may have more to say about the plant policies and this, in turn, may lead to a change in the psychological climate.

Louis Costa came over from the Azores when he was twelve years old. He was apprenticed to a barber when he graduated from the eighth grade. Barbering is the only trade he has known. Today he is thirty-five and supports a wife and four children on his barber's wages. He says that barbering gives him the feeling of being "cooped up" but that he must stay with it in order to support his family. He is therefore a conscientious, hard-working barber forty hours of the week, but he spends every week end out of doors, weather permitting. Sometimes he takes his family on a picnic, sometimes he goes crab fishing, sometimes he gardens, sometimes he hunts, and sometimes he goes out with his brother, who is a commercial fisherman. On rainy week ends he works on his fishing or hunting gear. True, going back to work on Mondays is always depressing, but his week is brightened by the plans he makes and remakes for the week end. Perhaps his adjustment to life would be better if he were a game warden or a landscape gardener, but his life is richer, fuller, and less frustrating with his outdoor activities than it would be if he spent his week ends in passive frustration, watching television or listening to the radio.

The men in Eva Mahoney's family all worked in the mines, and the girls worked in the mills until they were old enough to marry and sometimes after that. Eva was different. She was alert and intelligent, and she liked to read. Encouraged by her teachers, she went to high school, graduated with honors, and won a scholarship to a nearby college. She completed work for a degree and a teaching credential and came back to her home town to teach in the elementary schools. At first her family was proud of her, but soon they began to make fun of her "highbrow ideas." At the same time, she found herself becoming more critical of their way of doing things. At the end of her second year of teaching she married the high-school chemistry teacher. She hoped that her withdrawal from teaching and settling down as a homemaker would improve her relations with her family, but it did not. The Mahoneys were constantly engaged in violent quarrels that split the family into several factions, and, try as she might, she could not seem to keep herself from becoming involved. Furthermore, the criticism of her by the family continued unabated. When her husband was offered a position in a distant town at the same salary he was making, she persuaded him to accept, because she had discovered that living in the same town with her family was resulting in anxieties, exasperations, and general nervous strain.

Mr. Hicks is meeting his problem by modifying his immediate social environment as much as possible; Mr. Costa has built a psychological "escape hatch" for himself; and Eva Mahoney is solving her problem by running away from it. Each of these solutions is a good one for the person concerned, because it is realistic and meets his personal needs. Some of us do not tend to be so realistic; we react to frustrating situations in accordance with our characteristic pattern of response, without considering whether it is appropriate. That is, there are some who always try to change the situation, there are others who always accept the situation and develop outside interests, and there are those who consistently run away. There are some, too, who tend to regard all situations as intolerable and oppressive, who would have difficulties in *any* situation, because of neurotic conflicts. The emotionally mature person, on the other hand, is one who is able to evaluate his problems realistically and to take appropriate action. He does not shrink from changing situations, even though changes may be resisted or discouraged by his fellow citizens or co-workers; he does not feel overresentful at having to accept a situation which cannot be changed and from which there is no escape; and he does not feel stigmatized and inferior if he has to admit failure and escape from a situation that is producing problems he cannot handle.

Disintegrative Factors

This section is concerned with some of the factors in everyday life and in the general world situation that constitute active or potential threats to mental health. Sometimes we are generally aware of danger but are incapable of dealing with it directly; at other times, we are not even aware of the existence of the threat or of the effect it has upon us. The attempt in this section is not to present a complete catalog of those forces and influences that threaten mental health and emotional adjustment, but rather to mention a few focal points in our social experience that predispose us to inner conflict, neurotic anxiety, and emotionally immature behavior.

The "Power" Orientation. The fact that the culture in which we live is power-oriented plays a major part in the neurotic patterns that most of us develop in our attempts to adjust our needs to the demands of our social environment. The power factor expresses itself in a variety of ways. We compete because we seek power. We worry about security because we wish to protect ourselves against the power of others. We scheme and work and manipulate others in order to accumulate more and more money, which is symbolic of economic power. We make sacrifices to the automobile as a kind of household god — it symbolizes our power-oriented culture. We join together in groups either to seek power or to defend ourselves against the power of others, or both. We try to rise in social status because we realize that the higher the social class, the greater the power. When we build an organization, we construct a hierarchy ranging from those few with the most power on top to those many with the least power at the bottom. The assumption underlying much of our thinking is that workers do their jobs because they fear or respect the power of their superiors rather than because they are responsible, intelligent, or proud of their work. Even the struggle that exists between the adolescent and his parents can be reduced to the power factor: the adolescent wants power without responsibility, whereas the parents attempt to develop responsibility in the adolescent without giving him any power.

We become involved in the struggle for power through no fault of our own; merely to grow up in our culture is to find ourselves drawn into the frenzy and the scramble that result from our pursuit of power. As we grow into adulthood, we find that those who have the least power run the risk of being manipulated by those who have the most power. As children and adolescents, we have had the experience of constantly being under the control and direction of others. Basically, we do not like such experiences — we much prefer to be free. We see the solution as that of getting power for ourselves, so that we cannot be manipulated by others. So we set forth in our search for power, as expressed in status and wealth. It comes very slowly; eventually some of us succeed, but others do not. Even those of us who succeed find that there are always others more powerful than we. Furthermore, those who feel deprived of power always stand ready to take it away from us; therefore, we strive for *more* status and wealth, with the idea that if we get enough power, we will be safe. We never reach this point. In the meantime, those of us who are unsuccessful in our quest for power fear and resent the ones who are successful. Thus the struggle goes on and on, with some of us accumulating larger and larger shares of power, and others of us fearing those who are successful in acquiring power.

The quest for power over others is a game that has few winners and many losers. It is frustrating and anxiety-producing. It is destructive of the mutual trust and satisfactions that can develop from sound human relationships, because it overvalues material rewards and undervalues psychological rewards. The person who is completely imbued with the lust for power says, in effect, "Nothing really matters in this dog-eat-dog world but money, status, and power. If you don't have these, you are nothing and people will walk all over you. If you do have them, you can do anything."

Prejudice. The person who is completely absorbed in his search for power, who sincerely believes that the only kind of success that is worth while is measured in terms of status and money, and who believes the myth that "anyone can be successful who works hard enough," is likely to suffer the most severe psychic shocks. His orientation is so unrealistic, so emotionally immature, that it is likely to result in some pronounced form of neurotic distortion. In some cases this orientation may even develop into a psychosis, and it routinely produces prejudice and intolerance. N. W. Ackerman and Marie Jahoda, who have made a study of anti-Semitism among persons undergoing psychotherapy, learned that the outstanding feature of our culture, as it motivated the lives of the patients in their sample, was the emphasis on intense economic and social competitiveness. These patients had set up vague goals for themselves that might be described as "success," "wealth," and "authority," goals they were unable to attain to any degree of satisfaction. Because of their sense of unrelieved frustration, they were unable to obtain satisfaction from their everyday work, they experienced bitter loneliness, and they rejected religious values. It is not surprising that they became warped by prejudice (11).

Another study, by Bruno Bettelheim and Morris Janowitz, of a random sampling of World War II veterans in Chicago, revealed that a high percentage displayed prejudice against Jews and Negroes. The findings of this study are similar to those of Ackerman and Jahoda, in that the prejudice appeared to be based on the anxiety resulting from their frustrated attempts to attain "success." "Success" to these individuals was conceived of as income, status, and economic security, and they were convinced that in a competitive society anyone can succeed if he tries hard enough. Those who were not making progress toward their goal of "success," or who were actually slipping backward, naturally fell into patterns of frustration and resentment, coupled with the feeling of having been cheated and deprived of their birthright. Thus they, too, tended to express their hostility by displacing it with prejudice against minority groups (12).

Although there are factors in ourselves and in our culture that prevent most of us from being completely corrupted by the quest for power, it is well to be aware of this force, inasmuch as it operates so subtly and pervasively. For instance, many persons who are otherwise well-adjusted firmly believe that they work primarily for wages, or that they "simply cannot live on $5,000 a year." Or we assume as a matter of course that no "sensible person" would enter a job that would not lead to promotion or advancement unless such a move were dictated by economic necessity, for we cannot imagine a "normal" person being uninterested in attaining higher status. These tacit assumptions are frequently at variance with the observable facts, and for this reason we should endeavor to avoid making them, or at least we should recognize the irrational and unrealistic bases underlying such assumptions. The facts of the matter are, of course, that many people do live useful and happy lives on much less than $5,000 a year, and there are millions who find contentment and satisfaction in so-called "blind-alley jobs."

American business has sometimes been accused of forcing competitive and authoritarian ways of life on individuals. Actually, business is no more guilty in this respect than is any other portion of our culture. The power orientation has left its mark on every variety of group endeavor — government agencies, churches, schools, social clubs, and even families. The truth is that business is power-oriented because *we* are power-oriented rather than vice versa. As a matter of fact, there are a growing number of business establishments that are conducting their affairs on a democratic basis, who literally make their employees "partners in production" and who foster the human and therapeutic element inherent in all productive activity (13).

Distortions in Communication. Although communication may have a potentially therapeutic function, it may also be used as a means of manipulation and control. Sometimes society needs to manipulate or control the individual for his own benefit or for the protection of others, but often manipulation benefits only the manipulator.

Much research has gone into perfecting the techniques of propaganda; proportionately little research is concerned with discovering how people's real needs can be met more effectively. The result is that we are saturated with propaganda and publicity of all kinds — propaganda which begs us to act, which appeals to our vanity, and which promises us everything we ever dreamed for. Because this propaganda is so skillfully conceived, we buy a special soap in the hope that it will eliminate pimples, we vote for Garnix in the hope that he will really give us lower taxes and better schools, and we buy our children television sets so that they will not feel inferior and deprived. Then there is the formula propagandized by the movies, radio, and the slick-paper magazines: "If you are beautiful and fragrant, men will love you; if men love you, they will marry you; if men marry you, you will be happy (14)." The soap does not cure the pimples, Garnix increases taxes without improving the schools, and we buy television sets but our children still feel inferior to the children around the corner who have a pony. Some pretty girls aren't loved, some do not marry, and many married people are unhappy. Thus we find from experience that not being alert to the pitfalls of propaganda leads to disappointment. After a while, we become cynical; we say, "Never believe a politician. Never believe an ad writer. You can't trust Hollywood." And, inevitably, "You can't trust anyone."

If we suffer too many disappointments of this kind we come to feel after a while that everyone intends to exploit us. Sometimes we express this feeling with a gay cynicism or a wry smile, but the psychic hurt is there, nevertheless. In order for us to be effective and mature, to understand and accept ourselves and others, it is necessary for us to trust one another. Therefore, the barrage of propaganda to which we are subjected during our waking hours really does not aid communication — it actually prevents communication by driving wedges of disappointment and mistrust between us and our fellow men.

The Flight from Others. Because we have learned not to trust others, because we find the wear and tear of everyday life painful, and because we sometimes need to draw apart from others to recover from the psychic wounds we have received in life's struggles, many of us in the middle-class, urban culture have come to lead withdrawn, inactive lives, sheltered in the privacy of our apartments, flats, or "row houses." It is a very common thing to hear an apartment dweller say with an air of gloomy pride, "I've lived in this building for three years, and I don't know a person in it by name." Essentially this is a self-centered sort of existence; it offers little opportunity for creativity and growth. Privacy is a necessary part of the well-rounded life; the mature person is one who can be alone without becoming anxious or upset. But deliberately arranging one's life so as to achieve the maximum in loneliness is a form of emotional immaturity. This pattern of life is related to the cultural norm that leads us to repress all emotions, good or bad, and to over-intellectualize our lives.

Overconformity. The mature person is one who can conform to the reasonable demands of society without giving up his individuality and his creativity. However, in order to do this, he must be aware of the forces in the culture that insist that everything individual or different or original is wrong and should be destroyed or banned. He should also be aware that we are inconsistent in our intolerance, for we tend to accept new ideas in the field of technology and science, but not in the field of human relations. Even so, we have progressed beyond the closed minds of the men who imprisoned Galileo because his scientific discoveries and theories did not conform to the accepted beliefs of the time.

Conformity is something we learn as children, when we discover that we incur disapproval if we behave in a manner contrary to parental expectations. This disapproval produces anxiety, which is very painful. In order to avoid anxiety, we attempt to find out what kind of behavior is expected of us and conform to that pattern. Soon we learn that we can avoid disapproval most easily by identifying ourselves with significant adults and copying their behavior.

The difficulty is that many of us learn this lesson too well, so that we are not self-directed, but other-directed, so that we cannot adjust to new situations easily, but must anxiously wait for some braver, more aggressive person to work out a solution, which we then may copy. The complete conformist is incapable of learning in the deeper sense of the word; he can only copy the behavior of others. Thus he cannot meet life on anything like even terms but is completely dependent on others for solutions to life's problems.

The conforming person is a willing tool of authoritarian persons, because he is afraid to think for himself, is submissive, and finds it easier and safer to obey the suggestions and instructions of others. For many people, this way of life sometimes works satisfactorily in a sterile sort of way, until they have to cope with problems that they must solve without help from others, or until they innocently become involved in the tug of war between two conflicting authority-figures. At such times, they are thrown on their inadequate personal resources, sometimes with disastrous results.

Fear of Reality. Absolute conformists have a strong fear of unpleasant truths that happen to be at variance with popular belief. They are satisfied with simple, superficial explanations of essentially complex matters; they are strong partisans of "common sense"; and they prefer to divide all situations into "good" or "bad" or some other dual classification. This feeling is expressed in such popular statements as "let sleeping dogs lie," "don't rock the boat," "if you can't boost, don't knock," or "you're either for us or against us." This fear of learning the facts, of gaining insight, is in essence a neurotic mechanism that protects the conformist individual from the necessity of learning. Since learning necessitates growth and growth necessitates change and change implies something new and possibly unknown, the conformist feels that only by the suppression of disturbing facts can he be protected from the unknown and dangerous.

The conformist impedes the progress of mental health by insisting that all social problems be solved by the use of reward and punishment, a system that produces remarkably little permanent and socially useful learning, considering the money and energy expended in its activities. (See Chapter 16.) Punishment-reward approaches to learning, too, are well attuned to the power structure, in that the assumption is that it is necessary to *force or persuade* people to be "good," law-abiding, productive, or even intelligent.

The Threat of War. The conformist conforms because he is trying to "play safe" and avoid threat. Yet because he cannot deal adequately with reality and because he cannot accurately evaluate and understand the facts of his social environment, he is psychologically vulnerable during times of rapid social change (such as the rapid swing from economic depression to wartime prosperity) and periods of international tension (such as the "war of nerves" of the first part of World War II and the cold war of recent years). During such periods of stress and rapid change, the conformist is confused, because he hears such differing interpretations of the "situation" by columnists, senators, and news analysts that he does not know what to think or believe. Some conformists solve this problem by selecting one radio commentator and staying with him.

The mature person, too, has his difficulties. He must avoid being rushed into a premature evaluation of the situation and he must gather as much factual information as he can before he decides on his course of action. In times of stress this is difficult, because news stories from usually reliable sources are frequently contam-

inated by rumor, and the imponderable and unpredictable factors of the international scene produce insecurity and anxiety. Conditions of tension and anxiety, if they persist over a long period of time, will have their effect, even on mature individuals.

One of the dangers during a long period of armed truce is that tensions and anxieties arise to such a peak that the advent of war seems welcome, because it ends the anxiety of waiting for war. At such times, even disaster seems less painful than anxiety. Thus nations plunge into war, sometimes prematurely, because they cannot bear the tension and anxiety of lengthy negotiations.

One of the questions that persistently comes up is whether war itself can be eliminated. Probably most of us feel that war is inevitable, since we have always had wars. Yet anthropologists have discovered areas where tribes have lived in peace for centuries. Even Europe, during a prehistoric period, was evidently populated by groups who did not wage war (15). War, like so many of our behavior patterns, appears to be culturally determined. Nations whose people live an aggressive pattern of life, and whose citizens lead lives embittered by suppressed or repressed hostility, tend to act aggressively toward one another. This pattern of values is reflected in attitudes toward peace and war. Nations are likely to justify their wars by pleading necessity to defend themselves against other nations who are attacking them or who might attack them or who might help other nations attack them. Peace is, according to this system of values, merely the absence of war; peace is an opportunity to carry on competition somewhat less aggressively, an opportunity to rest up from wars. If peace were to be perceived in a more positive light, if it were seen as the opportunity for peoples to communicate with one another and to aid one another toward greater economic and social security, peace would have greater value, it would no longer mean merely the absence of armed conflict.

The "Lunatic Fringe." Although most civilized nations are sufficiently aware of the dangers of war to avoid gestures that might lead to armed violence, there are within each country groups of people who are a potential threat to peace and to the mental health of the world. In Germany, during the 1930's, such people formed a group large enough to take over the country by quasi-legal means. These are the people whose minds are so warped by feelings of having been deprived, cheated, and frustrated that they are ready to follow any agitator or would-be dictator whose propaganda appeals to them. They live in a world of slogans and misrepresentations, of half-truths and sheer nonsense. Their psychological world has been described as follows:

> This is a world in which a "Jew" may at once be a "Communist," "a high government official," and "international banker," in which the [political] agitator may be "a plain little man" (complete with a wife named Lulu and a son who wants a bicycle), a Christ-like martyr on a perpetual pilgrimage to a Calvary he never quite reaches, and a tough guy with a blackjack on his hip. It is a world in which the "discovery" . . . that Walter Winchell's "real" name is, possibly, Velvele Weinschul assumes enormous importance. In short, this is most clearly a deranged universe . . . a cosmos in which un-sanity and non-sense are as inescapable as air (16).

Perhaps our first reaction to people in such groups is one of puzzled apprehension. Then we realize that they constitute an active threat to peace, for they are the ones who are most likely to be so carried away by fanaticism as to take over the established government by violence or subversive action, and we wonder how we may best control them and defend ourselves against them. We should also be concerned about the conditions in our society that produce persons whose neurotic needs are so strong that they can be easily swayed and manipulated by a clever, fanatical agitator. Although our immediate task may seem to be to take steps calculated to defend ourselves against revolution and violence, the more rewarding approach in the long run would be to work for (a) the changing of those features in the culture that produce personality disintegration and neurotic conflict and (b) the development of the kind of life that provides for more therapeutic relationships. The people who form the backbone of a potential revolutionary movement, the so-called "lunatic fringe," are not basically different from the rest of us. Their neurotic needs are similar to ours, the difference being that some of their neurotic needs are more exaggerated, their defenses are more elaborate, and the distortion in their perception is more marked. They differ from the normal person in the same way that the antisocial deviants differ. The differences are ones of degree, rather than of kind. As is the case with the social deviant, their illness is a difficult one to treat, because it is a part of the sickness of our whole society.

SUMMARY

There are several factors in everyday life that are actual or potential forces in the promotion of better mental health. The most important of these is the normal human tendency to recover from wounds and shocks, both psychic and physical. This may be termed "the drive toward health." One of the tools available to man as an aid to the improvement of mental health is that of verbal communication, which enables him to relate himself to his fellows and to take advantage of the therapeutic aspects of everyday situations. Recent developments in the techniques of better communication include nondirective counseling methods, general semantics, and experiments in the dynamics of group behavior. Everyday experiences offer opportunities for therapeutic relations and for learning to get along with oneself and with others. Religion, too, can provide therapeutic experiences, although the extent to which it does so depends on the ability of the individual to find a religious leader and a group with whom he can communicate easily. The individual owes it to himself to select as therapeutic a social environment as possible. Sometimes this means that he must avoid or reduce the disintegrative forces of his social environment by making changes within the existing framework. Sometimes he must sublimate his frustrations or actually leave the disturbing situation for what promises to be a better one.

Factors in everyday life that may have a disintegrative effect on mental health are to a large extent related to the "power orientation" of our culture — the high value we place upon power, our striving for power through competition, our unrealistic aspirations for wealth and status, and our anxieties about economic security. Since competition for status and economic power is a game at which few win and many lose, frustrations inevitably result. These frustrations are commonly expressed through prejudices directed against minority groups.

Other factors in everyday life that are disintegrative in their effect are the tendency to isolate ourselves from others, the forces in our culture that attempt to require overconformity from everyone, the fear of unpleasant realities, and the threat of war. We have come to regard war as inevitable, though there have been groups of people who have been able to live without it.

REFERENCES

1. K. Goldstein, *Human Nature in the Light of Psychopathology.* Cambridge: Harvard University Press, 1940.
2. W. U. Snyder, "Client-Centered Therapy," in L. A. Pennington and I. A. Berg, eds., *An Introduction to Clinical Psychology.* New York: Ronald, 1948. Pp. 465–497.
3. C. R. Rogers, *Counseling and Psychotherapy.* Boston: Houghton Mifflin, 1942.
4. C. R. Rogers, *Client-Centered Therapy.* Boston: Houghton Mifflin, 1951.
5. S. I. Hayakawa, "New Techniques of Agreement," *Etc.: A Review of General Semantics.* 8:3–12; 1950.
6. A. Korzybski, *Science and Sanity: An Introduction to Non-Aristotelian Systems and General Semantics,* 3d edition. Lakeville, Conn.: International Non-Aristotelian Library Publishing Co., 1948.
7. S. I. Hayakawa, *Language in Thought and Action.* New York: Harcourt, Brace, 1950.
8. K. Lewin, *Resolving Social Conflicts,* edited by G. W. Lewin. New York: Harper, 1948.
9. C. G. Jung, *Modern Man in Search of a Soul,* tr. by W. S. Dell and C. F. Baynes. New York: Harcourt, Brace, 1933. P. 264.
10. H. M. Bell, *Youth Tell Their Story.* Washington, D.C.: American Council on Education, 1938. P. 21.
11. N. W. Ackerman and M. Jahoda, *Anti-Semitism and Emotional Disorder.* New York: Harper, 1950.
12. B. Bettelheim and M. Janowitz, *Dynamics of Prejudice: A Psychological and Sociological Study of Veterans.* New York: Harper, 1950.
13. "52 Paychecks a Year." A film produced by the Cooley Company for the Nunn-Bush Shoe Co.
14. Committee on Preventive Psychiatry of the Group for the Advancement of Psychiatry, *Promotion of Mental Health in the Primary and Secondary Schools: An Evaluation of Four Projects,* Report No. 18; January, 1951. P. 7.
15. C. Kluckhohn, *Mirror for Man.* New York: McGraw-Hill, 1949. P. 45.
16. M. J. Maloney, "Four Studies in Prejudice," *Etc.: A Review of General Semantics.* 8:50; 1950. (In a review of *Prophets of Deceit: A Study of the Techniques of the American Agitator* by L. Lowenthal and N. Guterman. New York: Harper, 1949). Reprinted by permission of *Etc.*

SUGGESTED READINGS

C. R. Rogers, *Client-Centered Therapy.* Boston: Houghton Mifflin, 1951.
C. R. Rogers, *Counseling and Psychotherapy.* Boston: Houghton Mifflin, 1942.
W. U. Snyder, "Client-Centered Therapy," in L. A. Pennington and I. A. Berg, eds., *An Introduction to Clinical Psychology.* New York: Ronald, 1948. Pp. 465–497. The books by C. R. Rogers and the chapter by W. U. Snyder provide a clear picture of the contributions of the nondirective or client-centered schools of counseling.

I. J. Lee, *How Do You Talk about People?* New York: The Anti-Defamation League of B'nai B'rith, 1950. A pamphlet that deals with prejudice from the standpoint of general semantics.

R. Lippitt, *Training in Community Relations.* New York: Harper, 1949. Description of a workshop conducted for the purpose of helping people learn the ways and means of reducing intergroup tensions.

A. McC. Lee, "Can the Individual Protect Himself against Propaganda Not in His Interest?" *Social Forces.* 29:56–61; 1950. Reassurance for those who are looking for answers to this question.

K. Young, *Personality and Problems of Adjustment.* New York: Appleton-Century-Crofts, 1940. Chapter 29 is entitled "Integration and Balance through Religion, Art, and Avocation."

T. H. Pear, ed., *Psychological Factors of Peace and War.* New York: Philosophical Library, 1951. A collection of essays prepared for the United Nations Association, dealing with war as a phenomenon of cultural behavior.

T. W. Adorno, *et al.*, *The Authoritarian Personality.* New York: Harper, 1950. Also recommended for reading in the field of prejudice.

E. Fromm, *Psychoanalysis and Religion.* New Haven: Yale University Press, 1950.

T. Benedek, *Insight and Personality Adjustment.* New York: Ronald, 1946. An analysis of personality problems growing out of war.

H. C. Lindgren, *The Art of Human Relations.* New York: Hermitage, 1953. See Chapter 14, "The Therapy of Everyday Life."

S. Chase, *Roads to Agreement.* New York: Harper, 1951. A popularized presentation of what may be done in promoting better understanding in the world today.

H. A. Overstreet, *The Mature Mind.* New York: Norton, 1949. A well-written argument for the development of emotional maturity. A best seller.

J. Liebman, *Peace of Mind.* New York: Simon and Schuster, 1946. The contribution that religion can make toward many of the problems we face. The author sees psychiatry and religion aiming toward a common goal.

S. H. Britt, *Selected Readings in Social Psychology.* New York: Rinehart, 1950. Section VI, "Social Conflict," contains selections on prejudice, psychological warfare, war and peace, and propaganda.

H. Cantril, *The Psychology of Social Movements.* New York: Wiley, 1941. The first portion of the book deals with the individual's relationship to social movements; the second portion deals with specific phenomena like the lynching mob, the Nazis, and the Kingdom of Father Divine.

H. Cantril, *The "Why" of Man's Experience.* New York: Macmillan, 1950. A probing, insightful investigation of man from the viewpoint of the psychologist.

S. S. Sargent, *Social Psychology.* New York: Ronald, 1950. See Part IV, "Understanding Social Phenomena," particularly the chapters on prejudice, propaganda, and applications in the area of social issues.

S. H. Britt, *Social Psychology of Modern Life*, Rev. edition. New York: Rinehart, 1949. See Chapters 23 and 24, which deal with prejudice, nationalism and war.

T. M. Newcomb, *Social Psychology.* New York: Dryden, 1950. Chapter 16 deals with various aspects of group conflict, including prejudice.

XX ... *Toward Better*

Mental Health

What Can We Do about Better Mental Health for Ourselves?

As stated in the initial chapter of this book, mental health and emotional maturity are attained by a process of growth, a necessarily slow process. It is a process both exasperatingly slow and often painful. If neurotic defenses are well-developed, growth in the direction of greater emotional maturity may frequently be accompanied by considerable anxiety. Therefore, we should not be surprised or upset when we have difficulty in improving or maturing in accordance with our expectations. After all, our goals should not be to bring about a major change in personality but to attain a reasonable level of emotional maturity. It is unreasonable to strive to be completely free from neurotic needs and defenses, but it is reasonable to strive for such goals as more effective relations with others, a higher level of productivity and creativity, and a richer and more satisfying life as a student, citizen, spouse, parent, or worker.

Understanding and Insight. One of the objectives of the study of mental hygiene as developed by this text is the promotion of a better understanding of oneself and others. Understanding is basic, because knowledge of the causes of behavior of oneself and others constitutes the entering wedge of insight and acceptance. Hatred and intolerance, as well as the other attitudes that keep people apart and prevent co-operation and agreement, diminish under the impact of understanding and insight into one's own feelings and attitudes and the motivation of others. Understanding everything

458

may not constitute forgiving everything, but it is the first step on the road leading to acceptance, tolerance, and respect.

Insight has been described as the perception of new meaning in one's experience, the awareness of new relationships of cause and effect (1). This kind of perception or awareness is more than merely having all the facts; it involves putting the facts together in a new way, a way that changes things and makes for better learning. Although awareness helps learning, it does not make it simpler or easier. Usually it reveals things as actually more complicated, because understanding human problems means avoiding easy, superficial, and "obvious" explanations of them. The facts of human behavior are not simple and obvious; they are complex and obscure.

Clifford Miguel's case serves as an example of how one individual was able to obtain insight into and understanding of his own problems of adjustment.

Clifford worked as a salesman for a small printing plant, which was eventually forced to close because of the death of the senior partner. Since Clifford had an excellent work record, he had no difficulty in getting another job as a printing salesman with a large concern that employed a dozen or more salesmen. Although Clifford's sales record was good and his relations with each of the other salesmen were pleasant and friendly, he was not happy. On his previous job he had been able to make many suggestions about procedure, layout, and sales policy that were readily accepted by management and put into effect. At the new plant it was quite different. Clifford would make suggestions at the bi-weekly staff meeting, but they were criticized, rejected, or ignored by the other members of the sales staff. He took to brooding over this, wondering whether his ideas really were any good or whether there was something wrong in his manner of presentation. He spent hours going over his recollections of the staff meetings without finding any clue to the difficulty. His relations with the other salesmen continued on a pleasant plane, although he noticed that their attitudes were different in staff meetings.

One day he overheard someone casually remark after a particularly unproductive staff meeting, "You know, this gang reminds me of my family — they can't agree on anything either." All at once the pieces of the puzzle fell into place, and Clifford realized that the trouble was that this staff *was* very much like a large, bickering family, with each child attempting to compete with the others for a place in the sun. The sales manager was a paternalistic, fatherly person who favored first one, then the other, of the salesmen. Whereas the managers at Clifford's old place of employment were relaxed, democratic individuals, who were willing to accept a good idea no matter who suggested it, each member of the staff at the larger plant seemed intent on building himself up at the expense of others, and sometimes at the expense of the business. All these *facts* had been apparent to Clifford before, but until he overheard this chance remark, he was unable to put them together in any kind of sensible pattern.

Clifford used this insight in getting another job, working for people who were receptive to ideas and suggestions. However, before he accepted his new position, he carefully studied the people he would have to work with, in order to be sure that they were more co-operative than competitive.

When insight is achieved, it comes much as it did to Clifford. There is a period of puzzlement, sometimes brief and sometimes lengthy, and then suddenly the pieces fall into place. This is the "aha! phenomenon," or learning through the discovery of relationships, described by the Gestalt psychologists who developed the concept of insight in learning. (See Chapter 16.)

There is no standard procedure that is certain to produce insight into personal problems, but it can sometimes be accelerated by the following:

1. *Becoming aware of the problem.* Clifford could have reacted to the situation by deciding that his fellow workers did not like him personally or that his ideas really were not very good. But he avoided the trap of the simple interpretation. He did not accept the easy explanation of what was happening. He was very much aware that a problem existed that had hitherto defied analysis.

2. *Trial-and-error activity.* For some, the "working phase" of insightful learning is the blundering of trial and error; for others, it is a systematic eliminating of false leads. In any event, learning frequently comes when it is least expected, sometimes aided by an otherwise irrelevant remark or thought. Clifford could have looked for clues by asking himself these questions: What other life situation does this remind me of? What exactly was it that made me so resentful during our last staff meeting? Joe's words? Or was it his tone of voice? Why do my fellow workers and I get along when we are drinking coffee together, but not when we are in a meeting?

3. *Talking to others.* Clifford did not use this method, but it usually

helps, particularly if you can get a good listener, one who does not make too many suggestions but reacts just enough to help you solve your own problem. As a matter of fact, if someone *had* given Clifford the solution to his problem before he was ready to see it, it would not have helped him and he would have had to persist until he had solved the problem himself.

Insight and understanding are usually aided by an awareness of the undercurrents in human behavior. (See Chapter 10.) Clifford was sensitive to this factor. He was fairly certain that when a fellow salesman criticized an idea of his, it did not necessarily mean that the other salesman was reacting to the *idea*. The criticism meant, rather, that the salesman was attacking Clifford as a way of building himself up at Clifford's expense, because he regarded Clifford's ideas as a menace to his own security.

We have a better chance to understand our own motives and those of others when we recognize that there are multiple motives in what we say or do. Indeed, one might almost say that the *most obvious explanation* of any act — that is, the explanation that seems apparent at first glance — *is probably of minor importance and actually serves as a blind for motives of major importance.* This sort of self-deception is practiced frequently in everyday life.

YOUNG PHYSICIAN: "I traded in my Ford on a Cadillac because I wanted a more comfortable car."

CHILD: "I took the money out of Mommy's purse because I wanted to buy some candy."

STUDENT: "I would have done that assignment, but I just didn't have time."

HUSBAND: "I know we never go out any more, dear, but after eight hours' work and two hours' commuting, I'm just too tired."

We can speculate at length as to the nature of real motives that lie behind the above statements without necessarily hitting on the crucial ones, but we can be sure that each of the reasons given is actually of minor importance to the speaker. It serves largely to obscure the essential reason, which is largely unconscious.

One area of life that we might fruitfully explore to gain self-understanding and insight is our own childhood. One can learn much about himself by pondering such questions as these:

In what ways do my behavior and attitudes resemble the behavior and attitudes of my parents?

Is my attitude toward persons in authority similar to my feeling toward my father? My mother? My teachers in school?

When I am in a group of people, do I feel toward them the way I used to feel toward my brothers and sisters?

Attitudes toward power and authority are especially significant, for these relationships cause far more than their share of emotional conflict and neurotic disturbance. Insight may be aided by questions like these:

What kind of relations do I have with authority figures (teachers, employers, persons of high status and prestige)? Do I treat them as equals? Do I try to compete with them? Am I uneasy when I am with them? Do I always do as I am told? Do I try to do *what* I am told but not in the way prescribed?

How do *I* handle authority when I have it? Am I at ease? Am I nervous and tense? Do I enjoy it? Do others resent my leadership?

How do I react to the competitive side of life? Do I work hard at competition? Do I try to avoid competitive situations? Am I afraid to compete? If so, is it because I am afraid that I will hurt someone? Or is it because I am afraid that *I* will be hurt?

What are my feelings about money? Do I feel that everyone has his price? Do I see my life goal as an amount of money I expect to earn and save? How do I feel about lending money to others? How do I feel about giving money away?

How do I feel about status? If I take a job, will it have to offer opportunities for promotion? What does attending college have to do with my status needs? How do I feel when I am demoted or lose status through no fault of my own?

Admittedly these questions do not unerringly point out the road to better self-understanding and insight, but perhaps they can serve to stimulate contemplation and self-examination that may lead in that general direction.

Acceptance and Tolerance. Levels of maturity represented by acceptance and tolerance necessitate more emotional involvement than do understanding and insight, which are more intellectual. In general, a mature person is an accepting, tolerant person, although not all persons who appear to be accepting and tolerant are mature. Some persons adopt a superficially easygoing and permissive attitude as a way of compensating for an essentially rejecting personality. They appear to accept, but this acceptance is tinged with an aroma of "sweet hostility."

A reasonably mature person is one who can accept weaknesses in himself and others. He can accept the fact of failure without feeling inferior or defeated. At the same time, he can accept and enjoy success, whereas the immature person will often belittle or overlook or exaggerate his successes.

Because the mature person is aware of his own pattern of motivation and has insight into the motives of others, he is less anxious about what others might do to him. He does not see the acts of others as threats, unless he has some realistic reason to do so. If something makes him angry or afraid, he accepts his fear or his anger as a reasonable thing. The mature person assumes that it is legitimate to express feelings and that they should be expressed in a manner as socially acceptable as possible, out of respect for the feelings of others. Sometimes this means sublimation into some form of symbolic behavior; sometimes it means commenting humorously on one's irritation; and sometimes it means standing up for one's rights frankly and honestly. At the same time the mature person also realizes that strong emotions may be aroused not so much by what others may be doing to him as by his own more or less neurotic needs, for no person is so mature as to be entirely free from immature lapses.

Respect and Love. Because of the mature person's success in understanding, accepting, and tolerating himself and others, he finds that there are some things about himself and some things about most people that he can like, appreciate, and enjoy. He takes frank pride in his ability to sink basketballs or get A's in biology. He does not feel the need to boast about these things, but he is able to talk about them with pleasure. Furthermore, he finds that he is very fond of himself — not to the point of anxious and selfish preoccupation with his welfare and activities, but rather to the point of feeling that basically he is a *good* person, one who is worthy of the respect and love of others. He can feel this way even though he knows that sometimes he disappoints himself and others, that sometimes he fails, that sometimes he is irritating, that not every one likes him, and that in many ways he could be more effective and more likable.

Since he can feel this way toward himself, he can feel this way toward others. Since he can respect himself, he can respect others as individuals. Since he can feel love for himself, he can love those persons with whom he shares his life.

Self-direction. The more emotional maturity an individual possesses, the less "vulnerable" he is. In other words, greater emotional maturity enables him to resist exploitation and manipulation by others. A less mature person can be manipulated through his neurotic needs. For example, a person with a strong feeling of inferiority, compensated for by an exaggerated need for status, is more vulnerable to a sales appeal that has an aura of prestige. Door-to-door encyclopedia salesmen frequently find that their wares are more attractive when they mention that the leader of the town's social set has purchased a set of their books. The rabble-rousers mentioned in the section on war owe their success to their ability to appeal to the immature individual's chronic feeling of having been cheated, defrauded, and deprived of success. In the film "Feeling of Rejection," the heroine, Margaret, is saddled with overtime at the office and with the dishwashing at home because she cannot say no (2).

The complete conformist, a less mature person, is afraid to think different or original thoughts, because they make him feel anxious. He has great difficulty in making life plans, in standing up for his rights, and in making important decisions. He is completely immobilized by rapidly changing conditions, by situations that appear to call for several kinds of actions, some of them contradictory. The mature person, being self-directing, is better able to cope with such ambiguous situations. Because he is flexible, willing to learn, and not afraid to make mistakes, he moves aggressively into the problem, confident in the feeling that it is better to grapple with life than to let it run over him. Because he is learning how to understand and accept others, he is less likely to fear them. If he is afraid, he knows what he is afraid of. However, because he has confidence in himself, he has confidence in others, and he imbues others with this feeling of confidence.

The farther we move in the pattern of life from the intellectual to the emotional, the less we have to say about the *methods* of attaining maturity. We can make suggestions about some of the ways in which persons might go about *learning to understand* others, but we are at a loss when it comes to suggesting how one should go about respecting himself and others or becoming self-directing. We can discuss knowledge, understanding, and insight, because these concepts are at a verbal or a semiverbal level, but emotion and feeling, being at a subverbal level, defy adequate description and discussion. Perhaps the best we can do is to assume that those persons who initially are sufficiently motivated to attempt a real understanding of themselves and others, who intelligently seek out therapeutic situations and avoid or change those situations that are less therapeutic or disintegrative, who approach learning situations with enthusiasm and humility, and who persist in spite of the discouragement, frustration, and anxiety that accompany much of the process of emotional and intellectual growth, are likely to make the most progress toward the goal of greater emotional maturity and self-direction.

What We Can Do about Mental Health for Others

Our first responsibility in promoting better mental health for others is to take steps to improve our own mental health in order that our relations with others may be more therapeutic. Because those who know the mature person know they can trust him, they are enabled to trust themselves; because he is tolerant, they are helped to tolerance; because he can accept them, they are better able to accept themselves. Furthermore, mature persons, singly or in groups, can make decisions and solve problems that aid the cause of mental health for the many.

Group Action. Most of the changes that make the world a healthier place to live in come from group action. In a democratic society we would not want this to come about in any other way, because decisions made by a single individual on behalf of all society usually end in failure, unless they happen to reflect the will of the people. Thus the campaign for better mental health is not a matter merely of building mental hospitals, establishing clinics for psychotherapy, and developing a program of child guidance in the schools; it is also a problem of educating the general public. Of course, the public may be educated through campaigns aimed specifically at promoting special programs like those named above. But until the rank and file of the electorate know what is really involved in

Board of Education, Chicago, Ill.

Most of the changes to make the world a healthier place to live will come from group action.

mental health and are convinced that it is worth paying for, the process of educating the public must continue.

As this is being written, the child-care centers in California, which were established during World War II to take care of the children of working mothers, have just won, for perhaps the tenth time, a fight for existence. The dividends in mental health that accrue from the child-care centers — therapeutic environment for children, relief of parental anxieties, and evening educational programs in child care for parents — are enormous. The human value of this simple social device extends far beyond the relatively small expense required to operate it. Yet each year the State Legislature reaffirms a policy of maintaining child-care centers on a temporary, year-to-year basis, in spite of demands from civic leaders that they be put on a more permanent footing. The Legislature would not do this if the rank and file of the electorate were vitally interested in child-care centers to the point of lending them moral support. Public interest at present is barely sufficient to keep them operating on a year-to-year basis. If public interest should lag, the centers would be dropped. This is what happens when the public has not been sufficiently educated in matters of mental health.

Virtually every community of any size has its mental health society, or some similar organization that performs the same function. These relatively small but active groups are beginning to exert a powerful influence, in proportion to their size, in educating the public in the need for improved mental health facilities. In some instances their campaigns have directly effected the establishment and improvement of such facilities. Membership in these organizations is open to the general public, and they present excellent opportunities for the individual to render community service.

Also to be commended and recommended are the Service Leagues, Councils for Civic Unity, Anti-Defamation Leagues, and similar organizations that provide more specialized functions. Some groups provide rehabilitational care and facilities for the inmates of jails and prisons, some attempt to fight prejudice and discrimination against minority groups by fostering legislation and by public education, and others are interested in combating juvenile delinquency by providing supervised recreational facilities.

Improvement of Public Education. Although our system of mass public education is a strong force for social cohesiveness, its casualty rate in the area of emotional maladjustment is all too high.   However, one of the most encouraging trends is the tendency of education to humanize itself.   Schools are doing a very imperfect job of meeting human needs, but they meet them much better than they did fifty or even twenty-five years ago.   Changes in the desired direction come slowly, almost imperceptibly, but they are nevertheless taking place.   Every year fewer children are "held back" in the elementary grades; every year the number of guidance workers grows; every year sees a little more liberalization of the curriculum.   Considering the size of public education, the inadequate teacher-training curricula, and the vast amount of public apathy toward education, the schools do very well.   But they need help in doing better.   The mature individual will have his hands full if he attempts to make education more therapeutic and less disintegrative, but doing so presents a challenge he cannot ignore.

Actually, education is in many ways the white hope of the mental hygienist, because through educational facilities he has access to the individuals who will constitute the public that will be asked to support more complete and more thorough mental health programs. The dream of the mental hygienist is that if he can improve the mental health of the children who are now in school, the alcoholic clinics, mental hospitals, jails, race tracks, prisons, courts, and gambling halls of tomorrow will lack customers.   However, the actualization of such a dream is not within our grasp; its attainment lies, at the very best, some decades ahead.

Parent Education.   Mental hygienists are generally agreed that education for mental health should begin with parents, since it is their influence at the earliest stages of the child's life that seems to destine the child for emotional health or neurosis.   The difficulty generally is that the parents who need education the least are the ones who can be most easily persuaded to participate in learning activities, and the ones who need it the most are the ones who resist all attempts made to interest them in these activities.   The parents who participate in any kind of formalized parent education constitute a very small percentage of the total number of parents, and there does not seem to be any sure way of remedying this situation, unless it is to give parent education to high school students.   There is an increasing tendency to provide such instruction, but the movement is handicapped by the opposition of politically powerful groups who decry what they call "frills in education," as well as by a shortage of trained instructors. The question also arises: Is this the best time to give such instruction? Perhaps it is needed at *both* the late adolescent and young adult stages of life. One trend, however, that awakens optimism is the large number of mental-health articles, interestingly written by competent persons, appearing in magazines of national circulation during recent years. If such wide publicity continues, it may in the end prove to be the most potent force in public education for mental health.

The co-operative nursery school or play center is a recent development that so far affects relatively few people, but is worthy of mention because it represents parent education in the best sense. These schools are organized and managed by parents for the purpose of providing group-play opportunities for children in the preschool years. They are supervised by trained nursery-school teachers, who are also responsible for providing education in child care and development for the participating parents. The schools are staffed by the mothers, who serve as mother-teachers one day a week. One evening a week is set aside for education for both mothers and fathers. These schools provide opportunities for parents to work co-operatively on a project of great mutual interest — the welfare of their children. The idea that parents can play an intimate role in education, with therapeutic results for themselves and the child, seems rather obvious, but so far very few schools above the nursery level have accepted this philosophy.

The Group Process. Perhaps the most promising development in our struggle to solve the world's problems in an emotionally mature way rather than through violence is our growth in understanding of the principles underlying the dynamics of group behavior, mentioned at various points throughout this book. The possibility that solutions to problems achieved through the group process are superior to those attained by an individual is an intriguing one, particularly in view of the fact that it runs counter to our "common sense" principle of concentrating the power of decision in one person at the top of the hierarchy of power and authority. From the standpoint of the principles of mental health as described in this text, the group-process approach appears to be a sound one. It is highly therapeutic for the individuals concerned in that they are provided with opportunities to clarify their thinking, to express their feelings, to understand and accept the thoughts and the feelings of others, and to learn to see matters from the points of view of others. The group process would seem to have great promise if used in industrial disputes or even in international negotiations. Perhaps if discussions of international affairs were conducted in the light of what we know now about the dynamics of groups instead of on a formal, legalistic basis, as at present, we might have a real opportunity to substitute peace for war as a way of life for the world.

SUMMARY

The individual who wishes to progress toward a greater emotional maturity must first work toward understanding of and insight into himself and others. Insight and understanding are evolved not so much from information and knowledge as from a desire to grow and change one's relations with oneself and with others for the better. This is a slow and difficult process, because everything that is immature and neurotic within one obstructs the learning process. Acceptance and tolerance of oneself and others constitutes the next step on the road to greater emotional maturity, and the final step is the attainment of the ability to love and respect oneself and others. The steps toward emotional maturity become more and more involved in the unconscious processes — the areas of feeling and emotion — as they progress from understanding to love. Self-direction, too, is a goal of the maturing person, because ability to be self-directing implies freedom from irrational and neurotic restraints and dependence upon intelligence, perception, empathy, and other processes of the healthy self-structure.

Obligations to oneself also involve obligations to society; our own chances for better mental health are directly and indirectly aided by our participation in programs and movements aimed at the improvement of the mental health of the general public. Most of these improvements come from some kind of group action. The chief function of the groups is to conduct a program of public education, for, without public education, little progress can be expected in the mental health field. Much needs to be done with the schools themselves. If experiences in school were more therapeutic, many mental health problems of adults — problems involving psychoneurosis, psychosis, crime and delinquency, narcotics and alcohol, labor unrest — would be eliminated before they develop. Parent education is also a field that attracts the mental hygienist, inasmuch as problem parents tend to produce problem children, but here the difficulty is that of involving the parent voluntarily in his own education.

The development giving most hope for the promotion of better mental health for everyone is the dynamic approach to group functioning. This new branch of psychology promises to make group activity not only more therapeutic and personally rewarding for its participants, but also more effective and productive. Perhaps our improved understanding of the group process will eventually lead to the abolition of war and the building of a permanent peace.

REFERENCES

1. C. R. Rogers, *Counseling and Psychotherapy*. Boston: Houghton Mifflin, 1942. P. 174.
2. C. G. Stogdill and B. Ruddick, "The Feeling of Rejection," a film. Montreal: National Film Board of Canada. Produced for the Mental Health Division of the Department of National Health and Welfare, 1946.

SUGGESTED READINGS

H. W. Bernard, *Toward Better Personal Adjustment*. New York: McGraw-Hill, 1951. Chapter 16. (Chapter 15 also deals with religion as a factor in mental health.)

C. G. Wrenn, *Building Self-Confidence*. Stanford: Stanford University Press, 1948.

F. McKinney, *Psychology of Personal Adjustment*, 2d edition. New York: Wiley, 1949. See Chapter 16.

P. N. Symonds, *Dynamic Psychology*. New York: Appleton-Century-Crofts, 1949. See Chapter 20.

H. A. Carroll, *Mental Hygiene*. New York: Prentice-Hall, 1947. Chapter 14.

W. C. Langer, *Psychology and Human Living*. New York: Appleton-Century-Crofts, 1943. Chapter 14.

L. C. Steckle, *Problems of Human Adjustment*. New York: Harper, 1949. Chapter 13. (Chapter 11 also deals with the search for God.)

L. F. Shaffer, *The Psychology of Adjustment*. Boston: Houghton Mifflin, 1936. See Chapter 17.

K. Horney, *Self-Analysis*. New York: Norton, 1942.

D. S. Arbuckle, *Teacher Counseling*. Cambridge: Addison-Wesley, 1950. A description of some of the ways in which public schools may provide more therapeutic experiences for children. Nondirective and child-centered in its approach.

F. Redl and W. W. Wattenberg, *Mental Hygiene in Teaching*. New York: Harcourt, Brace, 1951. A humanized and therapeutic approach to public-school · education along the lines suggested in this chapter.

G. Thorman, *Toward Mental Health*, Public Affairs Pamphlet No. 120, 1946. Prepared and distributed by the National Mental Health Foundation to promote better understanding of the problems of mental health on the part of the general public.

W. C. Menninger, *There Is Something You Can Do about Mental Health*. New York: The National Committee for Mental Hygiene, 1949. A pamphlet published and distributed to educate the public as to its role in promoting better mental health.

Albert Deutsch, *Mental Hygiene in Review*. New York: The National Committee for Mental Hygiene, 1949. Another pamphlet prepared and distributed for the purpose of educating the public. Deals with the contributions of psychiatry and mental health organizations.

Index